THE

RESTITUTION

OF

METAPHYSICS

THE

RESTITUTION

OF

METAPHYSICS

ERROL E. HARRIS

Humanity
Books

an imprint of Prometheus Books
59 John Glenn Drive, Amherst, New York 14228-2197

Published 2000 by Humanity Books, an imprint of Prometheus Books

04 03 02 01 00   5 4 3 2 1

Library of Congress Cataloging-in-Publication Data

Harris, Errol E.
        The restitution of metaphysics / Errol E. Harris.
            p.   cm.
        Includes bibliographical references and index.
        ISBN 1–57392–663–9
        1. Metaphysics. 2. Physics—Philosophy. 3. Science—Philosophy.
4. Empiricism. I. Title.
BD111.H275   1999
110—dc20   96–028610
                                                                CIP

To the loving memory of my father,
Samuel Jack Harris.

"His life was gentle, and the elements
So mixed in him that Nature might stand up
And say to all the world, 'This was a man.'"

"... what in me is dark
illumine, what is low raise and support;
That to the height of this great argument,
I may assert Eternal Providence,
And justify the ways of God to men."

—John Milton

Contents

Preface

The conceptual scheme within which science operates in any historical period is all embracing. It determines the prevalent conception of the universe as a whole, and involves a comprehensive metaphysic. The Copernican revolution in astronomy, which introduced the conceptual scheme characteristic of the modern period completely subverted the previous Aristotelian conception of the world as a besouled living being centered on the Earth and governed by a prime mover who rotated the outer heaven imparting its movement to everything else. Each of these conceptual schemes dominated the thinking and practice of an entire civilization, having consequences for its religion, its philosophy, its morality, and its politics.

As may well be expected, when a revolution occurs in the prevailing conceptual scheme, as it did with the publication of the Copernican hypothesis, it takes a long time for the new "paradigm" to penetrate and pervade the affected civilization. Copernicus published *De Revolutionibus Orbium Celestium* in the declining years of the fifteenth century, but it was not until almost two hundred years later that the Copernican system attained its maturity in the hands of Isaac Newton, and it took another hundred years to penetrate the philosophical, moral, political, and religious thought of the age of Enlightenment.

The opening of the twentieth century introduced a new conceptual scheme founded upon Albert Einstein's discovery of relativity and Max Planck's discovery of the quantum, but while the new paradigm has revolutionized science, it has as yet had little effect on philosophy and social order. The difference between our own epoch and that of the sixteenth century is that today the survival of the human race is threatened by the technological developments from Newtonian science, as it never was by the prevalence of the Aristotelian scheme, and no solution of the global problems which beset our civilization at the present time can be found until the implications of the Einsteinian revolution in science are widely understood and absorbed to effect a similar revolution in philosophical, religious, moral, and political thinking.

The idea of the natural world characteristic of Newtonian science was that of a vast machine, in which the mind of the observer found no place. Consequently, mind became unbridgeably separated from matter and the subjective from the objectively real. This alienation of the external world from the observing and manipulating activity of the scientist generated the notion that nature was at the disposal of human beings and could be exploited at will as the discovery of the laws governing natural processes enabled men and women to control and utilize natural products.

The parts of the celestial mechanism were separable bodies moving under the influence of impressed forces. In the final analysis, the bodies were mass-points, or irreducible atoms, mutually separable and independent. Under the aegis of this conceptual scheme science made spectacular advances and, as generally presupposed, it deeply affected the thought and practice of the modern age in all its branches. Atomism dominated the thinking of the period in every field. In philosophy, under the influence of Descartes and the rationalists, the central concept became that of a unitary self, or ego, centered upon itself, as the source of all certainty, all knowledge and all action. This concept underpinned a radical individualism that came to infect moral and political thinking. Under the influence of the British empiricists, in contrast, epistemology was founded upon psychological atomism, which came to fruition in the work of David Hume, and dissolved away the self altogether. In morality it was subjective satisfaction, whether in the enjoyment of pleasure or in the attainment of self-realization, that determined ethical theory and codes of conduct. In politics and economics a radical individualism prevailed as expounded in the work of John Locke and later in that of Adam Smith, of John Stuart Mill and of Herbert Spencer.

All these currents of thought have continued to the present day. In philosophy Hume's atomistic empiricism has been followed. Like him, contemporary philosophers have castigated and abandoned metaphysics, with the final result that their philosophy, like Hume's own, has collapsed into complete skepticism. The cult of the ego, in phenomenology and existentialism, has had a similar issue by way of hermeneutics in deconstructionism. Morality has declined due to the insidious belief in relativism resulting on the one hand from the Newtonian subjectivization of value judgments and the demand for value-free science and on the other from the self-centered subjectivizing tendency of utilitarian hedonism and the individualism of Locke and Mill. From this also a political "liberalism" has developed that is radically individualistic and issues in a tension between individual rights and government action with consequent resistance to all government as such and the pursuit of factional demands. The same individualism has spawned the capitalist self-interested pursuit of profit in economics, to which all else has been subordinated, creating an ever widening gulf between the rich and the poor. In international relations the nation-state, in keeping with the prevailing separatism, insists on its independence and gives precedence to its own national interests at the expense of the common interests of humanity. The results have been breakdown of moral standards, corruption in government, increase in crime, the exacerbation of economic inequality, civil and international conflict, rampant terrorism, and the betrayal in practice of religious principles, be they Christian, Muslim, or Buddhist.

Meanwhile the exploitation of natural resources causes untold damage to the planetary ecology that threatens the survival of all life on Earth. Natural science made enormous advances after Newton's synthesis of the Copernican developments, and the mechanistic paradigm generated a technology that produced the industrial revolution. Production has increased beyond all precedent until, today, excessive exploitation of natural resources, over-cultivation of arable land, widespread extraction of mineral wealth and increasing use of fossil fuels are disrupting the planetary environment. The ozone layer is being depleted, the rain forests are being destroyed, and living species are being decimated at an alarming rate. Industrialization is polluting rivers, lakes, the ocean, and the atmosphere; green-house gases emitted in vast quantities are producing global warming that threatens calamitous climate change. Thus the advance of technology facilitated by Newtonian science is threatening the very survival of the civilization it has helped to create, and is destroying the conditions on which all life on Earth depends.

This is the sorry aftermath of renaissance science and the Enlightenment, the deleterious consequences of an outmoded scientific paradigm—outmoded, because it has now long been superseded by the physics of relativity and quanta and an organismic biology, whose dominant concept is an all-embracing unity that has reversed and cancelled out the atomism of Newtonianism. The new conceptual scheme has not yet borne fruit in philosophical thinking, nor has it permeated the social structure of our culture. If it were to do so, the holism characteristic of the new physics would revolutionize all our thinking, would produce a new metaphysic and with it a new moral philosophy. Our current problems are global in scope and can be solved only by adopting a global outlook, by instituting global government, and by taking global action. The social and political world, like the biosphere and the physical universe, must be seen as a single whole, and global social solidarity has become the prerequisite of human salvation.

The new scientific paradigm ushered in this new outlook almost a century ago, but aside from the sciences its implications have not been appreciated. We cannot, however, wait for the normally slow processes of history by which the new conceptual scheme becomes absorbed into our common way of life, because until this happens the survival of the race will be in serious jeopardy, due to the destruction of the life-sustaining global environment, now proceeding at a rate which is fast becoming irreversible.

In the chapters that follow I have tried to demonstrate the failure of empiricism and the philosophical outgrowths from classical Newtonian science, and I have endeavored to outline the sort of metaphysic demanded by the new physics of our own day. I have not discussed phenomenology and existentialism or their various offshoots as much, or given them as close attention, as I have given to contemporary empiricism because my main objective has been to expose the dependence of the theories denigrating metaphysics on the scientific presuppositions of a bygone era. This is less marked, although not altogether absent, in the thought of Husserl and Heidegger, who were both impressed by the limitations of Newtonian science. The persistence of the spell over them of Newtonian ideas is due to their inheritance from Kant and Nietzsche. Nor is their objection to metaphysics so vocal or vituperative, although, in the Continental movements that have developed out of their thought, it is strong. The typical anti-metaphysical stance is that of empiricism, which is the direct product of renaissance science; so it is to empiricism that my critique is chiefly directed.

My hope is to accelerate the permeation of contemporary culture by the conceptual scheme initiated by the twentieth century scientific revolution, the effects of which have been delayed by the hangover from inebriation by the scientific progress that the Newtonian paradigm stimulated.

In this book I have drawn together and interwoven the various threads that have led me to the philosophical position I have striven to develop over the past sixty years. It contains the fruit of my latest reflection and presents a world view that I think I can claim is genuinely post modern, where "modern" is taken to indicate the outlook and cast of thought typical of Western civilization after the Renaissance. If there is little sign at the present time of widespread adoption of a fresh philosophical outlook, I can but hope that what I have written may catch the attention of some of the younger generation, in whose hands the direction of the future lies.

Acknowledgments

The publisher gratefully acknowledges permission to use the following material:

In Chapter 1, from *Impressions of Empiricism* (London: Macmillan, 1976).

In Chapters 2 and 3, from *Philosophical Quarterly*, vols. 2 (1952) and 3 (1953).

In Chapter 4, from *Dialectica*, vol. 17, no. 1 (1963).

In Chapter 6, from *Proceedings of the American Catholic Philosophical Association*, 1967.

In Chapter 10, from *Journal of Philosophy*, vol. 56, no. 1, (1959).

In Chapter 12, from the *International Philosophical Quarterly*, vol. 6, no. 4 (1966), and *Proceedings of the XIIth International Congress of Philosophy*, 1968.

In Chapters 15 and 16, from *Idealistic Studies*, vol. 19, no. 2 (1979), and vol. 5 no. 3 (1975).

Introduction: Attacks on Metaphysics

Philosophy in the twentieth century has been marked by the repudiation of metaphysics as a possible discipline. This is, of course, nothing new, and, in the current century, its various forms of attack have all been revivals of similar attacks in the past, for they have not been infrequent throughout the history of Western thought. Even if we do not go back to the Ancients, to Lucretius, or to the Sophists, modern philosophy affords recurrent denials of the viability of metaphysics. We are all familiar with David Hume's denunciation:

> If we take in our hand any volume; of divinity or school metaphysics, for instance; let us ask, *Does it contain any abstract reasoning concerning quantity or number?* No. *does it contain any experimental reasoning concerning matter of fact?* No. Commit it then to the flames: for it can contain nothing but sophistry and illusion.[1]

Twentieth-century empiricism stemming from the logical positivism of the Vienna Circle revived this rejection of metaphysics for like reasons: that its statements could not be verified by empirical observation, and so were castigated as senseless.

Immanuel Kant's rejection of metaphysics (qualified as it is) has been followed in effect by Edmund Husserl and the phenomenologists, as has Friedrich Nietzsche's by the existentialists; and all these tendencies have converged and have culminated in the radical nihilism of such thinkers as Richard Rorty and the poststructuralism and postmodernism of Michel Foucault and Jacques Derrida, reviving in large measure a positivism akin to that of Auguste Comte.

The final outcome is a self-defeating skepticism, for the principles adopted by each of these trends, if applied to its own position, renders it untenable on its own showing. The logical positivists soon realized that their verification principle was itself unverifiable and thus, by their own criterion, metaphysical. They attempted to escape by resorting to linguistic analysis, seeking to show that metaphysical questions were pseudoquestions arising from the misapplication of technical, or the misuse of ordinary, language; but this eventually also turned against itself in Rorty's evacuating "pragmaticism," which refuses to take any philosophy, including itself, seriously.

Moreover, all these philosophical movements are themselves metaphysical, although the metaphysical bases on which they rest are not often acknowledged. That of positivism is empiricism, the metaphysical presumption that all

1

knowledge is derived from sensation—the effect on the mind (or brain) of causal influences from external things—resting again on the prior metaphysical presupposition of materialism. This was succinctly stated by Thomas Hobbes:

> There is no conception in a man's mind, which hath not at first, totally, or by parts, been begotten upon the organs of *Sense*.
> All which qualities called *Sensible*, are in the object that causeth them, but so many several motions of the matter, by which it presseth our organs diversely. Neither in us that are pressed, are they any thing else but diverse motions; (for motion produceth nothing but motion). But their appearance to us is Fancy, the same waking that dreaming.[2]

Here we have pure assumptions, which are not only metaphysical but also mutually inconsistent (for the "appearance to us" remains totally inexplicable on the premises stated).

That nothing exists except matter is not empirically verifiable, and the assumption that sensation is nothing other than motion produced by the pressure on our sense organs of external objects is incoherent, for as even John Locke was aware, the causes of our sensations "appear not to our senses to operate in their production"[3]—not even as "Fancy." Consequently, the conceptions of the mind cannot include any awareness of organs of sense, and Hobbes' contention, if true, would be unknowable and, if known, must for that very reason be false. Yet this palpably untenable metaphysic is the underpinning of every version of empiricism.

Contemporary empiricists became uncomfortably aware of the crumbly condition of their theories' foundation but were reluctant to abandon them altogether, so they changed their tactics and put the blame for the defects on linguistic aberrations. The new stance, however, still rested upon the same presuppositions. The original rejection of all statements unverifiable by sense observation led them to contend that knowledge about matters of fact could be gained solely from empirical science, and to restrict the task of philosophy to logic and the analysis of language. Logic (at first) was regarded as a special, ideal language displaying the logical structure of the facts. Later, this was also denied as a deception generated by the form of mathematical language. Accordingly, in this persistent reliance on linguistic analysis as the panacea of all ills, the empiricist assumption remained fundamental to analytic philosophy (but unacknowledged) to the end.

Presumably it was a repressed sense of guilt about this unacknowledged foundation that led Rorty to argue that every quest for "foundations" was futile and illegitimate, because there were none. Knowledge has no discoverable undergirding, not even, it would seem, the knowledge that it has none. Like all skeptical claims, Rorty's denials must apply to his own contentions if they are to be self-consistent. They can, if they are to be heeded, have no foundation, and there will be no basis for their truth. If all philosophy is indefensible and insupportable, Rorty's included, his own submissions, as he himself confesses, cannot be taken seriously.

Kant's objections were not to metaphysics as such but only to the kind of metaphysics that, in his day, had become current in the schools—mainly the sort purveyed by Christian Wolff. Kant recognized that his own position was metaphysical and claimed that its aim was the only "scientifically" justifiable task that metaphysics could perform: namely, to set the proper limits to the scope of the understanding and the use of reason. Husserl takes a very similar route, closely following Kant and Johann Fichte (though without acknowledgment), and while claiming that phenomenology is an exact science, he declares it to be metaphysically neutral; but he does not disguise its derivation from René Descartes's *cogito* and its dependence on the metaphysical postulation of a transcendental ego.

Much the same is true of the existentialists, whose insistence on absolute freedom and authenticity is reminiscent of Fichte's argument in *Die Bestimmung der Menchen*; for them, however, the confession is not so clearly made that it is the transcendental ego that underlies free action, as it is for Kant and Fichte. The efforts of both Martin Heidegger and Maurice Merleau-Ponty to avoid commitment to a transcendental ego fail—in Heidegger's case because it is the necessary (if unrecognized) presupposition of the existential awareness of "being-in-the-world," implying the distinction indicated by the hyphenation between *Dasein* and its surroundings. The consciousness of being-in-the-world must transcend this distinction if we are to be aware of it, so that consciousness cannot be identified with the natural self. The choice of *Seinkönnen* from among what is conceived as "coming toward" *Dasein* out of a projected future involves the same implication. Only a transcendental ego, no natural self confined to what is "ready to hand," could so conceive them.[4]

In the case of Merleau-Ponty, who rejects the notion of a transcendental ego as too intellectualistic, implying a transparency in consciousness that it can never claim, the attempt to avoid commitment to a transcendental ego fails because the ambiguous use of the French *corps vecu*, which in English becomes "lived body," implies some sort of awareness, even if prepredicative, that must be able somehow to grasp the "being-in-the-world" of the lived body, as no feeling or activity confined to a merely physiological body could.[5] The verb "live" in English cannot be made transitive, so the use of "lived body" by translators is a solecism. The legitimate sense of the phrase is "felt body," or bodily feeling, and that does indeed include the whole content of consciousness (as Benedict Spinoza, G. W. F. Hegel, F. H. Bradley, and R. G. Collingwood were all well aware), but its discrimination into self and other, and the habitation of the first in the distinguished surrounding world, necessarily imply a transcendent subject that is not the same as either. The metaphysical substrate of the implicit denial of metaphysics is again evident.

Phenomenology purports to be pure description of what direct inspection of consciousness reveals. The immediate awareness of being-in-the-world is its product. From this it is a short step to the notion of *Verstehen*, which Wilhelm Dilthey insists is the necessary condition of historiography. *Verstehen* involves not just intellectual understanding but also all emotional and spiritual experience; it is the projection of the historian into the entire state of mind of the people of whom he or she writes and must be the substance of all interpretation. Here (as with Merleau-Ponty), intellectualism is played down; but more than this, objectivity is denied, and a descent into historicism and relativism is the inevitable consequence.

The next step, taken by H-G. Gadamer, is to apply this principle to the historian himself, and to any other sort of writer, including especially the philosopher. It thus becomes a hermeneutical principle, and the doctrine is promoted that all history and all philosophy are to be reduced to hermeneutics, the sole object of which is the text to be interpreted.

The outcome of this current of thought is a dialectical opposition: first, a radical historicism, which renounces all objectivity and makes all interpretation relative to the social context; and second, a detachment of the interpreter from the text as a distinct object. The first results in the structuralism of Claude Lévi-Strauss, a curious and somewhat perverted form of holism, which insists on *Verstehen* in the sense of understanding all human activity in terms of the social structure to which it belongs, while denying to the participants awareness of the social structures within which they think and act and to the influence of which they are inevitably subject. The very possibility of history is then denied, and its whole temporal structure is relativized and condemned; and with it, the objectivity of any kind of knowledge goes by the board.

The second results in a neopositivism surfacing as poststructuralism, or deconstructionism, as we find it in the work of Foucault and Derrida, repudiating all subjectivity, all meaning, all interpretation, and all transcendental *a prioris* and professing to regard every subject matter of research purely "objectively."

Historicism and relativism conceal an underlying subjectivism in their denial of objectivity, yet they revert into the opposite by detaching the investigator from his or her object and encouraging behaviorism and objectivism. So the protest of Husserl and Heidegger against objectivation has, by stages, been turned upside down and transformed into a complete renunciation of subjectivity.

But none of this is of any avail. Relativism is inextricably entangled with skepticism. The denial of objectivity is the denial of truth, and that cannot but infect the asseverations of the relativist and the skeptic themselves. The same applies to the radical positivism and deconstructionism of the postmodernists; the requirement of consistency dictates that their own works be regarded "objectively," without respect to meaning, as "discourse" (according to Foucault) or as "writing" (according to Derrida), the significance of which (if any) is determined purely by the current practice in their field of activity. If so, the claims they make with respect to other doctrines will be applicable to their own and are immediately relativized. Or else they commit the Epistemologist's Fallacy by exempting their own theory from the strictures it imposes upon all others and that, if allowed, would prove it false of theory in general.

Once again, attacks on metaphysics, overt or implied, have proved self-destructive, and the barrenness of contemporary philosophy has become apparent. In fact, philosophy, as a constructive and enlightening study, has virtually disappeared from the schools, giving way to sciences, exact and empirical, natural and social. Yet the sciences themselves, in the twentieth century, have been revolutionized and are demanding a new metaphysic in harmony with and definitive of their developing conceptual scheme (or "paradigm," in Thomas Kuhn's terminology). This will not be a return to the old metaphysics of empiricism or rationalism, realism and idealism, but will be one demanding a holistic conception of the real, which reconciles all these oppositions, absolves metaphysics from all the current misconceived defamations, and so far from substituting empirical science for metaphysical speculation, is itself the consequence of the current scientific paradigm.

In the chapters which follow, first the attack on metaphysics made by the empiricists is examined and criticized. Then a new metaphysic is outlined, concordant with the scientific revolution of the twentieth century, and certain aspects of it are further developed, promising a more constructive and productive prospect for philosophical progress. No special consideration has been given to phenomenology and existentialism, nor is there any detailed assessment of them and their various offshoots, because the main object of discussion is to expose the dependence of the theories denigrating metaphysics on the scientific presuppositions of a bygone age. This is less marked, although not altogether absent, in the thought of Husserl, Heidegger and their followers than in that of the Vienna Circle and theirs. So far as it is implicit in Husserl, it is inherited from Kant and, in existentialism, from Nietzsche. Nor is the antipathy to metaphysics so vocal or so vituperative in these thinkers, even though it is strong in the most recent Continental writers. The typical antimetaphysical stance is that of empiricism, which is the direct product of the Copernican revolution of the sixteenth century and the consequent Newtonian conceptual scheme. So it is at empiricism that the ensuing critique is chiefly directed.

What follows should be read in conjunction with what I have written elsewhere, in *Nature, Mind and Modern Science*, in *Formal Transcendental and Dialectical Thinking*, in *The Reality of Time*, and *in Cosmos and Athropos*, and is intended as a complement to those works.

Notes

1. David Hume, *An Enquiry Concerning Human Understanding*, sec. XII, pt. III.
2. Thomas Hobbes, *Leviathan*, chap. I.
3. John Locke, *An Essay Concerning Human Understanding*, bk. II, chaps. 8, 25.
4. Cf. E. E. Harris, *The Reality of Time*, pp. 30–1.
5. Cf. Harris, *The Reality of Time*, p. 97f.

Part 1
Errors of Empiricism

1

Empiricism in Philosophy and in Science

The term "empiricism" has had at least two different, though not unconnected, applications in modern thought, one to scientific method and the other to philosophical theory. I shall try to show that although these two applications of the term have a common source, their actual referents are widely divergent and in large measure even mutually incompatible.

The birth of modern science in the seventeenth century brought with it a firm conviction that scientific theory must be founded upon and supported by observed factual and experimental evidence. Since then, no respectable scientist has ever regarded a theory as established until some experimental confirmation, considered sufficient by the scientific community, has been produced. This dependence of scientific knowledge upon observation and experiment is what is meant by empiricism in science. But the precise function of observation and its relation to theory in the methodology of science are matters to be further investigated.

Philosophical empiricism, on the other hand, is something much more radical and deep-seated. It is a theory of knowledge, an epistemology, which carries with it implications for scientific method but which can itself claim empirical support only if and so far as the actual practice of scientists conforms to its requirements. Philosophical empiricism is not just a methodology of science; it is a theory of the nature of knowledge as such, and whether it is empirical in the first sense I have distinguished is a further question.

I do not propose to review the long history of philosophical empiricism or to list its numerous varieties—for not all theories that accept the title agree in detail. It will be enough to observe that in its modern forms, the philosophic theory was largely inspired by the new emphasis on empirical evidence in seventeenth-century science, and especially by the enthusiasm for experimental methods expressed by Francis Bacon in his *Novum Organum*. It must be noticed, however, that Bacon did not develop an epistemoloy but only a methodology of science, and one that does not necessarily involve empiricism in the second sense of the term. He protested against the prejudices of the learned and of the vulgar, against fruitless debate without systematic investigation, and he insisted upon the importance of experiment, but he did not ground these views on any explicit philosophical theory of knowledge or reality.

Modern philosophical empiricism proper was founded by Thomas Hobbes and John Locke, but there is no need for me to expound their theories here, or that of any other individual philosopher. I shall merely outline in brief (and I hope without undue misrepresentation of any particular thinker) the main and most typical tenets of philosophical empiricism in general, note its implications for metaphysics and scientific method, and then turn to the actual procedure of practicing scientists to discover whether it supports the philosophical theory.

The first and most fundamental principle of theoretical empiricism is that all factual knowledge about the world ultimately derives from sensation. This is, perhaps, a rather crude statement of the principle, but although it may need refinement and qualification, it does not seriously misrepresent the tradition. Sensations are held to be passively received by the knowing subject and to reveal those basic qualities (sometimes called sense-data, or sensa) by combination of which physical objects are built up. The rest is a matter of construction, arrangement, and concatenation of these, which issues as a picture of a world of material things in specific relations.

Some may wish to deny that empiricists derive all knowledge from sensation. Logical and mathematical truths, what Hume called 'relations of ideas," as opposed to "matters of fact," are, as he put it, "discoverable by the mere operation of thought without dependence on what is anywhere existent in the universe."[1] But for empiricists, such truths are devoid of factual content and express, in the last resort, only linguistic equivalences, so that it is doubtful whether they should rank as knowledge in any proper sense of the word. Even so, if statements of linguistic equivalence are to have any content whatever, that content must, on this theory, be derived from sense. As for Hume's "relations of ideas," he was quite adamant in his insistence that all ideas are merely fainter copies of sensory impressions, and "what is discoverable by the mere operation of thought" is, for him, the result only of the comparison of impressions or ideas, for there is nothing else for thought to work upon. Abstract ideas, apart from particular impressions or their ideal replicas, Hume, following George Berkeley, rejects without reserve. So I think I can leave my initial statement standing: for empiricism, the original source of all knowledge is sense.

If more testimony is desired, I have only to quote Hume once again. In his *Treatise of Human Nature* he writes:

> Now since nothing is ever present to the mind but perceptions, and since all ideas are derived from something antecedently present to the mind; it follows, that 'tis impossible for us so much as to conceive or form an idea of anything specifically different from ideas and impressions. Let us fix our attention

out of ourselves as much as possible: Let us chace our imagination to the heavens, or the utmost limits of the universe; we never really advance a step beyond ourselves, nor can we conceive any kind of existence, but those perceptions, which have appeared in that narrow compass. This is the universe of the imagination, nor have we any idea but what is there produced.[2]

Hume's final conclusion—that metaphysics, containing neither content derived from sensible data nor pure mathematics, is worthless sophistry—follows immediately. The universe of the imagination may, presumably, include artifacts, fiction, and poetry, but there can be no justification for imputing reality to any of these. The speculations of metaphysics, having no empirical base, can be nothing but fantastic concoctions of the mind.

It is further maintained that all sensuous impressions are "particular existences," and so likewise are the simple ideas derived from them. The former, in more recent terminology, are called sense-data, and the latter their imaginative reproduction. Although our minds can combine or separate them in any way they please in imagination and can compare and relate their qualities, they cannot create them ab initio and can accept impressions only as they occur, in continuous succession. Moreover, their intrinsic character reveals no feature which can determine how, or in what order, they should occur; so that there is no evident connection between any two of them, and in consequence, the occurrence of none of them can be inferred from that of any other.

It follows that the only ground we can have for predicting future experience is our expectation that conjunctions of impressions and ideas, which have happened frequently in the past, will recur in the future. For apart from the frequent conjunction of impressions and ideas in the past, there is nothing to indicate in what order they may occur in the future. But frequent conjunction leads the mind to expect similar recurrences: thus, if thunder has, in past experience, constantly followed lightning, we expect that this conjunction will recur, and when we see the flash we listen for the rumble as its consequent, or if we hear the crash we presume that the lightning immediately preceded it. Accordingly, all inference to matters of fact, according to empiricist doctrine, is and can only be of this inductive type.

Inference of any other kind depends, according to Hume, upon comparison between ideas and impressions that are immediately present to the mind. Other writers have stressed its purely analytic character. They maintain, following Hobbes, that it can do no more than develop the consequences of the definitions of terms and is thus essentially tautological, affording no new information. This is the character, for empiricism, of all deductive reasoning; while any and every inference yielding conclusions that are not contained in the premises can only be inductive.

It would be altogether mistaken to form the impression (should anybody be so inclined) that, because I have quoted Hume, empiricism may be dismissed as a philosophical doctrine that went out of commission in the eighteenth century. Not only did John Suart Mill and others continue the tradition in the nineteenth, but it has been predominant among philosophers of our own day in the English-speaking world and very influential outside it. But although contemporary thinkers such as Bertrand Russell, G. E. Moore, Ludwig Wittgenstein, and Rudolf Carnap have introduced complications and sophistications, the fundamental tenets remain the same, and Hume's statement of the theory is still the most consistent, most uncompromising, and most powerful.

Accordingly, at least until the 1960s, philosophy of science was largely concerned with developing the consequences of philosophical empiricism for scientific methodology and has concluded, in conformity with the outline I have given, that scientific reasoning is—and, like any other reasoning, only can be—either deductive, which is purely analytic and tautological, or inductive, deriving general laws from particular observed instances and making predictions on the basis of such laws. An elegant and detailed account of how these two types of reasoning are combined in scientific method is set out in Professor R. B. Braithwaite's book *Scientific Explanation*, as well as in many other modern texts, which leave no doubt about the prevalence of the theory at the time.

Difficulties, however, immediately suggest themselves, for the main pride and special achievement of science has been the making of discoveries, and if its methods were restricted to the two forms of reasoning alleged, it could never discover anything new, unless by direct observation, for which no special method seems necessary. That nothing new can be discovered by purely analytic deduction everybody will agree—and all empiricists insist. But it is less obvious that inductive inference is equally sterile, though that must surely be the case. For all that can legitimize its conclusions is the frequent conjunction of events in past experience, and the only conclusion that can support is the probable repetition of the past conjunction. Consequently, induction can do no more than underline what is already known. Neither of these forms of reasoning could predict the occurrence of a conjunction that has never previously been observed, nor do empiricists claim that either of them could.

It may be said, however, that although new knowledge cannot be reached by deduction alone, or by induction alone, yet in combination they can reveal the unexpected. If this is so, I cannot understand how. It is usually maintained that the purely formal structure of a deductive system is an uninterpreted calculus, consisting of formulae constructed from symbols representing variables. The calculus operates according to set rules prescribing the method of transformation of formulae, so that from certain equivalences others can be derived. We interpret the calculus by substituting empirical terms, denoting observables, for the variables; then we can deduce from certain empirical statements others which we have not yet observed to be true but which can now be put to the test of experiment.

This, however, does not seem to me to be feasible, because the deductive system is purely analytic, and the transformation of any formula results only in another which is equivalent to the first. No conclusion can be drawn by its means which contains anything not already included in the premises. So even if empirical terms are substituted for the variables to provide, as premises, statements of what has been observed, all that could be derived from them by pure deduction would be equivalent statements of the same observations. The meaning of any statement resulting from the replacement of variables by empirical terms must necessarily be the same as that of any other from which it could be validly derived. If new information is to be derived by "deduction," it must be some other kind of deduction than what empiricists will allow.

How then does the scientist make discoveries? Must (s)he wait until (s)he observes new phenomena by chance? Some scientific discoveries do seem to have been accidental, but serendipity is exceptional, and its accidental character is largely a deceptive appearance, for observations that the scientist is not theoretically equipped to make are never recorded (for reasons we shall presently have occasion to note). Is it, perhaps, that the methodology of scientific experimentation, on the necessity of which Bacon was so insistent, holds the secret of discovery? In some measure, I believe that it does, although it is not sufficient by itself. But if it does, traditional empiricists have not revealed that secret, for it cannot be with the help of the deduction or induction they are prepared to countenance that experiment can discover anything *new*, and if it does not do so by sheer accident, some other kind of logic must be involved.

Moreover, a very little reflection on the history of science soon reveals that some of the most significant and spectacular discoveries have been made independently of any new observations, and others again have been of objects or processes that could not have been observed at all. In some cases, the discoveries were of facts which could not at the time be observed with the means then at the disposal of scientists; in other cases, they were literally unobservable. Numerous examples are available of both types. One example of the first is the discovery of molecular structure, and an example of the second is the discovery of the precession of the perihelion of Mercury.

Even a less controversial case, like the discovery of Uranus, was not just the direct observation of a new phenomenon. In fact it was not a new observation at all, for Uranus had been sighted twenty-two times before it was 'discovered." Even Sir William Herschel, when he came upon the unexpected object while mapping the heavens, took it to be a comet. And he did so not entirely on the basis of what he saw but largely in consequence of theoretical assumptions. Only after elaborate mathematical calculations to determine the orbit of the alleged comet was it discovered to be a planet, and needless to say, no orbit as such can be observed; it has to be inferred from a conjunction of observation, measurement, and calculation. Thus discovery is the fruit of inference, but not of purely analytic deduction, which cannot produce new knowledge, nor of induction, which can only repeat the old. At no stage in Herschel's proceeding did he, or anybody else, argue that because the new celestial body appeared as it did, or moved as calculated, it could be expected to do so again in the future. Such an inference would have been of no interest. What excited the astronomers and the world at large was that an eighth planet had swum into the ken of humankind. A new and hitherto unknown fact had been revealed.

I am not suggesting that observation and experiment are unimportant factors in scientific method; quite the contrary. They are undoubtedly indispensable, and it is precisely to them that the description of science as empirical refers. But the relation between observation and theory is not what traditional empiricism alleges. No observation is intelligible and no experiment would be made apart from theory, which is not only the conclusion drawn from repeated observations but is also the means of recognizing and interpreting what is observed, as well as of conceiving and designing experiments. Observation cannot be merely random and haphazard if it is to be scientific; but without a prior hypothesis, random and haphazard is all it could be. Experiment is, in fact, the question that the scientist puts to nature, and no question arises unless some theory is already being entertained. Further, all observation, even the most naive, is an interpretation, in the light of prior knowledge, of presented "data" (though I use that word with reservation, because nothing intelligible is ever merely "given"). Experiment is part of the scientist's endeavor to develop the implications of hypotheses already conceived. And it is in terms of theories already established and accepted that he or she interprets the results.

In fact, recent developments in the philosophy of science have established that all observation is theory laden, and it is only in the light of accepted theories that the objects of scientific theory are recognized when encountered. Charles Darwin, investigating with Sedgewick the geology of Cwm Idwal in Wales, records in his autobiography that neither of them saw any of the glacial phenomena surrounding them which, he says, "are so conspicuous that . . . a house on fire did not tell its story more plainly than this valley." Thomas Kuhn has shown from the history of science that the interpretation of all that is observed depends on the current "paradigm" accepted by the scientific community of the day, and that this includes its conception of the fundamental elements of nature and the general character of the universe at large. What does not conform to this accepted conceptual scheme is simply not observed at all. This contention completely demolishes the fundamental belief of philosophical empiricism that all knowledge is derived from passively received sense impressions, a belief that has been further discredited by investigations in the psychology of perception by Sir Frederick Bartlett, M. D. Vernon, and many others.

Furthermore, neither accepted theories nor hypotheses to be tested are a product of inductive inference of the sort envisaged by philosophical empiricism.

Arguments of the form "AB frequently, therefore, probably AB always" may be encountered in therapeutic sciences such as medicine, but they are never more than preliminary, and no scientist bent on discovery will be content with any such reasoning. Practitioners may for a time rely on what are called "purely empirical" conjunctions. For instance, acupuncture has been found, when skillfully applied, to have certain beneficial effects; therefore, if similarly applied again, similar effects may be expected. But the scientific physiologist will want to discover why acupuncture has these effects and will look for more systematic connections. Constant conjunction is indeed an indication that systematic relationships exist and may be discovered, so that the argument "AB frequently, therefore perhaps AB always," although not unimportant or irrelevant, is only a first step.

Even so, some prior theory, some suggested hypothesis, is necessary before a constant conjunction appears significant, and without the theory, no correlation may even be noticed. Moreover, an important condition is that the prior theory should be in some way defective and should have given rise to difficulties and conflicts. For example, in the early days of chemistry, it was only when the phlogiston theory began to give trouble that attention was paid to the fact that substances increased in weight when burned. The fact itself had been noticed as early as 1630, by Jean Rey, but as long as the idea of phlogiston seemed useful (and in its day, it was far more fruitful than is often imagined), the only interest the augmentation in weight aroused was as a slight anomaly to be explained away, as it was by assuming that phlogiston had negative weight. However, as the pneumatic chemists in the eighteenth century came upon various "airs," some of which supported combustion and some of which did not, some of which burned in air and some of which did not, the phlogiston explanation gave rise to numerous contradictions, a list of which is given by Lavoisier in the first section of his *Opuscules Physique et Chemique*. He therefore proposed the hypothesis that when substances burned and metals calcined, they absorbed some portion of the surrounding air. At the same time, Guyton de Morveau performed a series of experiments demonstrating the constant augmentation of weight accompanying combustion, the clue that Lavoisier (among others) followed in a more famous series of experiments establishing the theory of oxidation.

We can observe from this example first that there existed a prior theory which was proving unsatisfactory (because it led to contradictions) and next that the contradictions arising from it raised new questions, which prompted experimentation and fresh observation, revealing constant conjunctions. Then these gave rise to a new tentative hypothesis, followed, finally, by further experiments to test and confirm the new theory.

An important feature of this development is that, if de Morveau's experiments seemed to reveal a constant conjunction, Lavoisier's were neither designed to do so nor produced one as their result. The experiments were diverse in character, each produced a different result, and none was merely repetitive; but all the results fitted together systematically, and each supported all the rest, so that they formed an interrelated system of evidence, of mutually interdependent facts. The new theory stated the principle of relationship that made the diverse phenomena hang together coherently, as the old theory had tried but failed to do.

To these characteristics of scientific method I shall have occasion to refer again, but we may immediately observe that so-called inductive argument plays a relatively minor part. In fact, it is demonstrably false that scientists always derive their theories by generalization from repeated conjunction of particular observed phenomena. Undoubtedly they do, on appropriate occasions, use statistical methods to evaluate evidence. But not all, and not the most important, scientific theories have been reached by any method remotely resembling induction of the traditional empiricist pattern. An outstanding example (but certainly not the only one) is the heliocentric hypothesis of Copernicus, which was not prompted by any special observations. In fact, it would be difficult to imagine any naked-eye observations of the heavens (and none other were available at the time) from which such a hypothesis could have been generalized. No observation of the diurnal motion of the heavenly bodies reveals the fact that the earth (or any other planet) revolves around the sun, and no inductive generalization from what is constantly observed gives this conclusion. What Copernicus did was to revive a theory suggested centuries earlier by Aristarchus of Samos to explain data which, as sensuously observed (visible points of light against the dark background of the heavens), could mean nothing intelligible without some theory in terms of which they could be interpreted. Nor was Copernicus's system for interpreting the movement of the heavenly bodies less complicated or more successful as a means of prediction than Ptolemy's, which it was designed to replace. Its sole claim to superiority, and the source of its appeal to Copernicus' followers, was its greater coherent unity, the merit that he himself emphasized in recommending it to Pope Pius III.

Among contemporary philosophers, Sir Karl Popper was the first to draw attention to the fact that induction was not the typical form of scientific reasoning. He rejected it also for philosophical reasons, which, important as they are, I do not propose to review.[3] Scientific method, in his view, is hypothetico-deductive, and he would respond to my question about discovery by denying that it is ever a matter of logic. What scientists discover are new theories, and these (Popper maintains) are pure conjecture, to which logic does not apply. Once conceived, consequences that are subject to observation and experiment can be deduced from the conjectured hypothesis. Thus we may test the hypothesis, but favorable observations, however many, can never verify it. They only leave it unrefuted, for verification by inductive reasoning is never possible;

no amount of favorable evidence ever being enough. Yet one unfavorable instance is sufficient to falsify the hypothesis. The endeavor of science, then, is always to falsify, and hypotheses survive as long as that endeavor fails.

The answer to the question about the logic of discovery, on this view, would be that there is none, for no logical account can ever be given. Logic becomes applicable only in assessing the arguments by which scientists seek to falsify theories or, when occasion arises, to justify their retention. Hypotheses are discovered by the exercise of scientific genius, which is explicable, if at all, only by psychology, and follows no logical rules. This, today, is a widely accepted doctrine, and of course it is true both that arguments in defense or in refutation of scientific theories must be logically validated and that genius is largely unaccountable, in the sense that insight is a talent for the acquisition of which there are no rules. But if genius is needed to make scientific discoveries, it does not follow that no logical process is involved in the activity, any more than it follows that because genius is needed for the composition of a symphony, the composer may ignore the rules of harmony and counterpoint.

There are good reasons for denying the division of scientific procedure into what have been called "the context of discovery" and "the context of justification." The two processes are inextricably intertwined, and I hope to be able to indicate here, if not to demonstrate conclusively, that a logic of some kind is intrinsic to both.

Popper seems to me to be certainly right in maintaining that consequences are deduced from hypotheses which are then tested by observation. But if so, the deduction must be of a kind that can disclose new facts. If it were purely analytic, all we could derive by its means would be either alternative forms of the hypothesis or alternative formulations of initial conditions brought under the supposed law (the assumed hypothesis having the form of a law of nature). But this would give us nothing to investigate experimentally. The argument should run thus:

> If hypothesis H is true, under conditions a, b, and c (which we have experienced and can reproduce), result R would occur (which has not yet been observed).

This is a synthetic proposition that could not be the product of purely formal deduction. Nobody, least at all Popper, would regard it as an inductive argument. So the question remains: what kind of logic is involved? Even in hypothetico-deductive procedure, it is not what empiricism could consistently admit.

Sir Karl has put us on a new path, but he has not led us out of the woods. Hypotheses are not as a rule, or typically, mere guesses, and they are prompted by rational considerations. Some kind of logical account of them should therefore be possible. In the history of science, we constantly find that new hypotheses are modifications and adaptations of older ones, the breakdown of which is heralded by the emergence of contradiction in the course of developing their consequences. The success or failure of a hypothesis depends on the extent to which it can disclose systematic relationships among observed phenomena consistently and over a comprehensive range; when it fails, it gives rise to new questions and efforts at reconstruction in order to resolve the conflicts.

Further, the method of empirical testing does not center purely on efforts at falsification. When awkward cases are found in the course of scientific research, the theory is not immediately rejected. The matter is usually held in abeyance, pending closer investigation, for scientists do not—they cannot afford to—reject an effective explanatory system in response to isolated unassimilable instances. The anomalies are not altogether ignored, but a persistent effort is made to adjust and modify the principles of the system so that the difficulties will be overcome, usually, at first, by adopting some ad hoc explanation. When many such anomalies have accumulated, and when they involve serious contradictions within the system, drastic modifications of the conceptual scheme may be demanded, and when such epoch-marking changes do occur, they alter the whole aspect of the science concerned. But contrary to the belief that has become since Thomas Kuhn declared consecutive paradigms to be incommensurable, such revolutions do not give rise to theories that are altogether discontinuous with those they replace.

These features of scientific advance have already been noted in Lavoisier's demolition of the phlogiston theory, and they can be discerned in the still more dramatic transition from Aristotelian to Galilean and Newtonian mechanics.

Aristotle, as is well known, taught that bodies moved only if violently dislodged from their normal place. They moved, therefore, either under impulsion or naturally if returning to their proper place in the universe. Two major difficulties, however, arose from this theory. First, falling bodies moved continuously faster as they approached the earth. The Aristotelian explanation, that they increased their speed from joy at the nearer approach to their natural home, would not account for the fact that a body dropped from a greater height accelerated more than one falling from a lower point, despite equal proximity to the earth. Second, the theory could give no plausible account of the motion of projectiles. Why did the arrow, for instance, not drop directly form the released bowstring? Peripatetics had tried to argue that the force of the air rushing into the space left by the moving arrow (to prevent the formation of a vacuum) kept it in motion, but why, then, should it ever stop? (Observe that in each case the attempt to keep the theory self-consistent was made by proposing an ad hoc explanation.) In answer to the last question, one could not, without contradiction, invoke air pressure to bring the arrow to rest as well as to propel it forward. Attempts to apply the theory had led to contradictions.

Buridan solved these problems by propounding the theory of impetus, according to which motion automatically engendered in the body a nisus to continue in its course. This impetus would gradually die out, as does heat in a red-hot poker as it cools. Falling bodies would thus gather impetus as they fell, and it would increase in proportion to the time and distance through which they moved. Likewise, projectiles would be kept in motion by the impetus initially imparted to them by the original impulse. Now, without contradiction, one could maintain that this impetus could be overcome by air resistance. The theory had thus been made, once more, self-consistent.

We find Galileo using the term "impetus" to explain the motion of a pendulum: how a weight suspended by a cord, when removed from the perpendicular (its position of rest) and then released, falls toward the original position and goes the same distance beyond it.[4] Elsewhere he uses the word "momentum" to mean the quantity of motion proportional to time and distance, clearly having in mind the "impetus" gathered by falling bodies in Buridan's account. The connection of this with the modern conception of momentum is obvious. Further, it is natural to conceive a moving body, so long as it is unimpeded by air pressure or any other force, continuing in motion by its own impetus uniformly in a straight line—the Newtonian conception of inertial motion.

Thus we may trace a continuous conceptual development from Aristotelian physics to Newtonian mechanics. Aristotle systematized the observed phenomena in one way, but his system was not coherent and led to contradictions. Buridan removed these by a slight adjustment of the system, introducing a new but not alien conception. Impetus was a sort of modified natural motion. But when Copernicus introduced the heliocentric hypothesis, new conflicts arose due to the alleged motion of the earth: for instance, if the earth rotated on its axis, one would expect a body falling vertically to land behind the point of original ascent—which does not occur; and if the earth was not the center, how could it be the natural place of heavy bodies? Galileo was concerned to remove these conflicts and was in the process of evolving a new mechanics which would account for everything that the old theory had accommodated as well as conform to the new celestial hypothesis. Here we find our clue to the origin of new theories. It is not simply guesswork or mere conjecture, nor is it generalization from numerous similar conjunctions of events, but it is the adjustment of an explanatory system in order to remove internal contradictions.

We may gather from the above examination of scientific method that a scientific theory is designed to organize experience in the relevant field and to provide an explanatory system within which phenomena can be rendered intelligible. When discrepancies and anomalies occur, hypotheses are proposed to remove them, and to test these hypotheses, experiments are devised that marshal diverse evidence fitting together in systematic fashion, so that no one factor can be denied without bringing down the entire structure. When this is achieved, the hypothesis is considered to have been established. The reasoning is constructive of system rather than inductive or deductive, although it contains elements of both, and the logic involved needs further investigation. It is certainly a logic of system, of a whole whose parts are interdependent, to which traditional formal deduction is not appropriate, because it is based on the conception of direct comparison between bare disconnected particulars and is so far purely tautological, and to which empiricist inductive logic is at most peripheral.

The historical example most frequently appealed to in support of empiricism is Galileo's discovery of the law of falling bodies. This is usually taken as the turning point at which science adopted empirical methods and broke away from metaphysics. It may be useful, therefore, to consider the facts with some care. The law was, until recently, widely believed to have been a generalization from experimental results obtained by Galileo when he dropped weights from the Leaning Tower of Pisa and rolled balls down inclined planes. Just what experiments Galileo performed we do not precisely know, for he does not describe them in the treatise in which he set out his theory, and he demonstrates it, for the most part, without reference to experimental results.[5] Moreover, if he did perform the appropriate experiments, he could not with the means at his disposal have measured distances and velocities with sufficient accuracy to derive his laws. Worse still, if he had been able to measure precisely, he would have obtained results that refuted his theories and supported those of his opponents. We may assert with confidence, therefore, that the law was not the conclusion of an inductive argument. Nor is it pure conjecture or random guesswork. The theory is set out in deductive form by Galileo, but the deduction is not used to derive observable consequences, and neither Galileo nor his successors made experimental attempts to falsify the theory. Had they done so, the results of the alleged experiments from the Leaning Tower, accurately measured, would have been sufficient refutation, and the hypothesis should have been rejected. When we examine Galileo's argument, we find that method of derivation relates empirical facts and deductive reasoning in a manner quite foreign to the teaching of philosophical empiricism; for according to that, deduction is purely analytic and cannot produce new factual information. Yet this is what Galileo succeeds in doing.

I shall confine myself to just one of his demonstrations, which seems especially typical and illuminating. The law to be established is stated as follows:

> The momenta or speeds of one and the same moving body [falling along an inclined plane] vary with the inclination of the plane.[6]

We may note in passing that Galileo uses the Italian words *il momento* and *l'impeto* as synonyms throughout the discussion. Still echoing Aristotle, he points out that all heavy bodies tend toward "the common center" and that no heavy body can, of itself, move upward. Accordingly, a body at rest on a horizontal plane will have no tendency to move and will offer no resistance to external lateral forces. If the plane is inclined, the body will tend to move downward, but the "momentum" acquired by a falling body will be greatest when it falls vertically. If it falls along an inclined plane, this momentum will be proportionately less.

Now imagine two weights hanging vertically over a pulley. To balance each other, they must be equal. But if one of them is placed on an inclined plane, in order to balance the other which hangs vertically, it will have to be heavier, because its momentum will be decreased by the support of the incline. If the supporting surface were horizontal, it would need no weight at all hanging vertically to balance it; but as the plane inclines from the horizontal, the balancing weight must increase. The momenta of the bodies are represented by the distance each would fall freely in equal times. The force, in both cases, acts along the vertical and so is proportional to the vertical distance moved. Thus, moving freely, an equal weight falling vertically would, in the same time, move further than one on an incline, in the proportion of the length of the incline to its height. The relation of the weights of two bodies mutually attached so as to balance each other would, therefore, be in inverse proportion to these lengths; that is, the weight of the body hanging vertically must be to that of the one on the inclined plane as the height of the inclined plane is to its length. Hence the momentum of a body falling along an inclined plane will vary with the inclination of the plane.

The reasoning is obviously deductive, partly geometrical and partly arithmetical, but the conclusion concerns matters of fact and gives factual information about the movement of a body along an inclined plane that is not contained in the premise about vertical motion. Whether or not Galileo ever performed the experiment he describes, he does not base the reasoning on any record of experimental results, nor does he claim that he ever checked his conclusion experimentally. Clearly, the reasoning is cogent without any such support. Yet it does depend on empirical knowledge about falling bodies and is not purely a priori. He assumes the knowledge that bodies fall more rapidly on a vertical course than along an incline and that in both cases they accelerate. The reasoning is neither inductive nor purely analytic, yet it does not seem to be a merely additive combination of the two. Galileo does not argue or assume the argument that bodies have been frequently observed to fall thus and so, and will therefore do so as a general rule. Nor does he substitute empirical quantities for the variables in an algoritm and calculate the answer.

What he is doing is presuming a systematic relationship between certain concepts—weight, time, distance, and motion, as well as geometric and arithmetic relationships mathematically determined—and, by applying to this system certain defined configurations of weights mutually balanced, reading off a determinate conclusion. The reasoning is *constructive* of system rather than either inductive or formally deductive, and it demands a logic akin to both yet identical with neither.

It has now become evident that the account of scientific method given by philosophical empiricism does not conform to the actual practice of empirical science—to the experimental procedure that scientists pursue. Scientific method is not induction, as that is described by philosophical empiricism; and, for science, that is just as well, because Hume himself demonstrated incontrovertibly that inductive argument cannot be rationally justified, and every subsequent attempt to vindicate it has failed.[7] Nor, so far as science is hypothetico-deductive, is its deduction what philosophical empiricism prescribes. Furthermore, experimentation implies a prior theory out of which a question has arisen due to discovered inconsistencies, and all observation turns out to be theory laden. Moreover the devisal of the experiment and the results of observation are all dependent on and relative to a constellation of presuppositions (what Kuhn calls a "paradigm"), a conceptual scheme, in terms of which whatever is observed is interpreted. This theory ladenness of observation belies the empiricist assumption that all knowledge is derived from purely sense-given data. But it was this assumption that led to the pronouncement that all factual knowledge is derived from the empirical sciences and to the banishment of metaphysics. That prohibition, we can now see, was totally indefensible.

I have argued that scientific method, in contrast to what philosophical empiricism contends, is the construction of a systematic explanatory scheme, and every system is a whole of interdependent elements. Such a whole must be complete, and no scientific theory is complete until it embraces the entire universe. At that stage it becomes a cosmology and implies a metaphysic. Indeed, the conceptual background of all observation and scientific experimentation is ultimately all-embracing, and when made explicit, it is seen to be a worldview: that of the Ancients and Medievals, for example, was of a cosmos that was alive and besouled; that of Newtonian science was the conception of the universe as a vast machine (or celestial clockwork). Every such worldview is a metaphysic; so the edict of empiricism against metaphysics is without a shred of justification, for intrinsic to all science and all experimental method a metaphysic is presupposed.

Notes

A modified version of this chapter was originally delivered as a lecture to the Royal Institute of Philosophy in London and published by Macmillan in the volume entitled *Impressions of Empiricism* in 1976.

1. David Hume, *An Enquiry Concerning Human Understanding.* Sect. IV. Part I, § 20. (Oxford, Clarendon Press, 1955), p. 25.
2. David Hume, *A Treatise of Human Nature*, bk. I, pt. II, sec. vi.
3. I have done so elsewhere. See E. E. Harris, *Hypothesis and Perception*, chaps. 2 and 4.

4. Cf. Galileo Galilei, *Dialogue Concerning the two Chief World Systems*, pp. 22f.
5. Cf. Galileo Galilei, *Dialogues Concerning Two New Sciences*.
6. Galilei, *Dialogues Concerning Two New Sciences*, p. 181.
7. Cf. Harris, *Hypothesis and Perception*, pt. I.

2

Scientific Philosophy

The progress of science is today the outstanding achievement of the human race. In no other field can we claim without question to have advanced: in art, the claim could not be established without dispute; in economics and politics, we have failed miserably to solve our most pressing problems; in morality and religion, we seem rather to have retrogressed. No doubt there will be differences of opinion about the degree of pessimism that is appropriate, but difference of opinion is itself usually held to be a mark of frustration rather than one of advance. To the casual observer, the history of philosophy appears to be the supreme example of such frustration—a long tale of dispute and contradiction leading nowhere but to greater doubt. Scientists may occasionally disagree, but they pursue a method proved by its successes and built upon a foundation of established fact which that method has certified. Can philosophy not emulate this example, adopt similar methods, achieve similarly reliable results, and "tread the sure path of a science"—the sure path of progress?

Philosophers have cherished this hope at least since Kant, but dispute and disagreement have continued. In the mid-twentieth century, however, there were some who confidently claimed that the hope had been realized, that philosophy now did tread the sure path of a science—not indeed metaphysics, as with Kant, but a new philosophy that had abandoned metaphysics as egregiously unscientific.

1. THE CRITERIA OF SCIENCE

If, however, the modern philosopher's claim to be scientific is traced in this way to a desire for progress, we might justifiably suspect "scientific philosophy" to be a product of pretentious emulation, the result of the emotional appeal of the idea of progress and the desire for the satisfaction of believing oneself to be "in the swim" and to be advancing with the inexorable tide. A theory that was no more than the product of such ulterior motives could hardly be scientific, for science is not based on wishful thinking but on systematically established fact, and its results can be substantiated only by the use of rigorous logic.

So far, at least, we may agree with Hans Reichenbach in his condemnation of philosophy as unscientific if it substitutes for logical analysis "superficial analogies" and "fanciful pictures" prompted by "extralogical motives." He calls for a psychology of philosophers (and he is not the first to do so) as the surest way of explaining their errors and disagreements, and he claims that contemporary philosophers have discovered a scientific method that is free from the effects of emotional appeal.[1] But unless we are supplied with a *scientific criterion* of scientific method, this claim cannot be countenanced, and the modern "scientific" philosopher too must submit to a psychological analysis of his motives. I have suggested a little of what that might reveal.[2] But until the criteria of scientific philosophy have been examined, we should not be justified in calling in the psychoanalyst.

The mere absence of disagreement is no good criterion, for persons actuated by similar "extralogical motives" will naturally agree, and Reichenbach does not claim that modern scientific philosophy is universally accepted. He is, in fact, astonished at the persistent opposition to it, which, he feels, can only be explained psychologically.[3] Accordingly, we must look for other criteria.

Reichenbach offers us two criteria, the first of which is the use of logical analysis: "In the face of error we can ask only for psychological explanation; truth calls for logical analysis." Science, he says, is the logical development of problems.[4] Just what he means by logical analysis or logical development he does not explain, although he has much to say about the development of symbolic logic and the general nature of its operation. Without committing myself to agreement with him on that matter, I am prepared to accept, as the hallmark of scientific method, reasoning that is rigorous and self-consistent and that follows the argument wherever it leads in the search for truth, undiverted by expediency or interested desire.

This requirement of science has been recognized and accepted at least since the time of Socrates, who (if Plato is to be believed) persistently stated it and emphasized its importance. All the great philosophers of the Western tradition demand its observance—certainly all those adversely criticized in the first part of Reichenbach's book. His criticism can be accepted, therefore, only if it is successful in showing that their theories are incoherent. It must not be simply an attempt to impute motives for which the evidence can of necessity be extremely meager. Before considering his critique of traditional philosophy in these terms, however, I shall examine the claim of the type of philosophy Reichenbach advocates to be scientific, using as my standard the extent to which it satisfies the requirements of rigorous logic. If it is found that the so-called scientific philosophy is the result of inconsistent and confused thinking, the epithet will certainly have been misapplied—and then, if we wish, we may account for the error psychologically.

The second criterion that Reichenbach offers of scientific procedure is adherence to "the verifiability theory of meaning."[5] In fact, despite his reiteration of the demand for logical analysis, this principle of verifiability is the only test he really applies, oblivious of the facts that, (1) in the sense of "verifiability" used, it is in conflict with the demand for logical consistency, and (2) the effect of its application is to destroy the efficacy of logic.

The principle is in conflict with the requirements of logic, first, because the verifiability theory of meaning depends upon a tacitly assumed metaphysical doctrine which is self-contradictory and incoherent; and secondly because, if verification is taken (as in the theory under discussion) to depend on sensory experience, logical analysis soon reveals the impossibility of verifying any statement that is commonly thought to have meaning. This becomes apparent from Reichenbach's account.

"Human beings." he writes, "are things among other things of nature, and they are affected by other things through the mediation of their sense organs."[6] The "reactions of the human body" so produced include the invention and use of signs (that is, physical things used to symbolize other physical things) in such a way that the correspondence of a sign combination with an actual state of affairs makes it true, and failure so to correspond makes it false. Only sign combinations that are either true or false are meaningful. The direct verification of meaningful sign combinations is affected by "direct observation," on which indirect verification also ultimately depends, for it involves "inductive inferences based on direct observation."[7] Direct observation is thus the final test of truth. From what follows in the succeeding pages,[8] it becomes clear that "my body" and "other things" (later called "other physical things") are constructions produced by "a process of internal ordering" of sentences reporting direct observations (called "report sentences") so as to distinguish those that are "objective" from those that are "subjective." The first will fit into a systematic order according to general laws, and the second will not (except by extension of the system in a special way which gives psychological interpretation of "subjective" report sentences). All report sentences are said to be "immediately true."[9] And so it becomes plain that "physical things," including all signs, are no more than what others have called "logical constructions" out of "direct observations" reportable in immediately true sentences. Such direct observations are presumably among the reactions of the human body to effects upon it through the mediation of the sense organs of other physical things. But our bodies and sense organs, as well as other physical things that affect them (producing whatever is recorded in report sentences), are no more than constructs out of "direct observations" so recorded. The whole doctrine is, therefore, circular and cannot be maintained without petitio principii. If judged by the standard of logical consistency, it must be pronounced unscientific.

It is, moreover, unverifiable in the manner prescribed; for no particular observation can directly inform us that observations can be systematically ordered according to general laws. General laws are not revealed by direct observation, and if derived from inductive inference, they cannot be confirmed by any one particular observation, nor are any number sufficient. No direct observation can tell us which observations can be systematically ordered, how they can be ordered, or that, when they are so ordered, they are "objective." Reichenbach, in fact, uses the word "objective" in two different senses: on page 261, it means what belongs to a certain order or system of report sentences; on the next page, it means what is reported when "my body" is causally affected by "other physical things." But the presence of the causal relation is never revealed by the observation reported or by any observation that can be reported in a sentence immediately true; nor can it be discovered by inductive inference, which (if Hume is credited) can never reveal any causal connection.[10] Consequently, the theory is not only incoherent but, by its own criterion, also unverifiable, and so must be pronounced meaningless and unscientific.

The examples that Reichenbach gives of report sentences[11] are, moreover, misleading. "It rains," "There is a dog," "Peter came to see me"—etc., are, none of them, immediately true. They are all assertions of more or less complex facts, each implying the interpretation and interconnection of a great many observations. A. J. Ayer is more precise when he tells us that an immediately true sentence (an "incorrigible" proposition) would be the bare report of the occurrence of a single experience.[12] This would state an "ostensive" proposition, the possibility of which Ayer at one time denied on the ground that it could contain only demonstrative symbols.[13]

Whenever a sentence conveys information, as do the examples of report sentences given by Reichenbach, it does more than express an ostensive proposition, for even a sentence that only describes a present sense experience necessarily goes beyond what is immediately given. It implies classification of the elements (or data) contained in the experience and relation of them in various way to those of numerous other experiences.[14] This is the case with Reichenbach's examples of report sentences. "Peter came to see me" is the report of a past occurrence which, on his own showing, can only be indirectly verified.[15] Even the sentence "It rains" is not directly verifiable. Presumably it is intended to convey the fact that here and now drops of water are falling from the clouds to earth, and this involves a number of relations between various objects: earth, clouds, raindrops, my body (all of which imply the classification of the sense-data referred to them), spatial interrelations among themselves and with other objects (not necessarily immediately sensed) defining "here", relations of before and after, simultaneity and succession (which cannot all be sensed at once) defining "now", and so forth. None of these complex meanings can be directly observed in a single sense-percept (which is all that can ever be reported in an ostensive proposition). The so-called report sentences are, therefore, all empirical hypotheses, and all of them require further verification. None is immediately true. And they cannot be verified by any sentence that is immediately true, because neither the fact that the objects of direct experience belong to classes, nor the fact that they are mutually related in complex ways, is given in direct experience or in any experience that can be reported in an immediately true sentence. If they are not verifiable in this way, they are not (according to the theory) verifiable at all and should be set aside as meaningless. And if report sentences are not verifiable, nothing else can be. The criterion of meaning has become inapplicable—has proved to be unmeaning—and cannot be accepted as scientific.

Furthermore, the restriction of meaning to statements empirically verifiable leads Reichenbach (and others of like mind) to deny the existence of what it pleases him to call "the synthetic a priori"—that is, universal and necessary propositions with informative content. All necessary propositions thus become analytic and so ultimately tautological. The propositions of logic and mathematics (being universal and necessary) are assigned to this class. But because a tautology is self-evident, it depends for its truth on no other proposition,[16] and consistency in logic becomes a meaningless term. On this theory, consistency is no more than synonymity, and the demand that science should be logically consistent reduces to the demand that it should tell us nothing. This must inevitably be the case, because synthetic (informative) propositions, ex hypothesi, cannot be necessary; any conjunction of matters of fact may occur, and no prediction can be made by pure logical deduction. Logic can never be concerned with the factual content of any statement. Empirical or otherwise, therefore, science can conform to the requirements of logic only so far as its statements are tautologous and empty or factual information: so far as it excludes everything of scientific interest.

Moreover, as a tautology can have no logical connection with any other tautology, there can be no universal rules connecting one set of synonymous sentences with any other set. The interconnection of implications requisite to show that direct observation is entailed by an empirical hypothesis consequently cannot be found, and logic is powerless to assist us in any investigation the scientific character of which is to depend on the verifiability of its assertions. "It rains," as has been shown, cannot be synonymous with any one sentence reporting direct observation (i.e., any sentence that is immediately true); nor can it be synonymous with a set of such sentences, unless the sentences of the set are not mutually synonymous and are necessarily connected. The possibility of just this sort of connection is what Reichenbach persistently denies, yet the analytic necessity that he admits is useless for the purpose of verification.

This reduction of logic to futility is the direct result of the adoption of the verifiability theory of meaning, which is now seen to be totally unscientific even by its own standards. Why then is it so confidently asserted to be "an indispensable part of scientific philosophy"?[17] May we not with reason suspect that, because the method of empirical science includes observation and experiment (impossible in philosophy), Reichenbach, with a vocal group of colleagues, hopes to share in the respect and prestige enjoyed by the scientists if he proclaims a doctrine that rejects as meaningless whatever is unverifiable by sense-observation? To do so, however, without scientific examination of the nature of verification, and simply to assert dogmatically that what is verifiable must entail a sentence immediately true (reporting direct observation), is no part of scientific procedure. The desire to be scientific accordingly reveals itself as an extralogical motive for a thoroughly unsound and unscientific theory.

2. SCIENTIFIC VERIFICATION

Verification is no more nor less than the establishment of the truth of what is verified; it is therefore obvious that if every meaningful statement is either true or false, meaning must depend on the possibility in principle of verification. But that what verifies is "ostensive propositions" or "report sentences" has been sufficiently disproved. What then is the nature of verification? So that we may make no mistake about what is and what is not scientific, let us consider the actual process by which a scientist establishes a hypothesis.

I take as my example Lavoisier's classic experiments which established the theory of oxidation. By heating a definite weight of mercury in a retort, the outlet of which led into a vessel containing air and inverted over water, he found that, as the metal calcined, the volume of air in the vessel decreased by a measurable amount and the weight of the calx exceeded that of the mercury. He then reversed the process by heating the calx in a crucible enclosed in a vessel similarly inverted over water and found that the volume of air in the vessel increased by the same amount as, in the previous experiment, it had decreased, and the weight of the recovered mercury was the same as it had been originally. These results showed that the increase in weight in the first experiment could be correlated with the absorption of a portion of the air, and the loss of weight in the second experiment with the emission of the same volume of a gas, later to be identified as oxygen.

What, in these experiments, is the evidence relevant to the establishment of the oxidation theory? It is the facts that (1) the air in the enclosed vessel first decreases as the mercury calcines, (2) it then increases as the calx is reconverted into metal, (3) these changes are in the same quantity, and (4) they correlate with the observed changes in weight. None of these facts, however, is the bare occurrence of particular sense-data that might be reported in sentences immediately true. They are not even perceived as such. No doubt the movement of the water levels inside and outside the enclosed vessel is perceived, but it is not barely sensed. What is sensed is interpreted as such movement. If any of these data can be recorded by means of immediately true (ostensive) sentences, they do not in the least give us what we want. First, they must be interpreted as marks on a measuring scale and the meniscus indicating the level of the water in a vessel; then the relative positions of the relevant marks and lines must be interpreted as a reading on the measuring scale. The mere perception of a coincidence between a mark and a water level does not constitute such a reading, except when interpreted in the light of the whole system of knowledge about scales and units of measurement and the use and behavior of the measuring instrument, as well as the interpretation of a host of sensuous apprehensions as the perception of various recognizable bodies, movements of water levels, and the like.

Even so, the observation of pointer readings, or the coincidence between liquid levels and marks on a scale, is not by itself relevant as evidence for a theory unless it is interpreted in terms of an arrangement of objects and events that gives it significance as the measurement of just what is required. In the example under consideration, the position of the water levels on the scale has no relevance at all except as an indication of the volume of air enclosed in the vessel. It is such an indication only for an observer who comprehends the whole system of facts involved in the experiment, and it can be accepted as evidence only on certain quite definite (but unstated) assumptions which are not specifically observed (e.g., that the water does not itself emit or absorb gas, that the vessel is not porous, and so on). Again, the *correlation* of the changes in weight with those in volume cannot be directly observed but can only be inferred and must be calculated. In more complicated experiments, like the majority of those carried out in modern physics, the greater part of the evidence consists in the results of calculation, results that could never be obtained from direct observation.

All this goes to show that any attempt to reduce scientific evidence to bare direct observation deprives it of everything that makes it scientifically significant—namely, its interpretation in terms of a developed and developing body of systematic knowledge, apart from which no purely sensuous apprehension can have any scientific value. Scientific verification, in short, is not (as is so frequently alleged) comparison of a theory with the observed facts. The observation of the fact is itself an interpretation involving theory, and the scientist's purpose is to develop that interpretation, to adjust and correct it, to render it coherent whenever some elements collide with others, and to integrate it into a single systematic body of scientific knowledge.

But the systematic interconnection of facts which makes both science and verification possible is no given in "direct observation". It is, moreover, impossible without necessary connection between matters of fact and universal rules of correlation. It cannot be built up by means of tautologies, and it depends on just that principle of a priori synthesis which Reichenbach seeks to exclude from all scientific thinking.

This a priori synthesis is what it was once fashionable to call the universal, and Reichenbach attacks all past notions of universality other than empirical generalization. We are now in a position to see that scientific method implies a universal which is not only synthetic but also both universal and necessary, so that if philosophy is in any way unscientific, it cannot be because it accepts and tries to explain this kind of universality. Yet Reichenbach's main indictment of the philosophers of the classical tradition is for their belief in a priori synthesis. His criticism, however, is not a logical analysis of the concept, but is an attempt to show that philosophers are moved by extralogical considerations in their use of picture thinking and false analogy as substitutes for explanation, in their search for certainty (which he considers unattainable in principle), and in their desire for moral direction. He himself refuses to admit the possibility of a priori synthesis and claims to have made empiricism consistent in a new theory of predictive knowledge, relinquishing all claim to certainty and finally solving the problem of inductive inference.

3. Prediction and the Problem of Induction

Explanation is defined by Reichenbach as generalization, which, he holds, is always empirical. Generalizations are statements of the *"if—then always"* variety derived from past experience of repeated factual conjunctions.[18] They are inductive inferences that are always reducible to induction by enumeration.[19] Such generalization, as Hume conclusively demonstrated, is logically unjustifiable, because it depends on the assumption that the course of experience is uniform and that the future will resemble the past, which cannot be deductively proved and for which there is no empirical evidence. Ex hypothesi, the assumption cannot be an empirical generalization from past experience, and if it is not true a priori, no empirical generalization has any rational basis. If the philosophers of the classical tradition preferred other forms of explanation, therefore, they can hardly be blamed, for no other form could be of less scientific value.

But Reichenbach claims to have solved the problem of inductive inference by means of a new account of prediction.[20] This proceeds from a calculation of probabilities, based on the frequency of past conjunctions, to a general statement of the *"if-then"* type. This general statement does not claim to be necessarily true (or certain); it is merely posited. The predictive value of such a posit is rated by the number (or ratio) expressing its degree of probability. When we predict, we do so on the ground of an inductive generalization, that is, a posit probable to a calculable degree. Our prediction is thus a kind of bet, justified by the rating of the posit.

What has been overlooked here is the tacit assumption that the frequency rating entitles us to expect the occurrence of one sort of conjunction rather than another *in the future*, an expectation that presupposes the uniformity of future experience with past. The frequency calculation is, and can only be, based on past experience, and what our posit amounts to is no more than that *in the past* some kind of conjunction of events has occurred with a certain degree of frequency. The presumption that this frequency will continue to occur in the future is no more justifiable than any other empirical generalization.

Again generalizing from past experience, Reichenbach asserts that prediction grounded on the frequency probability will probably be successful—that it is the best means of prediction that we have.[21] But as Hume showed,[22] this assertion itself can be made only on the assumption that the future will resemble the past. It is itself a posit which requires rating, and if it is to be relied on, we must make a further estimate of the probability that because past predictions of this kind have frequently succeeded they will do so in the future. We are thus led into an infinite regress which takes us ever further from the assurance that the future will resemble the past. Reichenbach's theory, accordingly, does not escape Hume's criticism—unless by the tacit assumption of a synthetic a priori, which he so deplores.

4. CERTAINTY

It is the search for certainty that is said to lead the unscientific philosopher into the doctrine of a priori synthesis, and we now see that even the abandonment of that search does not relieve the "scientific" philosopher of the incubus. Nor is this surprising. To abandon the belief in certain knowledge is ipso facto to relinquish the belief in probable knowledge. What *is* probable knowledge but that which is probably true? And truth in this context can mean no less than certainty.

What is probable is what the evidence permits us to believe to be the case under specified conditions. It is what, if the evidence were conclusive, would be certain. The statistical laws of modern physics are no exception to this rule. They imply a certainty that the modern physicist recognizes. Professor Roger Penrose is quite definite about this, declaring the view that uncertainty is an inherent property of physical reality to be "certainly wrong." And so is Max Planck, who insists that the Uncertainty Principle in physics is based on the principle of strict causation. Albert Einstein had the same conviction; and not even Bell's Theorem can dispose of certainty, as the strict logic and mathematical demonstrations of Henry Stapp have shown.[23]

The numerical measure of probability is the measure of its distance from certainty. It can have no other significance. The limit to which numerical probability moves as it increases is one, and that is the measure of certainty. If there is not, and cannot in principle be, certain knowledge, the whole series of fractions expressing frequency ratios is a meaningless concatenation of symbols.

Without one, there can be no half, or one-third, or any other fraction—in fact, no numerical system at all. So the entire frequency theory of probability that Reichenbach espouses tacitly assumes the existence of certain knowledge. The search for certainty, so much condemned as unscientific, is an indispensable condition of all knowledge, and even though the goal is only asymptotically approached, it is not thereby abolished.

The belief that the future will resemble the past cannot, as we saw, be founded on empirical generalization, and few generalizations worth making are ever confined to the past. Neither generalization nor prediction is the result of inductive enumeration. They depend on the construction of a systematic body of knowledge determining necessary connections and providing evidence for future occurrences that, to be sufficient, must be diverse and reciprocally corroborative. This elaboration of a coherent system is, as I have tried to show, the essence of scientific method, and it implies the belief in ultimate systematization—in a complete systematic whole of reality. Such a system would give the whole truth—would be certainty—if we could grasp it entire. Ludwig Wittgenstein, in his later philosophy, became aware that this was indeed the nature of certainty, although he did not manage to push the insight to its logical conclusion.[24] But human knowledge always falls far short of the ideal totality, although it must presuppose certainty and does approach it insofar as, in its continual advance, it becomes more coherent and more inclusive.

5. "OBJECTIVE" PRESENTATION

There is not space enough to make a detailed examination of Reichenbach's criticism of the great philosophers, desirable as that might be; but it is not difficult to show that the very faults he imputes to those whom he attacks are revealed in his own thinking: namely, failure to examine their subject with the detachment of a disinterested observer, and consequent excogitation of conclusions that are more the result of desire to discover what is congenial than of logical argument.

In his preface, Reichenbach warns us that it is not his intention to give an objective presentation of traditional philosophical material, except in the sense that his presentation will "be objective in the standards of its critique."[25] The value of these standards has already been considered, and they have been shown to be invalid and inapplicable. At the same time, objectivity, in the sense of accuracy in reporting the doctrines criticized, is entirely lacking in this work. His misrepresentation of the theories of the philosophers is so palpable that, unless it is the result of ignorance, it can be explained only as the blinding influence of a powerful (though unconscious) desire to obtain a preconceived result.

If the respect and admiration accorded to the triumphant scientist are to be shared by the modern philosopher, that philosopher must support the claim to be scientific, not merely by asserting the verifiability theory but by showing that those philosophers who have refuted empiricism were unscientific. To do this by scholarly examination of, and reply to, their arguments is a difficult and tedious undertaking, and might not produce the desired result. The extralogical motive of the "scientific" philosopher operates, therefore, as the source of inadvertent misrepresentation of the views of earlier philosophers to reveal ulterior motives behind the work of those whom he wishes to discredit—a projection on to them to his own unconscious cathexis.

A few examples will show that this is the case with Reichenbach. To Plato he attributes the argument that because the "Ideas" are accessible only to the eye of the mind, they must exist, for whatever we see with the bodily eye does exist.[26] The fact that Plato persistently denied reality to the things of the visible world is completely ignored. His reason for attributing superior reality to Ideas is exactly the opposite of what Reichenbach imputes to him. Roughly, Plato's argument is that because the things of the sensible world are in a constant state of flux, they cannot be clearly understood and are not wholly real; what is intelligible in them is due solely to their participation in ideas. Reality, for him, is that which is completely knowable and must therefore reside in the Ideas. Whatever its defects, this view is not the product (as Reichenbach alleges) of picture thinking and false analogy. It follows a carefully reasoned sequence of thought by a man who was deeply conscious of the difficulties involved in scientific verification and was fully aware that it depended on a universal of some sort. Reichenbach also asserts that Plato regarded mathematics as the supreme form of knowledge. It seems that he has omitted the sixth and seventh books of the *Republic* from his reading.

What could induce a scholar of Professor Reichenbach's standing so grossly to misrepresent the thought of a philosopher as well-known as Plato? Whether his motives are sincere or are "extralogical", it is evident that his argument is illogical.

Similarly, every reference to Kant's theory of causality in Reichenbach's *The Rise of Scientific Philosophy* displays misunderstanding:

> Applied to the problem of causality, [Kant's] argument would mean that we develop the notion of cause by finding particular causes, but that the knowledge of the general principle of causality is not logically derived from experiences. This principle, Kant argues, is the logical presupposition of every particular causal law; therefore it must be assumed true if we want to find such particular causal laws.[27]

Nothing like this, or like what follows in Reichenbach's next paragraph, can be found in the *Critique of Pure Reason*. Reichenbach contends that Kant bases his argument on our belief that every event must have some cause,[28] but Kant does nothing of the sort, nor does he base it on the necessity for presupposing the general principle if particular causes are to be sought. His argument is that if we did not presuppose a necessary connection between events (what cannot be given in sense), phenomena could not be objectively ordered in time, and we could thus have no experience of objects. Particular causal laws and our inveterate belief in their existence are all posterior to our experience of an objective world, and Kant is demonstrating that no such experience is possible—no empirical observation—without a priori synthesis, of which the necessary connection between cause and effect is one example.

Reichenbach never comes near to appreciating the force of this argument, and so his criticism of Kant is beside the point. "Assume it is correct," he writes, "that no experience can ever disprove the *a priori* principles. This means that whatever observations will be made, it will always be possible to interpret or order them in such a way that these principles are satisfied."[29] The cart precedes the horse. Kant's doctrine is that no empirical observation of any kind can be made unless the manifold of sensation is ordered and interpreted according to a priori categories. There is no observing of phenomena that do not conform to the categories followed by an ordering in terms of a priori principles. The ordering and interpreting are the implicit conditions of observation itself. Again, crass misrepresentation, unrelated to the criticized text, seems to conceal extralogical motives.

Possibly Kant gives an account of the categories that will not satisfy the modern scientist, but the remedy is to correct that account, not to attempt to abolish the a priori synthesis. That Kant's fundamental thesis is by no means unscientific or even outdated in this century many distinguished modern scientists testify.[30]

Reichenbach's criticism of Hegel can hardly be intended as serious and is certainly not worthy of serious comment. Hegel argues, it is alleged, "that the statement 'the rose is red' is a contradiction, because in it the same thing is said to be two different things," and so tries to establish the law of dialectics as a logical law.[31] The "primitive error" of such a grievous travesty can be corrected only by instruction, for which this is not the proper place.

These few examples of misrepresentation and unscholarly disregard for the text are unfortunately typical of nearly every reference to the great philosophers that Reichenbach makes.

6. MODERN SCIENCE

For the rest, Reichenbach's account of the results of "scientific" philosophy is little more than a description of the result of contemporary research in mathematical physics. What he has to say about biology is much less reliable; a little consideration of recent experimental results in that science and of the more important theories of the day would make his conclusion seem exceedingly doubtful—namely, that the calculus of probabilities is omnicompetent and, given the occurrence of heritable mutations, the laws of probability are sufficient to account for the whole course of biological evolution. The cogency of his proof of this conclusion cannot, he claims, be diminished by any criticism. Yet careful attention to experimental results has convinced a most influential body of modern biologists that no such hypothesis can be maintained in their science, that no "additive" account of living development can explain the facts, and that they can be adequately interpreted only in terms of "organism" and "system," which exclude the possibility of evolution by fractional change.[32]

In physics, however, Reichenbach is on his own ground, yet his survey of the contemporary position in this field brings him to a conclusion from which he should have drawn a different moral. It is that "the experiences offered by atomic phenomena make it necessary to abandon the idea of a corporeal substance and require a revision of the form of description by means of which we portray physical reality."[33] The nature of the required revision he does not explain. The great physicists of the age, however, from Einstein to Niels Bohr and Werner Heisenberg, have told us that physics is no longer "materialistic"; we have seen matter resolved into energy and energy into space-time curvature. The space-time (or metrical) field, moreover, is a structure of relations dependent on an act of thought—the choice of a frame of reference. The theory of relativity makes all measurement and all description of physical fact dependent upon this choice, an act of thought that is integral to the very nature of the facts described; so that physical reality can no longer be regarded as something apart from and independent of thought. It is not simply the effects of motion upon the measuring instrument, as some empiricists have tried to maintain,[34] that are relevant here, because the motion of the instrument cannot be determined absolutely, but only by reference to an arbitrarily chosen frame. Physical fact is and can only be what thinking makes it. The same conclusion emerges from the Copenhagen interpretation of the indeterminacy principle in quantum merchanics and from Eugene Wigner's contention that the collapse of the probability amplitude can occur only with the observer's consciousness of the result of the measurement.

But if, in physics, subject and object are thus united, as thinkers like Planck are convinced, and if Sir Arthur Eddington is right that physical reality turns out to be of the nature of intelligent mind, and revision of our description should lead us to substitute *thought* for corporeal substance. And that is precisely what was done by the much abused philosopher Hegel. A passage in which this substitution is made forms the opening quotation of Reichenbach's book, where it is derided as the preeminent example of unscientific nonsense. Hegel writes:

Reason is substance, as well as infinite power, its own infinite material underlying all natural and spiritual life; as also the infinite form; that which sets the material in motion. Reason is the substance from which all things derive their being.[35]

Hegel, moreover, in company with both earlier and later philosophers, propounded a theory of reality as a coherent and organic totality, and of knowledge as a system constructed on the same principle. These notions are implied in scientific method and are presupposed by both contemporary physics and the "organismic" biology of the present day; so Hegel's doctrine proves to be more in harmony with modern science that Reichenbach's own. If we seek for scientific philosophy, we must look for it in the works of the philosophers who followed Hegel in the classical tradition while they took account of and attempted to interpret the results of modern science. This tradition leads to such men as Bernard Bosanquet, Henri Bergson, Samuel Alexander, and A. N. Whitehead, whose work follows on those "systems of the nineteenth century" compared by Reichenbach to "the dead end of a river that after flowing through fertile lands finally dries out in the desert." The simile is tragically appropriate. The desert sands in which the river of philosophical thought is choked are the arid wastes of self-styled scientific philosophy.

Notes

Originally published in *Philosophical Quarterly*, vol. 2 (1952).

1. Cf. Hans Reichenbach, *The Rise of Scientific Philosophy*, (Berkeley and Los Angeles, University of California Press; London, Cambridge University Press, 1951), pp. 36, 308ff.
2. I have made other comments in E. E. Harris, *The Survival of Political Man*, (Johannesburg, Witwatersrand University Press, 1950), pp. 202–6.
3. Reichenbach, *The Rise of Scientific Philosophy*, p. 308.
4. Ibid., p. 117.
5. Cf. ibid., pp. 256–7.
6. Ibid., p. 255.
7. Ibid., p. 257.
8. Ibid., pp. 260–3.
9. Ibid., p. 261.
10. Cf. David Hume, *Treatise of Human Nature* bk. I, pt. IV, sec. ii.
11. Reichenbach, *The Rise of Scientific Philosophy*, pp. 257, 260.
12. A. J. Ayer, *Language, Truth and Logic*, p. 10.
13. Ibid., p. 91. Ayer has since modified his view to permit incorrigible propositions, with the proviso that they can give no information either to their enunciator or to their hearer.
14. Cf. ibid., pp. 91ff.
15. Reichenbach, *The Rise of Scientific Philosophy*, p. 257.

16. Cf. Ayer, *Language, Truth and Logic.*
17. Reichenbach, *The Rise of Scientific Philosophy*, pp. 256–7.
18. Ibid., pp. 5–7.
19. Ibid., pp. 82ff., 244.
20. Ibid., chap. 14.
21. Ibid., pp. 238ff., 246–7.
22. Hume, *Treatise of Human Nature.*, bk. I, pt. III, sec. iv.
23. Roger Penrose, *The Emperor's New Mind: Concerning Computers, Minds, and the Laws of Physics*, (Oxford, the Clarendon Press, 1989), p. 249. Cf. Max Planck, *Where is Science Going?* (London, G. Allen and Unwin, 1933), pp. 33f., 145 ff., and 201 ad fin., where, in an appendix, Einstein and Murphy discuss the issue; *The Universe in the Light of Modern Physics*, (London, G. Allen and Unwin, 1931, 1937), p. 84; *The Philosophy of Physics*, (London, Allen and Unwin, 1936, chap. 2. Cf. also Henry P. Stapp, "Are Faster-than-Light Influences Necessary," in *Quantum Mechanics versus Local Realism" The Einstein, Podolsky and Rosen Paradox*; Ed. P. Salleri (New York, Plenum Press, 1987) "Quantum Mechanics and the Physicist's Conception of Nature: Philosophical Implications of Bell's Theorem," in *The World View of Contemporary Physics: Does It Need a New Metaphysics?* Ed. R. Kitchener (Albany, NY., State University of New York Press, 1988).
24. L. Wittgenstein, *On Certainty.* (Oxford, Blackwell, 1969).
25. Reichenbach, *The Rise of Scientific Philosophy*, p. viii.
26. Ibid., p. 20f.
27. Ibid., p. 112.
28. Ibid., p. 42.
29. Ibid., p. 46.
30. See Sir Arthur Eddington, *The Nature of the Physical World*, (Cambridge, Cambridge University Press, 1948), p. 244; *Space, Time and Gravitation*, p. 200; *The Philosophy of Physical Science*, (Cambridge University Press, 1939), p. 188f. See also Henry Margenau, *The Nature of Physical Reality*, (New York, McGraw Hill, 1950), pp. 145, 419; D. W. Sciama, *The Unity of the Universe*, (New York, Doubleday, 1961), pp. 29–31; N. R. Hanson, *Patterns of Discovery.* (Cambridge, Cambridge University Press, 1958).
31. Reichenbach, *The Rise of Scientific Philosophy*, pp. 69ff.
32. See L. von Bertalanffy, *Modern Theories of Development*, (Oxford, Oxford University Press, 1933, New York, Harper, 1962), pp. 38ff. and *passim.* The case against chance mutation and natural selection has been greatly strengthened by Stuart Kaufman's recent book *The Origis of Order.* (Oxford, Oxford University Press, 1993).
33. Reichenbach, *The Rise of Scientific Philosophy*, p. 180.
34. See P. Frank, *Between Physics and Philosophy*, (Cambridge, MA., Harvard University Press, 1931), pp. 111–3.
35. G. W. F. Hegel, *Lectures on the Philosophy of World History* (1830), introduction. For Hegel, dialectical reason is the dynamic principle underlying physical energy as well as organic activity, both of which together constitute the process by which Mind, or Spirit, brings itself to consciousness through Nature. Today, physicists seek a fundamental law or mathematical equation from which all forces and elementary particles (each being an equivalent version of the other) can be deduced. Even Reichenbach recognizes that the probability waves, into which modern physics resolves matter, reduce to a mathematical formula (i.e., pure thought).

3

Misleading Analyses

When intimations of the decrepitude of the cornerstone of their teaching, the Verification Principle, began to seep into the consciousness of the logical positivists, they modified their stance somewhat and called themselves logical empiricists. But if they ceased to insist on the verification theory of meaning, they persisted in their abandonment of metaphysics and their renunciation of all speculation. Philosophy, in consequence, was restricted to logic, and the sort of logic that was espoused was symbolic logic. This claimed to be an ideal language, which, according to Wittgenstein's *Tractatus Logico-Philosophicus*, showed forth the form of the facts. Still following Hume, the facts were taken to be conjunctions, disjunctions, and interrelations between particular impressions and ideas, to whose qualitative content the logic was indifferent. They were regarded as bare particulars, and the linguistic statements of the relations between them were said to be atomic proposition—atomic because there was no logical connection between them: any one could be true (or false) without affecting the truth (or falsity) of any other.

Wittgenstein had now become the high priest of the movement, and he revised his original position on discovering that symbolic logic was not, indeed, an ideal logical language; in fact, many alternative logical languages could be devised, and the logical structure of discourse depended upon whatever language game one indulged in. The proper method of philosophy was then taken to be linguistic analysis, and the faults and defects of past philosophy were traced to the misconstrual of linguistic idiom.

The view that "the sole and whole function of philosophy" is "the detection of the sources in linguistic idiom of recurrent misconstructions and absurd theories" then became widespread among practicing philosophers in the English-speaking world. The absurd theories were, of course, metaphysical, for among these philosophers, absurdity came to be regarded more or less as the hallmark of metaphysics. And as the scope of philosophical investigation was limited to linguistic analysis, any other sort of philosophy was seen as metaphysical, so that as the movement advanced, and linguistic analysis was more widely practiced, every other sort of philosophy became discredited. In the words of Antony Flew:

The enterprises of metaphysical construction have seemed less and less practicable, less and less respectable. For anyone who has seen how much muddle and perplexity, how much paradox and absurdity, has already been traced back to its tainted sources in misleading idiom, or in unexplained and unnoticed distortions of standard English, must suspect that any further metaphysical construction which he might be tempted to erect would soon meet a similar humiliating and embarrassing débacle under the assaults of the new "logic and critic."[1]

One is led to reflect that English is not the only language in which metaphysics has been known to flourish, and it is surely remarkable that the uncritical use of languages differing widely in idiom and standard form should have given rise to the same absurdities and to similar metaphysical theories, or that metaphysical doctrines propounded in one language should so frequently appear plausible in another. Further, if the temptation to erect metaphysical constructions results from a conviction that has not been shaken by such linguistic analysis as has already been undertaken, the philosopher who is deterred from it by fear of humiliation under the attacks of new criticism is surely lacking both in moral courage and in intellectual integrity. If, and insofar as, we really do, as the result of our *façons de parler*, commit the sort of errors alleged and fall into the sort of muddle exhibited, linguistic analysis is performing a valuable and, indeed, a necessary service. If its method is sound and does not itself suffer from errors and confusions, we may pursue it with confidence. But are these conditions fulfilled? So devastating have the effects of the new "logic and critic" upon the old type of philosophizing seemed to be (even though, for the most part, the actual theories expounded by the older philosophers have not been directly subjected to it) that the new method has largely escaped criticism. Yet the more drastic its effects, the more important it is that it should not be accepted lightly or without critical examination.

In order to avoid the accusation of basing my criticism on assumptions that the exponents of the new method would reject, I shall confine myself to particular examples and shall choose for this purpose some of the papers published in Antony Flew's book *Logic and Language*, noting his warning that the contributors do not all claim to be in mutual agreement and that many of them would not, at the time of publication, still stand by all they had written in their essays. This does not matter as long as we criticize each on its own merits. If subsequent changes in the author's opinions serve to correct errors and nullify criticism, they are welcome (and should have been published); if they do not so modify the position as to make the criticism inapplicable, they do not affect the issue. Moreover, it would be readily admitted that all the essays have in common the claim to reveal ways in which linguistic forms can mislead us into propounding metaphysical doctrines that are disreputable, and insofar as any criticism affects this claim, it touches them all.

1. ANALYSIS OF MISLEADING EXPRESSIONS

I begin with what Gilbert Ryle calls "systematically misleading expressions," taking them in the order in which he deals with them. First, quasi-ontological statements, such as "God exists," "Satan does not exist," "Mr. Pickwick is a fiction or figment," "Mr. Baldwin is a genuine entity," are said to be systematically misleading because they do not assert or deny genuine characters of genuine subjects or record genuine facts, although they resemble in grammatical form statements that do (such as "Capone is not a philosopher"). " . . . is an entity," " . . . is an existent" are only bogus predicates, and that of which (in grammar) they are asserted is only a bogus subject.[2]

How then do we distinguish genuine subjects? Merely by the fact that we assert of them genuine predicates? If so, and if "real," "existent," and the like are not genuine predicates, the only genuine subjects are those of which reality, existence, or genuine being is *not* asserted. The case of Mr. Baldwin is significant (to be more up-to-date, let us take Mr. Clinton). If I say "Mr. Clinton is a good president," he is a genuine subject; but if I say "Mr. Clinton is a genuine entity," he ceases to be one. But "genuine subject," if it means anything, means "genuine entity." Ryle's protest is against the multiplication of bogus entities by the hypostatization of bogus subjects,[3] so by genuine subjects he must mean to refer to genuine entities. It would seem, therefore, that a genuine entity is genuine only when it is not stated to be so and becomes bogus as soon as it is identified as a genuine existent. But this is absurd.

This conclusion cannot be avoided by saying that, in the propositions quoted above, it is not Mr. Clinton himself who is either a genuine or a bogus subject but the name "Mr. Clinton," for in neither case is the assertion made of the name but, in both, of the person. Nevertheless, we are told that this is not so, that "Mr. Clinton is a genuine entity" is not about Mr. Clinton. But it is about something, for we are also explicitly warned that it is "not only significant but true," that it does not mislead its naive user and *need* not mislead the philosopher. Accordingly, it may be paraphrased somewhat like this: "There is somebody called Mr. Clinton." This, however, is only an oblique way of saying that somebody (who is called Mr. Clinton) is a genuine entity, since that is the whole force of the phrase "there is somebody." The somebody in question is no other than Mr. Clinton, and it must, therefore, be he who is the logical subject of the proposition. If the statement that he is a genuine entity were not about Mr. Clinton, we could not truly assert real predicates of him, for the ascription of real characters to a bogus entity must result in a false statement. But as we can ascribe real characters to Mr. Clinton, it must be about Mr. Clinton that we say he is a real entity, just as it is about him that we say he (and not merely his name) is a genuine logical subject whenever we predicate such characters of him.

The basis of any analysis like that made by Ryle is that we can truly ascribe genuine characters to certain objects in propositions with genuine logical subjects and predicates. These are the standards for recognizing genuineness in subjects and predicates. And, if this is so, the true ascription of genuine being or reality to some objects must be possible, for unless it were, there would be neither genuine subjects nor genuine predicates—and so also no bogus ones. The condition of the distinction between genuine and bogus subjects is the possibility of predicating reality or existence or genuine being of certain subjects. It is, therefore, ridiculous to maintain that such predication is bogus. It consequently transpires that the analysis of existence propositions itself presupposes the logical priority to all genuine subject-predicate statements of existence propositions, and it is therefore seriously misleading to allege that, because existence predicates are not characters, their subjects are not genuine subjects.

Now let us consider "Mr. Pickwick is a fiction." This statement also is said not to be about Mr. Pickwick—for, if it is true, there is no such person for it to be about. Then what am I denying when I say that Mr. Pickwick is not a real person? I cannot be denying that "Mr. Pickwick" is a proper name, for grammatically it certainly is, and if, in logic, proper names are, by definition, restricted to actually existing entities (which are not for that reason bogus), it may well be false that nobody is or ever has been called Pickwick, and it is certainly not *that* which I am asserting when I say that Dickens' Mr. Pickwick is a fiction. Am I then saying: "There was and is nobody called Mr. Pickwick identical with the character of that name in Dickens's novel"? No doubt I am, but this statement is not about "nobody," nor (despite what Ryle says) about Dickens, nor primarily about his novel, but about a certain character in the novel, namely, Mr. Pickwick.

But it is maintained that, if we say this, we may systematically mislead some philosopher into thinking that a fiction is some curious kind of entity. Yet, if "entity" means "existent," that is what is explicitly being denied in the statement "Mr. Pickwick is a fiction," and it must surely be a queer sort of wisdom beloved by the philosopher who is misled by not-*p* to believe *p*. "The world," says Ryle, "does not contain fictions in the way in which it contains statesmen." True indeed, and that is why I say, and what is presupposed when I say, that Mr. Pickwick is a fiction. If I understand the statement in the least, I cannot be misled into believing that the world contains fictions in the same way as it contains statesmen (and other things that are not fictions). And I submit that no sane person has ever believed any such thing. Whether the world contains fictions in some other way is a different question. If it did not, I suppose that there could be no novels.

It is clear, then, that ontological statements do not systematically mislead, for either they assert what must be presupposed if any genuine predicates are to be asserted of any genuine subjects, or else they deny of fictions and other nonentities that they are among the things contained in the world in the way in which actually existing things are contained in it. Only the insane or the hopelessly stupid could both understand such statements and believe that they deny what they assert or assert what they deny. And with all this Ryle is substantially in agreement, for he says that these statements are not only significant but true and that they do not mislead those who use and understand them, nor do I believe that he underestimates the intelligence either of his colleagues or of his predecessors. It is, therefore, difficult to understand who the philosophers may be who are apt to be misled by innocent statements. We should be gravely misled, however, if we believed "that those metaphysical philosophers are the greatest sinners who, as if they were saying something of importance, make 'Reality' or 'Being' the subject of their propositions, or 'real' the predicate," (Ryle in Flew, *Logic and Language*, p. 18) because these philosophers are attending to and are drawing our attention to just what makes any subject or any predicate a genuine one.

The analysis of "quasi-Platonic" statements is in like case. Philosophers (again, it is not stated which) are said to take such statements as "Unpunctuality is reprehensible" or "Virtue is its own reward" to be "precisely analogous" to statements like "Jones merits reproof" or "Smith has given himself a prize," and accordingly to believe that "universals" are "objects in the way that Mt Everest is an object." But no philosopher has ever thought anything of the kind. No sane person who at all understands the difference between universals and particulars could think that one was the same as the other. No sane person ever imagines that Unpunctuality or Virtue is a person like Jones or Smith, even though some allegorists and artists have so depicted them. If we are not apt to be misled by allegories, why should we be misled by the grammar of ordinary language? There is no "fraudulent pretense" in statements about universals that they are statements about particulars. This is precisely why the "plain man" is not deceived by them, and philosophers in the past have been so far from being deceived that the precise nature of the difference between universals and particulars has occupied much of their thought. Plato, in particular, was concerned with this difference (was, perhaps, the first to see its importance), and so great was his anxiety that the two should not be confused that he committed the error of assigning "ideas" to an altogether separate world of their own. But even that he did metaphorically, in a series of confessedly allegorical parables. Every serious discussion of the subject in the Dialogues is designed to emphasize the utter disparity between "ideas" and particular, sensible things, and there is nothing whatever in Plato's manner of speaking and of arguing about the "ideas" to lead us to think that he assumed, even unconsciously, that because so-called general words can be made subjects in sentences they therefore denote particular objects. And there is no sort of object like a particular that is not a particular. It is true that there are some defects in the Theory of Ideas which led Plato into serious difficulties (of which he was not entirely unaware), but what misled him was not linguistic idiom but the tendency to identify the universal with the common property of a class.

Other expressions recommended to our attention as systematically misleading are non-referential "the"-phrases of various kinds. I shall confine my discussion to the three kinds that are deemed to give rise to the most serious philosophical errors.

(i) Spatio-temporal "the"-phrases, such as "the top of the tree," "the center of the bush," are said to mislead us into thinking that they refer to a material part of the tree or the bush, whereas they indicate no more than relative position. Hence such other phrases—"the region occupied by x," "the path followed by y," "the moment or date at which z happened"—become the source of certain unspecified "Cartesian and perhaps Newtonian blunders about space and time."

In "the top of the tree" there is some ambiguity, for in common parlance, "the top" is sometimes used to refer to a part of the tree[4] and sometimes merely to a relative position. This is also true, but less often, of "the region occupied by." But it cannot be said of "the moment at which." We are not normally tempted to think that moments are material things or parts of them. When the phrase is ambiguous and there is a genuine sense in which it is used referentially, we can avoid error by clearly distinguishing the different usages. If we fail to do so, we shall be misled, but not *systematically* misled. On the other hand, when there is no ambiguity, it is difficult to see what sort of error could arise. Who would ever imagine that (except in special cases, in which an actual tract of land or an actual pathway is the referent) "the region occupied by x" (e.g., the Milky Way) referred to a tract of country, or "the path followed by y" (e.g., the planet Saturn) referred to some kind of roadway? It would be as apt to allege that it is a real garden path up which we are being led when it is suggested that Descartes or Newton made errors of this sort.

It is, of course, quite another matter to assert that Newton and Descartes may have paid too much attention, in framing their theories, to the perceptual appearance of material things, and to recommend a more Leibnizian doctrine that would treat such appearance as merely phenomenal though founded upon actual relations between immaterial substances. But this is by no means what the linguistic analyst wishes to do, and what Ryle is doing is misleading— perhaps systematically misleading.

(ii) Phrases such as "the thought of . . . ," "the idea of . . ." are held to have misled philosophers into believing in the existence of such entities as "thoughts," "ideas," "conceptions," and "judgments," all of which, like the members of "the Lockean demonology" are condemned as bogus. These "the"-phrases can be paraphrased into others which are not supposed to suggest such entities. "Jones hates the thought of going to the hospital" becomes "Jones is distressed whenever he thinks of what he will undergo if he goes to the hospital"; "The idea of having a holiday has just occurred to me" becomes "I have just been thinking that I might take a holiday."

But presumably when Jones thinks of what he will undergo, and when I think of taking a holiday, each has something before his mind as what he is thinking about. In neither case can it be the actual entities and events which have not yet occurred, so it must be something else. It is to these somethings that philosophers have referred by the words "ideas," "thoughts," "judgments," and the like, and the objects of our thought are not necessarily always bogus entities any more than are the objects of perception. Locke may have been mistaken in thinking that such objects were always mental images or something like them, but what misled him was faulty introspection rather than language.

(iii) Some philosophers, it is alleged, falsely imagine that "the meaning of x" refers "to a queer new entity"—presumably neither x nor what x means, but something other than these. Whatever, one must ask, could mislead any reasonable person to imagine any such thing? "The meaning of x" refers to precisely what x refers to, and nobody ever would or ever has thought otherwise. Meanings, as such, therefore, may quite legitimately occupy the minds of philosophers who try to understand just what is involved when a symbol, like x, refers us to something else—in fact, it is usually held that this is the proper subject of semantics. In the course of this study, it would be quite legitimate to inquire whether, for x to have a meaning, something or other must be "subjectively" entertained by the person for whom it had that meaning, and whether there must necessarily exist some "objective" thing to which it refers. So it may not be at all "pointless to discuss whether word meanings are subjective or objective", so long as we understand what we are about.

Accordingly, there is, after all, nothing specially seductive about these phrases, and the danger of being misled by them is a mere bogey. But this bogey has been dangerously used to discredit philosophers who have made important contributions to their subject, by the pretense that they have been misled and have made blunders in ways that they have never dreamed of. Philosophers make errors enough, and important ones too, which it is vital to discover and expose, but this makes it all the more necessary not to be led astray by a hunt for imaginary sins.

2. TREATMENT OF TIME-PUZZLES

John Findlay states with admirable lucidity many of the familiar problems about time, and it is not necessary to restate them here.[5] I shall deal with his treatment of only two problems that really underlie the rest. The first is the consequence of the infinite divisibility of the continuum: how can events that take time be made up of instants which do not? The second is the problem of understanding the passage of time: how can what is now present fade away into the past, what is now future emerge into the present, so that what is now true becomes false with the passage of time and what is now false true?

Findlay says that these puzzles arise "not because there is anything genuinely problematic in our experience, but because the ways in which we speak of that experience are lacking in harmony or otherwise unsatisfactory." They can therefore be avoided by applying linguistic remedies. It is not difficult, however, to show that the suggested remedies do not remove the problems. And this is not surprising if, as I maintain, it is not in language that these problems have their source.

The demand for consistency in the use of "now" and "present," if pressed to an extreme, results in the admission that "the present" has no duration; yet all events must occur in some present (or "now"), and it is only through the present that future events can be related to those of the past. Accordingly, we conclude that all events must be made up of successive "nows," none of which has any duration, and the question arises, how can events which take time be made up of "presents" or "nows" which do not? The suggested remedy is to realize that the facts themselves give us no trouble—"the facts are there," writes Findlay, "we can see and show them, and it is for us to talk of them in ways which will neither perplex nor embarrass us."[7] Moreover, we do not ordinarily use the words "now" and "present" with the extreme strictness the demand for which creates the problem. All we need do, therefore, is decide how we shall use them and to say of very brief events either that they take no time, and then "simply rule that events which take time *are* made up of events which take no time," or that they are short time-lapses which cannot be further divided.[8]

But will these decisions really remove the problems? Is this way of talking one that will neither perplex nor embarrass? We are exhorted by Findlay to avoid misleading pictures, but how is this to be done? If we are to rule that an event which takes time is made up of events which take none, we must assume either that there is a lapse between the timeless events, or that there is not. If there is no lapse, then it takes no time to pass from one timeless event to the next, and it will be impossible to understand how events which take time can be so constituted. If on the other hand, there is a lapse between timeless events, that lapse will itself be made up of events which take no time. Between each of these there will be a lapse similarly made up of timeless "moments," and again between each of these. So we shall have an infinite regress and should still fail to "picture" the way in which timeless events could add up to make those which filled some duration. To concede that the so-called timeless events are really of very short duration does not help, for if they are to *count* as timeless, they still add up together as timeless: $0 + 0 = 0$. And if they are not to count as timeless, they must be divisible. How then are we to understand the idiom by which we speak of the facts? The idiom, in fact, conflicts with our experience and can only cause perplexity and embarrassment to those who make the effort to understand what they are talking about.

Alternatively, if we decide to say that the present includes an indivisible brief period of time, are we to say also that between one "present" and the next there is a lapse or not? If we do, then between any two "presents" there will be other "presents," and again we have the infinite regress. If we do not, the transition from one "present" to the next will be timeless. But unless there is temporal change from one present to the next, there is no intelligible succession, and if there is temporal change, it must occur in time. Again, then our linguistic ruling has failed to save us from insoluble puzzles.

The second problem to be resolved is; how is it possible "for all the solid objects and people around us to melt away into the past, and for a new order of objects and persons to emerge mysteriously from the future," so that what is true of present facts ceases to be true when new events have occurred? Confused thinking is fairly obvious in the statement of this problem, but it is not removed simply by recommending a linguistic convention. Findlay points out that our ordinary system of tenses precludes confusion and leaves no room for puzzlement,[9] but the fact that we use a well-developed and precise system of tenses only records the passing away and coming to be of events, it does not explain how it comes about,[10] and the adoption of a different linguistic system purged of tenses and of subjectively relative adverbs and pronouns[11] would be beset by the difficulty of determining some impersonal points of reference from which to date and place events. Not even the physicist can do this, for "the observer" is always involved in the physical account. It is not true, therefore, that if we adopted this impersonal way of talking we should never be involved in difficulties. And there is good reason why we both try to talk in this way (as Findlay points out) and yet are uneasy in doing so. The nature of time is not altered by the way we speak about temporal events, and what is difficult to understand about it remains difficult whatever linguistic convention we adopt. In fact, philosophers in the past have tried all the suggested "forms of locution", and just because these have been found wanting, the puzzles have persisted.

J. E. McTaggart's problems with time were not engendered by the use of tenses but by the occurrence of events. To say of a man diving (Findlay's example) that he was about to dive, is now doing so, and then that he has already dived simply confirms that the same event is, at different times, future, present, and past; but what "moves" it from one to the other is not thereby made apparent. No linguistic convention will remove the problem presented by the fact that we cannot avoid speaking of time as moving on, or of passing, or of flowing like a stream, even when no material thing actually moves or passes or flows. Perplexity about the passage of time still persists. The mathematical physicist's spatialized four-dimensional picture of objects and events cannot solve the problem, for it still resorts to the idea of motion along a time line to explain our experience of succession. And motion inevitably takes time.

It does not help us to point out that we are quite familiar with temporal changes and habitually speak about them without confusion. Augustine was fully aware of this when he said that he knew what time was if nobody asked him but could not tell anybody who did ask. Because something presents no difficulty in practice, it does not follow that it is easy to understand or to explain. The difficulties that Findlay describes, of being desperately immobilized (because we cannot pass on to a future event before we have passed through an intervening one, and so on *ad infinitum*), or of casting about desperately for means to pass on to the next stage (for similar reasons), are difficulties that, of course, we never meet in practice. But that fact does not remove the intellectual difficulties of understanding how the passage of time is to be conceived, or how movement can be continuous. And these are neither caused nor relieved by linguistic usage. Mere familiarity with certain types of experience does not render them intelligible. We are, nowadays, all familiar with radio and television and have no difficulty in turning the knobs or pressing the buttons that provide us with our entertainment, but it does not follow that we understand how the results are brought about. It is true that, in this case, some of the difficulties can be removed by the study of observable phenomena—though not all the difficulties. Complete understanding of the phenomena of radiation demands the interpretation of facts, even when observation is frustrated by the nature of the facts themselves. It is the function of theory to explain observed facts; observation is not, by itself, explanation. Similarly, though we may all be familiar with changing and persistent objects, it does not follow that we easily understand what is presupposed in dating and relating them in temporal continuity and succession, or in distinguishing the permanent from the changing.

3. DISSIPATION OF DOUBTS ABOUT INDUCTION

Many contemporary philosophers seem to have been afflicted with a persistent blindness to the crucial point of the problem about induction, which the empiricist is bound to face. Yet this crucial point is not difficult to make clear. The inductive argument reaches a general conclusion about matters of fact from a number of particular premises. Or (what amounts to the same thing) from a number of occurrences (taken to be sufficient) of a certain phenomenon, it draws the conclusion that in similar circumstances that phenomenon will recur. In other words, the occurrence of a number of cases satisfying a rule is taken as evidence that the rule holds universally. That such an argument is not deductively valid is generally admitted, and nobody requires that it should be. Nor does anybody deny—neither the most radical of empiricists nor the most diehard of rationalists—that we do, in inductive reasoning, accept as sufficient evidence of a universal rule the fact that it has been fulfilled in the past in a large number of (or in all known) cases. This has not been called into question. But the empiricist, who wants to admit no factual knowledge that cannot be empirically derived, is faced by the problem that the principle of induction cannot be so derived, because it cannot, without question-begging, be *inductively* proved that a large number of favorable instances is evidence of the universal validity of a rule. To repeat: it is admitted by everybody that no deductively cogent reason can be given validating the inductive procedure; it is admitted likewise that in induction we do accept as sufficient evidence a large number of favorable instances; but what Hume and Bertrand Russell and others have stressed is that this acceptance of favorable instances as sufficient evidence is arbitrary, that it is not and cannot be the result of an inductive argument. It is, in fact, the generally accepted principle of inductive reasoning and cannot, *for that reason*, be inductively proved.

Paul Edwards, in his paper on the subject, accuses Russell of seeking unnecessarily for a deductive "justification" of inductive argument.[12] But the accusation is false. Russell is most emphatic that no such justification is possible. Further, Edwards asserts with much emphasis and repetition that we commonly do accept inductive evidence as sufficient reason for drawing conclusions, and that *that* is all we commonly mean by the phrase "good and sufficient reason." This nobody contests, but he goes further and claims to show that, "without in any way invoking a non-empirical principle, numbers of observed positive instances do frequently afford us evidence that unobserved instances . . . are also positive." And this claim he never makes good, for his argument is no more than that what we ordinarily mean by "good and sufficient reason" for predicting the occurrence of a phenomenon is precisely that we have observed this or an analogous phenomenon frequently in the past. But of course, our giving the phrase this meaning is nothing more nor less than our acceptance of the nonempirical (because not empirically or inductively demonstrable) principle that frequent past instances are evidence for future instances. The principle cannot be empirical, because it is inevitably presupposed in all inductive proof. The fact that consideration of a number of examples of inductive argument reveals our habitual acceptance of past favorable instances as evidence is not the reason why we accept past instances as evidence. Such an empirical investigation of inductive arguments is, therefore, not an empirical proof that numbers of observed favorable instances do afford us evidence of unobserved favorable instances, but only that they are habitually *taken* to do so.

Once this point is firmly grasped, it becomes plain that Edwards' appeal to the ordinary use of the phrase "good reason" is misleading, because it confuses the *fact* that we habitually accept past instances as evidence with our *reason* for accepting them. Only this confusion makes the contention seem plausible that inductive argument is not dependent on a nonempirical principle and consequently presents no problem for the empiricist. He castigates Russell for asserting the contrary, yet his whole argument is evidence in favor of Russell's case, and he has produced the impression that the problem has been disposed of simply by failing to see what it is.

4. DISPOSAL OF SENSE-DATA

The linguistic analyst suggests that the question whether there are sense-data is misleading because it seems to refer to a peculiar kind of entity distinguished from, yet specially related to, material objects, whereas it is really a question about the terminology we intend to use for describing perceptual experiences. Here again, it is held, we are familiar with and all clearly understand the facts, but we argue whether we should say "I see a round penny that looks elliptical to me," or "I see an elliptical sense-datum 'of' a round penny." These reports of the same fact are said to be equally good, and each useful for a different purpose, but the second is misleading because it makes us think that there are peculiar things called sense-data, which are like material things in that they are sensible, but unlike them in that they cannot appear to be other than they are.

It is hardly for one who does not believe that knowledge is based on data of any kind to come to the assistance of sense-data theories when they are attacked, but it is one thing to reject a particular view of perception because it involves an untenable assumption, and quite another to allege that perception and the knowledge it gives us of material things present no problem whatsoever. Those who postulate the existence of sense-data at least draw attention to the undoubted fact that the perceptual act is not as simple as it appears to common sense and to the naive realist. They are at least aware that to be apprised of the existence of a material object by direct perception is not just a matter of looking or feeling or listening; that what we become aware of directly by sense is not itself sufficient to acquaint us even with the actual presence, let alone inform us of the nature, of a material object. But it does make us aware of something, and the sense-datum is one answer to the question, aware of what?

G. A. Paul (not the only one who has done so) suggests by his analysis that this is not the case. He does not actually say, but the leaves us with the strong impression, that in every perceptual act, we know quite plainly exactly what it is that we immediately perceive, and that this is always some material object; but that we do not know, and no amount of experiment (or consideration?) will help us to discover, what sort of thing we directly perceive when we see a material thing "by means of" a sense-datum which differs from the thing in appearance. The talk of sense-data is said to be just a special way of saying what we all always clearly understand: that we are perceiving a so-and-so which looks (feels or sounds) such-like to us.

Now this is very misleading, because it overlooks the facts that (1) if we were always so clearly and easily familiar with what actually occurs in sense perception, nothing would ever have induced philosophers to invent the sense-datum vocabulary, and (2) if I know that I am perceiving a so-and-so (e.g., a round brown penny) and that it appears such-like (e.g., elliptical and red) to me, I know far more than I ever directly sense. It is the attempt to analyze such a situation into what I know and assume about what I directly sense, and what I do actually and directly sense (and how they relate one to the other), that has led some philosophers to use sense-datum terminology. They may or may not be right to contend that sense-data are special entities specially related to material things, but they do not mislead us about the nature of the problem they are tackling as much as those who suggest that it is the illusory effect of our peculiar use of words.

CONCLUSION

First, the allegation that philosophers (and possibly even others) are confused by the forms of ordinary language and misled into the formulation of absurd theories is not proven. In fact, the errors imputed to the philosophers are errors they have not made and are such as would be committed only by the intellectually deficient.

Secondly, the imputation of these errors to the allegedly misleading character of language forms is itself the result of confusions, such as the mistaken belief that we can assign a status in language to words without assigning a corresponding status to the things for which they stand: that we can, for instance, identify, either in language or in logic, a genuine subject of attributes without claiming for it a status in the actual world as "a substance," or "a real thing," or "a reality."

Thirdly, the attempt to show that some traditional philosophical problems are only apparent and arise only from the way in which we talk about certain matters fails, because the problems remain, however we choose to alter our way of speaking, so long as we continue by our words to refer to the same subjects.

Fourthly, at least some attempts by linguistic analysts to deny the existence of philosophical problems are the result of *ignoratio elenchi*—as when the fact that we commonly accept empirical evidence as sufficient to establish a general conclusion is taken to show that empirical justification of induction presents no problem.

Finally, the attempt to explain away problems as the result of linguistic usage, in virtually every case, has been a disguised attempt to bolster up empiricist presuppositions without taking seriously the objections that have hitherto been brought against them by serious philosophers. It is simply a clandestine attempt to adhere to empiricism while ignoring, or speciously explaining away, the philosophical obstacles that have been pointed out, sometimes even by its own adherents.

Notes

Originally published in *Philosophical Quarterly*, vol. 3, no. 13 (October 1953).

1. Antony Flew, ed., *Logic and Language*, (Oxford, Blackwell, 1952), p. 9.
2. Ibid., p. 17.
3. Cf. ibid., p. 32.
4. As when we speak of cutting off the top of (or "topping") a tree, and in "Rock-a-bye baby in the treetop."
5. Flew, *Logic and Language*, pp. 44, 48–9, 51. Cf. my discussion in *The Reality of Time*. (Albany, NY., State University of New York Press, 1988).
6. Flew, *Logic and Language*, p. 38.
7. Ibid., p. 46.
8. Ibid., p. 47.
9. Ibid., p. 52.
10. It can be more easily explained as soon as we realize that it is not the passage of time that causes things to change but something in the nature of the things themselves, and it is more nearly (but not altogether) true that the changes cause the passage of time.
11. Cf. Flew, *Logic and Language*, p. 53.
12. Ibid., p. 66.

4

The End of the Phase

What we are destroying is nothing but a house of cards and we are clearing the ground of language on which they stand.
—Ludwig Wittgenstein, *Philosophical Investigations*

1. HISTORICAL BACKGROUND

The linguistic philosophy which for some time has been prevalent in Europe and the United States has at various times espoused certain doctrines, changed and abandoned them; at others eschewed all doctrine and professed only to use certain methods, and these too it has changed and sometimes abandoned; but there are still those who practice what they call and always have called "philosophy," even while castigating and condemning what (in some other sense) they call philosophy, and while renouncing, denouncing, and explaining away what they say philosophers do. However this may be, whether one disavows any theory or point of view, if one adopts some recognized method of "doing philosophy," there must be some reason for accepting the method and some pretext for continuing the practice, which should somehow be defensible by argument. To deny this would be to forfeit all claim to respect or attention. Yet if we accept the pronouncements of some linguistic philosophers and credit and account given of the development of their own positions, we are forced to the conclusion that, on their own showing, all reason and every pretext for continuing "analysis" under the guise of philosophy have long since vanished.

I am aware that as long ago as 1959 Ernest Gellner forcibly argued a similar thesis in his book *Words and Things*, in which he explicated the doctrines and arguments embedded or presupposed in the process of linguistic analysis and submitted them to criticism. This was a timely and much needed task, for whether or not one agrees with the criticism, the doctrines and arguments, thus stripped of all disguise, can be recognized for what they are and considered on their merits. But little heed was given to Gellner's critique, which was, with the usual *ad hominem* argument, dismissed by those criticized as personal abuse.

52

I propose to take a different course, in large measure to allow linguistic philosophers to speak for themselves, and then to draw what I take to be the natural and inevitable conclusions from their explicit statements about themselves.

Concerning the origins of the type of philosophy under consideration, there is no serious difference of opinion. It grew by stages out of the early work of Bertrand Russell and G. E. Moore as that was developed by Wittgenstein, and in its earlier phases it was closely associated with the theory of logical atomism. For this we have the testimony of both J. O. Urmson and G. J. Warnock in the accounts they have given of its growth.[1] The theory was admittedly empiricist, unashamedly metaphysical, and held that the world was a collection of particular facts, each independent of and in no way necessarily connected to any other, so that any one could either be or not be the case, with everything else remaining the same. That it derives originally from Hume's epistemological theory is obvious, and that it harbours metaphysical presuppositions cannot be denied. Each fact was said to be constituted by "objects" that were particulars qualified by particular properties and standing in various relations to one another. So far as the particular objects are concerned, their mutual relations are "external" (in the sense of not being essential or necessary), although, according to some versions of the doctrine, relations between some properties (those of the "formal" kind) are internal to their terms—that is, they would not be what they are if their terms were not what they are.[2] Atomic facts are, then, facts that certain objects have certain properties and (or) stand in certain relations, and the propositions stating such facts are atomic propositions. It was held, further, that all facts are in the last resort atomic. This was how the world is constituted—in Wittgenstein's words, "the world divides into facts"[3]— but propositions that are atomic may be variously combined to form molecular propositions, which are reducible to or analyzable into, and whose truth is a function of, their atomic constituents.

Further, it was maintained that ordinary language often obscures the form and character of the propositions as well as the logical relations between them, but a logical language can be devised so as to display more or less exactly the logical form of the facts. Such a language would be truth functional and would operate, or be operable, as a calculus. It is just such a language that is set out in *Principia Mathematica*, which claimed to be the logical basis of mathematics and so the form of symbolism in which everything "that can be accurately said at all" can be expressed.[4]

Urmson and Warnock both assert that Russell adopted he metaphysic of logical atomism, partly in reaction against F. H. Bradley's philosophy, and partly because it was suggested to Russell by his early researches into the foundations of mathematics. They assert that in the course of these researches, Russell constructed a logical system whose structure, he came to believe, was the key to the nature and relations of things in the world. To me it is clear that this is a reversal of the natural order of thought, and that without the prior conception of a world of atomic facts constituted of particulars variously related, he would not have embarked upon the construction of the logical system. The logic moreover unless it presupposes the metaphysical doctrine, not only fails of application but also ceases to function. That this is so I have argued at length in *Formal, Transcendental, and Dialectical Thinking*, and I need not repeat the arguments here but will shortly summarize the main points before developing my main theme.

The priority of logical atomism to the symbolic logic of *Principia Mathematica* can be demonstrated in a number of ways, a few examples of which will serve my present purpose. The recognition of its priority is of special importance, for if it is overlooked, it is possible to create the impression (as is done by implication in Wittgenstein's *Philosophical Investigations*, as well as by Urmson and Warnock) that the whole process of the development of analytic philosophy was one of changing conceptions of linguistic analysis, first founded upon the belief that an ideal logical language is possible to which ordinary language can be reduced, or at least compared, and by reference to which its obscurities can be clarified, and later modified by the discovery, through the investigation of the nature of ordinary, natural language, that no logical notation that can be constructed has any claim to linguistic preference, that none is ideal, and that ordinary language cannot in fact be reduced to any symbolic calculus.

In this process, the metaphysical doctrine of atomic facts is represented as a mistaken and inessential by-product adopted first by Russell and then, through his influence, by Wittgenstein of the *Tractatus* period, because they were misled by certain notational and linguistic forms[5] into giving a peculiar description of the world, which was later seen to have been unwarranted. I contend that this is a misrepresentation of the case and that, without logical atomism and the empiricism of which it is the offshoot, linguistic analysis would never have been thought the special sphere of philosophy or exclusively its method, that all later developments of the movement have followed as corollaries from this original metaphysical doctrine, and that the subsequent linguistic attacks on logical atomism and associated features of empiricism are consequently suicidal.

2. METAPHYSICAL PRESUPPOSITIONS OF *PRINCIPIA MATHEMATICA*

The authors of *Principia Mathematica* themselves stand witness to their presumption in formulating their logical calculus of logical atomism. They say in their introduction that the ideas employed in the logic are too abstract for ordinary language, the grammatical structure of which does not represent uniquely the relations between the ideas involved.[6] Thus the structure of the symbolism is taken to represent, and so to resemble, the structure and relations of the ideas—that is, the subject matter to which the logic applies. If the subject-matter had not the structure that it has, the symbolism would not have served. Hence the basis of the "language" or symbolic notation is the character of the subject-matter. In this context, the subject-matter is taken to be mathematics ("it is framed with a view to the perfectly precise expression, in its symbols, of mathematical propositions"; p. 1). A decision is therefore needed as to the nature of the subject-matter of mathematics. If this were to transpire to be no more than the invention and manipulation of symbols according to arbitrarily chosen rules (as some have alleged), it would give no pretext for the preference of one scheme of symbolization over any other, and the reasons given by the authors of *Principia Mathematica* for their adoption of the one they have chosen would fall away. If, however, mathematics is taken to schematize in some way the structure (however skeletal) of the world, then some metaphysic is being presupposed. Consequently, Russell could not have been led to the metaphysical doctrine of logical atomism by the nature of the symbolic notation in *Principia Mathematica*, for the symbolic notation, we are explicitly told, was selected as most appropriate to some presumed structure in the subject-matter of mathematics.

Now Russell has admitted that he was led to the position he espouses by a study of the work of Gottlob Frege, and Frege's theory of the concept, in his definition of number, is of a set or class the members of which are particulars unrelated to one another, except insofar as they all belong to the class: that is, the relations between them are purely external. Frege's definition of number is explicitly adopted by Russell,[7] and it becomes clear that the assumed structure of the subject-matter of mathematics (or, at least, of arithmetic) is, in consequence, that of classes, or sets, of externally related particulars. This is simply another way of describing, in rather more abstract terms, the atomic facts defined by Wittgenstein in the *Tractatus*. They are particular objects externally related one to another (as each is to any properties it may contingently possess).

On page 8 of *Principia Mathematica*, we are told that the entire system is such that the truth value of $f(p)$ is dependent only on the truth of p, not on its being p. Accordingly, if p is equivalent to q, $f(p)$ is equivalent to $f(p)$. Now as two propositions are said to be equivalent if they are either both true or both false (p. 7), the system is such that any true proposition can be substituted for any other true proposition in any function or proof without invalidating it. Clearly the propositions are regarded as atomic propositions, any one of which can be true or false without making any difference to any other, so that any two true propositions can be regarded as equivalent (i.e., true) in value, as can any two false propositions. If the facts were such that they were interdependent for their truth or falsehood, if things or events were parts of wholes the organizing principles of which determined their character, this could not be the case, for then the truth value of p would depend on its being p and on its relations to other statements of fact. In such a situation, it would be impossible validly to substitute any true proposition for any other true proposition in any function or proof. In the argument that Socrates is mortal because Socrates is a man and all men are mortal, it is not permissible to substitute "the sun is hot" for "all men are mortal." Thus the entire system of logic developed in *Principia Mathematica* depends on treating propositions as atomic and rests on the metaphysical doctrine of logical atomism. This can be further demonstrated by examining the way in which material implication is defined and operates in the system, as I have shown at some length in *Formal, Transcendental and Dialectical Thinking*.[8] The same presupposition lies behind formal implication as supports material implication, and every operation throughout the logical calculus depends on these two functions.

Of the four logical functions fundamental to the whole of the propositional calculus, material implication is the most important, because it combines the other three: $p \supset q$ is defined as equivalent to $\sim p \ q$ and to $\sim(p.\sim q)$, so the logical sum, the logical product, and the contradictory function are all involved in it. The whole of the system is built up on these four functions, as the authors of *Principia Mathematica* say, "step by step."

But material implication can hold only between atomic propositions that are bound together by no internal relations, between which there are no connections (necessary or even contingent) but only contingent associations or conjunctions. This is evident from the way the function is defined. The implicative relation is said to hold between p and q whenever both p and q are true, or both are false, or when the first is false and the second true (i.e., whenever the first is false or the second is true). Thus "Socrates was a woman" (being false) materially implies any other proposition (true or false), and "All men are mortal" is implied by every other proposition (true or false). This could be so only if the truth values of the propositions were all entirely independent one of another.

In normal reasoning, when we say that some truth implies some other, we mean exactly the opposite of material implication. That a patient shows the symptoms of malaria implies that he or she has been bitten by an anopheles mosquito, because only in human blood can the parasite which develops in the blood of the mosquito complete its life cycle. Here there is a necessary connection, and one could not substitute for "the patient shows symptoms of malaria" any other true proposition, such as "Socrates was a Greek philosopher" (which does not imply, in the usual sense, that he was bitten by an anopheles mosquito). Likewise, "Newton's mother was not a woman" (being false) does not normally imply that the sun is hot or that Newton had malaria, but it does imply both these propositions "materially." It follows that material implication can hold only between unconnected atomic propositions.

If the consequent is internally related to the antecedent, the relation between them cannot be material implication, because no other propositions can legitimately be substituted for either of them if the relation is to continue to hold, and although they may satisfy the definition of material implication (both being true), the sign ⊃ does not indicate the internal relation presupposed in common reasoning, which assumes that the *implicans* necessitates the *implicatum*. Hence only atomic propositions can serve as components of the material implicative function.

There is no need to multiply examples, for in the introduction to the second edition of *Principia Mathematica*, we read that atomic propositions are accepted as a datum and that such terms as can occur in any atomic proposition are "particulars".[9] This is reaffirmed by Russell in his paper "Logical Atomism" in *Contemporary British Philosophy* (1924), where he maintains that although facts are not simple, all complexes must be composed of simples, which are the limits of analysis. The logical uses, he says, of the old notion of substance can be applied, if at all, only to simples, and such are what the simple symbols in symbolic logic represent. In fact, it is clear from the way in which Russell writes in this paper, both of symbolic logic and of the world, that he considers the justification of the logical procedures to be their appropriateness to the structure of the real. There can, moreover, be no doubt that the account given of atomic propositions on page xv of *Principia Mathematica* is meant to reveal what the authors consider to be the structure of the facts that such propositions state.

Wittgenstein, in his *Tractatus Logico-Philosophicus*, asserts quite frankly that the logical notation shows forth the form of the facts and makes no suggestion that it is independent of, or could be justified except by, the metaphysical doctrine there developed. There is no need whatever to think that he was misled into this position by any linguistic error or confusion of Russell's, for unless the notation did represent the form of the facts, symbolic logic would be the logic of nothing whatsoever, not even of mathematics (in which the facts are assumed to be as represented by Frege).

That Russell and Wittgenstein were misled by the language of mathematics to adopt the theory of logical atomism is further disproved by the fact that the language of mathematics does not support the metaphysical theory. The structure and procedure of mathematics depend throughout, and in all its branches, on the nature of numbers, of which the foundation is the series of natural integers. Although Frege defined number in a way that encouraged belief in the metaphysical doctrine of atomism, he seems to have overlooked the fact that the relations between the numbers, as such, is not purely external but rather the opposite. The most compelling characteristic of the series of natural integers is the logical interdependence of the mutual relations of its terms. Wittgenstein was aware of this when he included numbers among those formal series between whose members relations are internal (*Tractatus* 4.1252). It is therefore *only* to atomic facts, not to the truths of mathematics, that the logical notation of *Principia Mathematica* can be appropriate, a circumstance which again becomes apparent from the reduction of mathematical propositions to tautologies (*Tractatus* 6.2–6.22). They "express no thoughts," picture no facts; they are not the atomic propositions that the notation is designed to symbolize and to whose form it corresponds. If this be so, no analogy from the language of mathematics could have suggested either the "ideal" logical language or the atomic metaphysic to Russell, much less to Wittgenstein himself.

Moreover, mathematics makes quite different use of symbols similar to those of symbolic logic. In the logic, $f(p)$ is a function, the truth of which, when substitution is made for p, depends on the truth-value of the proposition substituted. "If p then q" is true if q is true. But in this molecular proposition, the logical character of p is quite different from what it is when p occurs alone. "You are ill" makes an assertion about "you." "If you are ill you should go to bed" makes no such assertion but makes a quite different one about the treatment of illness. Here, "you are ill" is not asserted, nor is "you should go to bed", but something different from either concerning the connection between being ill and going to bed. It is of the nature of propositions (even when only entertained) to assert something, and it is clear, therefore, that in symbolic logic, what is represented by p has a different logical significance when it occurs alone from when it is included in a logical function such as $f(p)$. In mathematics this is not the case. The variable x is precisely the same when it occurs alone as when it occurs in x^2, or $2x = y$, or in any other function; θ is the same in $\sin\theta$, $\cos\theta$, or $\tan\theta$, or when it is considered simply as an angle of a particular magnitude. It is not true, therefore, that the notation of symbolic logic is like mathematical notation in anything but superficial appearance. It is not especially suited to express or reveal the relations between mathematical concepts, but it is appropriate and is designed to represent the structure of a world of atomic facts, any one of which may be, or may not be, what it is, irrespective of all the rest. The notation follows essentially from logical atomism.

Why then did the authors of *Principia Mathematica* maintain that their notation was "framed with a view to the perfectly precise expression of mathematical propositions," and why did they believe that the whole of mathematics could be deduced from certain fundamental logical postulates? The answer is that they were led to these beliefs by their adoption of logical atomism, and not vice versa. If they were misled, it was by Frege's doctrine of the concept and not by mathematical linguistic usages. Their admiration for Hume, also, may well have been partly responsible.

3. EMPIRICIST FOUNDATIONS OF ANALYSIS

From the conception of a world of atomic particulars, the denial of ontological status to round squares, universals, whatever is denoted by a definite description, and all other denizens of what Urmson called "the Meinongian under-world" is a natural consequence. So, likewise, is Russell's attempt to eliminate them from accurate discourse by demonstrating that the common expressions for them are incomplete symbols. It was natural also that his technique for doing so should have involved notation borrowed from symbolic logic. The typical phrase in the translation of such expressions is, "There is an object x such that . . . ," where the variable is replaceable only by the name of a genuine object—that is, a particular in a world of particulars. This is the pervading presumption of the notation.

It is an easy step from here to the contentions that linguistic forms mislead philosophers into the belief in bogus entities, that attributes are reified as "universals" because abstract nouns are mistaken for proper names, that descriptions are given substantial force where none is warranted, and generally that idiomatic structures become systematically misleading. The proper method of clearing the metaphysical air was, by general agreement, analysis, but the conception of analysis became modified as time went on. At first, in the hands of Russell, it was the analysis of facts; in those of G. E. Moore, it was that of propositions, especially those whose obvious truth to common sense was frequently denied by philosophers. The termination of Russell's analysis was in the simples that constituted atomic facts; of Moore's it was sense-data.[10] That this involved no disagreement between them is amply proved by the link forged in Russell's *Our Knowledge of the External World* between the doctrine of logical atomism and the theory of perception in terms of sense-data and perspectives. The basis of logical atomism is essentially empiricism, and it is far more truly Hume's creation than Russell's. It is not, therefore, surprising that the next phase in the development of analytic philosophy was one in which elementary propositions were held to be ostensive, such as report the occurrence of an immediately present sense-datum.

The philosophical consequences of the metaphysics of logical atomism soon became apparent and were explicitly set out by Wittgenstein in the *Tractatus*. If all facts are atomic and if the ultimate simples into which they can be analyzed are sense-data, all atomic propositions are empirical. Further, if all factually significant propositions are either atomic or truth functions of atomic propositions, any form of words that is neither (unless it is tautological) is no genuine proposition and can at best be masquerading as a statement of fact. It was next observed that all possible genuine factual statements fall within the province of the natural sciences, and so none can be philosophical. Metaphysics, therefore, went by the board, and logical and mathematical propositions were still admissible only because, being tautological, they say nothing.

If now philosophers are ever to speak in their own character, what can they speak about? Clearly, only about logic, and logic must be concerned only with the devisal and manipulation of a notation that best displays the form of the facts. It will also be necessary to reveal and explain the relation between such a notation and other less rigorous forms of symbolization such as ordinary language. The logical notation will be regarded as the logically most adequate language, and the divergence from it of other systems is to be revealed by analysis. What we are now dealing with throughout is, therefore, always the analysis of language of one kind or another, and philosophy must be seen to be solely the analysis of language and to have no other function or field.

This, in effect, was the position when analytic philosophy was emerging from the positivistic stage of which the work of Rudolf Carnap is typical. It launched, henceforth, into what may be described as its therapeutic phase, which took two interrelated forms. One was the analysis conducted by the logical positivists, using technical linguistic notations, by translating sentences from the material mode into the formal mode of speech, unmasking in the process "pseudo-object" sentences (which were said to give rise to philosophical pseudo-problems) and revealing them to be syntactical sentences (which were reputed to occasion no such problems).[11]

The second form of therapy was conducted by John Wisdom and the immediate followers of Wittgenstein and consisted in the examination and comparison of the manifold uses of linguistic expressions to discover their mode of functioning and reveal their "logical geography" or position on the "language map".[12] The results were supposed to cure the philosopher of puzzlement and "mental cramp" by dissolving the philosophical problems—demonstrating "to him that he had given no meaning to certain signs in his propositions." The method was strongly influenced by the practice of G. E. Moore, who, confessing that he was unphilosophically minded himself,[13] set himself, through analysis of commonsense statements which he believed to be "obviously true," to discredit the surprisingly paradoxical affirmations current among philosophers. The appearance of paradox came to be regarded as an unquestionable symptom of intellectual malaise to which the therapy was to be applied.

Gilbert Ryle was the first to adopt this method in a full-scale attack on specific problems, whereas others had largely argued for its use on the ground that philosophical problems were only linguistically pathological and called for an analytic cure of this kind. But Ryle's practice does not depart from the view, that he himself had earlier expressed, that linguistic idioms mislead philosophers into beliefs in bogus entities (like ghosts inhabiting machines), although rightly understood, they imply something different (such as dispositions to behave in specific ways). We have seen that this view is rooted in the doctrine that the only genuine entities are empirically observable particulars in a world of such particulars. Warnock rightly insisted that the unexpressed yet pervasive assumption of Ryle's *The Concept of Mind* is an old-style materialism, a metaphysical position that, though not identical with empiricism, is one of its most common offshoots. The Rylian analysis, therefore, though not without its merits, does not differ in principle from other forms and phases of linguistic analysis, depends in the last resort on an unacknowledged metaphysic, and is liable to be infected by the faults of that metaphysic.

4. THE COLLAPSE OF ANALYSIS

From here on, a process of disintegration set in of which I must allow Warnock and Urmson to give evidence. The brief summary I have sketched of the development of the antimetaphysical and linguistic trends in the movement was intended to make clear their unmistakable dependence, from the first, on logical atomism and the empiricist interpretation that went with it. The doctrine of logical atomism leads to the belief in the need for analysis into elementary propositions; from the empirical character of elementary propositions, the denunciation of nonempirical propositions as factually nonsignificant derives; and from this the rejection of metaphysics follows. Similarly, from logical atomism is derived the conception of a symbolic notation as the logically ideal language (ideal because it mirrors the form of the facts) and the belief that the ordinary language in which we strive to communicate these same facts is a vaguer and more confused variant of the logical language—a sort of loose garment obscuring the proper form of the figure, the actual form of what it is supposed to convey.[14] Hence it is to logical atomism that we must trace back both the condemnation of metaphysics and the restriction of philosophy to the analysis of language.

Urmson tells us that logical atomism succumbed not to attack from without but to self-criticism. "There was," he says, "no outside attack which was sufficiently informed and sympathetic to have any effect."[15] Such, presumably was the criticism of Winston Barnes, who wrote:

> How . . . are we to regard statements in Wittgenstein's own work? *They* are neither mathematical nor matter of fact. They are philosophical. Wittgenstein's solution is to regard them as like metaphysical statements in being nonsense, but unlike them in being part of the proper elucidatory activity of philosophy. . . . The notion of elucidatory nonsense is one that only a very subtle mind in a very stupid moment could have conceived.[16]

Others pointed out that the rejection of metaphysics invalidates logical atomism itself and should therefore invalidate the conclusions drawn from it. And because one of these is the nonsignificance of metaphysical propositions, it is self-refuting. Urmson's own view hardly differs, for he writes:

> We have had cause to notice again and again that from the strict empiricist principles which the atomists often enunciated it would seem to follow that their metaphysics was devoid of meaning; for it could hardly be construed as empirical in content.[17]

Warnock agrees:

> According to the purest doctrines of Logical Atomism, a proposition can be significantly stated *either* if there is, or could be, an atomic fact to which it corresponds, *or* if it is a truth function, however complex, of propositions of that sort. But most of the propositions which Logical Atomists, including Wittgenstein himself, purported to assert were not of either of these kinds.

This fact, he goes on to say, recognized by Wittgenstein in his confession that his own statements were devoid of sense, was "laid quite early like a sort of time-bomb in the basement of Logical Atomism."[18] Lack of sympathy and information on the part of external critics does not seem, therefore, to have led them into very serious error.

The collapse of logical atomism, carrying with it the ruin of logical positivism, is attributed by Urmson to five main defects. In the first place, the whole notion of reductive analysis (analysis into simples or propositions about simples, be these what they may) was found to be untenable, because the statements to be analyzed could never be exhausted by, and were never equivalent to, elementary propositions, however many were produced. But worse than this, "the given" on which so much depended proved to be inaccessible.[19] Ostensive propositions could not be enunciated, and in consequence, the relation of fact to language proved, on the principles laid down, not to be a matter of possible significant discourse.[20] It was, of course, metaphysical (like the verification principle, which is only one way of stating that relation) and had to be abjured.[21] It is reassuring to discover that my own past efforts to draw attention to these difficulties in doctrines of logical empiricism were so little turned awry by ignorance and lack of sympathy.[22] Nor had the third disorder from which, according to Urmson, these theories suffered gone unnoticed by the allegedly uninformed and unsympathetic critics—that is, their entailment of solipsism.[23] Oddly enough, this feature was openly recognized and confessed without apparent remorse by Wittgenstein and by Ayer, despite its obvious metaphysical character. Fourthly, the central theory of language broke down. Not only did the invention of alternative logical calculi cast doubt on the ideality as a logical language of any particular one, but ordinary language resisted treatment as a truth-functional calculus altogether. General statements would not allow themselves to be satisfactorily resolved into a congeries of particular statements—$(x)\phi x$ into ϕa, ϕb, $\phi c, \ldots \phi n$. This we have observed, as well as the paradoxical doctrine of material implication. "When we make a statement of entailment," says Urmson, "we are not merely saying that it is not the case that the entailing proposition is false and the entailed proposition is true, but saying that the truth of the entailed proposition can be inferred from the truth of the other without independent knowledge of the truth of the entailed proposition."[24] But even before P. F. Strawson, "unsympathetic and uninformed" critics had noted these oddities in the logical doctrine.[25] Such propositions as "Jones believes that *p*" also proved intractable as truth functions of *p*. Wittgenstein's attempted resolution of this difficulty, if not altogether meaningless, seemed implausible, and Ayer's led back through a sort of behaviorism to solipsism.[26]

Fifthly, the picture theory of propositions could be given no clear sense, which is not a surprising consequence of the foregoing difficulties. Urmson expresses doubt that we find the world really divided into facts, for what we find are inseparable facts, as we have seen, is and the alleged form undiscoverable, and nothing in the forms of common speech could be found to answer to what it was alleged to be. "Is there not some danger," asks Urmson, "that in doing so [talking of the form of the fact] we are reading into the fact what is to be found in the language we use?"[27]

The wheel has come full circle. We began by extruding from the world the bogus entities of Meinongian and idealistic mythology as suggested by the forms of language. "The sole and whole function of philosophy," Ryle had declared, "was the detection of the sources in linguistic idioms of recurrent misconstructions and absurd theories." So we reformed our language to reflect the actual structure of the facts and reduced it to stark symbolic nudity, to discover at last that the anatomy of the fact itself is only a misconstruction and an absurd theory originating in linguistic idiom.

This is the conclusion reached, in effect, by Wittgenstein himself in *Philosophical Investigations*, a radical reconsideration of his earlier position. By a sort of quasi-empirical examination of the actual functioning of language, in which we are adjured not to think but to look, he is brought to the conclusions that language is not truth-functional and that no skeleton of an ideal language is shrouded by, or discoverable under, the looser garments of common speech. Language, he found, was not a calculus nor even a game, but a "form of life." His own and Russell's earlier beliefs were, he maintained, the result of their bewitchment by a pictorial and oversimplified conception of the activity of naming.[28] Philosophers in general tend to become bewitched in this way and so to talk paradoxically and to be tortured by intellectual bewilderment—they lose their way in the maze of language—so he contended. But by examining its interminable and incurably heterogeneous forms of usage, by copiously exemplifying the varieties of such forms, we can eventually help them to break the spell and to see their way, as we might help a fly to get out of a bottle. This, the legitimate philosophical procedure, "leaves everything as it is," except, of course, the sense of mystery.

There can be no doubt that in these afterthoughts Wittgenstein discovered some important truths about language corrective of his earlier errors. One would imagine that his new conclusions would be regarded as at least evidence against the truth of the doctrine of language presented in the *Tractatus* and, to that extent, a disproof of logical atomism. But, according to Warnock, he denied this. "He believed that what lay behind the old way of thinking was not a mistake of fact or logic, nor even a cluster of such mistakes, but something better called a *superstition*."[29] It is not easy to see the difference between a superstition and a cluster of factual and logical errors, but be that as it may, what was the source of the superstition? To our amazement, we are told that it was language. Language, it would seem, had led us into the superstitious belief that it is itself a propositional calculus in which the complex propositions are truth functions of the simple and atomic, so that we were mistakenly led to an analysis of language in order to discover which of its symbols had genuine meaning. The cure for this error, we now find, is to analyze language yet again, this time to discover that no precise and invariable meaning can ever be given to any symbol, but that meaning constantly shifts and varies as each locution is used in different contexts and for different purposes—every statement has its own logic.

But we saw earlier that the only reason it seemed plausible to assign to philosophy the sole task of analyzing language was the doctrine that language forms, by diverging from those of the facts, produced mystification. If this belief is now found to be superstitious, there can be no further reason to hold that language is the source of philosophical puzzlement and that its influence is the inspiration of metaphysical doctrines—logical atomism or any other. If there is no discoverable form of fact for language to mask or to mirror and no ideal language to mirror it, on what grounds is language held to produce confusion, and by what criterion are its misleading effects to be recognized as such? What possible ground can now remain for persisting in the belief that analysis of language will remedy the error? It was only the espousal of an atomistic empiricism that seemed to justify the contention that language misled philosophers into metaphysical fabrications that the correct analysis of language would dissipate. But now logical atomism has been unmasked as itself a metaphysical fabrication suggested by linguistic mystification. Is not this reasoning (if that is the name it merits) intolerably circular?

"The circle is of your own making," the linguistic philosopher might have retorted. "You and not we have insisted on the dependence of linguistic analysis on logical atomism. We see the metaphysical dogma as an illusion generated by language, not indeed ordinary language, but the language of mathematics." I have, however, shown that neither the procedure nor the language of mathematics could have suggested a logico-metaphysical atomism to anybody not already addicted to a belief in a world of atomic facts. This belief rested on the dogma that the original building blocks of all knowledge are sensa and that, therefore, statements that cannot be correlated with sense-data are senseless. To account for our addiction to such statements, some misleading influence had to be detected, and language was held to be the culprit. If the original belief is now rejected as a superstition, what followed from it must be rejected also.

Warnock, at least, was ready to make important concessions. He maintained that not only language bewitched and mesmerized the unwary into pictorial thinking and false metaphysics. Scientific discoveries, he thought, could do likewise, as the physiologists's description of the mechanisms of perception misled Russell into the belief that what we see is our own gray matter. Sometimes the limitations of our intellect and our failure to think clearly were the sources of our problems rather than bewitchment by language.[30] But if this is so, the remedy surely lies not in analysis of language but in clearer thinking and more careful reexamination of the subject matter (e.g., of the nature of perception).

Metaphysics, for a while, ceased to be anathema (although bad metaphysics is always to be deprecated). After F. Waissman's declaration that "to say that metaphysics is nonsense *is* nonsense," it became less imperative to exclude it from the fold of respectable philosophy. Warnock disowned any inclination to indulge in it himself and said that he noticed none among his linguistic colleagues. This, he said, was because they did not suffer from "cosmic anxieties." Precisely what sort of disorder this phrase denotes is not clearly explained, and in using it, Warnock almost laid himself open to the charge he leveled against F. H. Bradley of the inflation of language. The phrase suggests a need for attention from the psychiatrist rather than the metaphysician, and linguistic philosophers might well have been congratulated on their freedom from the ailment. But if by cosmic anxiety is meant interest in and curiosity about the nature of the universe, to confess lack of it is surely to acknowledge a sad deficiency of desire for any scientific or philosophical inquiry.

Nevertheless, there was a temporary reenfranchisement of metaphysics and a refreshing return by some philosophers associated with, or brought up in, the linguistic tradition to more constructive kinds of study. Not only did Strawson feel no scruple to call a work of his "a study in descriptive metaphysics," but Stuart Hampshire produced an important book *Thought and Action* which had no special linguistic bias and was even critical of much current linguistic practice. John Findlay produced a commentary on the work of that arch-metaphysician Hegel, full of insight and sympathetic understanding, which ranks among the best. Metaphysics was once again recognized as a way of gaining new and wider vision of old and familiar facts. Some philosophers will remember having read something like this before: ὁ μὲν γὰρ συνοπτικὸ ς διαλεκτικῆς δ δε μὴ 'όυ

John Austin's researches were described by Warnock as an attempt to "look through the workings of language at the facts of the world and our concerns with the world which have moulded, and continue to mould, our ways of speaking." (Warnock, *English Philosophy Since 1900*). Thus the ultimate interest of philosophy is finally admitted to be not language so much as the world, and our philosophical concern not with language but with the real. That our concepts are expressed in language and may be ill expressed, that the philosopher's task includes the examination of these modes of expression and their correction and improvement where they are at fault, few would wish to deny. But we must refuse to limit the philosophical enterprise to this linguistic propaedeutic. The important truth is that the philosopher's concern is with the concepts themselves and the realities that are their objects. If this is so, once the need for clarification has been admitted, what other philosophical pretext can we possibly allege for continuing the analysis of language? The classification in detail of kinds of statements and their varied uses is said to have an interest of its own, and this may well be so for meticulous minds. But what philosophical interest can it have beyond the initial clarification of concepts? As long as it was plausibly believed that misinterpretation of idiomatic forms gave rise to absurd and paradoxical theories, it seemed right and philosophically important to hunt down the subversive errors. But the plausibility of that view depended on the surreptitious adherence to a vicious metaphysical doctrine, which has now been exploded, about the nature and status of "genuine" and the identification of "bogus" entities. Consequently, analyses based on it were often more misleading than the confusions they were supposed to unveil. Moreover, the criterion by which the theories were judged to be absurd was never brought out into the open but was, for the most part, taken, by implication, to be common sense, no proof having been offered that common sense is infallible, nor any reason for accepting it as a criterion if it is not.

Despite all this, so-called analytic philosophy persisted and prevailed throughout the English-speaking world for decades, and as late as the 1980s, prominent philosophers were still denouncing metaphysics as "impossible," until the final product of the movement emerged as the self-destructive relativism and skepticism of Richard Rorty. Now, perhaps, we can claim that the view that linguistic analysis is the whole essence of philosophy has finally collapsed. The arguments of its own exponents knocked out from under it every philosophical support on which it could legitimately rest. If some would say that it needs no foundation, that is only a way of acknowledging that one has no reason for indulging in it beyond personal inclination. For such useful work as it may have done, let us applaud it as it bows out, and let us get back to work as genuine philosophers attacking problems that seriously affect our life and thought, seeking illumination that (as may now be generally admitted) competent metaphysical speculation can afford. Of the doctrines that gave rise to the adoption and practice of linguistic analysis that so long was current in Britain, the United States, and elsewhere, the final judgment is surely best epitomized in Collingwood's prophetic pronouncement (giving ironic point to the quotation from Wittgenstein that heads this chapter):

> this school, with all its ingenuity and pertinacity, is only building card houses out of a pack of lies.[31]

Notes

Originally published in *Dialectica*, vol. 17, no. 1 (1963).

1. J. O. Urmson, *Philosophical Analysis*, and G. J. Warnock, *English Philosophy Since 1900*.
2. Cf. L. Wittgenstein, *Tractatus Logico-Philosophicus*, 4.122 et seq.
3. Ibid., 1.2.
4. See Urmson, *Philosophical Analysis*, p. 7.
5. Ibid.
6. Cf. B. Russell and A. N. Whitehead, *Principia Mathematica*, vol. 1, pp. 2–3.
7. Cf. Bertrand Russell, *My Philosophical Development*, pp. 68–70.
8. Errol E. Harris, *Formal, Transcendental and Dialectical Thinking*, chap. 1.
9. Russell and Whitehead, *Principia Mathematica*, pp. xv, xix.
10. Cf. Warnock, *English Philosophy Since 1900*, p. 26, and G. E. Moore, *Philosophical Studies*, VII.
11. The method persisted, for instance, in the work of Gustav Bergman, who called it the "reconstruction" of metaphysics, see "The Revolt Against Logical Atomism," *Philosophical Quarterly*, vols. 7, 8 (1957–58).
12. Obvious allusions to Wittgenstein's "logical space"; see *Tractatus*, 1.13, 2.1, 2.202.
13. See Paul A. Schilpp, ed., *The Philosophy of G. E. Moore*, (New York, Tudor Publishing Co., 1952), p. 14.
14. Cf. Wittgenstein, *Tractatus*, 4.002.
15. Urmson, *Philosophical Analysis*, p. 100.
16. Winston H. Barnes, *The Philosophical Predicament*, p. 104.
17. Urmson, *Philosophical Analysis*, p. 53.
18. Warnock, *English Philosophy Since 1900*, pp. 41–2.
19. Analysts might have been forewarned of this calamity had they heeded H. H. Joachim, who demonstrated it in a detailed and incisive argument in *Logical Studies*. (Oxford, The Clarendon Press, 1944). Instead, the reviewer of the book, Stuart Hampshire, dismissed it as useless nonsense; see *Philosophy*, vol. 24 (1949).
20. Urmson, *Philosophical Analysis*, pp. 38–40, and Warnock, *English Philosophy Since 1900*, p. 50.
21. Cf. Barnes, *The Philosophical Predicament*, p. 117, and my own *Nature, Mind and Modern Science*, (London, G. Allen and Unwin, 1954), p. 328.
22. Cf. Harris, *Nature, Mind and Modern Science*, pp. 330–4.
23. See J. H. Weinberg, *An Examination of Logical Positivism* (London, Kegan Paul, Trench, 1936), chaps. 7, 8 and Harris, *Nature, Mind and Modern Science*, pp. 336–40.
24. Urmson, *Philosophical Analysis*, p. 132.
25. Cf. H. W. B. Joseph, "Internal and External Relations and the Philosophy of Analysis" (unpublished lectures delivered at Oxford in 1932), and "A Plea for Free-Thinking in Logistic," *Mind*, vols. 40–3; B. H. Blanshard, *The Nature of Thought*, (London, G. Allen and Unwin, 1939), chap. 29, and "The Philosophy of Analysis," in *Proceedings of the British Academy*, vol. 38, p. 56. P. F. Strawson, *Introduction to Logical Theory*, (London, Methuen, 1952), pp. 25 83.
26. See A. J. Ayer, *Thinking and Meaning*, (London, Macmillan, 1947), pp. 16ff., and my comment in *Nature, Mind and Modern Science*, pp. 336–7.
27. Urmson, *Philosophical Analysis*, pp. 145f.

28. Cf. L. Wittgenstein, *Philosophical Investigations*, p. 115, and Warnock, *English Philosophy Since 1900*, p. 76.
29. Warnock, *English Philosophy Since 1900*, pp. 73–4.
30. Ibid., p. 114.
31. R. G. Collingwood, *An Autobiography*, (Oxford, The Clarendon Press, 1939), p. 52.

5

Analysis and Insight

1. THE REVOLUTION IN PHILOSOPHY

In mid-century, philosophy was reputed to have undergone a revolution, and those who held themselves responsible for the change trumpeted it abroad with much aplomb. The history of this revolution, as sketched by Urmson and Warnock, was outlined in the last chapter, and its output was copiously illustrated in anthologies of essays by proponents of the new discipline (a word used here without prejudice to the rights of its critics). Indeed, a new and rather strange spirit ranged through the halls of philosophy, that still lingers in some of the major universities, although it is now much less strident. It may be appropriate at this point to look back and to compare what was then hailed as the new aspect of philosophy with its predecessors, and to consider the legacy it has left us.

For the Ancients, philosophy meant what it said: the love of wisdom. Wisdom was held to be the fruit of intelligence and thoughtful reflection upon as wide a range of experience as possible. It was held to bring insight into every aspect of human life and to give enlightenment in the face of every problem, both theoretical and practical. Perhaps this assumed too optimistic and pre-sumptuous an assessment of human capacity, but whether that be so or not, philosophy, as the love and practice of wisdom—for to love it must be to use it and not just to affirm its theoretical teachings—was not merely an intellec-tual pursuit but a way of life, a religion, a system of convictions, the holding of which must affect every facet of conduct, outlook, and attitude to the world and to one's fellow beings.

So it was for Socrates, who declared that to know the truth was to know how best to live, and that whosoever knew the good could not fail to practice it. So it was for Plato, whose philosopher-king was to embody the highest and best in human nature and to live the best of all possible lives in directing the best of all possible societies. So it was for Aristotle, who believed and asserted that the end, at least of moral philosophy, was not just knowledge but action, yet who saw the life of contemplation as the final aspiration of humankind and the only conceivable occupation for God.

This tradition was handed on to the later civilization of the West through the medieval church. Although some of the early fathers (notably Tertullian) tended to oppose faith to knowledge and to repudiate philosophy, reason and belief were united for St. Augustine, St. Anselm, and St. Thomas Aquinas; and faith was never divorced from practice. Philosophy was now explicitly combined with religion, even if it was subordinated to theology, and it was still regarded as a way of thinking that influenced and transformed every aspect of practical life.

Among the "moderns" of the Renaissance and after, the tradition persisted. The philosophy of Descartes embraced everything we now call science, as well as metaphysics and logic, and he believed it capable of revealing an infallible rule of conduct as surely as an indubitable system of theoretical principles. Spinoza knew that all philosophy was ethics and reasoned that human perfection and freedom consist in the intellectual love of God—uniting philosophy and science with morals and religion. Even the British empiricists were motivated in their philosophizing by the quest for a rational and satisfactory way of living.

Locke embarked upon his examination of the human understanding to discover how far its capabilities, within its limitations, were sufficient for the human condition. "Our business here," he writes in the introduction to *An Essay Concerning Human Understanding*, "is not to know all things, but those which concern our conduct." Similarly, Berkeley sought to combat skepticism and atheism and the perplexity in which they were liable to involve action. He considered true "the general opinion of the world . . . that the end of speculation be Practice," and that it was "the readiest preparation, as well as the strongest motive, to the study and practice of virtue."[1]

The very skepticism of Hume was largely a confession of failure in the quest for that knowledge which could inform and direct action. Complaining that he could find no opinion more probable or likely than any other, he asked:

> Where am I, or what? From what causes do I derive my existence, and to what condition shall I return? Whose favour shall I court, and whose anger must I dread? What beings surround me? and on whom have I any influence, or who have any influence on me? I am confounded with all these questions.[2]

They are practical questions on which he had hoped his philosophy would throw light. Yet for all his failure in epistemology to discover good grounds for trusting the senses or reason, he did not despair. He persisted in speculation about the passions and about the nature of morality. He writes:

> I am uneasy to think that I approve of one object and disapprove of another; call one thing beautiful and another deformed; decide concerning truth and falsehood, reason and folly, without knowing upon what principles I proceed. I am concerned for the condition of the learned world, which lies under such deplorable ignorance in all these particulars.[3]

The idea of philosophy as a study concerned with issues most important to human beings, and one in which no student could indulge without effects upon his or her entire life, continued among the German idealists and among the British utilitarians, who were themselves social reformers. It was also conspicuous at the turn of the nineteenth century among the British idealists, who gave their pupils to understand that philosophizing about the principles of practical life would help them to act better; "that some understanding of the nature of moral and political action," as R. G. Collingwood put it, "some attempt to formulate ideals and principles, was an indispensable condition of engaging creditably in these activities themselves."[4]

Nowadays we hear very little talk of this kind. The profession of contemporary philosophers has been very different, and their conception of philosophy has been quite remote from this belief in its practical bearing. According to Herbert Feigl:

> Neither the construction of a world view nor a vision of a way of living is its primary aim. If through the progress of knowledge and through social, political and educational reform one or other objective is pursued, philosophy in its critical and clarifying capacity may aid or guide such developments. But it cannot, by mere reflective analysis, prescribe or produce them.[5]

The contemplated guidance of social, political, and educational reform is clearly purely negative, and the presumption is that such practical reform either is possible without any "world view" or "vision of a way of living" or must derive these from some source other than philosophy. What other source, we are not told, but if we are inclined to think that it might be religion, we should apparently be wrong, for the theological, like the metaphysical, mode of explanation is castigated by Feigl as "pre-scientific." Nor could it be science itself, because science is not concerned with visions of a way of living and is reputed to eschew all considerations of value in its exclusive pursuit of fact.

Discussing the claims of philosophy, A. J. Ayer dismissed as "pontiffs" most of the great philosophers of the older tradition and described the contemporary species as "journeymen" content to "clear away the rubbish that lies in the way of knowledge" by attacking analytically special logical and linguistic puzzles, which, though theoretically important, are not impressive to the layman, and the solution of which can throw no light on moral or political problems. The question how one ought to live is one that Ayer considers moral philosophy incompetent to answer, and the answers that past philosophers have offered he finds wrongheaded and fallacious. Political philosophers of the past, he thinks, have done no more than express their preferences; they have never successfully justified them, nor are they, as philosophers, capable in principle of doing so. He writes:

No more than the scientist is the philosopher specially privileged to lay down the rules of conduct, or to prescribe an ideal form of life . . . whether or not the values that he recommends are found acceptable, it is not from his philosophy that they can derive their title to acceptance.[6]

The pursuit of wisdom has been emphatically repudiated by philosophers such as these, and there is even a distinguished group of contemporary writers who have treated that pursuit by the older "pontiffs" as a form of intellectual disease, for which their technique of analyzing language, they allege, is the treatment and the cure. The pupils of this diverse school are liable to have at least one conviction in common: that philosophy, whatever its theoretical impact might be, can have no practical influence of any importance. In Wittgenstein's words, it "leaves everything as it is."

One of these pupils is Richard Rorty, who confesses that he has reached his position through the practice of analytic philosophy. He has been brought to the conviction that the pursuit of "foundations" (i.e., metaphysics) is futile and can end only in failure; that all previous philosophy, analytic or other, has led to insuperable difficulties; and that none, including his own, is to be taken seriously. The final outcome of the twentieth-century revolution in philosophy is thus a skepticism, which disables even itself along with all the rest.[7]

2. EFFECTS OF ANALYSIS

The philosophy of analysis, widespread as it has become, has not wholly superseded the older philosophical tradition, but it is a typical expression of the spirit of the age, and it is a contributory cause of the parlous predicament in which the world finds itself today. The explanation goes deep into the roots of our modern scientific culture. Science today holds an unassailable position of authority and is the one field of human endeavor in which actual progress can be claimed without plausible contradiction. This progress is rightly attributed to the methods that science adopts, but just what these methods are have been variously misconceived, even by some scientists themselves. One such misconception dates from the very beginnings of modern science. The Copernican revolution and the developments that followed it gave rise to a conception of the world as a machine, and accentuated the contrast between matter and mind, so that knowledge was conceived as entering into the mind only through the senses, as light through the windows of a house. This was Locke's simile, and the notion is to a great extent what gave rise to the philosophy of empiricism. It also popularized the falsehood that the success of the physical sciences was exclusively the result of their dependence on sense perception. If this line of thought is followed to its logical conclusion, it issues in the paradox that only what can be sensuously perceived is scientifically (or rationally) knowable. The entire sphere of values and their criteria is thus excluded from what can be scientifically understood. That sphere was traditionally the main, if not the whole, province of philosophy. If scientific statements can be authentic only so far as they are derived from, and verified by, sense perception, no ultimate criticism or validation of value judgments can be scientific; and philosophy, if it professes to offer such rational criticism or validation, must be either sophistry or else a somewhat indirect and elaborate way of expressing personal preferences stemming from emotion and sentiment.

The spectacular progress of science after the seventeenth century fired the imagination of philosophers and engendered in them the aspiration to become scientific, so that their discipline might progress similarly. Some, like the late-nineteenth-century idealists T. H. Green and F. H. Bradley, tried to escape the stigma of unscientific thinking by relegating science to a lower level, as a second-grade form of knowledge, typical of what they called "the abstract understanding," and inferior to philosophy, which is the work of speculative reason. More recently, another group of philosophers, reacting violently against the idealists, have returned to the belief that empiricism, and empiricism alone, can provide a scientific method in philosophy. By an odd twist in the history of Western thought, they have become overwhelmingly influential just when a new revolution in science has made the errors of the earlier empiricism plainly apparent and its main position obviously untenable. To the philosophical implications of the twentieth-century revolution in physics, we shall return in a later chapter.

The type of philosophy that has emerged is one whose core is the tacit assumption, or the open assertion, of the purely instrumental function of reason. Reasoning is regarded only as a process of analysis that can have no constructive influence. It can perform no positive synthetic function in knowledge, a role (so far as it is recognized at all) that is reserved for sensation and feeling—unless recourse is had to some more recondite form of intuition. Philosophy thus professes to be simply and solely analytic and abjures any correlative synthetic, synoptic, or constructive capacity. It has never seriously been questioned that part of the function of reason is analysis of some kind, but two features distinguish the twentieth-century development: one is the restriction of philosophical thinking exclusively to analysis, and the other is the attempt to limit the form and method of analysis to a special kind of procedure, which, however, has varied from time to time in the history of the analytic movement and is differently conceived by each of its dominant figures.

Some details of the variety and differences that have characterized the various phases of the much-advertised philosophical revolution have already been noted. Here it is sufficient to reiterate that they all derive in the last resort from the empiricist doctrine that the primary source of factual knowledge is pure sensation, and that they are, as practiced by the majority of philosophers who advocate them, misleading and inadequate to the solution of philosophical problems. They commonly purport to *dis*solve such problems, to eliminate them by revealing them to be pseudo-problems and in some way illusory. I have sought to show that they do this either by subtle misrepresentation or by equally subtle evasion of the main issue in each case.

According to this conception, the purest form in which the analytic exercise of reason expresses itself is a symbolic calculus, to which the investigator has recourse when faced by a theoretical puzzle. He or she reduces the puzzle to symbolic form by replacing the empirical terms by variables and then resolves the problem by transforming the resulting formulas according to the rules of the calculus until a solution is reached in the same manner as an algebraical equation is solved. The name of logic is nowadays reserved for this sort of algorithm, but it has been established that there is not only one such logic, but any number. The postulates and rules that govern their several workings are arbitrary and may be chosen at will to suit the needs and convenience of the investigators. Logic, therefore, is simply a matter of convention, and if the use of one logic gives an answer to a problem that the investigator does not like, he or she is free to use a different logic and so to ring the changes on the postulates and rules until the desired answer can be deduced. What determines the preference for one answer over another cannot be logic as so conceived; it can only be sentiment, feeling, or prejudice, none of which is regarded as amenable to the influence of reason—*de gustibus non disputandum est*. There can thus be no such thing as rational choice.

This doctrine, however, undermines the very philosophy that propounds it, for it provides no rational criterion for the adoption of any theory whatsoever, but leaves us in the predicament described by Hume when he wrote:

> After the most accurate and exact of my reasonings, I can give no reason why I should assent to it; and feel nothing but a *strong* propensity to consider objects *strongly* in the view under which they appear to me.[8]

If we are free to adopt any logic that validates whatever theory may appeal to us, this must be true also of analysis, and the analytic practice itself must therefore be based, in the last resort, on prejudice and can claim no rational justification. The rational philosophical basis at one time claimed for it was the logical and metaphysical atomism of Bertrand Russell and the early Wittgenstein. But that was repudiated by more advanced exponents of the analytic method as a "superstition," leaving the whole technique without ground or pretext. The position is, therefore, self-refuting, and we are at liberty to set it aside as uncongenial or to reject it altogether as false.

3. ETHICAL IMPLICATIONS AND MORAL EFFECTS

This implication was not heeded, and the influence of analytic philosophy became dominant and has been widely destructive of the reflective disciplines of metaphysics and morals, Such ethical exercises as have been undertaken by analytic writers have been largely formal in character, concerned with analysis of the use of moral terms and linguistic expressions. In keeping with Ayer's strictures, they contribute nothing to our moral insight and make no pretense of justifying principles or validating ideals. To do this, it is held, is impossible by logical means, for all such "principles" and ideals are held to rest finally on feeling.

As the earlier moralists well knew, no ethical doctrine is ever without influence upon moral beliefs, and the presumption of recent ethical investigations— that moral appraisals and the adoption of value standards are incapable of rational validation—*is* an ethical doctrine, the influence of which in practice is to abandon us to the promptings of passion and to the habit of "thinking with our blood." In such an intellectual climate, popular morals and politics actually come to be largely a matter of feeling, prejudice, and (or) social conditioning. Moral codes are regarded as purely relative, and become so. They degenerate into what Karl Marx said they always were: ideologies—mere reflections of the current economic and social relations.

Early in this century, the forerunners of this movement at Oxford and its founders in Cambridge were already exerting an influence upon students that was felt by the young Collingwood and is described in his autobiography as follows:

> The pupils, whether or not they expected a philosophy that should give them, as that of Green's school had given their fathers, ideals to live for and principles to live by, did not get it; and were told that no philosopher (except of course a bogus philosopher) would even try to give it. The inference which any pupil could draw for himself was that for guidance in the problems of life, since one must not seek it from thinkers or from thinking, from ideals or from principles, one must look to people who were not thinkers (but fools), to processes that were not thinking (but passions), and to rules that were not principles (but rules of expediency). If the realists had wanted to train up a generation of men and women expressly as the potential dupes of every adventurer in morals or politics, commerce or religion, who should appeal to their emotions and promise them private gain which he neither could procure them nor even meant to procure them, no better way of doing it could have been discovered.[9]

Likewise, the influence of "analysis" is liable to raise up a generation of subtle arguers about the meanings of words who are completely devoid of rational insight into the nature and validity of standards of value. For all their cleverness, they are likely to become the dupes, of whom Collingwood speaks, who, without rational criteria of their own, are likely to be swayed by appeals to prejudice and passion and to follow any self-seeking or fantastic vogue that claims for the moment to be *de rigueur*.

Further, it is the intellectuals who should guide and influence popular opinions. The ideas of the intelligentsia, after some short time lag, seep down and become commonplace among the less learned. In the absence of moral guidance from the better instructed, and with the views ubiquitously expressed by academics (sources of which will be investigated more closely later) that morals are, after all, only relative, that there can be no objective standards, so that one personal choice is as good as any other, the mass of the people is even more liable to be swayed by passions of the moment and to fall victim to political and religious demagogues.

Today we witness with the utmost misgiving the common tendency throughout the world for peoples to swing toward extreme ideologies, most of which espouse or lead inevitably toward political dictatorship, and many of which advocate some form of irrationalism and antiobjectivism. If people are habituated to thinking with the blood, it is not surprising that they should be duped by doctrines whose appeal is largely to the emotions. We live today in a world torn by conflict between ideologies, with little evidence that reason and good sense are likely to prevail. These conflicts are fraught at the present time with dire consequences for humanity to which I will presently turn.

I am not suggesting that communism, fascism, fundamentalisms, and militant fanaticisms of all kinds are the immediate products of analytical philosophy—far from it. The fact seems rather to be that the philosophy of analysis, in its eagerness to clear away rubbish, has been so zealous that it has removed everything of any positive value and left a vacuum, into which the forces of extremism may move without effective resistance. The success of these irrationalisms is due to the hold they have over their supporters. This, I have argued elsewhere,[10] cannot be solely a tyranny of force. It depends on an enthusiasm for presented ideals and principles that, however bogus and deceptive they may be, are accepted without criticism. To combat them, some countervailing moral influence is required, not merely emotional, but a conviction rationally founded and more stable, such as was once possessed by the liberal democratic tradition but is now being steadily undermined and weakened by the influence, among other causes, of a skeptical, destructive, and disintegrating philosophizing, from both the empiricist right and the postmodernist left.

Conflicts of ideologies given free range in a philosophical vacuum would be evil enough, but when we consider that today the contestants are organized politically and tend to form opposing power blocs, depending for their defense on weapons of mass destruction—chemical, biological, and nuclear, as well as so-called conventional weapons, which are almost as vicious—the prospect for humankind is unrelievedly dismal. Unless rational counsels can prevail, the opposing forces are virtually bound, sooner or later, to come into open physical conflict, from which the chances of survival for human civilization are minimal.

4. REASON

If there is any feasible remedy for this, it is not likely to be simple, but I am firmly convinced that one factor in it must be the revival of a more satisfactory conception of reason—a conception that assigns to it a more positive role and acknowledges its efficacy in the attack on the practical, moral, and political problems that contemporary humanity faces. This would not be a return to the old faculty notion that separated reason from imagination and sense as affording different kinds of knowledge, but rather a recognition of the organizing and integrating activity of the mind in all its functioning. The operation and formulation of the principles of such organization are the proper activities of reason, and its process is both analytic and synthetic in mutually complementary phases. Thus it is the principle of insight and rational enlightenment, for that depends on the capacity to see the details of a complex situation or a tangled problem and to relate them in a unified and ordered structure. Mere analysis, by ignoring and dissipating the structural pattern, frustrates such insight, which depends on the ability to see things together without confusion or blurring. Analysis by itself presents us only with the separated details devoid of their bearing and dependence upon one another, and as their intrinsic character usually, if not always, depends on their mutual interrelation, isolating them from the context from which they have been dissected distorts our understanding of the whole. If I may be permitted to quote Collingwood again:

> One cannot abstract without falsifying. To think apart of things that are together, is to think of them as they are not, and to plead that this initial severance makes no essential difference to their inner nature is only to erect falsification into a principle.[11]

A rationality that is at once analytic and synthetic is both critical and constructive, and where it reveals errors and contradictions, it can also discover remedies and means of reconciliation. It is the source of insight, both corrective and directive, which can play a positive role in practical life. It can distinguish the right objectives of action and offer effective and constructive criticism of operative ideals in morals and politics, as well as theoretical interpretation of our experience of the world about us, upon which determination of practical principles is dependent and from which it is inseparable.

5. THE TASK OF PHILOSOPHY

The philosophical training that the rising generation is to receive must give them a capacity for critical and comprehensive insight if they are to escape from the predicament in which humanity currently finds itself. Teachers of philosophy need to be aware of the possibility of gaining enlightenment through philosophical reflection upon the major issues of ideological and political conflict.

They must be convinced of the competence of philosophy to illuminate, and of their duty to discover and critically examine, the principles of value involved. If this is not possible, the prospects for human survival on this planet will be diminished, for without deference to objective standards, valid for everybody, we are likely to drift steadily toward environmental disaster and international conflict from which only sanity and principled action can save us.

But I believe it can be shown that it is possible. A simple return to the doctrines of the past will not serve. It would fail of conviction and fall short in relation to current problems. A new philosophy must look more closely at the sciences, the most advanced of our theoretical disciplines, and must build upon them, combining the conclusions of the various sciences of nature to comprehend a view of the world as a whole. It does not require much investigation to discover how far contemporary scientific theories belie the confident assumptions of the philosophy of the recent past. When the errors of these assumptions have been corrected, we should be able to form new and more fruitful conceptions of the human mind, of logic, and of the function of rational thinking in human life. We should soon realize that science is not, never has been, and could not be founded on any bare, uninterpreted sense-data, for there is copious evidence that no such uninterpreted data can be distinguished in our conscious experience. It is possible to demonstrate that rational coherence and coordination are in some degree inherent in all human cognition from its very beginnings. In that case, it would not be surprising if, in its higher developments in science and philosophy, constructive principles were elaborated on which human life can be sensibly and harmoniously organized.

I believe, also, that it is possible to show that in all knowledge—natural science no less than any other—the role of thinking is in some sense evaluative, not simply an acceptance of brute fact. Science is not as value-free as is commonly believed. Intellectual integrity, which is an essential element of the scientific outlook, is a moral quality, not just a technical skill. Values, moreover, are always a matter of rational interpretation and never sheerly of feeling (although it is true enough that appraisals are always accompanied by feelings). In that case, moral and political, as well as intellectual, values and the derivative principles of action must be the fruit of reflection and constructive thinking, and never simply of instinct and passion. The task of moral philosophy (like all other philosophy) will be to carry the work of reflection forward, beyond the level of custom and common sense, by criticism and reorganization of concepts.

In all this the deliverances of the sciences can and must be included in our purview, for philosophy is no mere speculation in vacuo; despite frequent misconceptions, it is not just armchair contemplation. The philosopher (apart from common experience in the world of human action) does not work in the laboratory, but she or he has the right and indeed the duty to reflect upon and utilize all the results of empirical science that are relevant to the solution of philosophical problems. It is only by so doing that the metaphysician can form a comprehensive conception of the nature of reality, and the neglect of scientific findings would be fatal to the credibility of metaphysical speculation. It would not be wrong to say that metaphysics is built on and arises out of the sciences, without which it runs the risk of becoming what Collingwood contemptuously described as "flitting and gibbering."

If the metaphysician heeds and builds upon such groundwork, he or she should be able to arrive at a theory of the mind and a conception of human purposes compatible with the most reliable psychological findings; and reflection upon social and practical experience, coupled with the objective study of the social and political forms adopted in the past, should give grounds for a tenable and reliable theory of moral and political principles objective to all persons and societies. Such a theory cannot be simply descriptive; it must be critical and constructive, because what it is concerned with is value judgment, which is always a critical reflection upon human ends and purposes. Its essential subject is the criteria of value, their mutual coherence and internal consistency. It has been aptly designated a criteriological study.

6. PHILOSOPHY AND CURRENT PROBLEMS

A philosophical system so grounded ought to be sufficient to qualify the philosopher to give counsel, with all the humility that awareness of human limitations requires, on the pressing moral and political problems of our day. Of these the most urgent is probably that of conserving the global environment. While this is primarily a scientific problem, it is also essentially a practical, a moral, and a political issue, to which ethics and political philosophy are directly relevant. More obviously, the threat of nuclear warfare, far from having been eliminated by the end of the cold war, is a moral and political issue to the resolution of which philosophers, with the possible exception of Karl Jaspers, have as yet (to their shame) made no considerable contribution. Yet few topics are more relevant to their proper field, for it involves the philosophy of the state, of law, and of international order, as well as of moral obligation and human values.

Let us pause briefly to consider the implications of this menace. Modern warfare, and the destructive power of modern weapons, is such that, on any considerable scale, it threatens the very survival of civilization. Apart from the toll it invariably takes of human lives and the material structures of social order, the inevitable disruption of the ecology of the affected areas is an additional major threat to human survival. Warfare between small nations is always liable to escalate, and between the more powerful it cannot be limited, because no great nation at war with a major opponent can afford to refrain from using any weapon that would give it a calculable chance of avoiding defeat. Nations would not spend so much of their national income on armaments (nuclear and other) if they did not believe that they might have to use them. They arm because they fear that they will need to defend themselves against probable enemies. Yet today, we know that if we do fight we shall destroy not only our enemies but also our friends and ourselves. We do not know how to remove the danger of attack by others. We do not know how to reach trustworthy agreements with our potential opponents, or how to accommodate our differences and live and progress securely in peace. This is as true of Russians and Chinese as it is of Americans, British, Germans, and French, so the solution, if any, must be the same for all.

One reason, at least, why we are in this pathetic state of ignorance and perplexity is our failure to reflect fruitfully on the underlying principles of political organization, awareness of which enabled our forefathers to build our present political systems. Whereas they succeeded in setting up workable and durable state systems, we seem to be incapable of constructing an equally effective international political structure. The principles of political order are a legitimate part of the subject matter of philosophy (*pace* logical empiricism), and philosophers ought to be the most competent to guide and advise politicians how to respect and apply them. But the analysts have eliminated political theory from what they regard as the legitimate corpus of philosophical studies, and today there are virtually no philosophers capable of performing the necessary task. The very suggestion that they could perform it has so long been scouted that nowadays it is likely to be met with derision.

But this distrust of philosophy is surely misplaced. One of the main obstacles to the resolution of social and international conflict is ideology, and an ideology is a system of philosophy. We call it an ideology only when we disagree with it and wish to insinuate that it is bogus and false. The real problem today is how to combat a particular set of philosophical half-truths dogmatically asserted as a gospel. Or, alternatively, it is how to find means of accommodation and reconciliation between doctrines, each of which is plausible and partly true, whose opposition threatens to issue in violent conflict. Who is better equipped to resolve such a clash of ideologies than the professional philosopher? Why should the critique of philosophical systems and the practical consequences it entails be left to amateurs? It has been neglected by the professionals only because, with Ayer, they have been persuaded that political theory was not after all a philosophical subject but (so far as it was not a positive science eschewing value judgments) a texture of wishful thinking. So Ayer says of Karl Marx's call to philosophers to change the world rather than merely to interpret it: "The call . . . was needed to bring about something that Marx wished to happen"—as if any philosopher could fail to wish to bring about what he had convinced himself by systematic thinking was right.

Marx, however, was far from right or even self-consistent in all his very influential doctrines, and even this exhortation to philosophers to change the world is misleading. It commits the error of imagining that reflection upon the world leaves everything as it is—the same mistake as, in a different guise, infects the thought of Wittgenstein. Philosophy always does change the world, for better or for worse, because it is that reflection on the nature of values without which rational and considerate action is impossible. Action, as Aristotle well knew, is always for the sake of some good, something taken to be of value, and thought is always for the sake of action. Whatever theory we adopt, or tacitly assume, about the nature of value is bound to affect our conduct. Every such theory is a philosophical theory. So philosophy always changes the world, and only if this is clearly recognized and acknowledged by philosophers will they understand, and can they fulfill their proper function in society conscientiously and responsibly.

A theory of value, however, that reaches the conclusion that all moral judgments are relative, whether to culture, social grouping, or individual prejudice, destroys morality altogether. For morality consists in respect for an objective imperative that imposes obligation in despite of inclination. If all standards are purely relative, none can claim the necessary authority, and there can be no obligation to respect any one more than any other. Personal choice then becomes arbitrary, and in politics, might takes the place of right. Under such conditions, our current problems would obviously be insoluble and our future prospects wholly disastrous. But, as we have seen, the same line of argument that leads to moral relativism lands us also in theoretical skepticism, which demolishes its own underpinning. It is therefore imperative to make a fresh start and to seek more stable grounds for our convictions and beliefs.

I have drawn attention mostly to the need for a renewed recognition of moral and political philosophy at the present time. But it has rightly been said that all philosophy is metaphysics, because it is always self-reflective and is its own subject matter; it is the exercise of self-consciousness or reason (which is simply another name for the same activity). So let us proceed to consider more closely the nature and method of metaphysics.

Notes

The original version of this chapter was the inaugural lecture, delivered in 1963 at the University of Kansas, for the first Roy Roberts Professorship.

1. George Berkeley, *Three Dialogues Between Hylas and Philonous*, preface, in *Works*.
2. David Hume, *Treatise of Human Nature*, bk. I, chap. IV, p. 7.
3. Ibid.
4. R. G. Collingwood, *An Autobiography*, p. 47.
5. Herbert Feigl, "Logical Empiricism," in *Twentieth Century Philosophy*.

6. Cf. A. J. Ayer, "The Claims of Philosophy," *Polemic*, no. 7 (1947).
7. Cf. Richard Rorty, *Philosophy and the Mirror of Nature*. The same outcome in postmodernism and deconstructionism results from developments following upon existentialism and phenomenology, despite considerably more enlightenment shed on philosophical questions by thinkers such as Husserl, Merleau-Ponty, and Paul Ricoeur.
8. Hume, *Treaties of Human Nature*, loc. cit.
9. R. G. Collingwood, *An Autobiography*, p. 48f.
10. Cf. E. E. Harris, "Political Power", *Ethics*, vol. 68, no. 1, 1957.
11. R. G. Collingwood, *Speculum Mentis*, p. 160.

Part 2
Science and Metaphysics

6

Method and Explanation
in Science and Metaphysics

With the collapse of the verification principle and of all the consequent empiricist ploys, the ban on metaphysics should be altogether void and we should be able to proceed as was done before it was pronounced, and as our experience demands. One of its lasting effects, however, has been to discredit the methods and theories of older philosophies and to raise a generation of students partly ignorant of the older tradition and partly biased by ready-made criticisms, so that what was done in the past is both unfamiliar and suspect. If we are to rediscover an appropriate method for metaphysics, therefore, we should not be ill-advised to begin by glancing once again at the historical record.

By this I do not mean, so much, that we should remind ourselves what Plato or Aristotle or Descartes said was the correct method of speculation, but rather what was the practice of these and other great philosophers and its relation to other sciences. We are all aware that the very earliest Greek philosophers were at once both metaphysicians and natural scientists; not that they all pursued both disciplines as separate branches of study, but that for them, no distinction was drawn between science and philosophy, and none was imputed to them by later commentators. This state of affairs continued until Aristotle subdivided the forms of theoretical knowledge into different sciences, but even he did not regard metaphysics as really divorced from physics. The connection was so close that in the treatise that gives its name to the philosophical discipline, a large portion of the work that Aristotle himself called Physics is included. Right up to the eighteenth century, the term "philosophy" covered all the exact and the natural sciences, as well as everything that goes by that name today. Hegel complained that even such lowly pursuits as agriculture and haircutting were (in England) included under the name.[1] Even at the present time, in the Universities of Cambridge and Edinburgh, physics is still known as "natural philosophy."

Moreover, many of the great metaphysicians of the modern period—Descartes, Leibniz, Kant, Bergson, and Whitehead—were also scientists, and no consider-

84

able philosophical theory has been uninfluenced by scientific discovery or failed in its turn to have some effect on the course of scientific research. In the words of A. E. Taylor: "Every great metaphysical conception has exercised its influence on the general history of science, and, in return, every movement in science has affected the development of metaphysics"[2] This persistent historical association between science and metaphysics cannot be without significance and is symptomatic of an intimate relation between both their methods and their subject matter.

Curiously enough, the positivistic indictment against metaphysics is that it lacks what is taken to be the hallmark of science—empirical reference—and that its method is one of speculation and *a priori* deduction as opposed to induction and verification by empirical evidence. I attempt to defend the accused against these charges by showing that they misconceive the methods of science, on the one hand, and misrepresent that of metaphysics, on the other; and that the long historical association between metaphysics and the natural sciences is normal because their methods are in principle the same and their subject matters akin. I maintain that so far from neglecting empirical evidence, metaphysical theory rests upon it just to the extent that such evidence is provided and interpreted by the natural sciences, and that the relation between theory and observation is the same for both.

Observation is the deliverance of sense perception, and all current and most widely canvassed theories of perception today seem to agree in rejecting the notion that the percept is an immediately given atomic and simple datum that can be isolated from all others and from other elements in experience. Ryle's view that it is an achievement has come to be widely accepted among analysts, who point out that all verbs of perceiving, as used in reference to acts of perception, are achievement words. Such words imply that a piece of information has been attained, presumably as a result of some effort or process of trial. Verbs of perceiving are held to have intentionality and to imply the presence of an actual (material) object and the knowledge that it is present. No such knowledge can be given as a simple unmediated datum, for the presence of a physical object is a complex fact, involving the presumption of its solidity and persistence, as well as its causal efficacy and liability to be affected by extraneous causal influences. Without these, no material object would actually be presented. The achievement (for instance) of seeing such an object (even more so of hearing or feeling it) must thus be the end result of a discursive process of some kind, however rapidly accomplished, and could not be a direct revelation by any merely immediate intuition of an unprocessed datum.

The old idea of the existence and direct apprehension by sense-data has long been scouted, and philosophers today are more apt to regard material objects, in all their complexity of character and mutual relations, as the primary objects of perception. If this is not precisely what they say, it is the direct implication of the views set out at length by P. F. Strawson in *Individuals*, by Stuart Hampshire in *Thought and Action*, and by D. M. Armstrong in *Perception and the Physical World*. It is also implied in Alan Donagan's critique of Collingwood.[3]

In Armstrong's terms, an act of perception is an act of acquiring knowledge, or belief, about particular facts in the physical world by the use of the senses. But no knowledge of a particular fact in the physical world is a simple matter. Take Armstrong's favorite example: that the cat is on the mat. To know or believe this involves knowing what sort of things cats and mats are, and how they are distinguished from other, different things; it involves an understanding of spatial relations in general and that of "being on" in particular, and it presumes an acquaintance with a particular region of space with its contents, enabling the percipient to identify the particular cat and mat as belonging to the set of domestic furnishings to which implicit reference is being made (for, as expressing an actual percept, the statement is not just about any unspecified cat's being on any unidentified mat).

In short, the achievement that constitutes an act of perception of this kind is one that presupposes an already, to some extent, developed body of background knowledge, by reference to which what is present to the senses is recognized and interpreted. Apart from this, no perceptual achievement would be possible, for no recognition of any material object could take place, let alone appraisal of its relations to others.

From a somewhat different angle, a similar conclusion is reached by R. J. Hirst in his book *The Problems of Perception*. He considers perception to be a relation between a person and other public objects and events, which involves mental activity and so presents an inner and an outer aspect. On the inner side, it is the "(awareness or consciousness of) an external object," which must be distinguished as "a whole activity of the person."[4] To the person who is perceptually conscious, the content of his or her consciousness is an external object or scene. In short, perception is essentially an intentional activity. Hirst rejects any theory of sense-data and all suggestion of private objects, although he admits perceptual errors and hallucinations. For him, perception is a matter of degree, an activity that may be performed more or less successfully, in which the *percipienda* are elaborated in various ways and to different extents in order to produce *percepta*. In describing this process, he follows the psychologists, who assert that the percipient achieves percepts by the use of "cues" and correlations that modify the purely sentient elements of the experience, largely in accordance with past learning.

I have argued elsewhere[5] that the use of cues and correlations (some psychologists even speak of assumptions and hypotheses in this connection) cannot be reduced to mere physical or physiological processes but is essentially epistemological, implying an activity of reference and interpretation that again implies a body of more or less developed and organized knowledge to which reference is made and in terms of which what is presented is understood. It is not necessary, and would in fact be misguided, to regard this activity as intellectual in the sense that it requires the explicit use of abstract concepts and ratiocination. The suggestion, attributed to Brand Blanshard,[6] that it is a thought process and the view advanced by Hermann Helmholtz and some of the older psychologists that it is "unconscious inference" is often criticized (emphatically by Hirst) as too intellectualist. But these writers, Blanshard especially (who should be given credit for drawing attention to this essentially mediate character of perception long before the other philosophers mentioned above), by insisting that the judgment or inference is *implicit* or *unconscious*, themselves recognize its nonintellectual character. Unless we revert to sense-data (and perhaps even then), the recognition of some such process of mediation is inescapable. Equally inescapable is its logical and epistemological character as the reference of a focal object to a context, articulated in some degree, spatiotemporally extended, and significant for the perceiving subject as a body of knowledge, understood in a dispositional sense.

Corroboration of this conclusion comes from another quarter when we turn to the work of Maurice Merleau-Ponty,[7] for whom (as for Spinoza) perception is a functioning of the body as a whole, and not just of the sense organs. But the organism is sensitive not to separate, atomic stimuli but to a whole situation constituted by the constellation of effects upon it. Even below the level of self-awareness and intentionality proper, Merleau-Ponty points out, the body displays behaviors "as if oriented toward the meaning of certain elementary situations." The significant word here is "meaning." This orientation is no merely physical or physiological adjustment but involves an apprehension of the structure and significance of the presented situation. Every perception, he says, takes place within a certain "horizon" or setting (*entourage*) and ultimately "in the world," the perceived object itself being a unified and articulated texture of qualities and relations. If it is a visual object, it is given as "an infinite sum of an indefinite series of perspectival views," the interrelation of which is developed in a definite, recognizable order or form, so that the perceived thing is an inexhaustible system (*ensemble*). Consequently, perception is a synthesis performed by a subject able to relate and delimit perspectival aspects and to transcend the immediately given—a reference to a whole that can be grasped only through certain of its parts. No such synthesis is given directly by sense, and whatever is given must be complexly elaborated before it can be grasped as a percept.

In sum, the percept is an object apprehended in a setting as belonging to a world that must be grasped in some way as a whole or in general terms, however indefinite; and the logically prior condition of perceiving objects is the possession of some overall idea of this world, however vague, to which they belong and in which they are integrant. Observation, the fruit of perception, is thus embedded in and inseparable from interpretation, even at the level of common sense.

Science grows out of common sense and is continuous with it, in that the commonsense level is simply the progressive development and clarification of the interpretation of percepts through the perceptual and intellectual exploration of the setting that gives them significance. Science carries this process to higher levels by fuller, more explicit, and more precise exercise of the intellectual factor. *Pari passu* the observational aspect is sharpened and refined and becomes more accurate.

For scientific observation, moreover, the dependence on background knowledge is indispensable and especially important. The untutored savage, presented with the instruments of a scientific laboratory in an experimental situation, can make no scientific observation whatsoever. Even the educated layman can understand what is happening only with great difficulty, and only with help and explanation from the expert. Before any quantitative measurement can be made, the experimental situation as a whole has to be understood: What is being measured? In what connections? For what purpose? No instrument reading has significance unless its place in the experimental situation and its relevance to the questions that the experimenter is trying to answer are known. Only in answer to questions is any observation significant, and questions do not arise except out of a theory already entertained and a body of scientific knowledge already achieved.

Further, what precisely is being observed in any experiment can be known only to one who is versed in the science concerned. That a particular pointer stands opposite a particular number or mark on a scale is altogether without significance unless one knows that these things are part of, say, a galvanometer. That the indicated figure gives the measure of resistance to an electric current cannot be appreciated unless the observer understands the principles on which galvanometers are constructed and to what this one in particular is attached. Clearly, a considerable body of physical theory is presupposed in any one reading made with an instrument of this kind.

This is true at any level of scientific development. Observation is observation only if it answers relevant questions; these questions arise only out of prior knowledge—they are the *aporiae* of theories already adopted, or at least entertained. Apart from them, even though the objects are present to be observed, the investigator will not notice them, that is, will *not* observe them and whatever is observed will depend on the extent to which it is interpreted and illuminated by means of the theories to which the observation is contributing evidence. In short, theory always is and always must be prior to observation, and without it, science would have no relevant empirical basis.

In any given situation, the observable facts are infinite in number. Even those that are relevant to a particular problem in science may be innumerable. The scientist cannot observe them all and does not observe at random. To do so is strictly impossible, for the reasons already given, for to achieve knowledge of the observable facts, one has to bring to bear upon them knowledge already acquired. The investigator must, therefore, select and discriminate, and this can be done only in the light of the theories and hypotheses for which evidence is being sought, and only so far as the observations can be seen as significant in relation to them.

Scientists are well aware of all this. L. Bolzmann, the founder of modern thermodynamics, complained that "the lack of clarity in the principles of mechanics seems to be connected with the fact that one did not at once start with hypothetical pictures framed in our minds, but tried to strart from experience."[8] We have also the more recent testimony of Einstein and Eddington. The former writes:

> By and by I despaired of the possibility of discovering the true laws by means of constructive efforts based on known facts. The longer and the more despairingly I tried, the more I came to the conviction that only the discovery of a universal formal principle could lead us to assured results. . . . How then could such a universal principle be found?

There follows the description of a piece of imaginative thinking impossible to test in any experiment that gave him "the germ of the special theory of relativity."[9] Eddington is still more emphatic:

> A scientist commonly professes to base his beliefs on observation, not theories. Theories, it is said, are useful in suggesting new ideas and new lines of investigation for the experimenter; but "hard facts" are the only proper ground for conclusion. I have never come across anyone who carries this profession into practice—certainly not the hard-headed experimentalist, who is more swayed by his theories because he is less accustomed to scrutinize them. Observation is not sufficient. We do not believe our eyes unless we are first convinced that what they appear to tell us is credible. . . . For the reader resolved to eschew theory and admit only definite observational facts, *all* astronomical books are banned. *There are no purely observational facts about the heavenly bodies.*[10]

Lest we think that these physicists are prejudiced by their preoccupation with mathematics (although it is clear that this is not what inspired their remarks), let us hear that great biologist Charles Darwin: "Without hypotheses," he says, "there can be no useful observation."[11]

This is why the method of science is misconceived by those who persist in the view that, both for knowledge in general and for the natural sciences in particular, sense observation is primary and self-contained and must somehow be used as an independent check upon the accuracy of theories, and that the hallmark of scientific method in natural science is inductive reasoning from particular matters of fact to general laws—an invalid process of inference that, Karl Popper rightly asserts, is never actually used in science and cannot be validated in logic.

Scientific thinking, or for that matter thinking worthy of the name at any level, is the systematic development of a conceptual (or theoretic) scheme covering a field of investigation in terms of which percepts, or observations, are interpreted. Without such a scheme, we cannot even begin, and at every level of scientific development, an accepted scheme is already at hand. It is what Thomas Kuhn has called a "paradigm." This does not mean that it has its source in some mysterious *a priori*, independent of experience. It is itself experience as it has been organized up to that point; and experience is primitively sentient, becoming percipient only through organization (as the research of Gestalt psychologists has proved).[12] To ask which is temporally prior in this development, sense or thought, is to ask which came first, the hen or the egg.

Without attempting to penetrate to its origins, I shall try to illustrate how, at a relatively elementary stage of scientific development, theory served as the organizing factor in the construction of a coherent conception of its subject matter.

The order and return of the seasons have always been of vital importance to human (as well as all other) life. And they are obviously related to the movement of the sun, moon, and stars. Human beings, in consequence, have always had a keen interest in the heavenly cycles. The night sky presents the appearance of myriad bright points against a dark background, along with the moon as a superior luminary. (We need not pause to remind ourselves that this scene is itself the product of organization and discrimination, by attention, and cannot be perceived without the imposition of schemata upon primitive sentience, both innate and learned.)[13] The immediate presentation is one of completely random distribution, but more careful attention reveals recognizable patterns of spatial relation, some of which, if the observation is prolonged, remain constant, while others vary, so that over a protracted period the stars can be discovered to move across the heavens in various ways, some in circles, some along arcs that are greater or smaller segments of a circle, some in looping, oscillating courses, some faster and some more slowly. At first sight, this is a bewildering variety. But these apparent movements (which, let us note, do not appear to the senses but only to the thinking mind ordering the sensuous appearances), if they are related to the position of the sun at its rising and setting, and if we assume that the heaven is a great globe, at the center of which is the earth in the form of a relatively small sphere, and that the greater celestial sphere rotates about the small one on an axis one end of which is marked by the polestar, we can, in large measure, reduce this variety to order and regularity. By marking out among the stars the path of the sun around the celestial sphere during the twelve months of the year (namely, the ecliptic), we get a coherent conception that will account for the movement of the majority of the heavenly bodies. This conception (sometimes called the two-sphere view) was roughly the earliest astronomical theory, and since it was adopted, the history of astronomy up to the beginning of the nineteenth century, was almost exclusively that of successive attempts to develop it so as to account for the aberrant motions that this simple theory leaves inexplicable as contradictions within it—for example, the plenetary movements and the intermittent appearance of comets.

First the constellations were distinguished, then the movement of the moon and the sun in relation to them. In due course, the notion was conceived of concentric transparent spheres carrying the various heavenly bodies—the sun, the moon, the different planets, and the fixed stars. Originally these were assumed to revolve in unison, then at different speeds, then on different axes, and finally alternately in opposite directions. In each case, difficulties arose, giving rise to contradictions that the subsequent theory attempted to resolve and, in some measure, succeeded. The theory of spheres failed to account satisfactorily for the planetary motions, so Ptolemy introduced a system of epicycles, minor spheres carrying the planets which rolled along the surface of the major ones. Long before that, however, Aristarchus of Samos, modifying a much older Pythagorean theory (according to which all the heavenly bodies, including the earth, revolved around a central fire), had sought a solution of the problem by proposing that the sun and not the earth was at the center. Some sixteen centuries later, this hypothesis was resurrected by Copernicus, but it took three centuries more to weld together terrestrial and celestial mechanics and to make the entire conception of the physical universe tolerably coherent.

Astronomical theory, throughout its history, therefore has been a constant and continuous endeavor to organize human experience of the periodicity of the seasons and their relation to movements of the heavenly bodies by imposing upon it (or interpreting it in terms of) a system of concepts. Every science is a similar sustained effort to comprehend an area or aspect of human knowledge in terms of a conceptual system that will reduce the relative chaos of percipient awareness to coherent order. Success in this undertaking constitutes explanation. A fact or event is explained when it is seen in systematic context and is interpreted in terms of a systematic set of concepts. Explanation is not just "analysis," in the sense of "taking to pieces" or resolving into elements. Such analysis is, indeed, involved in explanation, but by itself, it explains little or nothing, for it ignores or demolishes the structural principles that originally held together the elementary parts into which the analysandum has been resolved. But it is only the elucidation of these structural principles that provides explanation. That is always synthesis as well as analysis (for each is necessary to the other).

As the sciences progress, they react on one another and tend to unite, so that the effort becomes general to relate all their conceptual schemes into a single all-embracing worldview. To describe the matter thus, however, may be misleading, for in the nature of the case, and as a matter of historical fact, the overarching conception is there from the beginning, first as a halting, naive, and largely pictorial synthesis, but one that becomes more conceptual, more systematic, and better articulated as the sciences develop. The discipline that produces this finally comprehensive synoptic view is metaphysics, which began in the West with Thales and Anaximander, gave birth to the sciences one by one, stimulated their development, and profited by it, so that each owed its successive advances to progress in the other, and the historical association between science and philosophy that I noted earlier was natural and necessary.

Accordingly, metaphysical explanation is the same in character as, and is continuous with, scientific explanation, and metaphysical method is in principle a development and a continuation of scientific method, as the latter may be said to be a specification of the former in different fields. The aim of metaphysics is a comprehensive conceptual scheme in the light of which the whole of experience can be organized and become intelligible. For this reason, it is sometimes said (for example, by Whitehead) to be concerned with the most general and pervasive features of the world, and at other times (for example, by Plato) to be the most synoptic of the sciences. But to quote A. E. Taylor again:

> Metaphysics does not profess to deal with a certain group of facts lying outside the province of the "sciences," but to deal with the same facts which form that province from a point of view which is not that of the experimental sciences.[14]

The phrase "the sciences" is meant here to refer to all the sciences, not just "the natural sciences," if that means only physics, chemistry, and biology. Not only must the social sciences and the sciences of the mind be included, but whatever others may be necessary to deal with any field or aspect of knowledge, for metaphysics seeks a conceptual scheme comprehensive of the whole of experience.

The differences between scientific and metaphysical method derive only from this difference of scope. The self-limitation of the special sciences permits, and is defined by, initial assumptions, which the absence of such limitation in metaphysics forbids. The special sciences do not examine these assumptions or call them into question, but metaphysics must do so and may not itself adopt any, unless provisionally. So Plato maintained that Dialectic eliminated hypotheses and was ἀνυπόθετος, and Kant declared that any hypothesis in metaphysics was contraband. Moreover, hypotheses are of two kinds, both in some measure relative to the limitation in scope of a science. There are working hypotheses, which scientists adopt consciously and deliberately, and which direct and canalize their research; and there are more fundamental presuppositions, often made as a matter of custom or tradition and without explicit reflection:

for instance, that every event has a cause and that all causation is efficient. Such presuppositions the scientist seldom examines and is often unaware of making, but it is one of the main functions of metaphysics to lay them bare, and an important part of the metaphysician's business is to submit them to critical examination.

Similarly, in the special sciences, theory is more directly related to observation, whereas metaphysical theory relates to observation only indirectly: it depends for its empirical evidence on what the natural sciences provide. This, to the casual observer, may give the impression that metaphysics is purely speculative and "deductive" in its method, "scorning the base degrees by which it did ascend" and producing empirically unverifiable theses. But this impression is false. Metaphysicians, if they do their job properly, use the special sciences and their discoveries as the material on which to reflect. They seek to uncover the absolute presuppositions made by the scientist and to examine them for consistency and tenability. They also seek to penetrate to the philosophical implications of what the sciences disclose about nature. Yet all science, special or philosophical, is speculative. Le Gros Clark writes: "Contrary to views which are sometimes expressed, speculation is by no means to be eschewed in scientific pursuits—indeed it is essential for progress since it is the generator of ideas and ideas stimulate inquiry."[15] In this respect, metaphysics does not differ from science, nor does it differ in its manner of verification.

Theory and observation in science are not two separate and independent factors, one of which may be used to check or test the other. A scientific theory is a more or less organized and coherent interpretation of what is observed, without which the observed facts lose their character and significance. Observation, as has already been noted, is saturated with interpretation, of which theory is no more than the development. Theory and observation together form a single whole of knowledge. But this is only more or less coherently organized, and the endeavor of science is constantly to make it more so over a wider field so that it becomes more comprehensive and more systematic. Verification, therefore, always consists in the assembly of diverse yet mutually corroborative evidence, the systematic interconnections of which make the denial of the theory impossible without breakdown of the entire conceptual scheme. Falsification consists in the failure of corroboration, which demands either modification of the theory or the discovery of new connections that will reconcile the conflicting evidence. The process, in science, obviously involves observation, for without it theory would have no content. In the case of astronomy, for instance, if no stars were observed, there would be no science. But the two-sphere view could not have been "verified" by comparison with some independently observed body of facts; it is simply the way in which the observed facts were organized. The Copernican system is another way of organizing them which can explain more satisfactorily and with less incoherence planetary and cometary movements, as the earlier theories could not. Verification in science is, therefore, nothing other than harmonious corroboration of all the available evidence.[16]

Metaphysics is neither more nor less than the attempt to organize comprehensively the deliverances of the sciences into a single worldview by means of a universal conceptual scheme in which all sciences can be integrated. And verification of metaphysical theory is achieved, as it is in science, by its coherence as a whole. Moreover, metaphysics includes epistemology and involves a theory of knowledge with which its own claim to truth must conform. If it does, this coherence, more than any other, is evidence of its truth.

That this can be adequately or successfully achieved without clarification of concepts is hardly to be expected; so part of the metaphysician's task, and part of the explanatory function of metaphysical theory, is conceptual analysis, which naturally considers the ways in which terms and concepts are used and how they function in science. But metaphysics cannot be restricted to such analysis, which is ancillary to its main constructive purpose of providing a systematic explanatory scheme in which all possible sciences can find their place.

Moreover, the extension of scope involved in metaphysical explanation is bound to require the modification of the use and application of concepts. What is appropriate in one science may well prove unacceptable in another, and still more so in a yet wider context. The term "evolution," for example, and its connotation are not the same in physics (as when physicists and astronomers speak of the evolution of stars, of galaxies, or of the universe as a whole) as they are in biology; and as Collingwood pointed out, when the idea is given philosophical significance (as it was by Herbert Spencer and by Henri Bergson), it is modified still further.[17] Analysis of concepts, therefore, also involves criticism, and adjustment in the light of such criticism. Consequently, metaphysics is inevitably "revisionary," and because the use of concepts in each science is not separate and independent of its use in the others, and because the transition from one science to the next is a continuous development, this revisionary function is essential to the descriptive, which cannot be properly or accurately carried out without it.

Furthermore, this process of critical analysis of concepts and presuppositions is bound to call into question the credentials and to prompt reassessment of the claims of the sciences concerned. Metaphysics, therefore, like all philosophy, is what Collingwood called a criteriological science and has a normative as well as a descriptive aspect. As it seeks what we may now, without mystification, accept as ultimate explanation, it will be concerned with and will inquire into the ultimate grounds—whatever they may be, and whether there are any (questions metaphysicians are obliged to raise)—of the existence and nature of the subject matter of all the special sciences that fall under its purview, as well as of its own.

Finally, the method of verifying metaphysicial theory, is no different in principle from what it is in the special sciences. It is to seek corroborative evidence among the sciences, which will naturally be, for the most part, theoretical evidence, itself an interpretation of observed fact. For the metaphysician to neglect the evidence, as science provides it, would be fatal, and through the mediation of science, this evidence is as empirical as any need be. Metaphysics, then, is an interpretation of interpretations; it is science of the second, or possibly even higher, degree. It is, in short, meta-science—and what else did the word "metaphysics" ever legitimately mean?

Notes

Originally published (in a modified version) in *Proceedings of the American Catholic Philosophical Association* (Washington, D.C., 1967) and reprinted in *The Future of Metaphysics*, ed. Robert E. Wood (Chicago: Quadrangle Books, 1970).

1. Cf. G. W. F. Hegel, *Encyclopaedia of Philosophical Sciences*, Part I, *Logic*, sec. 7.
2. A. E. Taylor, *Elements of Metaphysics*, p. 13.
3. Cf. A. Donagan, *The Later Philosophy of R. G. Collingwood*, p. 37. See also A. M. Quinton, "The Problems of Perception," *Mind*, vol. 44, 1955, pp. 28–51.
4. R. J. Hirst, *The Problems of Perception*, pp. 286, 287.
5. E. E. Harris, *The Foundations of Metaphysics in Science*, pp. 407ff.
6. Cf. Brand Blanshard, *The Nature of Thought*, vol. 1, and E. E. Harris, "Blanshard on Perception and Free Ideas," in *The Philosophy of Brand Blanshard*, pt. II, chap. 11.
7. M. Merleau-Ponty, *Phenomenology of Perception*.
8. I. Bolzmann, *Vorlesungen über die Principien der Mechanik*, p. 2.
9. Paul Schilpp, ed., *Albert Einstein, Philosopher Scientist*, pp. 52–3.
10. Sir Arthur Eddington, *The Expanding Universe*, p. 17; emphasis in original.
11. Quoted by W. E. le Gros Clark in "Anatomical Perspectives in Neuropsychiatry," in *Perspectives in Neurophysiology*.
12. Cf. Harris, *The Foundations of Metaphysics in Science*, chap. 20.
13. Ibid., chap. 19, pp. 373ff.
14. Taylor, *Elements of Metaphysics*, p. 10.
15. Le Gros Clark, "Anatomical Perspectives in Neuropsychiatry," p. 10.
16. Karl Popper has implicitly subscribed to a similar view in a significant footnote in *The Logic of Scientific Discovery*, p. 87: "If I assert that there is a family of white ravens in the New York zoo, then I assert something which can be tested *in principle*. If somebody wishes to test it, and is informed, upon arrival, that the family has died, or has never been heard of, it is left to him to accept or reject my falsifying... statement. As a rule, he will have means of forming an opinion by examining witnesses, documents, etc.; that is to say by appealing to other intersubjectively testable and reproducible facts."
17. R. G. Collingwood, *An Essay on Philosophical Method*, p. 34.

7

The New Physics and the Need
for a New Metaphysics

1. HISTORICAL ANOMALY

In Chapter 5, I remarked that it was an odd twist in the history of Western thought that gave empiricism overwhelming influence in philosophical circles just when a new revolution in science had made its errors apparent and its general position untenable. It is now time to substantiate this submission. It will then become apparent what kind of new metaphysics is demanded by the new physics.

Contemporary empiricism is a reversion to, and an elaboration of, that of Hume, which had grown from seeds planted by Hobbes and Locke a century earlier. These philosophers had been inspired by the sixteenth- and seventeenth-century scientific revolution, establishing what may, without undue misrepresentation (although not with complete historical accuracy), be termed the Renaissance worldview. The universe was envisioned as a collection of particulate bodies moving under the influence of external forces. The doctrines of Aristotle, Joseph Glanvil said, had given place to "the more excellent Hypotheses of Democritus and Epicurus." Francis Bacon explicitly adopted the granular theory of matter, and John Locke (in conflict with his own first principles) spoke of "insensible particles" as constituting the "real internal constitution" of bodies (which is unknowable to us) and as the basis of their primary qualities.[1]

Newton's *Principia* eliminated, once and for all, Aristotle's distinction between sublunar and ethereal mechanics and established a conception of the universe as an assemblage of bodies, moved by forces (*vis insita* and *vis impressa*) acting through and upon their centers of gravity; as this is the focal point of all activity, each body is conceived as reduced (in the last resort) to a mass point. Thus was engendered the notion of things existing independently of one another, in an absolute space and time, indifferent to their positions or motions. So too, the bodies were mutually indifferent, except for the force of gravitation they exerted on one another. Relations between them were easily conceived as entirely external, unaffected by their intrinsic nature, which was entirely separable from them. (It was easy to overlook the fact, as was common, that gravity was proportional to mass and that the mutual gravitational attraction of bodies was universal. Relations, therefore, could not be altogether external, which was why Pierre-Simon Laplace, in the eighteenth century, could maintain that a supreme intelligence capable of perceiving the position and state of motion of every particle in the universe at any one time could deduce its position and state of motion at any other.) Hence the prevalent assumption of empiricists that all relations are external—what they call internal relations (if they ever do) are simply those between groups of externally related entities internal to aggregates or collections (sets).

Further, the physical world was now conceived as a vast machine, in which no place or provision could be found for the human mind, whose activity resisted subjection to mechanical laws. Although the importance of observation was stressed by the scientists, no account was taken, or could be given, of the place of the observer in the scientific panorama. The observer was set apart from the scene that was being surveyed, a scene viewed from the outside, as it were, through a telescope or a microscope, or at least through the portals of the senses. Yet what these delivered was something nonmechanical and nonmaterial—a conscious revelation for which no place was found in the terrestrial (or the celestial) mechanism. Hobbes tried to reduce sense to motion, but it still "appears to us as Fancy," which remained mechanistically unaccountable. The relation between mind and body remained an insoluble problem. The attempt to reduce mind to matter failed with the inability of the materialist to explain what was meant by "appearance to us," and the opposite attempt to reduce matter to mind, such as that made by George Berkeley, collapsed into skepticism under Hume's devastating analysis.

Whether human consciousness could be reduced to matter and motion, or matter be reduced to *percipi*, some way had to be surmised how consciousness could reflect and record the events and bodies in an external world. The obvious answer seemed to be: through the senses. Hence arose the primary postulate of empiricism. From this it followed inevitably, as Hume demonstrated, that simple sense impressions and ideas were separate existences, between which, although they might be variously associated, no necessary connection could be found. From a world composed of particulate bodies in external relation, experience of which was built up out of unconnected sense-data, it is but a short step to Wittgenstein's description of the world as composed of facts any one of which could or could not be the case without making any difference to any other. Logical atomism follows directly, along with the formal symbolic logic of *Principia Mathematica*.

2. THE TWENTIETH-CENTURY SCIENTIFIC REVOLUTION

The Renaissance worldview, however, has been completely subverted by the revolution in physics initiated at the beginning of the twentieth century by Max Planck and Albert Einstein. Even before that, some premonition of the change had been indicated by Ernst Mach, who asserted that inertial forces (centrifugal and Coriolis) were the effects of gravitational attraction exerted by the fixed stars, and that inertial frames were, in consequence, those that were unaccelerated relative to some suitably defined average of all the matter in the universe. This meant that all motion was the result of effects permeating the entire universe, and that events were all necessarily interrelated. Thus the conception of external relations began to crumble.

RELATIVITY

This identification of inertial forces with gravitation impressed Einstein, who called it the Principle of Equivalence, and it implanted in his mind ideas that led to the theory of relativity. With the special theory, external relations ceased to be significant. The discovery that the velocity of light and other electromagnetic radiation was constant relative to all reference frames, whatever their motion, rendered the presumption of simultaneity at a distance no longer valid; and because the only way of measuring length and time over large distances is by light signals, all such measurements differ for observers moving relatively to one another. They can nevertheless be related mathematically by the Lorenz transformations. Consequently, measurements of space, time, and velocity are inseparably interdependent, and, for the special theory, space-time becomes a single four-dimensional manifold in which coordinates of measurement vary for observers moving at different speeds. Émile Borel writes: "The essential point is the absolute impossibility of separating the measurement of space from the measurement of time."[2]

Not only space, time, and consequently velocity thus become interdependent, but so does mass. Einstein was able to show that mass increases with velocity, and that as velocity, approaches the speed of light, mass approaches infinity. Now velocity is relative to the reference frame, and that of the reference frame to every other; so measurements of mass are as dependent on those of length and duration as each of those is on the other. Accordingly, all the intrinsic physical properties of bodies are mutually dependent, and all physical relations are internal to their terms.

The theory of relativity gave precedence to the concept of the field over that of the particle. This development also had been anticipated in the nineteenth century by the theory of electrodynamics due to J. Clerk Maxwell. The electromagnetic field in principle fills the whole of space, and in accordance with the general theory of relativity, space-time itself is regarded as the metrical field from which the measured quantities are inseparable, and in which the elements that have them are inextricably embedded. Energy and mass thus become degrees of curvature in space-time, and matter, having been equated with energy in Einstein's equation $e = mc^2$, is a singularity in space-time.

The entire universe, therefore, is conceived as a single space-time whole in which the radius of curvature is found to determine all the physical constants and to rank as a natural unit of measurement. It is, moreover, a whole that is not indefinitely extensive, for the curvature introduced by the presence of energy and matter bends it in upon itself to form a four-dimensional hypersphere with finite volume but no spatiotemporal boundary.

Physicists are agreed (for more powerful reasons still to be examined) that, within this self-enclosed whole, every occurrence and every phenomenon effects every other, and there are, in the last resort, no isolable entities or events. The physical world is a single whole, the parts of which are inseparable and interlocking, in which the primary principle of order determines all physical laws and governs all occurrences and relationships within it. What this fundamental ordering principle is, scientists are now well on the way to discovering; that there is one, and that their paramount aim is to discover what it is, all the major physicists of the age have been convinced: Einstein, Eddington, Sciama, and Heisenberg, to mention only a few.[3]

QUANTUM THEORY

Quantum theory and research into the physics of elementary particles have confirmed and reinforced this holism. Max Planck had discovered that energy could be transmitted only in distinct quanta of action, which could not be further subdivided. Particles were found sometimes to behave like waves and came to be conceived as superposed waves, or wave packets, and every wave field is now associated with some type of particle, while every kind of energy is quantized in particulate form. In short, the concepts of wave and particle have become interchangeable and they overlap; again, the notion of field takes precedence (the atom, for instance, is conceived more as a complex field of forces than as a system of moving particles: the electron shells as standing waves in the electromagnetic field of the nucleus, itself a field of the strong nuclear force). All this is organized and structured by Pauli's Principle of Exclusion, which decrees that in any system no two particles can have the same quantum numbers (or state of motion). Physical entities thus have come to be viewed as wholes of integrated and interdependent parts, rather than as separate and isolable particles.

Further, these wholes are themselves interconnected so that they cannot be treated separately. The Heisenberg Indeterminacy Principle has raised the problem of the existence of conjunct (or complementary) quantities prior to observation; for these quantities cannot be precisely determined separately, but only as features of a single energy system, and one inseparable from the observer with his or her measuring apparatus. An interpretation offered by David Bohm and B. J. Hiley postulates a "quantum field" and conceives the measuring instrument and what it measures as a single indivisible complex, within which the measured property comes into being. What the measuring instrument registers, however, has meaning as a value only when (and as) read by the investigator. Hence observer and observed are united in the experimental result, which, according to Eugene Wigner, occurs only with the observer's consciousness of it. Thus matter and mind can no longer be treated as separate.

Bell's Theorem has disposed of the presumption of hidden variables, and the modification of the Einstein, Podolsky, and Rosen experiment by Bohm and Aharanov has established the need to postulate faster-than-light influences, which are not signals, linking distant events. The conception of nonlocality has been introduced to describe this linkage, other evidence of which has been discovered in quasi-crystalline structures.[4] Such nonlocality implies an inseparability of entities and events that binds them together into a unity. In the words of Bohm and Hiley: "One is led to a new notion of unbroken wholeness which denies the classical idea of analysability of the world into separately and independently existing parts."[5]

We must conclude, with Fritjof Capra, that "quantum theory forces us to see the universe not as a collection of physical objects, but rather as a complicated web of relations between various parts of a unified whole."[6]

CONTEMPORARY DEVELOPMENTS

In recent years, the unified field theory, originally conceived by Einstein, Schroedinger, and Weyl, and on which Einstein spent the latter part of his life trying unsuccessfully to formulate, has come back into prominence. S-matrix theory, quantum electrodynamic theory, and grand unified theories have united the electromagnetic, electroweak, and strong forces, leaving only gravity still to be accommodated, and the superstring theory promises to encompass all four. So physicists are approaching that universal equation envisaged by Heisenberg from which all the physical forces and types of particle can be derived, and even the constants of nature might be deducible. Eddington's attempts to discover these constants from purely theoretical considerations, and E. A. Milne's derivation of Einstein's and Newton's laws solely from the assumption that there are no privileged observers, seem less extravagant than scientists have believed since the 1930s.

CHAOS THEORY

The same conviction of holism has emerged from the study of turbulence in what has come to be known as chaos theory, which has revealed the delicate sensitivity of complex, dynamic systems to initial conditions and the unexpectedly intricate and beautiful patterns of order underlying what seem at first sight to be chaotic processes. The discovery of what came to be called "strange attractors" operative in turbulence led investigators to seek patterns amid apparent randomness rather than local mechanisms. When found, these proved to be ordered in fractal geometric structures, reviving the idea of self-representative systems originally suggested in the last century by Dedekind and Royce. So the study of complex, dynamic systems has persuaded its pursuers that no reductionist program in science can produce genuine explanation, and that only the grasp of the entire system can render the details intelligible.[7]

ECOLOGY

The revelation of the unity of the physical universe has been augmented by the development in biology of the science of ecology, which has established the existence of biological communities, in both small and large compass. These are organic systems, each relatively self-contained but all interactive, so that ultimately the entire biosphere is one single organic whole. As physics and chemistry are mutually continuous, and with them biochemistry, the interlock between this biological totality and the physicochemical system is unquestionable and is underlined by the concurrent demonstration that organism and environment cannot be separated, but are similarly organically integrated. At the same time, developments in genetic and evolution theory have taken an organismic turn, culminating in Stuart Kaufman's call for a reconsideration of Darwinism to make room for principles of active self-organization interacting with the processes of mutation and natural selection.

HOLISM

Twentieth-century science has thus established a view of the world as a systematic whole of parts and elements mutually adapted one to another according to a principle of organization that is implicated in each and every one of them. At the physical level, Bohm has described it as a "holomovement," in which the whole is implicit in every part, as occurs in a holograph. In the continuous process, this implicate order expresses itself in various ways—as radiation, as elementary particles, as atoms and molecules, and so forth. In such a whole, all relations are internal to their terms and determine the nature of the entities related, and both are governed by the ordering principle that is universal to the whole and is implicated in every part.

3. The Need for a New Metaphysic

The metaphysical presuppositions of empiricism are altogether unsuited to this worldview and are flatly controverted by it. Ayer's pronouncement that "if two states of affairs are distinct, a statement which refers to only one of them does not entail anything about the other"[8] is totally belied. There can be no atomic facts and no atomic propositions. The logic that assumes their existence may still be of use—if the subject matter to which it relates is to be regarded (for theoretical convenience) as a mere aggregate, but to the system of the real world, as science now conceives it, such a logic must be wholly inappropriate. The assumption that human consciousness is separate from its objects and receives its ideas by transmission through the senses, as Locke imagined, like light penetrating a dark room through a window, can no longer be entertained. What is called for is a completely different metaphysic, a different sort of logic and a new epistemology.

The required metaphysic, however, is not altogether new. Prompted partly by purely epistemological considerations, and partly in response to difficulties arising out of the Newtonian presuppositions, some philosophers in the eighteenth and nineteenth centuries anticipated present-day demands. Leibniz identified "two labyrinths in which the human mind is caught." One concerns the infinite divisibility of the continuum (particularly space and time), the other the nature of freedom. Both arise directly from the presuppositions of Newtonian science outlined above. If space, time, and matter are continuous, into what units are they to be divided, and what can the nature of these units be? If the physical world is a machine, how can human beings act freely in it? We need not pursue Leibniz' reasoning in his attempts to solve these two puzzles; what is of interest is that he reintroduced the notions of final causation and substantial forms, both of which the Newtonians and the empiricists had long since rejected. Both these ideas imply some kind of holism, final causes for reasons we shall notice in a moment. Substantial forms, Leibniz says, are the principles of true unity, which cannot be found in matter.

Kant, roused from dogmatic slumber by Hume's skepticism, sought to restore the objectivity to scientific knowledge that Hume had sacrificed. He did this by attributing it to the spontaneous organizing (or synthesizing) activity of the transcendental subject, resulting in an indefeasible unity of experience, without which no objects at all could be presented in sensation. Once again, unity is the key term, and on the subjective side, Kant established the necessity for coherent wholeness as the condition for any knowledge whatsoever:

> If each representation were completely foreign to every other, standing apart in isolation, no such thing as knowledge would ever arise. For knowledge is [essentially] a whole in which representations stand compared and connected.[9] (Kemp Smith's translation).

Further, he realized with profound perspicacity that such wholeness involved teleological explanation (Leibniz's final causes). In the *Critique of Judgement*, he writes:

> It is requisite to a thing as a natural end (or purpose) first that the parts (as regards their existence and their form) are possible through their relation to the whole. For, consequently, the thing itself is an end conceived under a concept or an idea which must determine *a priori* everything that is to be contained in it. (Sec. 63)

From this point, Schelling and Hegel developed their doctrine of the Concept as the whole (which Hegel identifies as "the Truth"), and of Nature as an organic totality, in which the gamut of natural forms constitutes the process of development of the Idea, as manifested in the form of externality, to self-consciousness, or Spirit, thus resolving the controversy between realism and idealism and the problem of the relation of body (Nature) to mind. Hegel's emphasis on holism goes hand in hand with, and necessarily gives rise to, the dialectic, which is, for him, not merely a method of exposition but, as he puts it, "the principle of all life, all movement and all activity in the actual world." The essential elements of this metaphysic—holism, teleology, and dialectic—need to be revived and developed in the light of what contemporary science has disclosed.

In the twentieth century, two philosophers began to do this before the empiricist takeover. They were A. N. Whitehead and R. G. Collingwood, but neither of them carried out the project completely. Whitehead returned to a metaphysic very similar in many respects to that of Leibniz, identifying actual entities with events and substituting the conception of process for that of substance. His actual entities "prehend" all others in the entire universe into a unity and, as "superjects," transmit this unity continuously to their successors. All potentialities of definiteness ("eternal objects"), the prehensions of which constitute the "mental pole" of an actual entity, are ordered in God's primordial nature, and the whole process is summed up in the Consequent Nature of God, in which all actual entities are progressively prehended. The holistic character of this conception of the universe is pretty obvious.[10] Whitehead also, somewhat vaguely, discerned that the unity of the universe and the knowledge of it implied a dialectic of opposites: "Throughout the Universe there reigns the union of opposites which is the ground of dualism," he writes in *Adventures of Ideas*.[11]

In his remarkable *Essay on Philosophical Method*, Collingwood developed a theory of the scale of forms that specifies what he identifies as the philosophical universal. This is really what Hegel and his successors had called the concrete universal, of which Bernard Bosanquet had striven manfully to give an adequate account. It was Collingwood who completed this task, and his scale of forms is nothing other than the dialectical scale characteristic of Hegel's philosophy and intrinsic to the Concept, or the whole that he declared to be the ultimate truth or Absolute. Collingwood, however, confined his analysis to the philosophical universal and rightly assumed that it did not apply to the abstract universal of science. What he did not observe, considering himself unqualified to pronounce upon it, was that scientific thinking was not confined to the abstract universal but was concrete in significant ways, as was philosophical thinking, which he himself proclaimed to be essentially metaphysical.[12]

Notes

1. Cf. John Locke, *An Essay Concerning Human Understanding*, bk. II, chap. 8, sec. 13; chap. 23, secs. 2, 3.
2. E. Borel, *Space and Time*, p. 161.
3. Cf. A. Einstein, *The World as I See It*, p. 125: "The supreme task of the physicist is to arrive at those universal elementary laws from which the cosmos can be built up by pure deduction." Sir A. Eddington, *The Expanding Universe*, pp. 104–5: "I only want to make vivid the wide inter-relatedness of things. . . . Our goal is not to reach an ultimate conception, but to complete the full circle of relationships." D. W. Sciama, *The Unity of the Universe*, p. 167: "What the cosmologist requires . . . is a theory which is able to account in detail for the contents of the universe. To do this completely it should imply that the universe contains no accidental features whatsoever." Werner Heisenberg, *Physics and Philosophy*, p. 72: "The final equation of motion for matter will probably be some quantized nonlinear wave equation for a wave field of operators that simply represents matter, not any kind of waves or particles. This wave equation will probably be equivalent to rather complicated, sets of integral equations, which have 'Eigenvalues' and 'Eigensolutions' as the physicists call it. These Eigensolutions will finally represent the elementary particles." Werner Heisenberg, *Philosophical Problems of Nuclear Science*, p. 105: "It is quite conceivable that in the not too distant future we shall be able to write down a single equation from which will follow the properties of matter in general."
4. Cf. Henry Stapp, "Are Faster-than-Light Influences Necessary," in *Quantum Mechanics versus Local Realism: The Einstein, Podolsky and Rosen Paradox*; "Quantum Theory and the Physicist's Conception of Nature: Philosophical Implications of Bell's Theorem," *The World View of Contemporary Physics: Does It Need a New Metaphysics?* Roger Penrose, *The Emperor's New Mind*, p. 436.
5. D. Bohm and B. Hiley, "On the Intuitive Understanding of Non-Locality as implied by Quantum Theory," *Foundations of Physics*, vol. 5 (1975).
6. F. Capra, *The Tao of Physics*, p. 150.
7. Cf. J. Gleick, *Chaos: Making a New Science*, p. 304.
8. A. J. Ayer, *The Problem of Knowledge*, p. 29.
9. Immanuel Kant, *Critique of Pure Reason*, A97 Trans. Norman Kemp Smith p. 130.
10. Cf. E. E. Harris, *The Spirit of Hegel*, appendix, and E. E. Harris, and *Nature, Mind and Modern Science*, chap. 19.
11. A. N. Whitehead, *Adventures of Ideas*, chap. 11, sec. xxiii.
12. Cf. R. G. Collingwood, *An Essay on Philosophical Method*, pp. 14, 127.

8

The Logic and Metaphysics of Holism

1. UNITY OF DIFFERENCES

As the basic presupposition of contemporary science is that the universe is a whole, the first task of the philosopher is to examine the concept of wholeness to discover what it entails. This should uncover the logical structure not only of the concept but equally of the world the nature of which the concept expresses.

Whatever we normally call a whole clearly is thought of as unitary, one and cohesive. But at the same time, it also implies that it has parts that are mutually distinct, even though they are united and cohere within the whole. A whole, therefore, is always a one of many. What has no parts, a mathematical point, for example, is not appropriately called a whole, nor is a blank, undifferentiated uniformity. So far as we may be inclined to call either of these whole, it is because we tacitly impute diversity to them. A mathematical point, if it is conceivable, must have position, and that implies relations to other points situated elsewhere in various directions. A point, in consequence, is as it were, many faceted, or better, it is the starting point of motion in one or another of numerous directions, and so is strictly a one of many. Only as thus conceived can it properly be regarded as a whole. Much the same is true of a blank uniformity. If it is spread out (whether spatially, temporally, or both), parts must be distinguishable within it—parts that, no doubt, we say are all exactly alike, yet they could not even be that unless they were distinct. It is immaterial how we distinguish the parts, whether by position in space, as before or after in time, or however else; a uniform expanse must have them in order to be expanded.[1] It too is then a one of many, and if so, we may think of it as at least potentially a whole.

If multiplicity is as characteristic of a whole as unity, the question arises of the sort of relationship existing between the parts, and whether our inclination to call the set a whole depends upon it. Some relationships are very loose, as, for instance, those among the grains in a heap of sand or among marbles in a bag or sticks in a pile. Yet for certain purposes, we may be inclined to call these assemblages wholes, because they can each be regarded as one unity. If we do, however, that immediately affects our view of the relationship among the parts, be it their juxtaposition (as with the sticks), their spatial restriction (as with the marbles), or their congregation (as with the grains of sand). In short, the nature of the whole dictates the nature of the relationship among the parts.

For the most part, however, we are less inclined to think of such collections as wholes than as assemblages whose parts are more intimately connected, such as the pattern on a rug, a machine, or an organism. It is, moreover, clear that intimacy of relationship among the parts of a whole is a matter of degree, as the examples offered illustrate, and this is an important feature of the concept of wholeness to which we shall have occasion to return. But generally speaking, as wholeness necessarily implies unity as well as multiplicity, a whole is always a group of different parts in relation; vice versa, terms in relation always constitute some sort of unity or whole. We should do well, then, to proceed by considering next what is meant by, and involved in, being in relation.

2. RELATIONS

Whatever function relations perform, they always connect their terms together; even when they are relations of difference or separation, the terms are inevitably conjoined by the relation. If I say that the sun is ninety-three million miles away from the earth, that relation connects the earth with the sun in a spatial context (dynamically, of course, there is another relation between these heavenly bodies that holds them together in the solar system, but that is a further consideration). If I say that no two persons could be more different in character than were Hitler and Mahatma Gandhi, I associate these two people (by contrast) with respect to their conduct and beliefs in a historical context. Terms in relation, therefore, constitute a whole, and a whole always consists of terms in relation, a unity of differences. The relations are, as it were, the glue that holds the parts of the whole together. Yet, as the parts are, and must be, distinct, the relations between them also serve to differentiate them, or at least to imply that they are not the same. Even when we relate two terms as being exactly alike, we can do so only if there are *two* terms and not just one. It is the relations, then, that ensure the unity as well as the differences within a whole.

There may still be some who remember F. H. Bradley's brilliant discussion of relations in *Appearance and Reality*.[2] He argued that whichever way we tried to understand relations, whether as external or internal, they proved incoherent and strictly unintelligible. They are, therefore, Bradley concluded, no better than an appearance and are not features of reality. If conceived as external, relations, which purport to connect their terms, fall between them; but then a new relation must be postulated between each of the terms and the intervening relation. So an infinite regress is generated, and no connection between the terms is ever reached. In short, external relations do not and cannot relate. On the other hand, if relations are held to be internal to their terms, either the terms dissolve away altogether into relations, which then have nothing to relate, or a distinction must be drawn between that portion of the terms which is affected by the relation and that which is not. In that case, once again, a new relation has to be postulated between the affected and the unaffected portions, which will be subject to the same difficulties, and an infinite regress again results. So either internal relations have no terms, and so relate nothing (but terms altogether without relations—unrelated qualities—Bradley contends, are inconceivable), or else the relations dissipate the potential terms *ad infinitum*.

Bradley is usually credited with defending internal relations and rejecting external, but it is clear from his argument that he rejects both and relegates all relations to the relative limbo of appearance. I say "relative" because, for Bradley, appearance is always of the real, and only the real can appear. Relations, therefore, should give some indication of reality, although it is not apparent from Bradley's doctrine just how this is possible.

Bradley's criticism, however, assumes that relations, whether external or internal, fall between their terms and, in some sense, are distinct from them. There is an echo in his argument of Hume's doctrine that what can be distinguished must be different, and what are different must be separate existents, whereas we now have good reason to hold that this is not the case. Relations are the way in which the terms stand to one another; they are how distinctions are made within a whole, and this is what we must investigate.

3. RELATIONS AND CONTINUA

If we consider terms in relation carefully, we find that they are always elements within a continuum of some sort, and that if they were not, they could not be related. To begin with the simplest example, the relation between two points in space: obviously, space is a continuum, without which the points could not even exist, let alone be related to one another. And their relation is the distance between them, which is nothing other than the traversal of the intervening continuum. Exactly the same is true of two events in time.

Two natural numbers are related in terms of the continuum of natural numbers, and the relation between two colors is expressed in terms of the color series, or of the number series, if wavelength or frequency is cited. Both these series are continuous. Sounds are similarly related through a continuum of pitch and volume.

Other examples are less obvious, yet no less apt. Family relations are dependent upon the marital conjugation of husband and wife and are determined by the continuous development of the germ plasm, due to meiosis and mitosis, and the resulting continuum of the family tree. In biology, we express the relation of different species through evolution which we take to be continuous, and we establish the relation by looking for "missing links" that will establish the continuity definitively.

Social relations involve a continuous social structure and continuous social processes of action. To demonstrate this may be somewhat more complicated, but it is no less true. The continuum is largely historical and is thus a structure of temporal relations, but it is more than that: society is a continuum of social functions and social positions, which, as has been demonstrated by political philosophers from Plato and Aristotle to Bernard Bosanquet, merge into one another. There is a continuous development from family to clan, and thence to tribe and to polity. There is a continuum of status from the member of a family to one of civil society and political administration. Each member of the society exemplifies several such positions and fulfills several such functions. For instance, a schoolgirl becomes a wife and a mother and may be a breadwinner and (or) a member of the legislature. Margaret Thatcher's career is a continuum of such social positions exemplified in one person, and numerous persons make up the social continuum.

As Zeno demonstrated long ago, it is never possible to identify a terminal least fraction in any continuum, nor to extricate any element within it from its neighbors. Every segment of a continuum necessarily overlaps with some other, otherwise it is not continuous with its neighbors. It follows that the terms of a relation overlap, or are dependent for their relatedness on the overlap of intervening portions of the continuum to which they belong. One may be inclined immediately to deny this, but closer consideration shows it to be correct.

The relation between two points in space is the distance between them, which is continuous with both of them and with which they both overlap. How so? you may ask. A point, regarded as the terminus of a line, is common to any other coterminous line, and to any line intersecting the first in that point. Whitehead defines a point in terms of "abstract sets," and an abstract set he defines as a set of regions any two members of which are such that one of them includes the other nontangentially and there is no region included in every member of the set. A geometrical element he defines as a complete group of abstractive sets equivalent to each other but not equivalent to any outside the group. A geometrical element is said to be incident in another when the latter covers every member of the former but the two are not identical. A point is then a geometrical element that has no others incident in it. In short, a point is to be understood in terms of the overlap of regions in an abstractive set, and the relation between two points must involve the overlap of two such sets. Two regular polygons are related to one another by the number of their sides, and number, we have observed, is a continuum of magnitudes. But, more properly, the relation between them is demonstrable by inscribing one within the other and observing the overlap between them.

The relation between marbles in a bag is not only juxtaposition, which is spatial and so participates in the overlap of spacial shapes, but also causal due to the pressure each exerts on the other and on the bag, and causal relations are always an overlap between cause and effect: physically (as in this case) through some continuous field of force.

We may press this point further. The atoms in a hydrogen molecule are held together by an electromagnetic force because they share an electron, and so overlap. Chemical combination is due to similar sharing of electrons by the atoms of two or more different chemical elements. The molecules in the leptocosm of a crystal overlap. In chemical reactions brought about by a catalyst, each reagent overlaps with the catalyst. The metabolism of a living organism consists of overlapping chemical cycles within its body, such as respiration, digestion, and the Krebs cycle, each of which is interwoven with the others. These diverse causal relations all require overlap between cause and effect.

These, a captious critic may object, are specially chosen cases. What of the relation, let us say, of my dining-room chair to a leaf in the garden hedge? There are, of course, several sorts of relation between these two objects: Spatial relations would involve the spatial continuum, temporal relations entailed in reaching one from the other would involve both spatial and temporal continua. Property relations (they both belong to me) invoke the continuum of my personality and activities as well as a continuous texture of legal and customary principles, recognitions, and practices. These different continua lie on different levels of structural integration, the nature and interrelation of which we shall consider anon. In each of them, the kind of overlap is not the same and is certainly not always spatial. The traits in my character certainly overlap in my personality, and my attitude to my dining-room chair may well overlap with any interest I take in the leaves of my garden hedge. For instance, I may wish to cut back the latter in order to improve the view from the former, and this may be motivated by any number of overlapping interests in gardening and interior decor.

Again, the captious critic may object: not all continua consist of overlapping elements. For instance, the number series is made up of discrete quanta, and the numbers do not overlap. But indeed they do: $1 + 1 = 2$, $2 + 1 = 3$; each successive number includes its predecessors. The only digit of which this is not true is 0, but with 0, the continuum has not yet begun. Yet 0 and 1 do overlap, for 0 is defined as the null class, which has only one member. Discrete magnitudes have to be dissected out of continuous magnitude, for if they are discrete, there must be some intervening magnitude that can again be divided into discrete magnitudes, and the continuum is inescapable.

At every level of complexity, the terms that are the related elements overlap, more obviously as the interlock and integrity of the whole increase. But we must not get too far ahead of the argument. We are concerned at this stage with continua; their bearing on wholes is yet to come. What should now be clear is that relations do not "fall between" their terms and are not external links. The terms merge into one another, they overlap, they are interwoven distincta.

Here two contrasting errors are to be avoided. One is to jump to the conclusion that because the terms of relation overlap, they coincide and are not distinguishable. That would be fatal, because it would destroy the continuum that makes them comparable. The other is to ignore the overlap as inessential to the terms and to treat them as if totally separable and disjoined. Bradley seems at least to have been in danger of falling into this trap. These errors correspond roughly to what Collingwood (to whose exposition I shall presently turn) called the fallacies of, respectively, precarious margins and false disjunction.[3] But Collingwood was referring to a somewhat different context, which still remains to be investigated.

It is essential to the nature of a continuum that its continuity consists in a pervasive common property that is continuously varied. In the number series, it is magnitude; in the color series, it is hue. In other cases, such as living processes, it is more difficult to designate but is nonetheless recognizable. A common property displaying itself in a number of different instances is the way in which a universal, or genus, is usually defined. If this definition is accepted, it will follow that the genus is a continuum in which the species are related differences, and that the species of the genus, the terms of a specific relation, overlap. And this is the doctrine that Collingwood advocates.

Examples are plentiful. Numbers are species of the universal magnitude (which is virtually synonymous with number); and Russell (following Frege) defined a number as a class of classes equivalent to a given class. Every number should then be a specific case of this universal. Red, orange, yellow, green, blue, and violet are species of the genus, color; they are obviously elements in a continuum which overlap, merging each into the next. Species of chemical elements are continuous in the periodic table, and the overlap in atomic and molecular terms has already been noted. Helium, for instance is the overlap of two atoms of hydrogen. In biological genera, the species are related genetically and through evolution, again evidencing continuity and overlap.

Collingwood, however, confined the overlap of classes to the philosophical universal, saying that in the empirical and exact sciences, classes were usually considered to be mutually exclusive, as might well (for those sciences) be appropriate. But closer inspection reveals that the overlap is not confined to philosophy, although, it will later appear, there are significant differences in the way species in the other disciplines are to be regarded. This overlap of classes has profound consequences.

While the compactness of the continuum ensures the overlap of terms, it also ensures that a sucession of elements will constitute a progression of some sort, because the terms must differ, and the divergence will of necessity, if the continuity is to be preserved, be progressive. This is clearly apparent in the case of the number series and of colors (which is dependent upon it), but not so immediately obvious in the case of spatiotemporal continua. Nevertheless, movement through space, the traversing of successive positions, is always in some direction, and temporal succession is unidirectional. Further, such motion through time and space can always be correlated with the number series, and every such example is a progressive increase in extensity (motion over distance, time-lapse over duration). Physical, chemical, and biological examples display this progressive tendency quite evidently, but more detailed consideration of them may be postponed to the next chapter.

Terms in relation within a continuum, or species in a genus, whichever way we wish to consider them (for each can be regarded as the other), can now be seen both as distinct differences within a uniformity or common character or universal and as degrees in a scale. As the scale progesses, the successive differences display more and more of the totality (the continuum, or the pervasive character): thus, movement through space and time traverses more of space and takes longer the further it progresses, spanning progressively greater extensity; the successive stages of material combination, from quarks to nucleons, from nucleons to atoms, and thence to molecules, progressively disclose the nature and diversity of matter. Hence the specific differences are degrees in a scale progressively revealing the universal more fully.

Further, because they are necessarily different, the related terms (or species) stands opposed to the next, each is other than the other and negates it. They are thus, at the same time, distincts, opposites, and degrees in a scale progressively unveiling the generic character, the universal essence, of the continuum. Some philosophers, like Benedetto Croce, have objected that distincts ought not to be confused with opposites, but Collingwood, in his discussion of the scale of forms, has shown that this objection is ill founded; because distinction and opposition are species of differentiation, and as such, they overlap, which has just been made evident from the fact that what is distinct from something else is not what that something else is: is its negation, and what negates a is opposed to a and cannot be predicated of it without contradiction. The continuum, therefore, or the genus, specifies itself in a scale of forms the relata in which are at once distinct, opposed, and ranged in a series of degrees that progressively reveal the universal character (or generic essence) more adequately. Moreover, because the scale is continuous and can be so only if each and every specific difference is related to the next in a definite way that sustains the continuity, they are mutually complementary.

4. WHOLES AND DIALECTIC

All this applies equally and directly to wholes. A whole is a one of many; it is a complex of interrelated parts and so will be a continuum, and its parts will be distinct, mutually opposed yet mutually complementary; they will overlap and be ranged in a scale of degrees progressively displaying more adequately the nature of the whole. To demonstrate this is our next task, and to dissipate initial doubts prompted by examples such as were instanced earlier, like the bag of marbles or the bundle of sticks. These, as was noted at the time, are examples of assemblages that are less appropriately thought of as wholes than others, such as living organisms; and, even so, it has transpired that the more dubious examples are not exempt from the characteristics of continua already outlined. Speaking more generally, let us now consider the nature of wholes as such.

What induces us to call any collection a whole is some common, pervasive, or universal character that bestows upon the parts a special sort of kinship. This may be more or less intimate, and the more intimate it is, the more inclined we are to regard the assemblage of parts as a whole. In general, in order to constitute a whole, the parts must be, in some way or other, mutually adapted, mutually interlocking, and interdependent. A bundle of sticks is not a bundle unless the sticks are in mutual contact (usually tied together) so that they are at least temporarily and in some degree inseparable. In the bundle, each stick must make room for those surrounding it, each will resist pressure from the others and will dispose itself accordingly, and the movement of each and all will be restrained by the ligatures. Within the whole, then, the membership of each part will be conditioned by its relations to the other parts, and it will be the member it is because of these relations and because the other parts are as they are. In short, to the extent that the assemblage is regarded as a whole, the relations between the parts are internal to their terms. In the case of continua, we found that all terms in relation overlapped, so all relations were in some sense or degree internal, and this is equally true of wholes, but for additional reasons.

The internality of relations among the parts of a whole is the special kind of kinship above mentioned that the integrity of the whole bestows upon them. It is now apparent that this kinship is a principle of organization or structure pervading the whole, which determines how the parts interlock and makes it the kind of whole it is. The principle of organization, therefore, has the status of a universal or generic essence; it determines the whole to be of a certain character. And this principle is specified in the relations between the parts, which, being internal, make each part what it is in distinction from the others. Each part is thus a specific application of the universal organizing principle, which is the primary reason why they all overlap.

A more immediate reason is the fact, undoubtedly consequent upon the organizing principle, that each part as such is determined by its relations to the other parts; thus, each is what it is because of the others, and as part of the whole, it cannot be isolated from the rest without ceasing to be what it is. It follows that in abstraction from the whole, any part (as such) contradicts itself. It purports to be what it is without its relations to the other parts that make it what it is. Moreover, the other parts, being other, negate it while they determine its membership in the whole, and so they are opposed to it even as they complement it.

This contradictory relationship is both logically and ontologically intolerable and demands resolution, which it achieves through the principle of organization, for that fits the parts together so that they support one another in constituting the whole. In assumed isolation, any part, as part of the whole, exemplifies the principle that constitutes the whole, but it does so inadequately and confusedly. The contradiction inherent in each separate part in isolation from the others is, however, resolved through its complementation by its neighbor, in combination with which it constitutes a subordinate whole (of parts in relation), which exemplifies the principle of organization more fully and more evidently, although not yet completely, for that combination again requires further complementation, for the same reasons as before. Until it is so complemented, the provisional whole so far attained again involves contradiction, and so the process of resolution continues until the totality is complete and the principle of organization is thoroughly fulfilled.

In this manner, the tension exerted by the immanence in the part of the organizing principle of the whole generates a series of wholes ranged in gradations of completeness and concretion. The scale of forms is thus a scale of wholes, every part is in some degree a whole, and every whole is made up of wholes in a graded succession of relative completeness. Leibniz grasped this fact when he conceived reality as a series of monads, each of which reflected all the rest, through perceptions that differed in degree of clearness and distinctness. The perceptions reflected the other monads, which were similarly ranged in a scale of degrees of clarity. So the universe was constituted of a scale of lesser universes (or, as Leibniz says, organisms made up of lesser organisms).

The contradiction involved in abstraction is the spur to augmentation of the isolated element and to progressive integration with complementary opposites. In thought, this progression is compelling, but it is also operative in fact. In every whole, each part has to assert itself as different from the rest, otherwise the continuous divergence of the elements is not maintained. The affirmation of this self-identity, however, at once invokes the relations of the part with its contrasting others, which is what both generates the contradiction and demands its resolution. So the process of successive unifications of opposites is propelled toward the generation and eventual achievement of greater wholeness.

The resulting series of intermediary wholes is thus ranged as a scale of forms into which the universal organizing principle has been specified. They negate and contradict one another, but they also complement one another because they overlap (insofar as they exemplify the universal), and, as the scale advances, each form displays the universal more adequately than its predecessor. They differ as distincts, as opposites, and as degrees, in a scale specifying a universal with progressive adequacy. A whole is thus *par excellence* a genus, or universal, expressed in and through its specific exemplifications as a scale of forms.

What directs the process is the organizing principle of the whole, and it is now evident that this principle is no mere static formula but is a dynamic urge, or nisus, to the whole; and because its driving power is contradiction, it is rightly described as dialectical. Hegel was the first to recognize this characteristic of wholeness and its importance both in reality and in thought. It was he who declared that dialectic is the principle of all movement, all life, and all activity.

The complex relationship of distinction, opposition, complementation, and gradation between the parts in the architecture of the whole (or better, the phases of its development) is the dialectical relationship. Further, as the nisus is toward completeness and the perfected whole is the end of the dialectical process, the pervasive causal influence is always proleptic. The elucidation of the part, taken in abstraction from its context, is always in its further elaboration in union with its other—in the succeeding phase of the dialectical process—and the ultimate principle of explanation is the universal principle of structure of the totality, which emerges in full only at the end. Accordingly, the process is teleological, as is the method of explanation that depends upon it.

The scale cannot begin from zero. Without parts, there is no whole, and from nothing, or nowhere, no continuum proceeds. Any beginning must exemplify some concept, and, as Hegel showed, even nothing, as soon as it is thought, becomes something. Likewise, in the case of the whole, the scale cannot proceed indefinitely, because it is a scale of wholes, more or less provisional, tending always to the full expression of an organizing principle, that is, a principle of wholeness, which, when completely realized, brings the scale to an end. This does not seem to be the case with continua, which, like the number series, appear to go on forever. But even here there are qualifications. The number series proceeds upon a base (two, ten, twelve, or whatever the mathematician may choose), and this constantly repeats itself; so there is a cyclical process in the endless progression. In physics, space-time has an inherent curvature and bends around into a hypersphere without boundaries but with a definite volume. Radiation has an absolute velocity that nothing can exceed. Organisms are restricted in size and extent to the requirements of organic integrity. In every case, the termination of the scale is a consummation imposed by the organizing principle of the appropriate whole.

Wholes, then, ordered as a scale of forms and organized according to a principle of structure, are, for that reason, systems, and every system is a whole. Each form in the scale is a provisional whole, hence the system is always (as

Leibniz recognized) a system of systems. As each is specified as a scale of forms, it is indifferent whether we refer to the universal principle as one of organization or of order—whether we apprehend the system synchronically or diachronically.

5. UNIVERSALS, CONCRETE, AND ABSTRACT

This principle, being universal to the whole and the determinant of its pervading character, functions as a generic essence. Every whole or system, therefore, is a case of the specification of a genus or universal, a generic essence or concept. Collingwood was undoubtedly right to find this structure in the philosophical universal. Other philosophers had distinguished the concrete from the abstract universal, contending (with Bernard Bosanquet) that the former was a system and the latter merely a common property. Here, however, we are asserting that every specification of every concept is systematically a scale of forms, which should imply that every universal is a system and so is concrete. Can this be justified?

Collingwood, similarly, distinguished between the philosophical and the scientific universal. He denied that the scientific concept displayed the overlap of classes, and if it was susceptible of scales of degrees, the variable and the genetic essence did not coincide, as they did in philosophy (e.g., ice, water, and steam mark nodal points in a scale of degrees of the variable, temperature, but throughout, the genus, water, remains H_2O; whereas pleasure, expediency, and duty differ as degrees of goodness, of which they are also specific examples, and here the generic essence and the variable are the same).

The explanation of this difference, however, does not violate the principles laid out above. The concept is itself a universal and is specified in a scale of forms, in which the philosophical (or concrete) concept ranks higher than the scientific. Systematicity is also a universal, and systems, accordingly, can be ranged in a scale from those which display the principle of order less adequately to those which do so in an eminent degree. Precisely the same is true of wholes. It was stated above that the type of relationship within an assemblage determines the extent to which we are inclined to call it truly a whole. Some relationships are looser than others. That obtaining in a bundle of sticks (though not absolutely unsystematic) is less systematic than that structuring the leptocosm of a crystal, and still less so than the interrelation of physiological cycles constituting the metabolism of a living thing.

Whenever it is found convenient to represent a collection of items as a mere aggregate, the concept may be regarded as an abstract common property, as it is by Frege in his definition of number. In such cases, the relations among the items are purely external. Thus Frege ranks the moons of Jupiter as a concept.[4] But when the system under inspection is more closely integrated and the relations between its elements are more evidently internal, the concept becomes more concrete, as it is today in physics and biology; the species overlap, and something more nearly akin to what is found in philosophy comes to the fore. The degree of abstraction in the scientific universal, therefore, will depend on the degree of wholeness displayed by the subject matter to which it applies. But this is no good reason to deny that in general the specification of concepts resolves itself into a scale of forms of the sort most eminently illustrated in philosophical speculation.

Nevertheless, to regard any assemblage as a mere aggregate and all relations as purely external is an extreme of abstraction, for whatever collection we examine, however loosely aggregated, involves difference among its elements, which implies mutual definition (what each is, the other is not, and each is defined by what it excludes). So all relations are bound to be in some sense and in some degree internal. As in every other case, the scale of wholes cannot begin with zero. The degree of abstraction can never be absolute. We have already noted this fact in the cases of points in space, grains in a pile of sand, sticks in a bundle, and marbles in a bag. In every collection, the relations among the associated entities must be such as to justify our treating the assemblage as one, and if they are, they will somehow affect the nature and behavior of their terms.

6. LOGIC AND METAPHYSICS

In this chapter, an outline has been given of a metaphysics grounded in the concept of a whole. At the same time, it is the basis for a logic of systematicity. The metaphysic envisages a universe dialectically ordered as a scale of forms— a system of systems—and one in which the dialectic is the causal dynamic. It follows that all causation will, in the last resort, be final causation, because it is the outcome of the dialectical process that reveals the true nature of the earlier phases. Efficient cause will then be revealed as peculiar to the lower phases and, being powered by the organizing principle of the whole, will be subsidiary to (while nevertheless overlapping with) final causes. Explanation in this kind of system is, then, ultimately teleological.

Far from being unverifiable, the metaphysical theory is prompted by the contemporary physicists' discovery that the universe is a whole and, accordingly, has the underpinning of empirical science. Moreover, it can be further supported by examining the structure of the world revealed by the sciences of nature. A brief attempt to demonstrate this follows in the next chapter.

The metaphysic is at the same time a logic, for it sets out the theory of the concrete universal and prescribes a scale of wholes or universals varying in degree of concreteness. This begins with the most abstract of universals: that which subsumes a collection of bare particulars gathered under it simply by virtue of their possessing a presumed common property, the abstract concept of which is the generic concept. On such a concept, the whole of traditional formal logic and its outgrowth, modern symbolic logic, are founded. At higher levels of concreteness, the universal represents the integrity of the whole more adequately, and the dialectical relationship of its phases is brought more fully into view. The logic of system, therefore, stresses the positive effect and influence of the negative and the dialectical power of contradiction.

Critics of dialectic have accused its advocates of tolerating contradiction as legitimate for rational thinking, but this is mistaken. It is the recognition that contradiction is irrational and unacceptable that fires the dialectical impulse and drives its logical progression. Moreover, formal logic is not wholly abandoned in dialectic, as the dialectical scale of concepts ensures. The prior phases of the process are not abolished entirely, even as they are superseded, for each successive whole in the scale includes and preserves its predecessors, although they are transformed in the new and more concrete context.

In this way, formal logic is preserved in dialectic, but its rules and procedures have to be modified with the adoption of a more concrete conception of the genus, as was foreshadowed above in the discussion of Collingwood's distinction between the philosophical and the scientific universals, and as is copiously illustrated in Hegel's *Science of Logic*. Thus the notions of deduction and induction are significantly transformed in dialectical logic from the way they are conceived in formal logic, as are those of the concept itself, of the proposition, and of inference. This is not the place to elaborate on these transformations. I have done so elsewhere.[5] Here my intention goes no further than to indicate the kind of logic and metaphysics instigated by the twentieth-century revolution in science.

Notes

1. Cf. my discussion in chap. 22 of *The Foundations of Metaphysics in Science*, where I argue that there is no such thing as a homogeneous continuum, because every continuum is a unity of differences.
2. Cf. F. H. Bradley, *Appearance and Reality*, chap. 3.
3. Cf. R. G. Collingwood, *An Essay on Philosophical Method*, chap. 2, sec. 3, pp. 46–50.
4. Cf. Gottlob Frege, *Grundlage der Arithmetik*, sec. 54.
5. Cf. my *Formal, Transcendental and Dialectical Thinking* and *An Interpretation of the Logic of Hegel*.

9

The Order of Nature

1. THE DISPENSATION OF THE PHYSICAL SCIENCES

When we turn to the sciences of nature today, we find that they give us a world picture that embodies the principles set out in the preceding chapter. Relativity theory presents space-time as the universal metrical field—a continuum, a diversified whole—and the whole that is the spatiotemporal universe is found to be a hypersphere, finite but unbounded. Within this continuum, fields of energy (or force) overlap and determine what the physicist describes as its curvature, and that again determines the metrical gauge.

Energy is radiation and is propagated in waves; waves overlap or are superposed in wave packets that manifest themselves as particles: matter and energy are equivalent, $e = mc^2$. Waves spread in concentric spheres, whereas particles travel along trajectories; they contradict each other, yet wave and particle have been shown to be complementary, each, in appropriate circumstances, behaving as the other.

Particle physicists, through the recognition of gauge and other symmetries, have discovered that elementary particles can be ranged in a progressive series, an eightfold scale (due to Murray Gell-Mann and Yuval Nee'man). Quarks overlap to form mesons and baryons; overlapping fields corresponding to protons and neutrons become atomic nuclei and, in overlapping correlation with electrons, form atoms. These again overlap, in the way we noticed earlier, to join into molecules of chemical elements and compounds, and the elements are ranged in a series of atomic weights and numbers, giving the Mendlejeff periodic table.

The overlapping fields constituting the four fundamental forces and their corresponding particles contrast with each other, as strong and weak; and these, with the electromagnetic force, contrast with gravitation. At the same time, they all overlap and are believed to have "frozen out" of a single unified field in the first few seconds of the universe's evolution.

The entire microscopic series, from elementary particles to molecules, is paralleled by a contrasting macroscopic series of vast gaseous and dust clouds that condense into galaxies and stars that are themselves ranged in species from white dwarfs to red giants. The two series, although opposed in scale, are mutually complementary, for without the internal furnaces in the stars, the heavier elements could not be synthesized, and the microscopic series would go no further than hydrogen atoms.

Thus the entire physical whole has resolved itself into a complex scale of overlapping, contrasting, and complementary forms, dialectically related. Without energy, there is no matter, and without either, there is no space-time, as Eddington explained:

> A region outside the field of action of matter could have no geodesics and consequently no intervals. . . . Now if all intervals vanished space-time would shrink to a point, then there would be no space, no time, no inertia, no anything. Thus a cause which creates intervals and geodesics must, so to speak, extend the world.[1]

Space-time specifies itself as energy and matter, which introduces curvature and determines geodesics. Each degree of curvature is a species of radiation or matter, and together they constitute a whole of wholes, a system of systems. The universe is held, by the physicists, to be organized on a single principle not yet discovered (although the superstring theory promises to achieve some such result), but it is dynamic throughout and self-specifying into the various forces and particles that are known.

At the present time, the Big Bang theory prevails, which contends that the universe began as an infinitesimal but extremely compact mass that exploded in a stupendous outburst, starting the current expansion and causing the recession of the galaxies. According to the superstring theory, the original nucleus was a ten-dimensional metrical field coiled up in a minute sphere and enclosing a single field of force at enormous temperature. This exploded, separating six dimensions, which remained minutely interlaced, from the other four, which spread out and expanded rapidly with corresponding reduction of temperature. As the mass cooled, the four forces (strong, weak, electromagnetic, and gravitational) froze out, and the scales of forms outlined above came successively into being: quarks, mesons, leptons and baryons, ions, hydrogen atoms, gas clouds, stars, and galaxies, which then generated the range of heavier elements.

Each succeeding phase is a complexification (what Pierre Teilhard de Chardin called *enroulement sur soi même*) of the previous level. Energy is a warping of space-time, and its further enfoldment is matter, which is a superposition of energy waves. Atoms are complexifications of overlapping elementary particles (or the fields they represent), molecules are overlapping atoms, and crystals are leptocosms of overlapping molecules. From here the complexification proceeds to macromolecules of organic compounds: peptides combining into polypeptides (amino acids), nucleotides into nucleic acids, the enfoldments of the radicals in the polypeptide and nucleic chains depending for their properties on the complex structure of the *enroulements*. Overlapping cycles of chemical activity involving these macromolecules then enter into the intricate unity of the living cell.

The physicochemical world is thus a whole of wholes, the self-specification of a dynamic principle into a dialectical scale of overlapping forms. Progressively they manifest more fully and adequately the structure and unity of the universal principle of order, which physicists hope in time to be able to set out in one single formula not yet discovered. This principle makes its appearance in the constants of nature and again in Pauli's Principle of Exclusion, which proves to be one of organization, determining the number of electron shells in the atom and the way in which they become interlinked in molecules.[2] It is a principle of activity that throughout the series governs the nature and behavior of all physical systems, processes, and entities.

But this physical whole is still incomplete and harbors contradiction. It is one and indivisible, for quantum physicists have shown that distant events are inseparably (nonlocally) interconnected. Yet it is essentially spatiotemporal; that is to say, it is extended in space-time. But to be so extended is to be self-external, with parts spread out and mutually exclusive. These two contrasting aspects contradict each other and demand reconciliation.

Partial reconciliation is achieved in chemical affinity, which to some extent overcomes the spatiotemporal externality of parts by the identity of the compound in its chemical properties and activity. But spatiotemporal self-externality can be fully overcome only if the terms of the relations are thoroughly indentified in their nonidentity, or contrast; and that is possible only if they become aware of themselves as related, which they can do only at the level of consciousness.

Now the rudiment of consciousness is sensibility, which does not occur until the level of organism is reached, where the whole maintains itself in dynamic equilibrium. Physical entities fail to do this, although, in some cases, they give a premonition of its possibility. A physical entity remains the same as long as the physical environment permits, but if conditions change so as to disrupt the attractive forces that bind its elements together, the entity is dissipated. So combined elements may be separated by electrolysis, or atoms split in very high temperatures. A living organism, on the other hand, can maintain its integrity in changing and (within limits) unfavorable conditions by adapting itself to its environment and modifying its activity to compensate for inimical changes. For example, if oxygen becomes scarce in the surrounding water, the protozoan *Arcella* secretes a bubble to float itself nearer to the surface where oxygen is more plentiful; and mammals regulate their internal temperature to compensate for external changes. It is this self-regulating self-maintenance that ushers in the sensitivity to the environment which becomes sensation and provides the basis for consciousness.

A whole, however, as I argued above, cannot be incomplete. The scale of forms cannot end abruptly, leaving the principle of organization only partly realized, nor can it go on forever always falling short. Partiality always generates contradiction, precisely because, by its partial nature, what is incomplete demands complementation in order to justify its claim to partialness within the whole. The physical scale, being incomplete, must therefore be continued from the inorganic into the organic—a further contrast that demands reconciliation—in order further to realize the overarching wholeness and for the principle of order to express itself more adequately.

2. LIFE

Although the organic contrasts with and, in some respects, contradicts the inorganic, there is continuity between them and they are closely conjoined. Physics is continuous with biology through biochemistry and microbiology. The complex, interwoven cycles of living metabolism are chemical throughout. Nevertheless, as soon as we move to the sphere of life, we enter a new phase in the scale. The unity of the organism is more close-knit and more intricate than anything at lower levels, and it has the curious and inscrutable capacity to adapt to changing conditions that, if it were not alive, would automatically destroy the system. Its reaction to its surroundings is not simply repetitive but is relevantly varied so as to maintain its internal integrity. Yet this is achieved without separation or independence from its physicochemical basis and in the closest possible interaction with its environment, both inorganic and organic. There is a constant interchange of energy and material between the living organism and its surroundings, so that strictly it is impossible to draw a sharp distinction between them; they are in organic interrelation.

In the sphere of life, the dominance of the whole over its constituent parts is more obvious and marked than in any of the inorganic forms. The organism is a dynamic, open system in which none of the metabolic processes can maintain itself, or even exist, apart from the totality. What it is and does are determined by the systematic organization of the living creature, which is not, however, fixed and unchanging—although it has a constant form and stability—but is plastic and adaptable. It is, moreover, essentially in process, and every phase and stage of its development (for instance, in morphogenesis) is governed by the specific nature of the mature individual.

3. EVOLUTION

The scale of forms disclosed in the biosphere is, for the most part, the product of evolution, which, since Charles Darwin until very recently, has been described in more or less mechanistic fashion as the result of random mutation and natural selection. Now, however, there is an impressive body of evidence that makes such neo-Darwinism quite implausible. In the first place, we must ask ourselves what it is that is selected. It cannot be less than a self-reproductive, self-maintaining organism, and self-reproduction is no more nor less than a method of self-maintenance. In other words, what is selected is a modification of an already adaptive system. It is therefore a *hysteron proteron* to attribute adaptation to the effects of natural selection.

In the second place, the facts to be explained are in most cases too complex to admit of the proffered explanation. The great majority of chance mutations are disadvantageous and often lethal, so selection should eliminate them from the population. Even potentially favorable mutations, if they occur purely by accident, are apt to be detrimental unless simultaneously accompanied by other, often quite complex, changes needed correlatively if the mutant is to gain selective advantage. Apart from these, they would in all probability be bred out, and once they had been, they could not be recovered.

For example, the modification of an area in the skin as a light-focusing lens will not be the rudiment of an eye if it does not appear immediately opposite a photosensitive nerve, and even if it does, it will be of little use without suitably attached muscles to focus it in response to the degree of acuity of the image. In fact, in embryogenesis (which often recapitulates evolution), the retinal nerve stimulates the development of the lens long before it is ever exposed to light, implying that neither is due to an independent chance variation. The random occurrence of any of these mutations in isolation would most probably disadvantage the animal in the struggle to survive, and so be bred out. Something more therefore, is needed to explain the development of the cephalopod and the mammalian eye than chance mutation.

In some cases, what has to be explained is far more complicated. *Hemipus picatus leggei*, the Ceylon black-backed pied shrike, for instance, does not simply have protective coloration, but it builds its nest on the bare branch of a tree, disguising it with materials that mimic the bark and its covering of lichen. The chicks, while waiting to be fed, sit immobile with upturned beaks and complete the camouflage, so that the whole ensemble resembles a broken branch. It would tax the ingenuity of anybody inclined toward neo-Darwinism to explain this combination of protective coloration and behavior—not just of one individual, but of several in cooperation—by an accumulation of chance mutations and natural selection. Of course, every advantageous change will naturally be selected—about that there can be no dispute. But that the sole source of the change is accidental mutation can seriously be questioned.

Recent developments in genetics have produced massive evidence supporting a more organismic explanation of evolutionary change. Chromosomes are no longer imagined to be a succession of genes like a string of beads. Separate characters have been found not always to be due to isolable genes. Genes are at times discovered to be divisible and scattered along the chromosome, with portions of DNA intervening between the parts. Some relatively simple characteristics have been found to result from the concerted activity of several genes. The genome has been shown to act as a whole and not as a collection of separable effects. Mutation, then, is no simple matter, and more is needed than isolated accidental modifications of single genes to explain changes in the phenotype with selective advantage.

This conclusion has been supported with copious evidence and cogent argument by Stuart Kauffman in his book *The Origins of Order: Self-Organization and Selection in Evolution*, where he contends that the doctrine of chance variation and natural selection must be supplemented by the recognition of self-organizing activity. Having referred to a mathematical demonstration that the chances against accidental production of a functioning enzyme in a time scale of two billion years would be one in $10^{40,000}$, he writes:

> The same sense of mystery surrounds the origin of a coupled metabolism, of the genetic code, of tissue organization. The general feature of these mysteries is that each exhibits, in one form or another, the evolutionary emergence of a mutually necessary set of processes. Each time we confront the evolutionary emergence of such a whole, whose parts are mutually necessary to one another, there is a tendency to reason. . . . What is the chance of obtaining the first part, of obtaining the second part—and since each is useless without the rest, what is the chance of obtaining them jointly? . . . I suggest throughout this book that many properties of organisms may be probable emergent collective properties of their constituents. The evolutionary origins of such properties, then, find their explanation in principles of self-organization rather than sufficiency of time.[3]

In the biotic sphere, we are always dealing with wholes whose parts are mutually necessary to one another, and biological evolution is always the development of such a whole; we should therefore expect it to proceed as a scale of forms such as has been described above. Let us consider first the ontogenetic process. It begins from a single cell, the union of two gametes. The cell is a complete organic whole, composed of a nucleus contrasting with its surrounding cytoplasm, each of which is itself complex; but in contrast to what it is about to become, it is relatively undifferentiated. The first stage of development is one of orientation within the egg, determining back and front, left and right. It then divides, and its daughter cells segment to become a collection of relatively disunited cells, forming the blastula. At this stage, there is nothing to indicate the sort of creature that is developing, and in the earlier stages of ontogenesis, it is difficult to distinguish the species of the embryo. (Recent research into the structure of the genetic code in the DNA has largely overcome this difficulty, but the general appearance of the early embryo does not reveal its genus). The process thus presents a single relatively undifferentiated cell, followed by a contrasting differentiated phase and then a multicellular collection without internal organization. Up to this point, the egg and the succeeding blastula are equipotential, and if divided in half, each half will develop into a complete adult. Next, after gastrulation, specialization takes place, with groups of cells irreversibly destined to become different organs and limbs. Each group develops relatively independently, and if transplanted, it will continue to produce the same limb or organ irrespective of its position in the body. In the final stage, this virtual mosaic of independent parts is reintegrated through the activity of common nervous and vascular systems, eventually subjecting the whole organism to control by a unified neurological system, concentrated in a single organ (the brain).

The entire process is governed and directed by the organized structure of the mature individual, which is immanent in every phase and differentiates itself in the process. It does so in a series of forms that are mutually continuous, mutually contrasting, and mutually complementary: the unitary with the multiple, the uniform with the specialized, the equipotential with the segregated, the disparate with the articulated and coordinated whole. Each phase presents the whole, but in a different and contraposed degree of integration and articulation. The scale is evidently dialectical.

Ontogenesis is the basis underlying the evolution of the species, which proceeds in comparable fashion, beginning from Protistans and unicellular forms which then congregate and colonize into multicellular organisms, more or less differentiated, such as slime molds, sponges, polyps, and hydra. Then there appear more individualized organisms, more differentiated, specialized, and integrated, branching out into the myriad species of the contrasting plant and animal kingdoms. Despite their patent opposition, these two major branches are complementary and interdependent, symbiotic at almost every stage of their development.

The scale of forms in which a universal specifies itself is not necessarily orthogonal. Wholes are not always restricted to straight lines, nor even to single ones. A tree is a whole, and its branches all belong to it and contribute to its organic integrity, although they do not all grow in a straight line or in the same direction. The specifying scale may similarly branch, without violating the rules of overlap and complementarity. A well-constructed novel has a plot that develops in a recognizable direction, but it also (especially if it is one by Charles Dickens) has subplots that interact with the main story, develop with it, and supply essential features of it. A symphony has many musical themes all interlaced and harmonizing, yet distinct, and all contributing to the ordered succession of symphonic sounds. So, likewise, does the evolutionary scale in biology branch out, with some branches coming to an end in *cul-de-sacs*. Nevertheless, each branch proceeds in a definite direction and continues orthogenetically, and the different branches are interdependent for their survival. Animals cannot do without plants, without which photosynthesis, using and supplying the all-generating energy from the sun, is impossible; and plants are often dependent upon animals (e.g., for the distribution of their seeds). Many invertebrates depend on vertebrates for their sustenance, and (directly or indirectly) vice versa.

What limits development along a special line is usually overspecialization, resulting in a certain rigidity admitting no further adaptation. Such is the case with plants, due to their immobility, and with arthropods, due to the restriction imposed on them by their external armor. The species that have developed furthest are those that have retained flexibility and the capacity for relevant variation, as have mammals and especially primates.

Invertebrate animals contrast with vertebrate, aquatic with terrestrial, cold-blooded with warm-blooded. Although the species branch off and evolve in separate directions, the process is continuous, and the species overlap. Invertebrate and vertebrate overlap in notochordata; fish and reptiles overlap in amphibians; reptiles and birds overlapped in pterodactyls; and birds and mammals overlap in the egg-laying duck-billed platypus. Overall and in each branch, the scale has the same character as the self-specification of an organized pattern by way of a series of overlapping, contrasting, and complementary forms progressively displaying the organizing principle more adequately.

Each form incorporates its predecessors. Multicellular creatures are made up of single cells organically similar to protozoa, and many developed organisms incorporate actual living protozoan forms (such as the phagocytes in mammalian blood). The higher animals and plants begin life as single cells, which segment and become colonial forms, then differentiate as the rudiments of distinct though interdependent organs in a single organic whole. The embryonic development of the mammal recapitulates in marked measure the evolution of the species, and many anatomical and physiological traits are vestiges of past structures and processes, as are numerous configurations of instinctive behavior. It is hardly necessary to repeat that all living forms incorporate the physical and chemical structures and processes that make up the physicochemical hierarchy, in which, in the same way, the more primitive are incorporated in the more complex.

In the evolving organism, metabolism merges with physiology and physiology with overt behavior. Behavior is primarily instinctive and repetitive but becomes more flexible, relevant to circumstances, and ultimately intelligent. On the subjective side, sensibility, possibly present from a very early stage, instigates learning and, through attention, matures as conscious perception, which develops further to intellection. Once more, we find interdependent and correlative series of scales of overlapping forms—physical, behavioral, and mental—each and all bringing to fruition a principle of organization through specific manifestations, successively displaying its activity in increasingly adequate degrees.

It must be borne in mind that the ordering principle is at every stage dynamic. In the sphere of life, it operates as an activity organizing what goes on at a lower level: metabolism is the activity of organizing the chemical cycles interwoven in the protoplasmic complex; physiology is the activity of organizing bodily functions so as to maintain the vitality of the system; behavior is patently organized activity directed to supplying the vital needs of the individual and the survival of the species. Sensation is more mysterious, but there is good reason to hold that it is the form taken by highly integrated physiological activity that has reached a critical threshold of intensity. Attention is further organizing activity, now of sentience, to constitute objects of perception; and consciousness is the activity of ordering and interrelating the perceived objects as the presentation of a coherently ordered world. As the most developed form of the active process, conscious thought is what most adequately and characteristically reveals the universal principle pervading the entire dialectical scale, a fact that is especially important for the doctrine here being expounded. But before I explain why, there is one more stage to be noticed in the biotic scale, which underlines and establishes its wholeness.

4. Ecology

From the outset, the realm of the life is that of organicism, and an organism is almost by definition a whole of internally related parts. Not only of the individuals is this true, but, through reproduction and sexual selection, it is also true of the species and, by inheritance, of the genus. The family tree and the system of classification are thus dialectically structured. Species and genus persist through time, but they also evolve to produce new genera and species, and, as we have seen, the evolutionary succession is one of dialectically related phases. There is, moreover, another dialectical series overlapping with all of these; namely, the biological community.

Apart from special conditions, every pond and lake in nature is a whole of interdependent and symbiotic organisms, of widely differing species and orders, from bacteria to diverse plants, fish, amphibia, and possibly, in some circumstances, birds and mammals. A tree in a field or a forest is an ecosystem of mutually sustaining creatures: parasitic epiphytes and fungi, ants and other insects, birds and small animals, all assisting and contributing to the maintenance of the conditions necessary to one another's health and survival. But none of these is isolable or completely self-contained. The whole forest is an ecosystem; a coral reef is as much or more so. Entire seas and oceans become biocoenoses, and ultimately the whole biosphere is a single biological community, delicately vulnerable to pollution of atmosphere and hydrosphere. Here is another dialectically specified system of systems, incorporating all the rest and uniting them into a single whole of mutually sustaining organisms and species—the disruption of which imperils all life within it.

That this biocoenotic whole is itself in dialectical relation with the physical whole is undeniable. It stands, indeed, in contrast to it; but, if only through its dependence on the outpouring of energy from the sun, the biosphere is inseparable from the astronomical system within which it is fostered. Furthermore, the physical and chemical environment prevailing on the earth, conditioned by its position in the solar system, as has many times been emphasized by scientists, is specially adapted to the generation and support of life. And living organisms, becoming progressively more adaptable and intelligent, evolve into self-conscious, rational human beings.

At the end of the last section, the point was reached at which the inadequacy of purely physical interrelation to the implicit wholeness of the system was recognized, and it was asserted that the nisus to the complete whole is thus stimulated to complexify yet further the structure of the physical basis. Hence emerges organism and the gamut of living forms. It has now become apparent that the biotic whole, involving adaptation of the organism to its environment, both inorganic and organic, sublates within itself the entire physical universe and becomes a focus of the total system. The surround of the living entity is registered in sentience, which develops into perception and intelligence; so consciousness becomes a further apprehension and elaboration of the environing totality. In short, the dialectical scale of forms thus outlined is the specification of the universal whole.

5. CONSUMMATION

So the final upshot of the scale is a compendium as well as a consummation of the whole scale. It is at once its last result or outcome and the entire gamut summed up in its own integrated structure. The living organism is in organic commerce with its environment, and it is subject to all the skyey influences flowing in upon it from every quarter, which include the effects of everything in the entire universe. All these influences are inwardized by the organism, which adjusts itself to them by suitable reaction and response, whether they be energy streaming in from outer space, gravitational forces, electromagnetic waves, vibrations in the air, temperature changes, or seasonal modifications of diurnal alternation. The organism is thus an epitomization of the universe as a whole, and it organizes and integrates all these multifarious influences, by its own activity, into its own systematic unity.

Physical and biological sciences now debouch into the psychological and social sciences, the special complexity and peculiar self-reference of which demand their own appropriate method, although their continuity with the other empirical sciences is not to be gainsaid. That psychical phenomena are internally related and coalesce into a whole is guaranteed by the fact that they are necessarily experienced by a unified, single, biological subject. Social relations are, likewise, reciprocal and interlaced in a systematic structure cemented by

mutual recognition. Here there are further scales of forms and dialectical relationships: sensation, perception, imagination, memory and learning, and intellect; belief, mythology, religion, kinship, social precedence, institutional structure.
It is not necessary to go into detail to illustrate further the fact that the empirical sciences bear out, provide evidence for, and demand a holistic and dialectical metaphysic. One further point, however, needs to be made, which is of
special significance.

Terms in relation, it was earlier maintained, are wholes, and wholes are relational complexes. But they are so only when taken together. In physical systems, relations are manifested in the reactions of the physical entities to each
others' states, but intimate though they are, they are not realized as relations
between terms, because they are not grasped as wholes by the entities involved.
The nisus toward this realization persists throughout the biotic realm, in which
relations assert themselves in the auturgic adaptation of metabolic processes
and the responses of the organism to environmental demands and stresses. But
here again, the organism, while it responds, does not grasp the connection of
response to stimulus as such. It falls short of this realization, even when it
perceives objects within the range of its senses, unless and until it becomes
aware of the fact that its perception springs from its own relationship to its
object. Only at this stage of developed and reflective consciousness are relations fully actualized.

It is this fact that gives special significance to scientific observation and ensures what has not been recognized until the current century: that until they
are scientifically measured, physical relations remain merely implicit or potential. More important still is the fact (consequent upon the dialectical sublation
of its predecessors by every form in the scale) that the whole immanent at the
physical and biotic levels cannot be completely actualized until its organizing
principle brings itself and its own self-specification to consciousness in intelligent mind.

Moreover, no whole can be whole and at the same time remain incomplete.
Throughout the natural order, wholes are ranged in degree of self-completion,
and it is because none is thoroughly self-sufficient that the scale progresses to
more complex and more intimately unified wholes. This process, due to its
dialectical nature, must continue until its universal principle of order is fully
actualized, which necessitates its bringing itself to consciousness as a mind, a
requirement that has profound ethical and theological implications. The metaphysics of the future, then, cannot neglect these implications and will necessarily include philosophy of mind, of social order and morality, and of religion.
Some consideration will be given to these subjects in the chapters that follow,
with special attention to problems arising from the doctrine so far set out.

To sum up: the whole of material nature is deployed as a system of systems
such as was outlined in the last chapter. It is a self-contained whole, which

differentiates itself into a scale of provisional wholes, each expressing the universal principle of organization in some degree, and successively expressing it more and more adequately, each phase continuous with and developing out of its predecessor, incorporating and superseding it, while at the same time transforming all that has gone before in the context of its more intricate and integral unity, so that the latest and most developed outcome comprehends the whole scale as it focuses within itself the entire system. In short, the natural world is a totality that specifies itself dialectically as a scale of physical, chemical, organic, living, ecological, and psychical forms.

Notes

1. Sir Arthur Eddington, *Space, Time and Gravitation*, pp. 157f.
2. Cf. Henry Margenau, *The Nature of Physical Reality*, chap. 20, and "The Exclusion Principle and Its Philosophical Importance," *Philosophy of Science*, vol. 11 (1944).
3. Stuart A. Kauffman, *The Origins of Order: Self-Organization and Selection in Evolution*, p. 22.

Part 3

Teleology

10

Teleology and Teleological Explanation

A consistently holistic metaphysic is necessarily dialectical, and as the universal of dialectical logic is concrete, the explanation of any stage is to be sought not in what precedes it but rather in what it is about to become. The concrete universal, moreover, becomes fully evident as such only at the end of the dialectic: it is what is specifying itself throughout the process, and as each successive specific form is a more adequate expression of the whole, it is the last that reveals it in toto. Explanation in such a system is, accordingly, teleological; and our next concern is to examine the meaning of teleology and the claims of teleological explanation.

1. THE RENAISSANCE REJECTION OF TELEOLOGY

Ever since Francis Bacon likened the fruitfulness of teleological explanation to that of vestal virgins, any suggestion that appeal should be made to anything other than efficient causation to explain phenomena has been suspect. Bacon's empiricist successors have generally applauded his criticism, despite the fact that Hume's analysis demonstrated conclusively that efficient causation, as he understood it, provided no explanation whatever—or at best one precisely similar to what Bacon had deprecated. For (as E. R. Guthrie has shown,[1]) if causation is reduced to constant conjunction, to explain the occurrence of B by saying that it is cause by A is to say that A is always followed or accompanied by B; in other words, that B occurs after A in this instance because it always does— which is much the same sort of explanation as that pilloried by Molière of the sleep-inducing properties of opium: that it has a sleep-inducing tendency—it always does induce sleep. It is thus the more remarkable that those who most energetically oppose teleological explanation today usually most strongly support Hume's analysis of cause.

Bacon and his contemporaries, however, were concerned with the methods of the newborn physical sciences of their day, the most triumphant of which was the classical mechanics, a science that rapidly became (and until the nineteenth century remained) the model for all others. It presumed that the world

132

was made up of solid material particles, the motion of which was governed by forces dependent solely on the masses and the inverse square of the distance between the bodies on which they acted. From the seventeenth century onward, therefore, efficient causation meant mechanical causation, and what was not reducible to this kind of mechanics was regarded as, to that extent, inexplicable.

Some thinkers, following Descartes, postulated another sphere of being of which a different account might be given—the sphere of conscious thought. But even they conceived everything else in terms of mechanical automatism, including the living bodies of animals and humans, so far in agreement with the materialists. "For what," asks Hobbes, "is the Heart, but a Spring; the Nerves, but so many Strings; and the Joynts, but so many Wheels, giving motion to the whole body?"[2]

Opposition to teleological explanation is thus a feature of the mechanistic outlook typical of seventeenth-century science, which, although it still persists, was somewhat shaken after the rise of biology a century and a half later. Progress in biology was accompanied by various forms of vitalism, which sought to reintroduce teleology into nature, at least so far as the phenomena of life were concerned, and dispute ensued between mechanists and vitalists. In effect, this was a dispute about where the Cartesian dividing line should be drawn, whether to assimilate living phenomena to mental or to material. But today, the Cartesian dualism is widely considered to be obsolete, and so is the classical mechanics. The debate about teleology is, consequently, liable to become sterile, whereas the persistent opposition to teleological explanation is a curious form of atavism. In fact, the contemporary participants in the debate are not really at variance, which becomes apparent as soon as the terms under dispute are suitably reinterpreted consonant with the holism of the sciences of our own day, and their apparent disagreement is largely misleading.

2. OBJECTIONS TO TELEOLOGICAL EXPLANATION

The two most common and telling objections to teleological explanation are, first, that teleology is supposed to be the operation in the present of a cause that will only occur in the future. A teleological process is one that is purposive and seeks a goal, so that every event in it must be explained by reference to this future objective, which determines the course of the whole process. The critic contends that to understand how a future event (the goal) can causally influence those that precede it is impossible; teleological explanation, therefore, is an attempt to explain *obscurum per obscurius*. The case of human action is understandable, it is alleged, in terms of conscious intention. We are aware of our purposes and aim at them consciously, so our actions are caused not by a future event but by our present awareness and the decision to act that we consciously form.[3] But, it is argued, teleological explanation in other cases, where consciousness may not be presumed, cannot be justified.

This leads to the second objection. Human action and possibly that of some higher vertebrates may be explicable in terms of consciousness, but in the case of invertebrates and lower species, such explanation becomes highly dubious. When we turn to physiological activity, metabolism, or the processes of morphology and phylogenesis, any account presuming conscious direction is plainly inadmissible, and teleological explanation is ruled out altogether. Yet it is just to these phenomena that some biologists and philosophers are most emphatic in asserting the inapplicability of mechanical principles and most insistent on the need for teleological description. Others steadfastly maintain that, in spite of the apparent difficulties and of our present ignorance of detail, there is no sufficient reason to deny that complete physicochemical explanations may in time be available for all biological phenomena.

Both these parties make assumptions about the nature of teleological processes which, though time-honored, are unwarranted; and when these misconceptions are dispelled and our view of teleology is suitably modified, it becomes apparent that there is no real issue between them. In the first place, purposive behavior is taken as the model for all teleological activity, and because such behavior is goal directed, it is assumed that the determining cause of any teleological process comes at the end. Until the process is completed, therefore, this directing cause lies in the future. In the second place, it is assumed that, in conscious purpose, the prevision of this end state is characteristic and is the stimulant to action.

Of course, both these assumptions have some justification. It is usually (although by no means necessarily) the case that the end state of a teleological process is the goal at which the activity is directed, but this is an incidental rather than an essential characteristic of the process. If an activity aims at a goal, it is liable to cease when the goal is attained, so that the attainment will mark the end of the process in time. But it is obvious (particularly in cases of failure) that the end of such a process is not necessarily that at which the activity aimed, and even when the end state and the goal are the same, what makes it the goal of the activity is not the fact that it come last in time but rather some character of fulfillment or "satisfaction."

Further, action with a conscious aim is often accompanied by the imagination of the state of affairs that the agent is trying to bring about, but this imagined state is not by any means always the one in which the activity actually terminates—obviously not when the aim is not reached, and frequently not when the activity is successful. Sometimes the agent is incapable of imagining what it would be like to attain the end sought and may not even know clearly what it is he or she is trying to produce until success is achieved; at other times, the goal is thought of in quite general terms while assiduous attention is given to the means.

Moreover, whatever sort of awareness a person may have of the goal that is sought in purposive conduct, this goal is not just an event or a set of events in the future, toward which the agent is being drawn by some mysterious kind of gravitation. It is something that, by his or her own effort and activity, the agent is engaged in bringing about. The event is not conceived as occurring (or at all liable to occur) in the future without this active participation. The activity is part and parcel of the goal, and the goal of the activity. In a genuine sense, the activity is the goal in the making, and the goal is what the activity is all the time generating.

For instance, the activity of an author writing a book is not related to its final product externally as means to an end. The book is the entire "work," and the whole process of activity generates and is summed up in what the publisher eventually distributes in print. Consequently, it is misleading to represent the process either as caused by a *future* event or as caused by a present conscious intention with no reference to the future. It is much more truly described as a process in which the outcome is all along immanent and potential, or through which the final state is being generated or is generating itself.

This, no doubt, is the sort of description that could equally be applied to many physicochemical processes, by which some end state is brought about; but here the assumption is being made that conscious purpose differs from merely physicochemical change in that the agent knows that the result depends on his or her action and is deliberately striving to produce it. In a physicochemical process we are not entitled to presume a conscious bond between cause and effect. Inorganic activity, we may say, proceeds according to a law, but conscious purposive behavior according to the idea of law. It is the conscious use of the knowledge of causal laws in order to bring about desired effects, as when a scientist or engineer uses his or her knowledge of physics and chemistry to construct a guided missile.

It is clear, then, that to appreciate the peculiar character of teleological activity, if human purposivenes is taken as the model, we must first consider the special character of the model, in particular the relation between the agent and the end and those properties of the goal in virtue of which it appeals to the agent as worthy of pursuit.

3. PURPOSIVE ACTION

It seems that some sort of conative impulse is essential to all purposive action, and this is provided by animal appetite. We are apt to say that appetite is "blind"—a sheer felt want that impels to activity aimed at removing the craving. Its object is, as John Locke holds, the removal of the uneasiness occasioned by the feeling of want. The extent to which, when actuated by appetite, we know what we want need not concern us here. Collingwood maintains hat we do not know, and that is why appetite is blind,[4] nevertheless, it is admittedly conscious, so far as we are aware of the feeling. When the object is known, appetite becomes desire, the explicit awareness of an object to be sought, in the attainment of which satisfaction is to be reached. Appetite is thus transformed in the light of self-consciousness, for to desire an object, we must be conscious of ourselves as seeking satisfaction in its attainment. We need not here consider by what process of mental development self-consciousness is reached. It is sufficient for our present purpose to note that unless I am aware of myself and my feelings as mine, I cannot conceive of an object as affording me satisfaction and I cannot, therefore, desire it as that which will satisfy *me*. Without self-consciousness, then, desire is not possible, although appetite certainly is.

Now it is common experience that our appetites are many and various and that they are not always mutually compatible, so that our effort to satisfy one may run counter to the impulse of another. At the bare appetitive level, this results in either the obliteration of the weaker by he stronger or an uneasy alternation between the two. But at the level of desire, this tug-of-war, although it survives as an element or moment in the experience and is still felt, is transformed by our awareness of the objects and of our desires for them into deliberate choice. We choose, when faced with alternative desirable objects, what we think will give us most satisfaction. Choice thus involves a grasp or view of two or more possibilities, an appreciation of their compatibility or incompatibility, and an estimate of the extent to which the adoption of any one, or of any combination of compatibles, will give us satisfaction.

This apprehension of our feelings and desires as our own and the activity of reviewing, comparing, and setting them in order of preference are typically the work of thought. It organizes our desires and directs our energies to the pursuit of their objects in such a manner as to attain what, through its activity, we anticipate as the total satisfaction of our person. Nothing less than this is involved in conscious, purposive conduct, for objects are consciously (or deliberately) pursued only as contributory to the satisfaction of the self, not simply (as in appetite) as the effort to remove a feeling of want.

Because desires frequently conflict, even in a single agent, and because no single human being can satisfy very many, let alone all, of his or her desires without the assistance and cooperation of others, the satisfaction of the self as a whole involves a complex and often arduous process of organization, ordering one's own priorities and adjusting one's objectives to those of others in the community that sustains our lives. This is what we normally call moral and political education (a lifelong endeavor). In its course, some kinds of activity are given up altogether as wholly in conflict with those from which the fullest satisfaction is expected; others may be postponed as incompatible with what is temporarily more urgent: others again may be admitted, but only when more important alternatives are not pressed; and some will be regarded as always necessary and constantly to be preferred to alternatives. The final result is a system of activities, or a way of life, that is found to be the most satisfactory on the whole, and the maintenance of which is our overruling aim. It is a system that involves our social relations and so intertwines our lives and activities with those of other people, and which provides us with the criterion by which we judge the value of possible actions and their aims and, consequently, is the directive of choice.

Conscious purposive action, therefore, is not impelled by any simple force or drive toward a single object simply imagined, nor is it drawn magnetically toward some single event or state of affairs to occur some time in the future, but is the continuous endeavor to maintain a dynamic system of activities and satisfactions in a self-conscious personality, which are continuous with a corresponding system of social relations. It must be observed that the objects that these activities pursue are satisfactory, on the whole and in the long run, only to the extent that they maintain the system; for so far as they fail to do so, so far as they run counter to its harmonious organization, they tend to be self-frustrating. It is only the pursuit of objects chosen for the sake of maintaining such a system that ranks as conscious purposive action. For in the course of organizing our desires in the manner described, we come to transfer them—with varying success, but often wholly—from objects that do not maintain the system to objects that do, and to regard *only* the latter as in a proper sense desirable.

It is, therefore, this fact of being a special sort of system or whole, or of contributing to or being an indispensable part of such a system, that renders the objects of conscious purposive action satisfactory; and the aims of such action are not "ends" in the temporal sense of finality, but rather the real and ultimate aim is the persistent maintenance of the system. The activity is not simply a linear process terminating in a state of satisfied quiescence, but a continuous striving, all of which is intrinsic to the satisfactory state of consciousness desired, so that the whole endeavor is at one and the same time both means and end. Our common substitution, in ordinary discourse, of the word "design" for "purpose" or "aim" supports this account. A design is a plan or pattern, a systematic arrangement of parts or elements, but we use the word with equal propriety for the intent of deliberate action. The object sought is the aim of the action so far as it fits into a plan; it is itself, or contributes to, a design or pattern. So we say of such action that it is done "by design," and we rank it as teleological.

Some may object that this description is of conscious activity at too sophisticated a level, and that the account given of purpose is too complicated to serve as a model for teleology. But no such objection is admissible, for anything less than what has been offered would not be deliberate action and so could not, without reserve, be described as consciously purposive. Merely impulsive or appetitive behavior might plausibly be attributed wholly to physiological processes, and that again to the purely physicochemical; and our consciousness of it might be regarded as simply epiphenomenal. If we were to assert that it was purposive and take it as a model for what is teleologically explicable, we should then be begging the question. But to allege that, when we choose deliberately, our awareness of what we are about it no more than an epiphenomenal accompaniment of physiological processes would, in effect, be to deny altogether that we choose, nor does it afford any plausible explanation of the deliberation. And we admit without reserve that teleological explanation is appropriate to action at this level of conscious choice, so we can with confidence extend such explanation to processes that bear relevant and significant resemblances to our own deliberate action.

The special peculiarity of such action is its high degree of variability in the maintenance of a constant direction. The aim or objective dominates the entire process, regulates its changes, and determines the alternative courses open to the agent. When the activity meets with obstacles, or is thwarted by the counteractivity of other persons, or is blocked by inanimate things, it is consciously modified to circumvent the opposition. This variability is never random but is governed and directed by the relevance of means to end, and is systematic. Moreover, as has been noted, the end is never a simple object but is always an element or factor in, or is the whole of, a more or less complex and systematic structure of objects and activities. In the last resort, the principle on which this structure is organized is the same as that which directs the variations in the activities seeking to construct the system. The aim of the activity, in consequence, serves to explain it.

When a person's behavior puzzles us, it is because we cannot see the systematic relevance of its variations to any governing principle or design. But when we discover what it is that he or she is trying to bring about, we are apt to say: "That explains everything." Similarly, our own and others' conduct is held to be reasonable when we can see how it is planned, how it is appropriate to a systematic design that it is bringing into being or a systematic state of affairs that it is trying to maintain. In such cases, no other sort of explanation will be adequate. It is no answer to the question what a man is doing who is groveling on the floor of his bedroom, to say that various chemical processes are going on in his body and that impulses passing along his nerves are causing his muscles to contract and relax in specific ways; whereas to say that he is dressing for a formal dinner and has lost his collar stud makes everything clear. So *if* a process is teleological in the sense described, no explanation will be complete that omits the principle regulating its variations and its course as a whole, or that overlooks the structural totality it is generating.

4. TELEOLOGY BELOW THE SELF-CONSCIOUS LEVEL

Teleological explanation, therefore, is not explanation in terms of an end state, or of a cause that succeeds its effect in time, but is an explanation of parts in terms of the whole, or processes in terms of a dynamic system to which they contribute, which they are maintaining, or which is being generated through them—a system whose principle of organization is the governing and directing principle of the processes to be explained. Whether such explanation is admissible in any particular case, and whether any other sort of explanation (e.g., one solely in terms of efficient causation) is sufficient, will depend on whether the explicandum has a character that is thus dependent upon some systematic totality or structure.

The claim is made by many biologists and some philosophers that all biological phenomena are of this sort, that they can, therefore, be adequately explained only teleologically and that any purely reductive explanation must, in the nature of the case, be incomplete and insufficient, however far-reaching it might be in detail. Other scientists, strongly supported by other philosophers (nowadays usually more influential), repudiate the claim and argue that nothing in the nature of biological phenomena warrants the belief that physics and chemistry are in principle incapable of accounting for them all. The former party seems sometimes to assume gratuitously that physicochemical explanation is always confined entirely to the explication of efficient causes, or even that it must inevitably be in terms of something like the classical mechanics. The latter party, on the other hand, is apt to support its case by showing that modern physics and chemistry have evolved in such a way as to explain physicochemical phenomena in terms of systematic wholes and might therefore be extended to cover biological facts, although they often confess that our present knowledge is insufficient to do this adequately and that new laws and theories would probably be needed. In short, the first party is protesting against a mechanism that is no longer scientifically current, and the second party, insofar as it seeks to repudiate teleology, is neatly giving away its case. I shall try to show that the first is right in what it affirms of biological phenomena, and the second is wrong in what it denies.

The account so far given of teleology should make it apparent that it involves no appeal to, or any need to postulate, mysterious entities like Driesch's entelechy or Bergson's *élan vital*. There is, therefore, no call to discuss this form of vitalism, which today finds no support. So far as I know, biologists, without exception, maintain that organization is the special characteristic of living matter and its behavior. According to E. W. Sinnott:

> It is not the *character* of the constituents of a living thing, but the *relations* between them which are most significant. An organism is an *organized* system, each part or quality so related to all the rest that in its growth the individual marches on . . . to a specific end or culmination, maintaining throughout its course a delicately balanced state of form and function which tends to restore itself when altered.[5]

He quotes in support a number of other biologists, by no means all of them in any sense "vitalists." Some, however, have claimed, on the strength of this organized character of living matter, that biology is an autonomous science with laws of its own, that these laws are not now and never will be reducible to physicochemical laws, even though they confess that the chemist and the physicist have much help to offer in the investigation of biological facts. But if the interpretation of teleology here proposed is correct, then it would follow that living things and living activity, inasmuch as organization is their dominant characteristic, could be fully explained only teleologically; and if physicochemical accounts of them were such as to omit or obscure their organized character, they would omit and obscure the very features that had to be explained. If, however, organization is discernible even in physical and chemical systems, if physicochemical laws and theories are evolved introducing principles of organization, even in the inorganic sphere, then biological phenomena might be adequately explained physicochemically without the explanation's ceasing to be teleological.

Description of a few examples of biological phenomena will help to show, first, that they are cases of what is here being called teleological activity, inasmuch as they are systematically organized, or are processes generating or maintaining systematically organized structures inasmuch as their course is regulated and directed by the whole that they are constituting and is capable of relevantly varying over a wide range. Further, in such phenomena, what primarily demands explanation are just those features consequent upon the wholeness and integrity of the system and its control of the processes that generate and subserve it. Consequently, any form of explanation that fails to make this organismic character intelligible fails of its object as explanation.

The slime mold is a lowly creature that shows little evidence of organization to the casual observer. The creature is a formless mass of protoplasm containing scattered nuclei and contractile vacuoles but is otherwise undifferentiated (except that the biochemist discovers protoplasm to be an organized substance). It is not divided into cells but is like an enormous amoeba reaching up to a square foot in area and two inches in thickness. It creeps along with a slow backward and forward motion, stronger in one direction than the other, so as to amount to locomotion. "Nevertheless," say G. P. Wells and Julian Huxley (on whose account this description is based), "it creeps with an appearance of appetite and purpose," turning aside to flow over and engulf any attractive lump of food.[6] Such a mold can be "strained" by being forced through dense cotton wool, so that in the process, its substance is divided into a multitude of fine parallel strands; but on emerging from the cotton, these strands coalesce again to form a continuous living mass. In unfavorable drought conditions, part of the slime mold's substance changes into a horny crust and forms a number of hollow capsules, each housing a portion of the protoplasm of its body. These can remain motionless and without external sign of life for up to three years, and then, when favorable conditions return, the hard capsules are absorbed, their contents flow together again, and the slow creeping activity is resumed. At a certain stage of its life history, the slime mold suddenly humps itself at intervals into wartlike knobs, which grow upward into stalks, solidifying at the core by hardening their own substance. The fluid protoplasm climbs up these stalks and at the top elaborates itself into vessels shaped according to the species of the slime mold—spherically, cylindrically, or like tiny umbrellas. These are the sporangia. They have hard outer shells filled with the spores and a tangle of minute coiled fibers, which, when the shell bursts, act as springs and propel the spores outward into the surrounding space. Each spore, if it falls into a damp place with a suitable food supply, hatches out a microscopic protozoan with its own means of locomotion, which, whenever it meets another of its own kind, fuses with it until the composite living mass grows to the size stated above.

The full description of this creature shows it to be, despite frequent appearances to the contrary, an organized structure, or one inherently capable of becoming organized at the appropriate time. Its activity varies always relevantly to the maintenance of its life and constitution. It pursues food; it encysts when food and moisture fail; it elaborates itself into organs adapted to the process of reproduction; and its infant protozoa unite to form a single mass behaving so as to preserve a typical character. Its very appearance of formlessness is belied by its organic behavior. To *explain* its activity, what we need to do is to account for its organization—how is a slimy, gelatinous mass capable of differentiating itself into delicately stalked and shaped sporangia at just the appropriate time? How is it capable of directing its course toward morsels that it can ingest and absorb, from which it can renew its substance? How does it succeed in distinguishing nutritious from non-nutritious matter? and so forth. The answer to these questions would have to be teleological in the sense we are adopting, and although that would not exclude reference to physicochemical processes, yet even if we could describe these in minute detail, that would help us only if it could inform us of the source and nature of their organization.

Another example is the growth of a conifer. The central shoot grows vertically upward to become the trunk of the tree, while the lateral shoots grow almost horizontally to form the branches. The branches grow more slowly than the trunk, but their rate of growth is maintained in a constant ratio so that the conical shape of the tree that results remains the same throughout. If the top of the central shoot is cut off, one of the lateral arms swings upward to take its place, its rate of growth increases, and its relation to that of the other branches is accordingly altered. Here again, we have a typical structure governing the process, reasserting itself when disturbed and maintaining its pattern by regulating appropriately its constituent factors. The activity is not simply uniform but is varied according to circumstance relevantly to the system to be preserved.

Even more typical examples can be found among the numerous phenomena of regeneration. If a flatworm is cut in half, the head end will grow a new tail and the tail end will grow a new head. If it is cut into three pieces, the middle piece will regenerate both head and tail. If the segment is irregular in shape, the new parts generated assume suitable spatial relations so that the normal shape of the creature is restored. If the worm is cut longitudinally, each half will regenerate a symmetrical other half, reducing in size as its tissue provides the requisite material for the regenerated portion. The impressive feature of these processes in every case is the dominance of the whole over the behavior of the part, which is precisely what I am here identifying as teleological.

Polyps and sponges can regenerate new individuals out of almost any sort of fragment of old ones, as long as the cells remain intact; in fact, a sponge rubbed through fine silk, so as to be disintegrated into single cells or very small groups of cells, can reorganize itself into a normal creature out of its disorganized fragments[7] or, alternatively, each cell or tiny group will grow and form itself into a new and perfect animal.[8] Here again, the whole governs the process throughout and makes it teleological. Nowadays we know that the reason for this is that the DNA included in every cell has encoded in it the entire structure of the organism, but what is yet to be explained is how the effects of the genetic code, which is the same in each cell, are varied relevantly to the differing circumstances in which regenerative demands are made.

Physiological processes characterized by what has been called homeostasis, where a complex of chemical or mechanical process (or both) is constantly varied so as to maintain some steady state in the organism, are outstanding cases of the same sort of organized and relevantly variable integration of heterogeneous parts and functions into a single typical whole. Examples are familiar and plentiful, and two or three will be enough to serve our present purpose. J. S. Haldane made famous the case of respiration and the varying means used to keep carbon dioxide and oxygen pressures constant in the lungs. The chemical action of the liver in regulating the supply of sugar in the blood varies according to the amount of different substances made available by the digestion of food. The action of the heart is regulated in complicated ways in order to adjust the blood supply to various parts of the body in differing conditions of heat, cold, exertion, fatigue, and the like. Such homeostasis is often explained as the effect of feedback mechanisms, which no doubt it may be, but it is as often forgotten that a feedback mechanism is a teleological device to regulate a process according to a set norm dictated by some purpose or the need to maintain some ordered complex.

In all such cases, it is important to notice their similarity to conscious intentional action in that they conserve and actively maintain a complex system by a process of relevant variation. So striking is this similarity that even the most tough-minded of scientists is liable, in describing them, to give way to anthropomorphic language and metaphor. Describing the growth of the embryo, Wells and Huxley, for instance, speak of the egg as "making up its mind" which part will be right and which left, which front and which back.[9] Sinnott, in a similar connection, *Writes*:

> Here is no random process but a steady march, each event in step with the rest as though to a definite and predetermined end. One gets the impression of some unseen craftsman who knows what he is about and molds the mass of growing cells according to a precise plan.[10]

Lewis Thomas, speaking of bacteria, writes:

> *Bdellovibrio* penetrate the walls of other bacteria, tuck themselves up inside, replicate, and burst out again as though they thought themselves phages.[11]

And that inveterate reductionist Jaques Monod speaks of "*le projet, réaliser le 'rêve' de toute cellule.*"[12]

The simulation in these biological phenomena of conscious purpose is what needs to be explained, not simply their physicochemical details; in other words, it is their organized character and their relevant variation. Certainly, that could not be fully understood without knowledge of their physicochemical character, but it is equally clear that it could not be explained by any physical or chemical analysis that dissipated the systematic interrelations. One that did not do this would have to be at least as much a synthesis as an analysis and would rank as teleological, whether or not it were given purely in physicochemical terms.

The obvious organic form of biological phenomena has induced many theorists to insist on what they call an organismic approach to biology, and while they acknowledge the value of the biochemist's research, they declare that, so far as it is merely mechanical, physicochemical explanation is in principle inappropriate to biology. The extent to which they are right has now been sufficiently indicated, but the door must be kept open for the possibility that physicochemical facts may themselves be holistic, so that explanation of organic phenomena in physicochemical terms would be as much teleological as mechanistic.

5. CRITICS OF TELEOLOGY

Some contemporary writers have submitted the views of the organismic school to severe criticism, but they seem, for the most part, to ignore the implications of the systematic character of the facts to be explained, or to propose possible types of physicochemical explanation that are still in essence teleological (so far as they are admitted to be holistic). R. B. Braithwaite, in his presidential address to the Aristotelian Society some years ago,[13] distinguished precisely between cases in which teleological explanation was useful and cases in which it was otiose. He agrees with E. S. Russell that persistence toward a goal in varying circumstances is what distinguishes teleological processes, but he contends that it is impossible to find any characteristic of the final state by itself of any teleological causal chain which is general enough to cover all goals of goal-directed actions and yet specific enough to differentiate such actions from other repeated cycles of behaviour

and that therefore, it is necessary "to look at the whole causal chain and not merely at its final state."

Braithwaite dimly discerns the distinguishing feature of teleological action (as opposed to other nonteleological cycles of behavior) to be not just its persistence toward an end state but some character of the whole causal chain. In an elaborate symbolic analysis, he defines the variancy of a teleological goal-directed sequence as the class of all those sets of field conditions (i.e., causally relevant factors in the environment of the system under consideration) which are such that every causal chain with the given initial state and determined by one of these sets attains the goal expected. He says that we may obtain our knowledge of this variancy in either of two ways: deductively from known causal laws, or else inductively from knowledge of previous sets of field conditions under which similar causal chains have attained the goal. Thus we may reasonably predict "that there will be a goal-attaining chain in the system." In the first case, he says, teleological explanation would be futile, for, in effect, physicochemical explanation would already be available; but in the second case, where this is not so, teleological explanation (i.e., in terms of the goal attained) is useful and appropriate. Cases in which our knowledge of the variancy can be deduced from known causal laws are the behavior of guided missiles and that of pilotless planes.[14] The maintenance of the body temperature in mammals is an instance of goal-directed action that can be predicted only on inductive evidence.

Here we must notice three points: (1) the holistic character of the goal-seeking process is recognized and admitted; (2) nevertheless, the case of the machine and the explanation of its behavior is not regarded as teleological; and (3) the presumption is made that biological processes might, with further scientific progress and more knowledge of detail, be reduced to cases in which teleological explanation was unnecessary. The difference, however, between the behavior of a guided missile and one moving freely under the influence of gravity and wind pressure is precisely that the former is governed by an elaborate system of mutually adjusted mechanisms which the latter lacks that are *designed* to direct it to its target; a physicochemical account of its action does not explain the source of this organization. For that, we should have to resort to the fact that the missile had been deliberately so constructed by an engineer, and this would be an explanation in terms of purpose. The system of mechanisms that maintain the mammalian body temperature is not designed by the mammal itself nor by anybody else, yet it is its simulation of deliberate purpose that has to be explained. It is not sufficient to be able to predict that there will be a goal-attaining chain of causes in the system. What is needed is to understand how such a chain of causes is possible, and if that is understandable at all, it can only be in terms of organization. Braithwaite should have concluded, therefore, that teleological explanation would be appropriate in both classes of cases which he describes. Neither can be made properly intelligible in any other way.

Moritz Schlick, in his "Philosophy of Organic Life,"[15] argues in the main against entelechies and vital forces with which we are not concerned. He contends, however, that finalism (that is, goal seeeking) does not distinguish the organic from the inorganic, and he cites the principle of least action as a purely physical example of the determination of a process as much by its end as by its beginning.[16] He might have given several other such examples from physics, not the least significant of which is Pauli's Principle of Exclusion. But these are evidences of teleological explanation in physics, not of the possibility or appropriateness of any other sort of explanation in biology.

Perhaps the most formidable and the most constructive critic of organicism among recent philosophers is Ernest Nagel, who attacks the belief that biological phenomena are irreducible to physics and chemistry and that explanation of them cannot be given solely by the laws of physics. He argues that this belief can be disposed of once it is shown either that biological concepts are definable purely in physicochemical terms or that biological laws are derivable from physical laws, or both. He admits that in the present state of our knowledge, neither is altogether possible, but he refuses to concede that both may not be possible at some future date. There is no evidence, he maintains, that such derivation is impossible in principle. The arguments, he confesses, that are the most weighty in support of the irreducibility of biology to physics are mainly three: (1) those that stress the goal-directed character of biological processes; (2) those that point to hierarchical order in living things; and (3) those that stress the wholeness of the organism—which maintain that, in biology, the whole is more than the sum of the parts. But he finds none of these arguments conclusive in establishing the claim, as he puts it, "that the mode of analysis required for understanding living phenomena is fundamentally different from that which obtains in the physical sciences."

Precisely what this mode of analysis is Nagel does not tell us, but his language strongly suggests that it is a sort of dissection, or taking to pieces, that renders a complex intelligible by examining each of its factors separately. This is suggested by his language, but it is belied by the account he gives of the conditions of biological explanation. Indeed, the use of the word "analysis" as more or less synonymous with "explanation" is misleading and question-begging where what has to be explained is the integration of an organized whole. In fact, no explanation is ever purely analytic, for it always involves at once both distinction and differentiation of parts within some complex, and the illumination of the way in which they are interrelated and unified. All explanation is at once analysis and synthesis. Let us now examine Nagel's criticism of each of the three arguments in favor of teleological explanation in turn.

(1) With respect to goal-directed behavior, he first maintains that the constructions of machines, which simulate it in varying degrees, proves that there is at any rate no absurdity in regarding goal-directed activity as possible for purely inorganic systems. But this argument, as has already been pointed out, overlooks the deliberate planning and construction of the machines by human beings to make them self-regulating or self-maintaining to the extent that they are, and its force, therefore, is the opposite of what is intended, inasmuch as it implies that some physicochemical systems require teleological explanation rather than that biological ones might not.

More formidable is Nagel's elaborate attempt, by symbolic formulation of the nature of goal-directed behavior (similar to but more complicated than Braithwaite's), to show that it can be adequately described without recourse to teleological explanation—that is, "without invoking purposes and goals as dynamic agents."[17] However, I have already shown that, properly speaking, teleology is not the dynamic agency of goals and purposes, if that means simply the causal efficacy of events occurring in the future. If, however, it means the actualization of an organized system, then it is doubtful whether Nagel's argument proves his point, for he assumes a system differentiated into a number of parts such that their activity jointly and severally is relevant to the maintenance of a certain property of the system, which he calls G (e.g., the body temperature of a mammal). Each of these parts is variable in state, and they are so connected that when the state of one changes so as to alter the property to be maintained, the others change concomitantly and in such a way that the property is, by their joint causation, restored. The first change of state Nagel calls a "primary variation," and the concomitant changes of the other parts of the system "adaptive variations." The conjoint state of the parts producing the constant property is said to be a G-state. It is merely assumed that the system is so constituted that the state-variables of the parts will compensate one another and (within certain more or less wide limits) always produce a G-state. It is then claimed that the "conditions for a directively organized system" have been stated "in a manner not requiring the adoption of teleology as a fundamental or unanalysable category."[18]

It is to be observed, however, that these conditions do not include the factor, whatever it might be, that determines the adaptive variations and causes them to be *adaptive*, or what one might call G-determining. We are simply asked to assume a system that is so constituted. Clearly, its constitution is intricately organized in order to bring about the result, and it is the maintenance of this organization that the G-state represents. Consequently, if the self-maintenance of a complex organization is what constitutes teleological activity, teleology has not been eliminated. This, in effect, Nagel himself admits when he says that teleological explanations

> view the operations of things from the perspective of certain selected wholes to which the things belong; and they are therefore concerned with properties of parts of such wholes only in so far as these properties are relevant to some complex features or activities assumed as characteristic for those wholes.[19]

Moreover, as this complex structural character of the system is merely assumed to be such as will maintain itself by the relevant adaptive variations of its parts, it has not been at all analyzed or explained, and therefore teleology is still required as an apparently unanalyzable category.

Moreover, Nagel's elaborate symbolic description fits, with equal elegance, both activities that are known to be consciously directed and those that are not. It does not preserve the distinction between what is generally acknowledged as purposive behavior and what is only claimed as such, because it proceeds *as if* it were consciously directed. Accordingly, it justifies our regarding both or neither as teleological. In fact, this symbolic account tells us nothing more than that if a system is so organized as persistently and in widely varying conditions to maintain a certain property, it is a goal-directed system. This we already knew to begin with, and the substitution of numerous mathematical symbols for ordinary words does not alter the position, although there is danger that it may bamboozle the innocent and unwary.

(2) Nagel meets the claim that hierarchical order is distinctive of teleological systems by pointing out that this is to be found in physicochemical systems as well as in biological organisms. It is, therefore, no obstacle, he contends, to the reduction of biological facts and explanations to physicochemical ones. But here he seems to have missed the point of the organicist argument. That is, first, that any sort of organization requires a special form of description and a special type of law to account for its attendant phenomena; and second, that organisms are hierarchically organized with physicochemical systems at the base of the hierarchy. Thus the difference between the sort of law that will explain phenomena low in the hierarchy and that which will be required to explain those at higher levels can be accounted for in terms of the increased degree of organized complexity. Consequently, the fact that physicochemical systems may be hierarchical in their structure would not necessarily permit the reduction of laws applicable at higher levels to those applicable lower down, even if it could be shown, as it has not, that this is the case within physicochemical hierarchies.

(3) The argument that the whole is more than the sum of the parts Nagel finds obscure, and again he suggests a symbolic interpretation to clarify the statement, which may be paraphrased as follows: if the behavior of a set of individuals forming a closed system, with respect to their manifesting a certain class of properties, can be explained by a given body of theory, which can

similarly explain the behavior of another set of individuals forming another closed system and manifesting the same class of properties, and if the behavior of these sets of individuals, when together they form part of a wider closed system, cannot be explained by laws derived from this given body of theory, then we should say that the whole is more than the sum of the parts; but if their behavior can be explained by laws derived from the given body of theory, the sum of the parts is equal to or the same thing as the whole.

The example Nagel gives of the first case is rather inept. The kinetic theory of gases, he says,. was able to explain certain of their thermal properties but not similarly to explain the same class of thermal properties in solids. This example does not seem to fit he model, for when the molecules of a gas are brought into a state of aggregation characteristic of a solid, they do not form part of a wider system in conjunction with another set of individuals, but merely themselves constitute a new system under different conditions. The ineptitude of the example, however, does not affect the argument that follows, for no doubt, better illustrations of what Nagel intends could easily be found. For instance, the typical absorption curve obtained from proteins when examined under the ultraviolet spectrometer is not obtained when these same proteins form part of a live seaurchin's egg, although if the egg is killed, the characteristic protein curve appears.[20]

Nagel points out that the distinction between wholes that are and those that are not the sums of their parts is relative to some assumed body of theory, so that what may be more than the sum of its parts relative to one theory may not be so relative to another and although it is true that there is now no physicochemical theory from which the behavior of living organisms can be deduced (even if the behavior of some of their parts can be), there is no reason to assume that the development of a body of theory that will explain organic phenomena physically is *in principle* impossible.

But what this reasoning proves is no less than that the behavior of the parts of a complex system is explicable only in the light of, and only by taking into account, the organization of the whole system. If a body of theory that can explain the behavior of two sets of individuals each forming a closed system cannot explain their joint behavior in a larger system, this is because it does not take the organization of the larger system into account, whereas a body of theory that did this might explain all. In short, the new body of theory (relative to the old) would have to be *organismic*. All that is meant by saying that the sum of the parts falls short of the whole is that the behavior of the parts taken severally or in isolation is not the same as their behavior when organized together, and that the latter can be understood only by reference to the organization of the total system. There are purely physical systems in which this does not seem to be the case; for instance, the motions of an aggregate of material points are directly derivable from the laws of dynamics governing that of a single material point (or at least a single pair). (This, however, is relative to the classical theory of dynamics and may not be the case when the theory of relativity is adopted.) In biology, on the other hand, we constantly find that the behavior of the several parts of an organism, though regularly describable in one way when they are taken singly, is liable to modification with variations in their interrelation within the living creature. Thus, particular cells in the developing embryo normally form certain tissues or organs, but if the embryo at an early stage in its development is cut in two, or if the cells are separated from the rest of the system, they develop entirely differently. It is therefore necessary to know the character of the whole system before we can predict the behavior of the several parts, and it is not possible, from mere addition of the normal behavior of the parts taken severally, to predict their behavior in the system, nor that of the system as a whole.

Of course, it does not follow that Nagel is wrong in his contention that what we here require is a new and more comprehensive body of theory; but this new type of theory, we may more than suspect, will provide explanations that are teleological, in the sense proposed. The fact that this has already proved to be the case in quantum physics only goes to show that the point at issue is no longer whether mechanism or teleology is more appropriate; but is the question of the sort of whole with which we are dealing, of the nature and degree of its complexity.

Nagel's next point has a similar bearing. He reminds us that no theory, physical or other, "can explain the operations of any concrete system unless various restrictive or boundary conditions are placed on the generality of the theory." Consequently, when we set out to explain by physicochemical laws the behavior of certain parts of the organism as they function within its total system, the boundary conditions within which the theory holds have been violated. "Accordingly," says Nagel, "a necessary requirement for the explanation of the unified behavior of organisms is that boundary and initial conditions bearing on the actual relations of the parts of the living organism be stated in *physicochemical* terms."

But this demand for appropriate boundary conditions is simply a demand that the system as a whole be taken into consideration. It is, in short, a demand for what we should here be calling a teleological explanation—one in terms of the maintenance of a total organized system. If it were possible to state it in physicochemical terms, this would not alter its teleological character. But it is admitted on all hands that the knowledge of physics and chemistry now at our disposal is insufficient, and that present physicochemical theories are inadequate to the task. Those that may be developed in the future and which may suffice, may well enunciate laws of quite a different sort from those now fruitful in physics and chemistry. As Schroedinger suggested in his book *What Is Life?* living activity may eventually come to be explicable in

physicochemical terms, but, he says, "We must be prepared to find it working
in a manner that cannot be reduced to the ordinary laws of physics." It is
guided "by a 'mechanism' entirely different from the 'probability mechanism'
of physics," and therefore "we must be prepared to find a new type of physical
law prevailing in it."[21] We may hazard a guess that when the new type of law
is discovered, it will turn out to be a law of final causation, in the sense here
proposed.

The proper meaning of teleology is that first given to it by Kant when, in
The Critique of Judgement, he wrote:

> It is requisite to a thing as natural end (or purpose) first that the parts (as
> regards their existence and their form) are possible through their relation to
> the whole. For, consequently, the thing itself is an end conceived under a
> concept or an idea which must determine a priori everything that is to be
> contained in it.

With like insight, he says in the preceding paragraph:

> a thing, which, as a product of nature, yet at the same time should possibly
> be regarded as purposive, must relate to itself reciprocally as cause and effect.[22]

It is the concept of the whole that thus operates as final cause, as Friedrich
Schelling, following up Kant's insight, recognized—the concept that Hegel el-
evated to the pinnacle of his logical dialectic.

Perhaps we may conclude that the adoption of this view of teleology, as the
governance of the part by the organizing principle of the whole, will prove
fruitful not only in disposing of old disputes but also in preserving the continuity in our conception of nature from the physicochemical to the biological,
and from the biological (since our model for teleology is consciously directed
action) to the psychological. To attempt by its means to solve the body-mind
problem might not seem too presumptuous; but that must be reserved for a
later chapter.

Notes

This chapter, with some modifications, originally appeared in *Journal of Philosophy*,
vol. 56, no. 1 (1959).

1. See E. R. Guthrie, "Purpose and Mechanism in Psychology", *Journal of Philosophy*,
   vol. 21, no. 25 (1924).
2. Thomas Hobbes, *Leviathan*, introduction.
3. Cf. R. B. Braithwaite, "Teleological Explanation," *Proceedings of the Aristotelian
   Society* vol. 47 (1946–47), p. iii.
4. R. G. Collingwood, *The New Leviathan*, 7.5.

5. E. W. Sinnott, *Cell and Psyche*, p. 20. He quotes in support, E. B. Wilson, J. H. Woodger, Herbert Muller, W. B. Cannon, R. G. Harrison, and Joseph Needham.

6. Cf. G. P. Wells and J. Huxley, *The Science of Life*, pp. 300–4.

7. Cf. Sinnott, *Cell and Psyche*, p. 27.

8. Cf. Wells and Huxley, *The Science of Life*, p. 512.

9. Ibid., p. 579.

10. Sinnott, *Cell and Psyche*, p. 24.

11. Lewis Thomas, *The Lives of a Cell*, p. 8.

12. Jaques Monod, *Le Hazard et la Necessité*, (Paris, 1970; Translated by A. Wainhouse as *Chance and Necessity*, p. 20.

13. Braithwaite, "Teleological Explanation," *Proceedings of the Aristotelian Society*, 157 (1946–7).

14. Ibid., p. 12.

15. Moritz Schlick, "Philosophy of Organic Life" reprinted in Feigl and Brodbeck, *Readings in the Philosophy of Science*, pp. 523–36.

16. Ibid., p. 530. It is interesting to note that Max Planck uses the same example as evidence from physical science of the existence of God in his *Scientific Autobiography*.

17. Ernest Nagel, "Teleological Explanation," reprinted in Feigl and Brodbeck, *Readings in the Philosophy of Science*, pp. 546, 550.

18. Ibid., p. 549.

19. bid., p. 553.

20. Cf. Joseph Needham, *Order and Life*, pp. 118–9.

21. E. Schroedinger, *What Is Life? and Other Scientific Essays*, pp. 76, 79, 81.

22. Cf. Immanuel Kant, *Kritik der Urteilskraft*, sec. 65:

> muß ein Ding, welches, als Naturprodukt, doch zugleich nur als Naturzweck möglich erkannt werden soll, sich zu sich wechselseitig als Ursach und Wirking verhalten....
>
> Zu einem Dinge als Naturzwecke wird nun erstlich erfordert, daß die Teile (ihrem Dasein und der Form nach) nur durch ihre Beziehung auf das Ganze möglich sind. Denn das Ding selbst ist ein Zweck, folglich unter einem Begriffe oder einer Idee befaßt, die alles, was in ihm enthalten sein soll, a priori bestimmen muß.

11

Mind and Teleology

1. ALTERNATIVES TO TELEOLOGY

By general consent, the model for teleological action is human self-conscious purpose, prompted by rational choice. That, we saw, is an activity of regulating impulses and desires to serve a harmonious and orderly life. Such an activity of organizing is the typical function of reason, about which more will have to be said in what follows. As a metaphysical theory undertakes to make the general nature of the real intelligible, it is obliged to account for every component of the world and must therefore give a coherent account of this organizing and regulating function of reason, along with all the other features of the real. This fact, of itself, imposes an inescapable character on metaphysical explanation, making teleology essential to its method. Why this should be so is what I propose next to explore, for it is far from being accepted by philosophers in general and is emphatically rejected by quite a few.

Metaphysical systems that place the ultimate principle of explanation in final causes, more especially in one ultimate final cause, are rightly described as teleological. Aristotle's and Hegel's systems, for example, attribute a teleological character to everything in the universe and to the universe as a whole. But there are others who either repudiate teleology altogether, maintaining that the only legitimate explanation that can be given of anything at all is by reference to efficient causation, including even mental events, or else tolerate teleological explanation for some kinds of processes but deny it of others.

A view of the world that countenances teleological explanation in some cases but does not require it in all would be obliged, in order to be consistent, to provide some explanation of the possibility and occurrence of the different types of process, teleological and nonteleological. It would be faced with the question how, in a nonteleological setting, teleological processes could arise. Some explanatory principle would have to be provided to bridge the gap between the two types of phenomena. At the other extreme, a view that denied the need for or the possibility of teleological explanation altogether would have to base its prohibition on some imputed or discovered general character of

152

things by virtue of which the alternative principle of explanation proved adequate in all cases.

Among the majority of scientists and philosophers today, teleology is largely taboo. A teleological account of biological processes, of evolution, or of physiological function (that term notwithstanding), or even of animal behavior is shunned as the hallmark of unscientific mystery-mongering, be the theory vitalistic, theistic, or whatever. If this rejection is well founded, it must be based on some alternative, presumably more reliable, conception of the nature of things, and one that is in itself more intelligible than that which supports teleology. It will rest, therefore, on the presupposition of some alternative metaphysic. That this is necessarily the case is an unpalatable suggestion to many scientists, who frequently despise metaphysics as unverifiable, or unfalsifiable, by experiment and observation; nor will it be welcomed by those philosophers who realize, or at least sense, the close connection between metaphysics and teleology and so repudiate both with equal emphasis. If teleological explanation rests on one kind of metaphysic, it can be opposed or disavowed only on the ground, acknowledged or latent, of some other kind of metaphysic, and any attempt to ignore or evade this fact can result only in indefensible dogmatism.

In recent times, certain non- and antiteleological views have been current among scientists and philosophers, that can be shown to be incoherent because they involve mutually conflicting assumptions, to which they are driven by the necessity of explaining undeniable facts. The undeniable facts that must be accounted for are human reflective awareness and the consequent possibility of orderly and systematic knowledge of the world, from which that of organized purposive behavior follows. They are undeniable, because any denial of them must be self-refuting.

Significantly, to deny the existence of self-reflective awareness (as Descartes showed), one must be reflectively aware. In order to deny the existence of orderly and systematic knowledge with any degree of credibility, one must possess some ordered and systematic knowledge on which to base the denial. To deny the occurrence of purposive behavior is itself to perform a purposive act. The phenomena of human experience are thus key facts that any view of the world must accommodate and, if it is to be intelligible, must satisfactorily explain. One may, therefore, take as a criterion of tenability the degree to which a metaphysical theory is able coherently to account for human self-awareness and rationality.

A teleological metaphysic is least likely to have difficulty in satisfying this criterion because human action is commonly recognized as the legitimate sphere of teleological explanation, and a metaphysic of this sort tends to explain the processes of lower nature, both physical and biological, in terms of an evolution that culminates in human mentality, and human mentality itself is explained by reference to transcendental ideas or ideals, or to some all-embracing holistic principle. Such a metaphysic, therefore, is usually (at least) humanistic and idealist, or theistic and transcendental, or is describable by some other suitable combination of these epithets.

A mixed doctrine, envisaging both teleological and nonteleological processes, tends when pressed to revert to one or the other, for unless it appeals to teleological principles to explain the nonteleological, or reduces the teleological processes to nonteleological, it is forced to maintain a radical dualism. Any attempt to account for interrelation and interaction between the two types of process then brings the consistency of the theory into jeopardy.

Consequently, the rejection of teleology is liable to be wholehearted and to attempt explanation of everything, not even excepting human mentality, solely by efficient causes. It is committed to a reduction of all processes to some nonteleological form, including any kind of evolution or development, any apparent purposive behavior, and even human subjectivity itself. Such a doctrine is physicalistic, commonly mechanistic in some significant sense, and atheistic—for clearly the introduction of God as creator or director of mundane events would be a new infiltration of teleology. Let us examine this type of theory to begin with. It is not necessary to criticize the work of any individual philosopher; all that is needed is to consider what may be (and usually is) held by anyone who resolutely sets out to exclude from the theory every suggestion of teleology. I shall try to show that this cannot consistently be done, and shall then give attention to the alternative view and outline briefly its salient characteristics.

2. NONTELEOLOGICAL METAPHYSICS

PHYSICALISM

The doctrine known as physicalism maintains that all events without exception can in the last resort be accurately described in the language of physical science. As the term was originally used by Carnap and the Vienna Circle, it was intended to refer only to semantic analysis and was not supposed to have any metaphysical implications, but it is clear that if language bears any significant relation to its referent, metaphysical implications are unavoidable. What is accurately describable in the language of physical science must be of the same nature as the object of physical science, so the implication is that if everything is so describable, everything must be simply physical, or reducible to what is simply physical, in actual fact. The direct effect of the doctrine, therefore, is to foster the belief that reality is purely material, that all events obey the laws of physics exclusively, and that they can be fully and satisfactorily explained by those laws.

Further, if teleology is to be rigidly excluded, the laws of physics cannot be regarded as laws of order and system, for there must be no immanent principle of organization in the nature of things to guide processes or to regulate the structure of facts. Any such principle would work teleologically, because it would have to be one that systematically brought into existence orderly arrangements of elements where none had previously existed. The laws of physics must therefore be taken as exclusively statistical laws from which the probability of occurrence may be deduced of specific randomly occurring events under stated initial conditions. Primordial physical processes would have to be some sort of purely random movement of particles or energy exchanges, and any semblance of order or structure would arise by chance in the primordial chaos. Thus physical laws would be the laws of probability stating the mathematical relationships between these chance events.

In a world of this nature, orderly structures occurring by chance would persist if circumstances permitted but would disintegrate if the random changes were such as to make their survival impossible. Any accidental structure that happened to include an arrangement resistant to dissolution would have relatively superior survival value and would be "naturally selected." Further chance complications in structure selected in this way could increase their survival value, and so more complex and "better adapted" entities could progressively come into being in an evolutionary sequence based entirely on chance variation and natural selection. We must emphasize at this stage that natural selection contributes nothing positive to the increase of complexity and adaptiveness of systems. It simply eliminates those that are least capable of surviving. Every positive addition is made by chance mutation, the probability of which is, presumably, to be statistically assessed. In this way, it has been submitted, the entire range of natural forms that we observe could have come into existence, from the starry heavens to living organisms, including (presumably) conscious, thinking, theorizing scientists.

The reduction by scientists of living processes to chemistry and physics is well advanced and may seem to support this sort of doctrine. Neo-Darwinism, the view of biological evolution as requiring nothing beyond chance mutation and natural selection, has been widespread among biologists in recent years. Behaviorism, which discounts introspective descriptions of conscious experience and claims to account for so-called intelligent activity solely by reference to publicly observable events (waiving any question about the nature of the public observation itself) is a further manifestation of the same metaphysical tendency, and associated with it is the enterprise of constructing purely mechanical theories of purposive behavior by means of cybernetics and servomechanisms; at the same time thinking is explained away as an operation at least analogous to that of digital computers. The degree of success or failure with which these several projects have met is not our present concern,[1] but there are certain general considerations that are fatal to the whole position.

What has so far been posited is a range of entities of increasingly complex

structure and behavior involving progressive advance in organization and mutually adjusted variety of form. By the time living organisms are reached, the
degree of this complexity and the intricacy and nicety of the adjustments becomes prodigious to the point of incalculability. But the fundamental assumption of the entire metaphysical outlook under scrutiny is that everything occurs
in accordance with laws that are statistical, and where statistical laws apply, the
overriding principle of activity is the second law of thermodynamics, according
to which, in any closed system, entropy (or disorder) continuously increases. It
is assumed that all activity is primarily random movement, and where random
movement prevails, the occurrence of nonrandom arrangement is improbable.
The improbability increases with the degree of order, and increases exponentially
as any series of events successively enhancing orderly structure continues.

   As the total sum of physical reality, the universe is more or less by definition
and nature a closed system; yet the account given by contemporary science of
its history is throughout evolutionary—the story of progressive increase in order and complication. That living species have evolved from less complex living forms is generally accepted, and nowadays it is confidently assumed that
living organisms have evolved from nonliving in a continuous process. But the
second law of thermodynamics should make all this so stupendously improbable as to amount to virtual impossibility.

   According to that law, the emergence of ordered wholes from the chaos of
random movement should be rare, and the probability of stable arrangements
should always be very low. If stable arrangement should ever occur, its modification in the direction of greater stability or more orderly complexity would
be more improbable than its first occurrence. The probability that this should
occur successively and with increasing stability, as has been said, decreases
exponentially, so that the emergence of life and the evolution of organisms as
staggeringly complex and as delicately adapted to changes in the environment
as are contemporary species is incalculably improbable. In point of fact, when
we come to living things we find that, by sacrificing stability to adaptability,
the system succeeds in maintaining a dynamic equilibrium of the most delicate
sensitivity, a state of affairs statistically improbable beyond belief. Thus the
whole conception of a purely physical universe subject to statistical laws but
including evolutionary series of events that generate increasingly complex orders
is incoherent and self-contradictory—or at the very best incredibly unlikely.

   Arguments to refute or to mitigate this judgment, however, have been offered. It has been said that the improbability of evolution is lessened by natural selection, for the multiplication of better adapted forms increases the probability
that one of them may change in the direction of advance. But first, the accumulation of ordered structure is itself highly improbable, and second, natural
selection is strictly inapplicable to anything except a self-reproducing system,
which is subject in its self-generation to mutations. What has no structure has

no clear individuality to preserve or select, and one that is self-reproducing must already be highly complex and adaptive. What does not reproduce itself, if it persists, has not been "selected"; and if it does not persist, it simply disintegrates. Self-replication by a complex system, however, is an event of immense improbability presupposing a whole train of extremely improbable events at the inorganic level. Even if this objection is waived, it remains true that natural selection, even if it is assumed to operate, has no positive effect and so cannot increase the probability of any kind of variation. Changes occur (it is presumed) by chance; if they have survival value, the changed entity is obviously more likely to survive, but it is not more likely to change in any manner either favorable or unfavorable to survival in subsequent hostile conditions. In a highly complicated and already unstable living organism, any change increasing survival value is always far less likely than the opposite. Nothing is really "selected" by natural selection (the word, in fact, implies conscious choice, and it was suggested to Charles Darwin by the deliberate practice of breeders of domestic animals; thus it surreptitiously reintroduces teleology); what cannot survive is simply eliminated. Accordingly, the probability of evolutionary advance is not increased by natural selection.

It may be argued in response that however improbable long evolutionary progressions may be, given enough time, they may still occur in an assemblage of randomly moving particles sufficiently numerous. The degree of improbability, however, may be judged from the calculation (quoted earlier from Kauffman) of the odds against the accidental assembling of a bacterium, estimated at 1 in $10^{20} \times 2000$. The time needed to actualize so minute a probability would far exceed what astrophysicists estimate to be the age of the universe. This is much too short to accommodate even the chance of assembling a single bacterium, let alone the whole course of human evolution, which has taken place within a few thousand million years.

A more serious objection however, than any so far offered to this metaphysical stance as a whole is fatal to its basic assumption—namely, the primordial occurrence of random activity. Random movement is conceivable only if there is some kind of particle or element the motion of which can be random. The idea could reasonably have been entertained in the nineteenth century and earlier, when physicists thought of fundamental particles as minute, hard, impenetrable spheres of matter moving about in space under the contingent influence of impressed forces. It can sensibly be assumed in the kinetic theory of gases, where one is dealing with large, but definitely denumerable, assemblages of molecules within a confined space. But in contemporary physics, particles are concomitant with energy fields, and their motion is integral to the energy system. Even free-moving particles attached to no particular group, such as neutrons expelled from atoms under bombardment, are seen as wave packets, presupposing some wave field in which the waves have become superposed. As soon as one speaks of waves, one is committed to the concept of periodicity and ordered structure, for that is precisely what a wave is. In the very nature of matter, then, order and system of some sort are prior to distinguishable particles. Hence it cannot be the case that order arises only by chance as a result of the random motion of preexistent particles.

The exclusion of teleology from any account of the world, moreover, forbids the admission of order and system as a necessary product of physical activity, for if it were to occur by necessity, as the result of an ordering principle inherent in the nature of energy and matter, the process would be teleological. In that case, it is not possible to found a nonteleological metaphysics on the presumption that all events obey the laws of physics, if those laws are the ones established by contemporary science.

AGNOSTIC COSMOLOGY

The antiteleologist may, nevertheless, think that there is still an avenue of escape, although it involves a somewhat drastic renunciation on the part of the scientist. Our science, it may be said, which discovers structure and order in the most elementary physical matrix, is simply constrained by the nature of our thinking, which necessarily imposes order on its subject matter. If we are to understand what we experience, we must subject it to some principles of organization, and our science is the result of this subjective ordering. What the actual nature of the world is we do not and cannot know, and it does not follow from the fact that our science offers a model of a structured and evolutionary world that reality is teleologically ordered. Edward Harrison goes so far as to say that none of our cosmologies is likely to be true of the real world. There have been, during the history of science, numerous world-pictures, he reminds us, all of which, except the most recent, have been rejected as false or even as ridiculous, and we have no assurance that the current one will not suffer a similar fate—rather the contrary.[2]

Other scientists have offered objections based on less speculative considerations. Modern quantum physics, they contend, reveals an ultimate indeterminacy and incomprehensibility in physical reality. All we can do is calculate the probability of the behavior of the ultimate entities, and all our knowledge is but statistical. Moreover, the probabilistic character of quantum physics, because it is fundamental to chemistry and biology, infects the whole of science. Thus, reality, so far as we have any indication of its nature, seems to be wholly random and unaccountable in its underlying activity. Witness the behavior of an atom in a radioactive substance. One may say with confidence that at some time within a calculable period it will disintegrate; but just when, or why, or why this atom rather than the next, or what cause or stimulus will set it off— these questions are simply, and in principle, unanswerable. Although there is thus in the final analysis no rational character in the behavior of the fundamental microentities of the world, the vast numbers of random movements involved allow of an averaging out and an appearance of uniformity and regularity that enable us to formulate general laws and make predictions reliable for practical purposes. But these are at best approximations and are useful to us in the conduct of our lives, giving us a measure of control over our environment. They are, however, no evidence of any ultimate or intrinsic order in the nature of things. The averaging out, however, is either solely the result of human thinking and calculation presenting nothing real or an actual effect of the allegedly random physical activity. If it is the latter, it must be due to some organizing influence producing order out of chaos, like the strange attractors revealed in complex dynamic systems by chaos theory. In that case, teleology would have to be admitted, and teleological explanation would be legitimized.

Kant, who adopted an epistemological position similar but not identical to this, left the question open whether things in themselves might after all constitute a teleological system. But modern philosophers, who hold similar views, seem ready to assert more dogmatically that the real is no more than a random succession of atomic particular events without any systematic order, although science imposes order on what we observe such as will make our experience of these bare particulars intelligible.

Any such theory is bound to be incoherent. If our minds (be it by averaging out or by the very nature of thinking) impose order upon experience, though the reality is utter chaos, then our science, and experience generally, are little better than sheer illusion, and it is hard to see how any such spurious ordering could enable us to act successfully in a really chaotic world—unless, of course, our experience of our own behavior were equally illusory, and we lived in a perpetual dreamworld of order and purpose. Even that, however, is an inconsistent presumption. For what we cannot deny is that we do experience a world and that it is, within tolerable limits, systematic and orderly, and that science, so far as it achieves its aim of understanding, subjects our experience of it to more rigorous ordering. Similarly, in our practical life, so far as we act intelligently, we act in an orderly and systematic fashion and strive to harmonize our relations with our environment, both natural and human. Accordingly, our intelligent activity is systematic. But we ourselves, and our activity, practical and intellectual, are part of the world and are actual events. This we cannot deny without self-refutation, because the denial itself would be evidence of its own contrary. But if the world, by nature and in essence, were chaotic, if it consisted merely of a random succession of bare particulars, intelligent, organizing minds could not arise within it. They could not evolve out of totally random motions of completely qualityless particles, for what does not contain within it the conditions of systematic activity cannot spontaneously produce system. We have already disposed of the argument that order of sufficient extent might have occurred by chance within the timescale available, and if some self-organizing principle is presupposed, that would reintroduce teleology, and a process running counter to the second law of thermodynamics. Add to all this the considerations put forward above that disorder is, in the final analysis, parasitic on order, because it presupposes some sort of ordered entities to be randomized (shuffling faceless cards creates neither order nor disorder), and the proposed metaphysic breaks down completely.

The only possible escape from this self-refutation is to hold that our minds are totally other than and different from the material world and are not part of it. But if we were to embrace this radical dualism, we should be hard put to understand what sort of relation could exist between our minds and our bodies. Either they could not belong to the same world and thus could not belong to one another, and any sort of interaction between them would be, if not wholly impossible, an inscrutable mystery; or what appear to us as our bodies must be mere figments of our imagination that do not in the least correspond to the real material entities to which our minds are somehow supposed to be attached. At the same time, the relation between our minds and the real world would be totally unintelligible, and what we claim to know as the material world would be just another figment. In short, we should have no knowledge or science, for what aspires to those names must be true. So we should be committed either to unmitigated skepticism or to a Berkelean subjective idealism tottering on the slippery slope that leads to solipsism and the ultimate abysm of incoherence. This is the sorry denouement of any attempt to account by a purely physicalist and nonteleological theory for the rational and orderly operation of our minds.

3. TELEOLOGICAL METAPHYSICS

Captious critics may call into question the meaning given to the world "teleology" throughout the foregoing discussion, for it embraces as teleological any active principle or process that creates order out of relative disorder—or, as communication engineers would say, extracts message from noise—any process, in fact, that reduces entropy or increases information (in the literal sense of imposing form on the unformed). Teleological activity, the critic may say, is only what seeks a goal, what pursues a purpose. Nevertheless, despite etymology, I believe that the extension of the meaning of the word to all organizing activity is legitimate; for although "*telos*" means "end," and we generally restrict the term "teleological" to processes that tend toward some preconceived goal, goal-seeking activities are only special cases of informed or informing behavior. What actively seeks a goal acts in accordance with a plan or rule of behavior, and rule implies order and system. Conscious purpose, which is the paradigm case of teleological activity, is explicitly action in accordance with a plan or by design. It is action variable according to some rule, which adapts itself to changing conditions in a systematic fashion in order to achieve its purposes, which is not necessarily its final stage (as already noticed) but which does involve the completion of some *pattern* of activity.

No metaphysical theory can overlook this systematic and ordering propensity of our own conscious life, if only because that is itself involved in the very attempt to excogitate a metaphysical theory. This is true even of an antisystematic philosophy like Existentialism, for a philosopher who reflects upon experience and finds it absurd must use some criterion of rationality by which to condemn it. If then he or she adopts a theory of life and action that enables him or her, as philosopher, to accept the absurd and be reconciled to it, to transcend and overcome its effects, he or she does so by virtue of a rational capacity. This rational capacity must somehow be the product of the irrational world and so must in some way mitigate its absurdity. Existentialism, in fact, by its refusal to surrender subjective freedom to an external and objective analysis, is insisting upon the very point here being made: that human conscious existence must be taken into account by any metaphysic, and that none that fails to accommodate it can stand. This failure is typical of every sort of nonteleological metaphysics, because it excludes from the fundamental nature of things any active principle of orderly creation.

It follows that a consistent and successful metaphysic has to be teleological. The metaphysician must expect to find some positive principle at work in the world that creates order, increases information, and reduces chaos or "noise"; this principle cannot be rejected, because in its absence, there could be no thinker in the world to seek philosophical comprehension of the nature of things, and so no metaphysician. This is an a priori reason for expecting the world to be teleological, and a sound one. It has surfaced in contemporary physics as the Anthropic Cosmological Principle, which states that we observe the universe to be as it is because we are here to observe; for, if the universe did not provide the conditions necessary for the emergence of intelligent life, there would be no scientists. In effect, this is a truism, but it is not, on that account, insignificant. And science provides the empirical evidence and empirical reasons for maintaining that there must be some teleological principle operative in the nature of things. It tells us that random activity increases entropy and that long evolutionary processes are too improbable to be accidental, and it also shows us that they occur. It discovers, besides, that elementary particles are features of energy systems, without which there could be no activity judged as random; and if we accept Schroedinger's arguments, the particles themselves are *Gestalten*, or relatively persistent patterns of wave motion. In short, the primary physical activity is already informed. If this be so, the fundamental assumption even of physics must be the prevalence of system and structure, and random activity can be conceived only in relation to some form of order.

Prima facie, order in the universe might be conceived in either of two ways:

it might be complete from the start and all-pervasive, or it might be thought to appear germinally in a chaotic matrix and realize itself progressively through an evolutionary process. These alternatives, however, are only apparent, for each requires and implies the other. It is not easy to demonstrate this in a short space, and the ensuing argument must be condensed to fit it into a single chapter.

That evolution can begin germinally within a chaotic matrix has now been discredited, because there is no chaotic matrix to be found. Further, the maintenance and augmentation of organic structures by a series of accidental variations have been shown to be too improbable to contemplate—unless, of course, one were prepared to assume some extraneous divine creative influence. Either way, any evolutionary account of the presence of order in the world must somehow accommodate the concept of an all-pervasive order. Order necessarily implies wholeness, for every pattern, structure, or system must be complete if it is to be such. The very concepts of incompleteness and partiality imply a whole to which the part belongs and that completes the unfinished fragment. Even a continuous series, like the series of natural numbers, which, although ordered in regular sequence, is endless, may be regarded as a totality or set, as in Cantor's conception of transfinite numbers. Further, the order of such a series consists in its being generated according to a precise rule. But this is not the paradigm case of order, in the sense of system, which requires structure, as it were, in depth, and self-closure, and which precludes endless progression. This is the reason why Hegel refers to unending series as false infinites, because they are, as he says, never complete but are endlessly finite.

The progressive realization of order, therefore, implies the existence (in some sense), the subsistence, or just the projection in idea of the totality that is being progressively realized and will, in principle, constitute the consummation of the process. The projection of the totality in idea presupposes an already high degree of realization, for only a thinker can conceive such a whole, and a thinker inhabits a highly developed, highly complex and integrated organism, performing an activity of ordering and structuring at an advanced level of coherence. What is being projected, therefore, is something already to a great extent realized, and the projection is possible only by virtue of that realization and by presupposition of the completed process. Thus Descartes could argue that to have the idea of a perfect being implies a cause of the idea which already contains "formally" or "eminently" as much reality as the idea contains "objectively." Apart from the actualized whole, it is not possible to conceive the part, projection from which would realize its complementation.

The process, moreover, is teleological—one in which the operative principle of progression must be a nisus to the whole and must be the principle of organization that pervades the whole. If it were not, the progressive realization of order would be accidental, and that, we have found, is virtually ruled out by the law of probability. Reality in some form, therefore, cannot be denied to that whole the ordering principle of which is actually operative in the process of generation, just as it is impossible to deny the existence of order prior to that of elementary particles because they are products of the energy field. As the process is teleological, it can be fully understood and explained only in the light of its completion.

Thus, unless the totality were in some sense real, nothing would be intelligible. It is not enough to call it simply potential, for what is potential is also in some sense actually present (however difficult it may be to understand in just what sense). The potential is what the actual has it in it to become, which, if it were not in some degree actual, would not be the case. It is not yet what Aristotle called *energeia*, but it is nevertheless present in potency in the process of actualization, and that is as much as to say that the actualized form is in some way operative (potent) from the start. It is, as Aristotle maintained, the final cause. To call it potential is to say that it is partially actual, but that is no less than, by implication, to claim reality for that whole of which it is the potential realization. The progressive evolution of a whole posits the reality of the form of the realized whole. This is the basis of the ontological argument for the existence of God.

If the universe is identified, as it is by Spinoza, with the actual ordered totality, the exclusion of evolution is only apparent (a fact that reveals itself in Spinoza's system, as I have tried to show in other contexts).[3] The totality cannot manifest itself as a whole in any one point or at any one time, nor can it be understood as a whole (in all its detail) in any one judgment. Both it and the knowledge of it must therefore, in order to be complete, unfold itself as a series or growth. Any part, or element, or phase, insofar as it is a part of the whole, implies the totality and so contains it in potentiality—it is a germ of the whole, from which the development can proceed. The totality is thus at once immanent in the part and transcendent beyond it. Further, it is transcendent beyond any mere sum or assemblage of parts, so far as it is an organizing principle that constitutes a form or configuration that is not realized in anything short of the consummated totality—just as the collection of lines and colors that make up a pattern when suitably arranged, apart from that arrangement, falls short of the pattern itself; or the elements and chemical processes that make up an organism, by themselves when disorganized, are not alive and, as a mere collection, are transcended by the life of the organic unity.

We come closer to the correct conception of such a system or ordered whole when we realize that it is not, and in the nature of the case could not be, a static quasi-spatial pattern but is a process or activity proceeding dialectically from less to more complex forms of organized unity. Even a spatial pattern is realized in this way. If it seems otherwise, it is only because we are unable to perceive any but relatively small patterns and are unaware of the eye movements involved in the perception. We learn from the theory of relativity that there is no simultaneity at a distance. Over large areas, distant positions cannot be grasped simultaneously, and any extended spatial arrangement can be realized only through motion between separate points.

The antithetical alternatives presented above turn out to be dialectically contrasting and opposed aspects of the same thing. An evolutionary series taken as a whole is an organic system, as is the growth of a germ cell into a mature animal. Each stage in the development is the whole organism at that stage; it is both a prefiguration of the ultimate totality, with a specific degree of adequacy to its fully developed character, and, as a specific stage in the process, it implies (through its relations to them) the other phases of the development. Accordingly, it is at once the implicate whole and a stage in its development.

However low in the scale we descend, we never reach zero, because there is no zero in the scale. "In order to be anything, it is necessary to begin by being something." As each phase is implicitly what is throughout coming to fulfillment, the whole is always immanent. As the development proceeds, nothing is lost and something is continually gained, so that at every stage the prior process is summed and preserved as well as (relatively) fulfilled and transcended. Consequently, the final phase must be at once "the end," transcendent beyond anything anterior to it in the process, and the entire process itself—the system or totality that sublates and enfolds the entire process and is one with it. It must be transcendentally and eternally whole, yet everlastingly self-realizing.

All this can be (and often is) alternatively expressed in the religious language of theism. God is the all-embracing *Ens realissimum* in whom everything lives and moves and has its being. He is the source and ground, the creative principle of all things, immanent in all things, and transcendent beyond all things—eternally real, eternally active, and everlastingly self-manifesting in and as the world.

The conclusion reached is that nonteleological metaphysic cannot escape self-contradiction and incoherence, and that an adequate and self-consistent metaphysic cannot be materialistic or atheistic but must be teleological, dialectical, theistic, and transcendental.

Notes

1. Cf., however, Hubert L. Dreyfus, "Why Computers Must Have Bodies in Order to Be Intelligent," *Review of Metaphysics*, vol. 21 (1967), and *What Computers Can't Do*; also Roger Penrose, *The Emperor's New Mind: Concerning Computers, Minds, and the Laws of Physics*.
2. Edward Harrison, *Masks of the Universe*.
3. Cf. E. E. Harris, *Nature, Mind and Modern Science*, chap. 11, and *Salvation from Despair: A Reappraisal of Spinoza's Philosophy*.

Part 4
Mind

12

The Relation of Mind to Body

1. DUALISM, PRO AND CON

The revolt against dualism is nothing new, as the title of Lovejoy's well-known book testifies, and belief in a dualism of body and mind is, for many persuasive reasons, seductive. In fact, the persistent appeal of the dualistic opinion may well be, in itself, evidence that something inexorable in the nature of mind requires us to retain some duality in our conception of personality. On the other hand, none of the various dualistic theories that have been offered has succeeded in making the relation between body and mind intelligible, and reaction against them is easily understandable. To find it, we need go back no further than to Hobbes and Gassendi, who resolved the problem by reducing the activity of the mind to matter and motion, which is one of the short ways of disposing of it; the other being Berkeley's, of reducing all matter to idea.

These are such easy, such economical, and such convenient ways of dispensing with the awkward and inexplicable concomitances of colors, sound, scents, and tastes with vibrations (electromagnetic or atmospheric) and chemical reactions that either the materialistic or the idealistic course would surely have gained universal acclaim long since, if intractable difficulties had not attended them both. Those who advocate the materialistic remedy seem never to face up to the problem implicit in Hobbes' inadvertent admission that, although sensible qualities are (as he says) no more than "so many several motions of the matter" pressing on our organs, "their appearance to us is Fancy." In what sense is an *appearance* of whatever kind a material motion? How can an electromagnetic vibration constitute a seeming? To what or whom, and in what manner, could neural activity (electrical discharges in nerve cells), *in* and *per se*, become representation (what Kant called *Vorstellung*) of some totally different object? On the other side, Berkeley and his followers leave unanswered the questions what our experience of our own bodies could possibly amount to, and why it is (as they themselves admit) the essential precondition of all our knowledge. If *esse est percipi*, how is it that whatever is perceived appears to be material?

166

The most obvious pretexts for rejecting either sort of monism are not far to seek. The activity of the body and, in particular, of the brain has spatiotemporal and physical characteristics that do not seem attributable to feelings, percepts, and thoughts or, if attributable at all, are so in quite different ways. Thus neural discharges travel along fibers and trace reticular patterns in the brain, but the experiences found to be concomitant with them do not. A sound has no spatial properties (or only such as are derived from extraneous associations), whereas discharges in the temporal lobe have. The apprehension of a mathematical relationship has no shape or position and might even, with some plausibility, be denied temporal predicates. The appreciation and enjoyment of a joke cannot be described in spatial terms.

Again, when what we call acts of mind, or experiences, do have spatiotemporal characters, they are not those of the neural processes thought or found to accompany them. A perceived or an imagined scene has a quite different spatial structure from the brain activity on which it is taken to be (and most probably is) dependent. A color patch, whether an afterimage, or a percept, or only imaginary, is seen "out there" and not inside the viewer's head. Even if it is argued that it might be inside the brain but appears to be "out there," because visual images are habitually projected to the external world, what is this *appearance* in terms of neural activity? How is what occurs in the brain "projected" into outer space? How could a pattern of neural activity (if that is what the image is) be conceived as projecting itself into a different spatial position, which it does not in fact occupy? Apart from appearances, afterimages and mental images of whatever sort, although extended, can hardly be said to occupy physical space in any valid sense; yet nobody doubts that the accompanying neural activity does so. Moreover, so-called secondary qualities generally give interminable trouble, for physical science can find no place for them, only for their neural counterparts. It knows only electromagnetic waves, atmospheric disturbances, and the like, entities with only primary qualities. Neurophysiology, at the same time, can do no better, for all it discovers is electrochemical activity, the transmission of electrical potential along nerve fibers. Where, then, are the secondary qualities to reside if not "in the mind"?

Further, what goes on in a person's brain does so for a limited time and occupies a relatively confined space within the skull, but the human mind can range, in perception, imagination, and thought, over the whole universe of space and time. Attempts are made to meet this difficulty, as a rule, by pointing to the symbolic and referential nature of mental (and, presumably, if less intelligibly, of brain) activity. But how does something spatiotemporally restricted refer beyond itself to what is spatiotemporally remote? A written or verbal symbol is by itself meaningless and inert—a mere mark on paper or a mere noise—unless interpreted and understood by a mind; otherwise, it can refer to nothing whatsoever. What sort of account can be given of interpretation purely in terms of neural activity? Here, no doubt, the contemporary materialist will appeal to behavior and will maintain that interpretation is reducible to the appropriate observable response to the presence of the symbol, and will contend that the behavior can be analyzed and described as neuromuscular. This is a subtle and attractive doctrine, but, as will presently be shown, it assumes a knowledge of appropriateness for which the proferred analysis finds no place.

In the face of these difficulties, dualistic theories retain their appeal, but it by no means follows that they remove them, or do not themselves give rise to others equally formidable, if not worse. We are all familiar with the disastrous epistemological consequences of causal, representative, and picture theories of perception, and of the frustrations of interactionism, parallelism, and epiphenomenalism. Modern advances in physiology have given scientists so much confidence in their ability to account for living movement entirely by physiological laws that the first of these three traditional theories nowadays finds least favor. If room is still found for experiences and mental phenomena, they can (so it seems) be regarded only as epiphenomenal, or as constituting a parallel series of events the causal connections of which with their physiological counterparts remain totally obscure. Consequently, Herbert Feigl, who demanded as the requirement of explanatory adequacy a coherent "nomological net" into which all events must fall, deplores the belief in mental events—as what he calls "nomological danglers"[1]—and seeks to tie them in by identifying them unreservedly with the neural activities from which they are alleged to dangle.

I propose to consider the arguments offered in favor of this kind of neural-identity and to show that they fail of their purpose. The theory as advocated by recent writers is inadequate and question-begging, but a monistic position can be set out, to which the neural-identity theory is a sort of halfway house, which is better able to account for our common experience and which can still accept the dualist's reasons for wishing to separate the mind from the body.

2. NEURAL-IDENTITY THEORIES

The main tenets of the view to be examined are as follows:

1. States of consciousness just are brain states. Mental activity is neural activity. They are identical, so there is only one set of events, not two; which, however, is describable in two different ways, or in two different languages.

2. The identity of the referents of the two descriptions is not logical or necessary but purely contingent. It just happens to be the case that conscious states are brain states, as it just happens to be a fact—not logically necessary—that clouds consist of minute water droplets.

3. The terms used in the neurophysiological description of brain states are not synonymous with those used in the phenomenological description of

conscious experiences. Their logic is not the same, and it is not (always, if ever) possible to translate sentences in the one language directly into sentences of the other.[2]

Because the identity is contingent, the credibility of the theory need not be impaired by the facts that statements about conscious states are not intended to be and are not, in fact, about brain processes,[3] and that we can describe the former without knowing of the existence of the latter.[4] Because the two sorts of statement do not *mean* the same (because their logical grammar is different), it is possible that our present theories of neural activity might even prove false, without prejudice to the neural-identity hypothesis; for "private" experiences might still be actually identical with some physiological functionings, though not with those we now think. The language of "private" experience has the logic we give it because we have (as yet) no better evidence of the occurrence of mental states (except our own) than the introspective reports of the experiencer.[5] So we may even imagine ourselves or others having experiences though our bodies were turned to stone or without any bodies at all.[6] In actual fact, however, nothing of the sort might be possible if the experiences happened to be identical with brain processes, as the theory alleges. Our being able to imagine it is simply evidence of the contingency of the identity.

The trouble with secondary qualities and the like is avoided by treating them behavioristically in terms of ability to discriminate, for which (so J. J. C. Smart contended) the precise nature of the *qualia* experienced is of little importance.[7] And the fact that the experiences seem to have quite different properties from those of brain processes is overcome by assigning some of the properties to the objects of experience and seeking to deny the rest or to explain them away in terms of behavior which can be described without reference to private phenomena.[8]

In outline, this is the position to be examined. How far is it proof against criticism?

The identity of conscious experiences with neural processes is said by Smart to be strict identity, not just a temporal (or spatiotemporal) coincidence. The neural process strictly is the experience and is all that it is. But when one examines the arguments used to meet the more obvious objections—that the description of experiences is not that of brain processes, that what we are aware of when we see colors, or feel pain, etc. is not a brain process—one is hard put to understand just what sort of identity it is that is to be called "strict." When *A* is identified with *a*, it is because they possess some common character, relation, or reference, despite different appearances. There must be some singular foundation of the identity. What this can be in the case of brain states and consciousness is difficult to determine. Place and Smart have tried to explain the nature of the identity by the help of analogous examples, such as the identity of the evening star with the morning star, of a flash of lightning with an electrical discharge, and of a cloud with a collection of minute water droplets.[9]

These examples are not uniform; the first is an identity of individuality, the second is not a genuine case of identity at all but is a confusion (presently to be exposed), and the third is an identity of composition. But the identity alleged of neural and mental process is not claimed to be any of these.

The evening and the morning stars are two different views of a single planet, obtained at different times. The identity of the planet can be established by various means. In both appearances it has identical properties and complementary sets of relations to other bodies from which its identity can be inferred. None of this is true of the alleged neuromental analogue.[10] The identity of the evening star with the morning star is, in fact, one of spatiotemporal continuity (like meeting Jones at breakfast and again at supper), and Smart denies that this is what he means by strict identity.

A flash of lightning is an electrical discharge, but it is not the discharge, as such, that is seen, but the flash. The flash is a bluish-white light, a sense-datum and not a physical entity. The physical entity is the emission of electromagnetic waves occasioned by the electrical discharge. Consequently, to identify either the flash of light, as seen, or the electromagnetic waves with the electrical discharge is to confuse cause with effect. Smart maintains that it is not the "look" of the lightning but the publicly observable flash that is identical with the electrical discharge. But the "look" and the flash (as seen) are the same thing. The publicly observable event is the discharge. There are only two terms in this relation, not three; there is the discharge and its visual appearance—the flash. Without and observer there can be no public observation, but also no observed flash, only an unobserved electrical discharge. So Smart is involved here with the relation between a secondary quality (color) and that in which it inheres, though he fails in this context to realize it. I shall return to this relationship presently, as it is crucial for his case.

The third analogy (used by Place) of the cloud of water droplets fails because nobody wishes to suggest that conscious states are *composed* of neural discharges in the way that the cloud is composed of droplets, or that wool is composed of fibers. Nor does anybody believe that brain states are made up of conscious experiences.

What sort of identity, then, is "strict identity" such as is said to obtain between mental and neural activity? We are told that it is an identity of the referent of two different languages, the physiological and the phenomenological. But can this be sustained? The languages are said to have different logical grammars, so that their terms and sentences have different meanings, although they both refer to the same identical events. Meaning, we are reminded (with due reference to Wittgenstein) is not a mental image or an external object for which a word stands but is the way in which it is used—its "logic." But it is surely false that the way in which a term is used (its logic) is entirely independent of, and indifferent to, that to which it refers. The use of the terms in a language is not wholly arbitrary (although it may be so in some cases); it is largely determined by the nature of the facts, or the feelings, that the language is used to express. If it is arbitrarily changed, what it conveys will be distorted. There may be considerable free play between usage and reference, but they cannot be wholly divorced. I may arbitrarily decide to use the word "cat" to refer to a wildflower and may make myself understood if the convention is consistently observed, but I could not communicate successfully if I made it refer indifferently to a feline quadruped, a wild flower, and a butterfly. If two different languages have the same referents, there must be some similarity or common character in their "logics." They must be mutually convertible in some way, as mathematically isomorphic calculi are mutually convertible. This is not the case with phenomenological and physiological languages. "I remember, I remember, the house where I was born" is not convertible into "There are such and such neural discharges occurring in my brain"; for to remember something is to distinguish and identify a past event, whereas the passage of ions along nerve fibers makes no reference to past events whatsoever. To say merely that the sentences do not mean the same because each language has it own peculiar logic may be true, but if so, it is to that extent at least prima facie evidence that they refer to quite different subjects and not to identical events.

If the terms do not mean the same, if what they describe have no properties in common, if their logics are diverse and the languages to which they belong are not mutually translatable, on what grounds can we identify their referents? What evidence of identity is there? In these circumstances, can "strict identity" have any significant meaning?

The sort of identity claimed is certainly ontological. An experience and a brain state are held to be ontologically one, and not two correlated events. In that case, experience as enjoyed must have either identical properties with the brain process or, if not, because they present different aspects of the same thing, then at least one would expect that some of the relations between experiences would be identical with corresponding relations between neural processes. And of this there should be scientific evidence. But such evidence as we have runs counter to this assumption. We assume, but do not know, that the temporal relations between them are identical, and even here, considerable doubts may be entertained in some cases, such for instance as remembering dream experiences. Beyond this there is definite evidence of considerable relational divergence between experiences and brain states.

In vision, the cortical projection of the retinal image is spread over a larger number of nerve cells in proportion to the acuity of vision appropriate to the stimulated area of the retina. Consequently, the spatial pattern of the neural excitation is quite different not only from that of the retinal image, but also from that of the visual object, and still more so from that of the physical entity seen. Quite apart from this, visual shapes are entirely different from the shapes of the neural activities that accompany them. The cortical excitation corresponding to a visually experienced circle occurs in two separated areas, one in each of the cerebral hemispheres, each shaped like a horseshoe, with the ventral end closed. Each horseshoe-shaped excitation corresponds to half of the circle, and although they are connected by fibers running through the *corpus callosum*, if these pathways are cut, the circle is still seen as a single whole. In what sense, then, are the brain process and the visual image identical? And how can we be justified in saying that they are?

Further, the nerve of a healthy tooth is delicately sensitive to the gentlest touch stimulus, and the neural activity of the response, as detected by insertion of a fine electrode into the nerve fiber, produces a stream of obvious potential waves. Laceration of the exposed nerve, however, which gives excruciating pain, causes a hardly noticeable difference in the electrical record, which a physiologist might well ignore if he or she knew nothing of the phenomenological facts.[11] It seems perverse to identify factually experiences and neural activities so widely different in quantitative and qualitative character.

One last consideration (although others could be cited) that tells heavily against identification of phenomenal and neural events is that all neural processes are of the same kind. They are all-or-nothing firings of neurons, transmitting negative potential along the fibers, in patterned arrangements whose spatial form is all that distinguishes them, whether their experienced counterpart is vision, hearing, touch, or some other affection; but the differences between these sensory modes are so radical as to make them virtually incomparable.

To all this, however, the protagonists of neural identity may retort that we are relying on the description of experience in terms of secondary qualities, which they consider as at best unimportant in the determination of behavior. We should replace them, they will say, by descriptions of discriminatory responses to stimuli, and these again can be analyzed into neural processes. Then it will become clear that what we commonly describe as an experience needs no phenomenal predicates but can be wholly identified with the neural activity that works the body's mechanisms and produces movement as well as more covert forms of behavior. Possibly even pain could be dealt with in this way and be classed with secondary qualities, for, as Berkeley showed, the effect of a less intense stimulus is attributed as a quality (or power) to the object (e.g., warmth), while the pain occasioned by a more intense stimulus (heat) is treated as purely subjective, although there is no essential difference between them other than intensity. A pain like toothache, accordingly, should be described entirely in terms of yelps and winces. Be that as it may, it is highly questionable whether a satisfactory account of behavior can ever be given that completely omits reference to secondary qualities (or experiences), though the implied reference may be obscure enough to be overlooked.

Smart objects to both of two views of the status of *qualia*: (i) that they are intrinsic to physical objects, and (ii) that they are properties of the sense-data produced in percipients by the action of physical objects upon their sense organs. He objects to the latter because it involves the nomological dangling to which Feigl has drawn attention, and also because if there were fundamental laws of science connecting *qualia* with the highly complex neural states supposed to produce them, they would have to relate simple entities with exceedingly complex structures. He objects to the former view because scientists have shown that the very complex visual mechanisms of human organisms respond to certain mixtures of wavelenghts arbitrarily determined by the structure of the neural apparatus, and it is on these mixtures that the colors depend. If the apparatus were different, quite different *qualia* would be experienced. This makes the view that *qualia* are intrinsic to the physical object highly implausible. Smart does admit that *qualia* are experienced[12] and play a part in the determination of behavior. What they are, however, he considers unimportant as long as, with their help, we can perform discriminatory responses. It is upon these alone that the concepts of the *qualia* (colors, in particular) depend.

This is so far true that in no way except by means of discriminatory responses (sometimes highly sophisticated) can any comparison be made between the private experiences of different persons, but it does not prove that the experienced *qualia* are identical with the discriminatory responses (rather the contrary, as we shall presently see) or with any part of them (e.g., the neural activity in the brain that is involved). Smart insists that the brain processes are not qualified by the *qualia*, the experiencing of which he holds them strictly to be; and if that is so, and if the *qualia* are not intrinsic to the physical objects *but are nevertheless experienced*, they become nomological danglers with no hooks to dangle from.

Yet it cannot be denied that they are experienced, for it is only by their means that the appropriate discriminations can be made. Smart seems to think that somehow he has evaded this fact because he can "elucidate the expression 'discriminate with respect to colour' without making use of the notion 'colour.'"[13] It means, he says, simply that the discrimination is made, but not with respect to shape, texture, smell, etc. However, the perception of shape, texture, and smell is just as much dependent on the sensing of *qualia* as is that of color; so if we know that a discrimination is made not with respect to these, it must surely be with respect to other *qualia*. Further, if we can distinguish the experience of these from the experience of color, how can we, without circularity, elucidate *this* discrimination while avoiding all reference to concepts of any of the types of *qualia* concerned?

Smart's account of color concepts dependent purely on the observation of discriminatory responses, begs the question in its key notion of "a normal percipient." This phrase is never directly defined. We are told only that one percipient is more normal than another if he or she can make discriminations that the other cannot. Unless this occurs consistently, as would probably be conceded, it would be insufficient, for if percipient *A* distinguished, shall we say, tomatoes from greengages on one occasion (which *B* failed to do) yet failed under similar conditions to distinguish chiles from french beans, we should hesitate to rate *A* more normal. But in order to know whether a percipient is discriminating consistently we must have some criterion of correct discrimination, and there is no such criterion of correct discrimination with *respect to color* except the experience and knowledge of the colors concerned. Smart knows that tomatoes are red and lettuce leaves green, so he can discern that those who distinguish them and who classify geraniums with tomatoes and grass with lettuce are normal; but unless he experienced the colors, or was taught the concepts and the right objects to which they should be applied by somebody who did experience colors, he could never distinguish normal percipients from abnormal. His ingenious account of the way in which blind men might acquire color concepts by observing the discriminatory reactions of their sighted slaves, even though the latter never used color terms in communicating with them, does not evade the ineluctable fact that the blind could do this only if they assumed that their sighted slaves were perceiving correctly and consistently whatever quality it was and according to which they discriminated.[14] If this were called into question, they would have no means of deciding the issue. Thus, if anybody tampered with the experiment by introducing new classifications not based on normal differences of hue but on some principle equally undetectable by the blind—let us say, saturation—the blind would be unable to distinguish one set of discriminatory responses from the other, and their assumed color concepts would become hopelessly confused.

In early Indo-European, color names referred to shades rather than to specific hues, a fact (possibly reflected in Homer's reference to "the wine-dark sea") that would give rise to very different color classifications from that based on simple hues. Yet both depend on the same color experiences, and nobody who lacked the experiences could explain the difference in principle between the two types of discrimination.

For a similar reason, no argument can legitimately be advanced that a sufficient criterion of correct and consistent discrimination would be its conformity to the practice of the majority of other people. For it has to be known that the majority are discriminating with *respect to color* and not (for instance) to visual texture or brightness or emotional tone, and there is no other criterion for establishing this than the experience of the relevant *qualia*. We can distinguish color from these other sorts of quality only if we can compare them in our experience.

Even though the capacity to discriminate would not be impaired if the *qualia* were altered or switched in a uniform and consistent manner, the indispensable condition for discrimination is the capacity to experience the *qualia*, and it is surely ridiculous to argue, as Smart does, that as long as we can discriminate, our inner experiences are of little importance, and that as long as people make the right discriminatory responses, they will be able to talk about colors even if they have no inner experience of colors at all.[15] For unless they could learn to discriminate colored objects by some criterion other than color (e.g., a mark invariably associated with the specific coloring)—and even then—they could not without experiencing the *qualia*, do it all.

Our belief that there are experiences as well as neural processes, and that mental activity has two different aspects difficult to relate one to another, U. T. Place attributes to what he calls the phenomenological fallacy: that is, the belief that "because our ability to describe things in our environment depends on or consciousness of them" our descriptions are primarily of our conscious experiences (looks, feels, and so forth) and only secondarily of things. The truth, he asserts, is the reverse: that only after we have learnt to describe the qualities of things can we describe our experiencing of them. Certainly, anybody who thought the description of sense-data was a prior necessity to the description of things would be wrong, but how does this go to prove that the experiencing, which is admitted to be the condition of the description, is nothing but a neural process in the brain? We all do, and know that we do, experience, *qualia*—they are the way things appear to us, and they do not appear as brain processes. The brain processes are emphatically not identical with the appearances, nor are the physical objects, for scientists tell us that these consist entirely of matter and energy, of imperceptible particles and waves. And if appearances are intrinsic to neither the physical objects nor the brain processes, to what category of beings do they belong? How could we account for them?

There can be little question that the neural-identity theory in the form presented and defended by Place, Smart, and Feigl signally fails to account for them.[16] The best that Smart can do is to suggest that we refrain from mentioning them and describe the occurrence of, for example, afterimages in "topic-neutral" language. When I see an orange patch, I am to say, "Something is going on in me like what goes on when with eyes open and in a good light I confront an orange." No doubt, this statement is true, but it throws not the faintest light on the question how what is going on in me is related to the appearance I experience. My omission to mention that appearance has not abolished it, and whatever brain process is going on, the appearance is obviously *not* identical with it. Meanwhile, the questions are begged how I identify the occasions when in a good light I confront an orange with my eyes open, unless I am able to make use of the visual appearances to me of oranges in various lights, and how I know what is going on in me on such occasions, so that I can compare it with what goes on when I experience afterimages.

3. MATTER AND FORM

The failure of the version of the neural-identity theory that we have considered does not reinstate old and unsatisfactory notions of dualism; and, set in a wider context, the physiological facts that have impressed the neural-identity theorists might point the way to a better solution to the problem of psychophysical relationship. Brain processes and neural activity generally constitute but one, albeit a most important one, of the organic functions that combine in the life of the organism. In that life, numerous functional processes are integrated into a single organized self-maintaining totality. The life process is differentiated in minute and complicated ways, each complementary to the rest, in a bewilderingly intricate system, which in all its multifarious internal diversity, is integrated as a unity of mutually dependent and inseparable functions. Originally, both in the evolutionary scale and in embryonic development, these functions are all performed by a single cell, but in the course of development, they are assigned to specifically differentiated groups of cells (nerve cells being but one such group) which severally form different anatomical organs, together constituting a highly complex structure. Yet they remain intimately interdependent and integral to the single system that is the living organism and that acts as one undivided agent.

The distinguishing characteristic of a living system is its propensity to maintain itself by automatic adjustment of its internal activity to changing conditions. Its activity is therefore a constant adaptive response to factors in its environment. The adaptive character of the response is defined and determined by what is requisite for the maintenance of the organic unity of the living creature, so that living activity is a progressive integration of an increasingly complex structures of interrelations between organism and environment.

There comes a stage in this progressive development at which the self-maintenance of the system is possible only if the organism's activity is informed by the character of the total situation within which it is reacting. At that stage, its organic responses must be so closely integrated that they become fused into a single unity. They reach a pitch of intensity of integration that goes beyond mere physicochemical reciprocity (although, of course, the integrated processes themselves need be nothing other than highly complex trains of physicochemical reaction). The thesis I wish to advocate is that, at this high intensity of unification, the *form* assumed by the unified organic activity is that of feeling or sentience.

We have seen that at every level of nature, natural forms are manifestations of some kind of organized activity constituting and expressing itself in structured wholes. At each level the appropriate whole is made up of elements on a lower level, the general character of which is quite different. A particular form of integration in a special pattern or organization gives rise to a new sort of

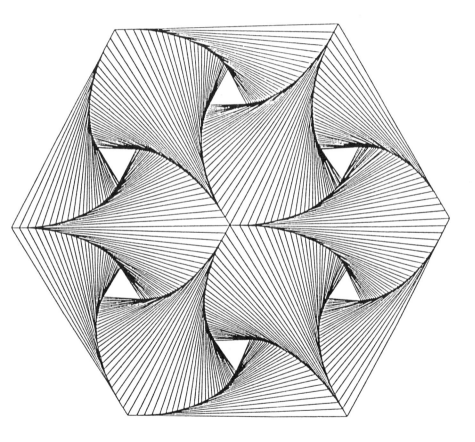

FIGURE 1 Mystery of the Vanishing Triangle. "In constructing the diagram, only triangles were drawn, yet the weird spade-like shape so dominates the result that the triangles pass unnoticed." (Design by Rutherford Boyd, "Mathematical Ideas in Design," *Scripta Mathematica*, vol. 14 [1948]. Reproduced by permission of Harriet R. Boyd.)

entity with new and unprecedented qualities. By way of analogy consider Figure 1. It is constructed entirely of triangles whose sides are straight lines, but they are organized and integrated in a special way, which produces the appearance of a complex pattern of fan-shaped curves, in which the triangular shape is virtually lost. Similarly, elementary particles take on a new form when they combine in a special pattern of order to become an atom. The atom has new properties that its elementary components taken severally do not possess, while those of the elementary particles are suppressed and hidden. Combinations of atoms produce yet further forms as molecules, which behave differently from single atoms. These, again, in appropriate combination form crystals with new properties and capacities not possible for their constituent molecules in separation. More complex molecules in larger and more elaborate combination become enzymes with more potent abilities and the capacity to react with and synthesize proteins and nucleic acids, which, in suitable associations, become living cells. These again have new characteristics not found among their separate constituents but dependent upon the complex way in which they are organized together.

At each successive level a new whole is constructed displaying a new form, the appearance and properties of which are different from those of its constituents, and in which those of the constituents have vanished or are at least suppressed and indiscernible. In the development of the organism there are gradations of activity similarly related. At the merely chemical level the interlaced cyclical processes are termed metabolism; but these, when more complexly interrelated become physiological functions such as digestion, circulation through the vascular system, neural discharges, and the like. These are regulated by complicated servomechanisms to maintain homeostatic levels of quantities and pressures off various substances (sugar, water, salt, etc., in the bloodstream; oxygen and carbon dioxide pressure in the lungs). When the substances are depleted and the homeostasis is disturbed, a new property manifests itself, registering the relevant need—hunger, thirst, pain, and so forth, stimulating the creature to overt behavior.

The sensations are differentiations of feeling or sentience, which supervenes on a certain high degree of integration of physiological functioning involving specially integrated patterns of activity at lower levels. Not only neural discharges are involved in these patterns but probably all, or most of, the metabolic and physiological functions of the body. At the physiological and metabolic levels the activity is automatic and unconscious, but at the level of behavior sensibility and perception are involved. My suggestion is that sentience is the new form assumed by the high degree of integration of physiological activity in a concentratedly organized structure.[17]

Just as the pattern of straight lines and triangles, when organized in a specially complex way, gives rise to a pattern of curves in which the triangles are no longer apparent, so a specially complex integration of physiological functioning may express itself as sentience, in which the physiological processes are not manifest as chemical activity but in a totally new form. No doubt, the main function of integration and organization is performed by the nervous system and is concentrated in the brain, but it seems clear that the whole system of the organism is involved—vascular, endocrine, and autonomic (for how could the central nervous system operate without the rest?)—and in the new emergent form of this systemic whole it becomes aware of itself, so to speak, in vague and confused totality as sentience.

Feeling is thus identical, not with any neural process taken in isolation, but with the entire organic system, of which neural process is only one of the most highly integrative functions; and it is identical, not in the sense that it simply is the material or the physiological system, but in the sense that it is not a new, different, or separate stuff or substance. It is identical with the physiological functioning in the sense that it is its form, as the form of a triangle is identical with the three lines and angles. The form is not a fourth line or angle, nor yet another ghostly collocation of lines and angles, yet it is something more and other than any of the parts, or than all of them considered as a mere collection. It is just the special way in which three straight lines are integrated into a single unitary figure.

The form of integration of organic processes, however, is not a spatial pattern or shape of this kind, but is a complex interplay of functional response, which can hardly be thought of otherwise than as sensibility. The elements of the integrated system are functioning processes that, although they involve spatial arrangements among trains of physicochemical reactions, derive their special character, not so much from these, as from the adaptive and adjustive function they serve in the self-maintenance of the system as a whole. The form of integration of a complex of such functional processes will be of a different order from that of geometrical or simple physical entities, or even of chemical cycles such as make up the organism's metabolism.

Adaptive or self-adjustive functioning is typically sensitivity, but what we are concerned with here is not just sensitivity as reaction (as a fine column of mercury is "sensitive" to changes of temperature), but as complex self-adjustment, to which the term "sensibility" more properly applies. This involves taking account of the mutual relationships of numerous interreacting factors within a single complex in which the totality, or structural principle, of the relational whole will be the dominant feature. It will be pervasive and will determine the general character of the whole as well as the special nature and behavior of the parts. A totality, in which the reciprocal influence of whole and parts along with the pervasive control and dominance of the principle of organic integration are apparent, is precisely the right description of awareness, and the form of integration characteristic of organic systems at the level of performance which is apposite here is, therefore, sentience, with the supervenient awareness that comes with the selective and organizing activity of attention.

"Awareness," however, is a term that at this stage should be used with caution. The *form* of organized physiological functioning at a high degree of intensity, I am claiming, is sentience, but sentience is not necessarily conscious. Primitive sentience is a confused totality of variegated but undiscriminated feeling, which may well be, and probably always is, subconscious. For it to become conscious, further activity of organization is required: specific instinctive impulses and the work of attention have to supervene before a definite object of awareness is discerned. Nevertheless, it is important to note that what is felt is not just the organic activity by itself, because the organic activity is not "by itself"; it is in intimate organic relation and reaction to the whole environing universe. What comes to consciousness through feeling, therefore, is certainly the bodily system of the organism, but as the focus of the entire world of nature at that point.

Despite material identity at the physiological and sentient levels, however, there is formal multiplicity. The formal properties of any selected level of organic activity will depend on how it is considered—as just physical, as chemical, or as biological. In each case the material involved may well be identically the same, but the properties of the totality will vary with the degree of integration and type of whole. Thus the movement of ions in a liquid medium may be described as a physical process without its significance as a neural impulse ever being noted; a neural discharge can be described as a physiological process without consideration of its contribution to behavior. So, likewise, the *form of integration* of the whole complex of neural and biochemical processes may be undetectable if description is limited to piecemeal physiological analysis.

The form at this level can be appreciated only by the psychologist concerned with feeling and response to stimulus, with movement as an expression of feeling, and with behavior as activity of the total organism in relation to a complete situation apprehended as a whole. If, somewhat arbitrarily, we lump together all forms up to the physiological level and attribute them to the body, and all forms at the psychological level and attribute them to the mind, we retain a dualistic position, but it is a somewhat artificial and unhelpful dualism produced by a factitious dichotomy in what is really a continuous scale of forms. Nevertheless, within the continuum there comes a critical point at which a definitive distinction may legitimately be made between "body" and "mind"— in fact, such critical points occur throughout the scale at intervals marking distinct qualitative differences that depend upon special degrees of structural integration. Hence we may legitimately distinguish the physicochemical from the biological, or physiological activity from conscious behavior in a perceived situation, although the development from one stage to the next is continuous throughout and the division between them is never sharp. Thus, although all physiological activity is physicochemical, what is alive is far more than merely a set of chemical reactions; although the psychological merges into the purely physiological—as when consciousness ebbs away under the influence of anesthetics or brain injury, leaving only reflex coordination—nevertheless, the sphere of mind is a new level, profoundly transforming the nature of all activity and behavior.

A possible criticism of this theory may be that the alleged form of integration is a metaphysical conceit, an invention of the speculative philosopher, for which there is no observable evidence, and that it should at once be excised by Occam's razor. This might be justified if there were in fact no observable evidence, and if the idea of an integrated organic system acting on a psychological level were unnecessary for the explanation of the facts. But clearly this is not the case. There is copious evidence that living structure and activity cannot be reproduced at the inorganic level, and that conscious and intelligent behavior is much more than mere physiological reaction.

Wherever the properties of a whole are dependent upon its structural integration and not simply on its material constituents, this argument should apply. So in physics, the properties of the atom, which derive from the number and arrangement of its nucleons and satellite electrons, should become suspect, because the structure or form is not another constituent that can be separately designated—or in chemistry, where the same is true of the compound molecule, or in crystallography, where the special properties of the crystal depend upon the internal lattice arrangement of its molecules. In these cases the critic would not be so ready to allege that the form is unobservable. But in the case of living organisms the complexity of the system is so fantastic that we lose sight of its integral wholeness when we consider it merely as a combination of interrelated physiological processes. Nevertheless, the true form of the totality is revealed and is observable in the pattern of behavior of the complete organism; and we are directly aware of it—and so observe it more immediately than anything else—as feeling, which (I am suggesting) is precisely the form of integration of its multifarious organic processes acting at a high level of intensity. These two ways of observing the form in question provide the appropriate subject matter for the science of psychology.

4. SECONDARY QUALITIES

Primitive sentience, the lowest psychological form, is not yet appearance and is not, properly speaking, consciousness. It is the terminus *a quo* of consciousness and is more properly, without the activity of attention, subconscious. It is unarticulated, though internally diverse, and only at a more developed stage are the apparently simple *qualia* of the different sense modalities distinguished within it by the selective activity of attention. Primitive sentience constitutes what psychologists call the psychical field, and attention organizes its contents into a system of objects in mutual relation. It is only in the course of this activity that sense-data can be identified, and that can be done only at a late stage of sophistication, when we subject our sensory experience to analysis. Sense-data are rather a theoretical abstraction than anything of which anybody is ever actually aware. So Place is right to maintain that we learn to describe objects before we learn how to extract, from our experience of them, the pure looks and feels by which we characterize them.

It is only when an element in the felt complex is singled out by selective attention and related to a background that it becomes an object of conscious perception—an appearance to us. What makes it appear is this very activity of setting it in a context that is in some degree articulated. The apprehension of an object in relation to a context of this sort is *cognition*, and with that, consciousness proper begins. Consciousness, it will be argued more at length in what follows, is nothing more nor less than the activity of selecting, grouping, structuring, and organizing the contents of the psychical field to constitute the perceived world of objects.

Secondary qualities are a product of this activity. They are not qualities either of the external thing or of any particular neural process, but are elements picked out by attention from the felt integration of the complete organic system and, within that psychic field, set against a vaguer and more general background of feeling. The account that the neural-identity theorist gives of them thus needs modification and development. Let us take an example from the version offered by Stephen Pepper, in one of the best statements of that position,[18] concerning the experience of hearing the sound of middle C:

> Both the physiologist's report and the introspectionist's report are symbolic statements. The peculiarity of these statements is that both are referring to an identical event.[19]

This contention is not strictly correct. The experience of the sound of middle C to which the introspectionist refers is not just the discharge of neurons in the temporal lobe. The neurons will not discharge unless the neural metabolism is functioning normally, and that is dependent on the blood supply and the general metabolism of the body, and that again on countless other organic processes that are equally dependent reciprocally upon it. We cannot dissect out the neurons and produce the experience of middle C with them alone. Probably the experience depends as much on patterns of neural discharge extending inward and outward from these neurons all over the cortex (to say nothing of the rest of the brain and the nervous system). If the hearer is not attending little or no consciousness of middle C may occur, even if the neurons in the temporal lobe discharge. The activating reticular system of the brain stem will also be involved. To go beyond merely hearing a sound, to identifying it as middle C requires much more, but as this may be thought ulterior to the question of secondary qualities, we need not discuss it here.

If there is to be an identity, it must be between the subjective experience and the total physiological functioning of the body at a given moment. It then obviously transpires that "the subjective experience" is much more than middle C and is the whole structure of content with middle C as the (temporary) focal dominating feature. Yet this complex as described by the physiologist is as different from the structure of the content of experience as anything could be, and strict identification seems more implausible than ever. The experienced content could well be (i) the specific form of organization into which the physiological functioning is integrated—a structure single and indivisible, though not necessarily "simple" or undifferentiated. The vibrations corresponding to middle C may well be a factor in the summed and integrated unity of a vast complex of physiological and physical activity. (ii) The form of this complex, qua sentience, will again have been structured by attention to highlight the sound of middle C against a background of noise and other sensations; and this second ordering will by no means be the same in character as the first.

The activity of attention, organizing and coordinating the distinguishable elements in primitive sentience, is a high-grade organic activity that is at once cognitive and practical. It is continous with, and part of, the general biological process of self-adaptation to and self-maintenance in the environment. Attention directs behavior and is prompted initially by biological needs, which are felt as tensions in the integrated form of organic activity in the ongoing process of self-maintenance. The outcome is the development of consciousness and the life of the mind. But mind and consciousness are not a new sort of stuff separate from, and unrelatable to, the matter of which our bodies are composed. They are a special sort of activity of organizing, at a specially high degree of integrated yet articulated wholeness, the extension and continuation of the organizing activity already operative at lower biological levels, which, at this higher level, constitutes the apprehension of objects in relation, makes possible behavior informed by the awareness of complete situations, and at the same time constructs a system of knowledge of the world in which we live.

5. CONSCIOUSNESS

There is a certain mystery enshrouding the nature of consciousness that seems to defeat all attempts to give an intelligible account of it. Bertrand Russell once suggested that all the *sensibilia* we experience are physical and physiological, and are present in the organism independently of the mind, which adds only awareness.[20] G. E. Moore expressed a similar thought when he wrote, "the object, when we are aware of it, is precisely what it would be if we were not aware of it,"[21] and insisted that consciousness is distinguishable from its object as that which all sensations have in common, is unique, and is related to its object in a unique and peculiar way. But what is this unique and peculiar relation? What is the added awareness? Moore tells us nothing about either, except that "it really is consciousness," and Russell gives no clue at all.

We are apt to imagine a special sort of light that reveals things to us, and we refer to consciousness, as a rule, by words conveying illumination and vision. Years ago, E. B. Holt put forward his once-famous searchlight theory,[22] and Samuel Alexander, in *Space, Time and Deity*, said he was almost tempted to adopt it.[23] The notion was of consciousness as illuminating, like a searchlight, that cross section of the world to which the organism responded, but how the response involved illumination or what sort of light it might radiate was never explained.

Nevertheless, our readiness to use metaphors of light and vision in speaking of consciousness is very easy to understand, and they serve a useful purpose in some contexts. Probably most of us think in visual images more than with the help of any other sense. We tend automatically to translate tactually felt shapes, as well as the sources of sounds, into visual imagery. The pressure of solid objects against the body conveys both their shape and that of the human body itself, which are apprehended at once as visual images. Even the tactual explorations of the tongue against the teeth reveal shapes and positions that are visualized in images such as a dentist might see. So constantly do we think visually and speak in terms of light, referring to awareness as a sort of luminosity and to unconsciousness as the dark, that we forget we are using metaphors. Yet a moment's reflection reminds us that vision, however important, is only one sense modality and is by no means essential to consciousness. The blind are fully aware, despite their disability, and darkness deprives us only of a single sensuous faculty. However common visualization may be, it obviously cannot be universal, for at least the congenitally blind must think in other than visual symbols. It is clear, therefore, that in order properly to understand the nature of consciousness, we must not allow ourselves to be misled by the all too ready metaphors of light but must seek to approach the matter in some other way.

Reliance on visual metaphors is, perhaps, fostered by too close a concentration on sense qualities. Philosophers are all too apt to talk of color patches; sounds, scents, and tastes taking a less prominent place in their discourse. They think of consciousness as what reveals pure sense-data and makes them appear to us, as light reveals colors that are invisible without it. True it is that consciousness reveals them, but not by playing upon them like a beam. None of the assumed sense-data is isolable, and the reduction of the content of consciousness to any one of them alone would at once destroy both the so-called datum and the awareness of it, which would not be the case if the awareness simply revealed the datum like a light. Moreover, this simile of light presupposes a prior consciousness able to cognize what the light reveals, and therefore tacitly begs the question: What then is the revelatory character of consciousness?

We may begin by observing that consciousness serves the purpose of bringing an ever-widening environment under the control of the conscious organism. The worm can react to and control little more than what comes into immediate contact with its skin. The mole can smell and hear the approach of an enemy and flee. The bird sees its prey from far, hears the crackle of twigs as a man approaches, and can react to a far wider expanse of surrounding influences. Humans add to all this the capacity to infer from what is present to what lies beyond their immediate purview, and, besides, can invent instruments to extend the reach of their senses over the whole surface of the earth and to the distant galaxies of outer space. Whatever else we may say of it, consciousness is thus a process of assimilation by the organism of the world in which it lives so that the most distant objects come under its surveillance and, in a significant way, become part of its own being. In other words, consciousness, so regarded, is a process of unification or concentration of a varied and complex universe within a single center.

It is clear that the condition of combining a plurality into unity is the introduction into it of relations so as to systematize its variety into a single complex whole. That consciousness does this is obvious, for it enables its subject to hold before itself a complex object and to grasp it as one, apprehending the interrelation of its parts. Interrelatedness exists, no doubt, apart from consciousness, but is not realized in the full sense until cognized. The unconscious interrelated terms are oblivious of the relations, even though they are affected and, indeed, determined by them. Only as cognized are the relations truly actualized as such. As cognized, however, the awareness of any object involves distinction of differences and their mutual interrelation. The possibility of a purely simple and undifferentiated object of consciousness has been called into question both by psychologists and by epistemologists and has been disproved by experiment. Any possible object is some form of *Gestalt*, a form or quality contrasted with a ground, if nothing more, a "this-not-that", which is cognized as a single complex pattern. The act of apprehension itself, therefore, must be complex, or discursive. It cannot be a merely immediate intuition but must always be a discursus that at one and the same time distinguishes and unites, analyzes and synthesizes. We may call it, using a phrase coined by H. H. Joachim, "an analytic-synthetic discursus."

Where there is no cognition, there is no consciousness; and even though psychologists insist that all experience is at once affective and conative as well as cognitive, affection and conation are aspects of sentience—they are felt rather than, in the first instance, perceived. Primitive sentience, we have said, is subconscious, for the very reason that it is undiscriminated. But the life of the organism is a constant endeavor to maintain itself, and that involves instinctive impulses—to feed, to grow, and to reproduce—supervening upon its inherent self-maintaining processes of metabolism and physiology. These instinctive urges direct attention to the elements in primitive sentience most apposite to their aims, such as feelings of hunger, thirst, pain, and the like, and to the appropriate felt conative impulses. So attention becomes engaged in distinguishing, selecting, and highlighting elements in the mass of feeling, against the general felt background of the sensory field. In this way, it creates objects for perception and brings its sentient content to consciousness.

In this manner bodily feelings are discriminated and the various sense modalities are distinguished; attention in every case creating the object perceived. The primitive object of consciousness is feeling, as R. G. Collingwood rightly maintained. But as the primitive form of feeling is a confused (if variegated) mass, only when, by a reflective act, the elements within it are selected for attention do they acquire the definition that reveals them as particular objects. This in itself is distinction and interrelation, and it is nothing other than this that reveals "data" to the mind.

"When I attend to a red patch in my here-and-now, my act of attention really makes the edges of that patch." So writes Collingwood.[24] In short, attention is the first step of the process, without which no definite object can be cognized. What reveals the object, therefore, is not a kind of illumination but the distinguishing and relating activity implicit in attention.

This activity is no more nor less than that of ordering and systematizing, setting a figure against a ground, discriminating objects and setting them in relation. It is the analytic-synthetic discursus typical of judgment and thinking. Consciousness is not an additional something that supervenes upon activities or is poured out over surrounding objects revealing them to some mysterious spectator. Being aware is an activity of identifying and relating objects within a context. Consciousness is not a special faculty or instrument with which we do this—doing it is being conscious. It is not a searchlight playing on the surrounding world, but an activity of distinguishing, relating, analyzing, and unifying: in short, organizing. It is no more and no less than the continuation at a higher level of the activity of organization that constitutes and characterizes all life. Consequently, the mind is not a separate "spiritual" entity but a very complex and highly integrated activity, raising to a higher level of concrescence and efficiency that of the organism as it assimilates its environment in the effort to maintain itself, an activity, the lower phases of which are metabolic and physiological—the body.

A theory of this sort avoids the inadequacies of the neural-identity theory yet also meets the objections of the dualist. It admits a duality of form between the physiological and the psychological and justifies the dualist's contention that subjective experience is something markedly different from neural process. Likewise, it accords with the patent facts that mental acts and experiences either have no spatiotemporal characteristics or, when they do, have very different ones from physical things. The organic functions integrated, as has been said, although they involve physicochemical processes, derive their character and significance primarily from their mutually adjustive and adaptive interplay. The form of their integration is, therefore, not necessarily spatial or temporal but rather sensitive and responsive. It issues as feeling, which, *in se*, has no spatiotemporal character but which, in the course of its further organization, as elements are picked out and set against a contrasting background and schemata are imposed upon it, acquires a spatiotemporal character of its own, not identical with that of the underlying physiological processes. At the same time, the form of integration of organic activity is not another entity; it adds no further constituent to the body, nor is it some ghostly epiphenomenon changing in parallel with its bodily counterpart.

Notes

Most of this chapter was adapted from material originally published in *International Philosophical Quarterly*, vol. 6, no. 4 (1966), as "The Neural Identity Theory and the Person," and in *Proceedings of the XIIth International Congress of Philosophy* (1968), as "Some Reflections on the Nature of Consciousness."

1. See Herbert Feigl, "The 'Mental' and the 'Physical'" in *Minnesota Studies in the Philosophy of Science*, vol. 2, pp. 370–97; and "Mind-Body, not a Pseudo-Problem," in *Dimensions of the Mind*, p. 29.
2. It is not clear to me whether the proponents of the theory would admit the possibility even of indirect translation in all cases.
3. Cf. U. T. Place, "Is Consciousness a Brain Process?" *British Journal of Psychology*, vol. 47 (1956), pp. 44–50.
4. Cf. J. J. C. Smart, "Sensations and Brain Processes," *Philosophical Review*, vol. 68 (1959), p. 146.
5. Ibid., p. 152.
6. Cf. P. F. Strawson, *Individuals*, pp. 115–6.
7. Cf. J. J. C. Smart, *Philosophy and Scientific Realism*, chap. 4, esp. pp. 82–83.
8. Cf. Smart, op. cit. and Feigl, op. cit.
9. Cf. Place, "Is Consciousness a Brain Process?" p. 47 and Smart, "Sensations and Brain Processes," pp. 145ff.
10. D. W. Hamlyn is substantially correct on this point, and Smart's reply to him is hardly effective. Cf. *Proceedings of the Aristotelian Society*, suppl. vol. 38 (1964), pp. 141, 144.
11. See Lord Adrian, *The Physical Background of Perception*, p. 27.
12. Smart, *Philosophy and Scientific Realism*, pp. 78–9.
13. Ibid.
14. Ibid. pp. 79–81.
15. Ibid., p. 82.
16. Readers of F. H. Bradley would have been forewarned of this:

> For nothing is actually removed from existence by being labelled appearance. What appears is there, and must be dealt with; but materialism has no rational way of dealing with appearance. Appearance must belong, and yet cannot belong, to the extended. It neither is able to fall somewhere apart, since there is no other real place; nor ought it, since, if so, the relation would vanish and appearance would cease to be derivative.
>
> *Appearance and Reality*, p. 12.

17. Here I follow Susanne Langer. Cf. *Philosophical Sketches*, chap. I, p. 9, and *Mind: An Essay on Human Feeling*, vol. 1, chap. 1.
18. Stephen Pepper, "A Neural-Identity Theory of Mind," in *Dimensions of the Mind*, Ed. Sydney Hook, chap. 3.
19. Ibid., p. 52.
20. Cf. Bertrand Russell, *Mysticism and Logic*, p. 150.
21. G. E. Moore, *Philosophical Studies*, p. 29.
22. E. B. Holt, *The Concept of Consciousness*.
23. Cf. Samuel Alexander, *Space, Time and Deity*, vol. 2, p. 111.
24. R. G. Collingwood, *The New Leviathan*, 4.53.

13

Activities of Mind

1. IDEALITY

The reality of a whole is not and cannot be made manifest in any one point in space or any one instant in time, although in any and every manifestation the whole is immanent. That is why it generates itself through a dialectical scale of forms, always beginning with the most inadequate and abstract representation, which, because of its inadequacy to the immanent principle of order, is impelled toward further growth and development. The beginning cannot be properly made with anything other than the most abstract form, because whatever is more concrete is already a whole that must specify itself in more elementary phases. It is only at the culmination of the dialectical process that the whole is fully active as such, and because it cannot be displayed spatiotemporally, and its totality cannot be materially present all at once, it is realized ideally and is operative as idea.

Thus, while the bodily organism is spatiotemporal and its activity is physicochemical, its life is the form in which its integrity actualizes itself; and this form expresses itself as sentience, which registers all the physical and chemical as well as the organic impingements upon it of the total environment in a single felt (quasi-ideal) totality. The implicit distinctions thus enfolded within the conglomerate field of primitive sentience are sorted out, identified, and related, by attention, in accordance with the principle of structure governing the organic whole, its design or concept. This concept is what comes to consciousness as idea and is active as mind.

2. DEGREES OF CONSCIOUSNESS

The psychical field, as pure sentience, is never what Koffka called "homogeneous." He sought in vain to isolate this undifferentiated field, insisting, in consequence, that no experience is ever completely homogeneous, and subsequent experiment has borne him out. In primitive sentience every kind of feeling is included, but none is distinguished as such: pleasure, pain, the emotions, and all the modalities of sense are felt, at first, as one indiscriminate mass, and they continue to qualify

189

one another even after they have been distinguished by the activity of attention. It is only with this activity that consciousness emerges, and it occurs on different levels of definition and intensity. Attention itself is a matter of degree, and all degrees of attention may exist at the same time, as when one concentrates on one object (say, the present sentence) while one is vaguely aware of sounds and other objects in one's vicinity, less so of more distant objects, and still more dimly of the pressure of one's clothes on the skin, the scents of flowers in the garden, and the like. But quite apart from that, consciousness itself has levels and degrees, as when one is coming around from the effects of an anesthetic or recovering from a concussion. We also have experiences of gradually losing consciousness, sinking into reverie, then into dream, and finally into deep sleep. Sometimes we are aware of straining to be conscious, to keep awake, to see or hear more clearly, or to understand more distinctly. As we have said, consciousness is not a light that can be switched on or off but an activity that may be performed with more or less adroitness and precision.

3. ORGANIZATION OF THE PSYCHICAL FIELD

In the course of discrimination, not only are particular objects discerned, but certain definite schemata are imposed upon the contents of the psychical field, examples of which are the spatiotemporal schema and the body image, making sensory location possible. Some of these schemata may be innate, but some are obviously acquired through the process of learning. The body image is one of these, and one that is closely associated with the distinction of the self from others, both animate and inanimate. This recognition of self then becomes a major factor in the organization of the psychical field. To this we must shortly give more attention. For the moment, let us continue a general review of the activities properly called mental.

4. PERCEPTION

Consciousness proper begins with perception, which is not simply the registering of separate stimuli, nor is it the apprehension of separable data, whether, with Locke, we call them "ideas" or, with later thinkers, sensa. First, this is because there are no simple separable data, only interconnected *Gestalten*, and second, because the organism does not react in simple separable ways to simple separate stimuli. The perceived object is always a total scene or situation, including all the sense media; it is imbued with affective tone and saturated with somatic and kinesthetic feeling. Of course, all these elements are not at the focus of attention, but they all bear upon what is. And what is at the focus is cognized only in its context, both contemporaneous and successive. How, and as what, it is perceived depends intimately upon this context, as well as, and just as much, upon past experience, including schemata both learned and innate, which are imposed by the mind's organizing activity on the presented content. That is to say, what is perceived is interpreted in relation both to immediate context and to what former experience has offered. Without such interpretation, there is no perception and no recognizable object.

We can thus dispose at once of the very prevalent misconception that perception is the transmission of bits of information from external objects through our sense organs and sensory nerves to the brain, where, presumably, it somehow lights up the aura called "consciousness," which is supposed to illuminate some kind of picture in the mind of the external thing—as if the mind were a camera obscura in which projected reflections of the outside world were recorded. Any such idea is self-stultifying, because what appears in a camera obscura does not reveal its relationship to the external objects it reflects. So, on any theory of transmission of this kind, what appears in the mind (or brain) could not reveal that relationship either, and so could not be apprised of the object as *external*. Ideas so acquired would not disclose the fact that they had been transmitted in the manner described. The mind of the theorist would therefore have had to acquire its knowledge of the process, and of the relation between the image and the reflected object, by some other means than that alleged. This theory cannot be true of the mind that forms it, and it must therefore be false for any mind. But if it were true, nobody could ever know that it was, and so would have no pretext for concocting it.

Neurophysiologists and cyberneticians, as well as even some psychologists, have been very prone to suggest some such theory as the above, imagining the sense organs, nervous system, and brain to behave analogously to computers, so as to construct models or encoded replicas of the objects projected on to the receptor, and presuming the body to be supplied with servomechanisms enabling it to move appropriately in response. What all such constructions overlook is that if signals, of whatever kind, from external bodies were transmitted to the brain, in whatever form, they must somehow be read and interpreted as representing the external objects. How and by whom is this supposed to be accomplished? The brain cannot interpret its own networks of neuronal firings as representing something quite different (let alone discover how they were caused), and no homunculus inhabits the skull to read the signals, decode them, and understand to what in the external world they correspond. Even if there were, how he could perceive them would still be an unsolved problem.[1]

We must conceive perception differently. Whatever effects reach our bodies from outside, they are not in the form of ready-made information about the world. They are, no doubt, electromagnetic waves and atmospheric vibrations, as well as chemical and other influences, and they are transmitted through the nervous system in the form of all-or-nothing electrical impulses. Precisely what happens in the brain we do not know. But if the hypothesis suggested in the last chapter is accepted—that sentience is the form of integration of all these physiological and neural processes acting as a single organic unity—we have plenty of evidence that the contents of sentience are differentiated, distinguished, interrelated, and organized by the activity of attention and thinking to form the perception of objects in the world around us. This is not purely a cerebral activity. It proceeds pari passu with practical movement directed toward the objects that we so construct and perceive, and the bodily movements contribute to the interpretation and construction. We think not only with the brain but with the whole body. The practical activity is itself registered in sentience (as somatic and kinesthetic sensations) and is structured along with other felt processes, so that our perceptions are all and always interpretations of impressions in the light of their context and their past history. This is a perpetual process of judging, the truth of which, as we shall presently see, is measured by its coherence and self-consistency.

There is a large body of psychological evidence supporting this view, to which I shall refer again in a later chapter, where the coherence theory of truth will be discussed at more length. Adelbert Ames, in a famous series of demonstrations, showed that all immediate sensory stimuli are ambiguous and that it is the perceiver who constructs the percept by relating the sensibilia to one another in a coherently systematic structure. He says:

> Our perceptual awarenesses are not determined by the characteristics of our physiological stimulus patterns, peripheral, or central, which can be thought of as completely "hieroglyphical," but are our own interpretations of these stimulus patterns in terms of our past experience, personal and inherited.[2]

Other psychologists whose experimental work supports the same view are Egon Brunswik, J. S. Bruner, L. Postman, H. Cantril, W. H. Ittleson, and Sir Frederick Bartlett, as well as the Gestalt psychologists, in particular, W. Köhler and K. Koffka. But the mass of experimental evidence far exceeds what is indicated by the mention of these few names. We may briefly summarize the results of numerous investigations as follows:

1. Perception is never instantaneous. There is always a short interval, varying in length according to conditions, between the presentation and the apprehension or recognition of an object. In this brief interval the mind undertakes an activity of structuring the contents of the perceptual field in accordance with schemata that are either innate or learned. These may be called perceptual dispositions. The structuring involves selection and correlation of elements (or what some psychologists call "cues"), and much of it goes on subconsciously. It is an activity essentially of the nature of judgment and inference, and one group of psychologists refers to it explicitly as entertaining "hypotheses" for the identification of the cues, and the modification of these hypotheses if the cues do not fit together coherently. Success in recognizing—that is, *perceiving*—the object depends on the coherence of this judgmental activity.

2. Experiments on the visual perception of distance provide convincing evidence of the influence of past experience and the operation of implicit or suppressed judgment and inference in perception. The assessment of distance has been found to depend on the assumption made by the perceiver of the normal size of the object based on familiarity with things of the same kind. Isolated objects, removed from their usual environment, provide no criterion for judgments of size or of distance, and their apparent distance will depend on prior knowledge of the sort of objects they are, not simply on their presented visual appearance.

3. One experiment proved that colors perceived on objects like playing cards depend more on expectation than on the presented objects themselves. For instance, black hearts will be seen either as spades, or as gray or purple hearts, or simply as red hearts. Sometimes the incongruity disrupts perception so that the subject is unable to identify the object at all. Only after prolonged exposure, permitting of sufficient thought and consideration, can it be recognized correctly. The appearance of the object is shown to depend on expectation built up from prior experience, as well as upon context, and the effort to perceive succeeds when all these form a coherent whole, but not if they conflict.

4. Experimenters have found that subjects wearing spectacles that invert the image or reverse left and right are completely disoriented at first, but soon, if they wear the spectacles continuously, begin to see everything normally. The perception of the objects clearly depends on reorganization of the sense field, reinterpretation of the images in accordance with practical needs and past experience.

As has been said, this activity of interpretation is not only theoretical but also practical. Ames constructed a model of a room that, when viewed through a peephole with one eye, looked normal and symmetrical, although in fact it was distorted in shape, with one corner lower than another and with walls oblique to one another and to the viewer. Although the room looked normal, people and furniture standing in it looked out of proportion: a small boy appeared taller than a man, and faces looking in at windows seemed to be the wrong size. This of course, was due to erroneous judgments of size and distance. However, if the viewer was allowed to make active contact with the walls, by bouncing a ball against them, or poking at objects with a stick, he or she came to *perceive* the room and the objects in it as they actually were. The appearance changed in response to the practical activity.

Sentience, therefore, is a totality registering the totality of organic activity in the body (which, again, registers in one way or another, however vaguely, all the influences impinging upon it from without) and providing the basis of all conscious experience. This felt mass develops by a process of self-organization, by attention and implicit interpretive judgment, into a perceived world, which is also a whole and is implicated as a whole in every perception.

5. THE LIFE-WORLD

This research shows that the percept is the product of an operation of organizing, continuous with that going on in the organism at lower physiological levels; but at the conscious stage, it has become incipient thinking—judging and inferring, the interpretation of "cues" (and we must note immediately that the very word "cue" implies a clue or guide to judgment). The activity, moreover, constructs and involves a structured context, both spatial and temporal. It is a perpetual interpretation of our sentient experience in terms of our accumulated knowledge of the world as we build it up throughout our lives. The conception of the world that we form, in consequence, is a whole more or less systematic, of interrelated and connected objects, all interdependent and mutually rendering one another intelligible.

This is the commonsense, perceptual world of everyday life, what Husserl and his followers called "the Life-World," typical of the natural attitude. It is a single world, intelligible to each of us as the experience of a single, unitary subject, and to all of us together as the common ground for mutual discourse. Thus, not only must the experience of each one of us taken severally be coherent if it is to make sense, but it must accord with what we learn of the experience of others, by practical and linguistic interaction with them, if we are to be able to communicate with them intelligibly and cooperate with them in action. Generally speaking, then, the commonsense perceptual world, as we normally experience it, is a relatively loosely ordered but generally coherent whole embracing all our experience and connecting together within it all commonly perceived objects.

For common sense, however, the life-world is only loosely ordered. Contradictions frequently arise, causing perplexity and demanding explanation and resolution. For instance, the moon, reflected in water, appears to be both above and below the surface of the earth; water exposed to sunlight dries up and disappears, yet is replenished by rain falling from the clouds—how is it both volatile and condensed in liquid form? Questions of this sort stimulate scientific investigation and the formulation of theories, in which the observed facts are organized and set in systematic relation that explains them. Science supervenes upon common sense as a higher phase of comprehension, its aim being to construct coherent explanatory systems, which eventually coalesce into a single scientific conception of the universe.

It may be as well here to pause to remember that the physical universe has been discovered by scientists to be a single indivisible whole; the biosphere has, likewise, proved to be a single ecosystem, in organic relation with its physical environment, all of which is focused in the unity of the living organism and, through its physiological integrity, is registered in primitive sentience. It is the same whole throughout, at different stages of dialectical development, which comes to consciousness as the life-world at a yet more advanced level. The activity of organizing is continuous throughout and is directed by the principle universal to the whole, which adjusts its parts one to another to make it one. As each phase expresses this principle more adequately than its predecessors, it is to the later phases that we must look to discover the true nature of the universal. So science is the truth of common sense and all that precedes it. It now begins to transpire that the organizing principle is of the nature of thought, as it emerges in perception and consciousness. This fact will lead to important conclusions at a later stage of our argument and must be constantly borne in mind as it proceeds.

6. INTELLECT

Perception, then, is an activity of self-organization, of discrimination, of identifying and distinguishing while at the same time synthesizing, the first product of which is a configuration against a background. The primary object is a "this-not-that," an analytic-synthetic discursus, which is the rudimentary form of judgment. In perception this judgment is implicit and largely subconscious, but as the stimulus is always ambiguous or hieroglyphic, the more difficult it is to identify, the more explicit the thinking activity becomes. To be completely explicit, it must be uttered—expressed, either in practical action, or in speech, or in both—and language (in the widest sense of the word, including music and dance) becomes the medium of activity at the intellectual level. Language, as Collingwood convincingly maintained,[3] is primarily the expression of feeling, and only secondarily the medium of communication, to which the conventional use of words and signs is ancillary. When it is used to explicate judgment and inference, implicit in all consciousness, it is ratiocination. But intellectual activity is far from being confined to the purely cognitive. It involves imagination and emotion and transforms behavior, raising it to the level of conduct. No experience (not even pure mathematics) is solely theoretical; none is altogether devoid of feeling and impulse. The sphere of the intellect thus includes morality, art, and religion, as well as science and philosophy.

What has been called the noosphere includes all activities at the conscious level, and it is the continuation of that same dialectical development the course of which we have all along been tracing. Each type of intellectual activity is driven by the universal nisus to the whole. In each successive phase, the endeavor is to make experience coherent, whether in social and moral practice, in science, in art, in religion, or in philosophy. Each level becomes the object for the next: sentience is the object of perception, perception is the object of science, science of metaphysics; instinctive impulse becomes the object of desire, and upon desires social and moral regulation is directed. Each constructs a comprehensive system or whole: perception discloses the life-world; morality

seeks a way of life satisfying the self as a whole; every science constructs a
system, that must be internally coherent and should be consistent with that of
every other science, if it is to be scientifically acceptable; art seeks to express
the intuition of the whole through the medium of imagination, in a work that
is balanced and harmonious; religion presents in dogmatic form the creative
and sustaining principle of reality, its absolute or divine nature, and the relation to it of the human spirit; metaphysics strives to see everything together as
one coherent whole of reality accommodating all the exploits of the above
intellectual pursuits.

7. Personality, Self-Consciousness, and Reason

A critical transition in the developmental progress occurs early in the sphere of
mind. This is the point at which the subject becomes aware of itself and self-
reflective. It is here that the intellectual level is truly reached, to which common sense is a prelude, although no hard distinction can be made between the
two, and common sense is continually affected by what is achieved by the
intellect.

The work of attention, distinguishing and constructing objects for perception, results at a certain stage in the distinction of the subject's own body from
others. As we have observed, both practical and cognitive activity is involved.
In the former, the subject experiences resistance by other bodies to the movement of his or her limbs, as well as the behavior of other living bodies in
contrast to his or her own. In the course of such experience, the self (or ego)
comes to be differentiated from the not-self. The process is highly complex,
and we need not enter into the details here but may be permitted to accept,
on the authority of neurophysiologists and psychologists, the fact that the body
image is central to the idea of the self, which is, however, not confined to it.[4]
Accordingly, the experiences, or mental acts, that the subject feels to be its
own and claims as *Erlebnis*, and in which it asserts its own agency, are assigned
at the same time both to the ego and to its body, with which that ego is at
least partially identified. So one tends naturally, as Strawson observes,[5] to assign to oneself both physical and mental predicates: for example, "I am lying
on the couch" (i.e., my body), and with equal assurance, "I am enjoying the
symphony" (i.e., my mind). Strawson is right to reject a separate subject for
mental predicates, because the mental acts are the acts, at a specially high
degree of integration, of the organism and not of any ghost-in-the-machine.
And he is right in stressing the importance of the body for human individuality. But his speculation about the conceivability of a disembodied ego, even
with the limitations on which he insists, is hardly coherent. How could one
conceive of a subject experiencing visual, auditory, and tactual sensations, as
well as the rest, without the relevant bodily organs if one fully understood the

dependence of such sensations upon physiological adjustments, on the state of the sense organs concerned, and on the physical position of the body as a whole. In most cases, perhaps in all, the sensations are as much sensations of the body itself as of external objects. The awareness of "a red patch over there," Russell Brain explains, depends upon the mutual relation of the images on the two retinas, the adjustment of the eye muscles, the accommodation of the eyes, the position of the head, and more, and "contains subjective somatic sense-data inextricably mingled with it."[6] For a disembodied spirit, it would therefore be impossible, as surely as would be an itch or an abdominal pain.

The person is the self-conscious totality of the physical and physiological organism, experiencing a world of which he or she is a member, through the medium and by self-organization of its feeling content. Spinoza, whose theory is usually and misguidedly interpreted as psychophysical dualism, had better insight into this matter than most philosophers when he declared: "The object of the idea constituting the human mind is a body, or certain mode of extension, actually existing, and nothing else."[7] The mind is the body's awareness of itself in organic relationship to the world at large.

However, once aware of itself and capable of distinguishing self from others, the thinker becomes self-reflective. Referring to oneself as "I" unites subject and object, with further far-reaching consequences. A new and critical point has been reached when the self becomes aware of itself as opposed to its object, yet claims that object as its own, as the content of its own experience. At this point, the whole character of consciousness is transformed.

Awareness of self is the kernel of personality and generates an entity of a new kind on a new level of being. It creates a reference point and a focus from which it is possible (as Plato said) to view all time and all existence, and so to transcend the physical and the merely biological limits of the living organism. Such a universal conspectus of the world is possible only for a subject able to relate to the world as object and to be aware of the relation, and so it is possible only for one who is conscious of self as an entity among others in the world, and as a self-conscious entity at that. In this awareness of self in relation to other, the subject cannot be confined to only one of the terms, because it is capable of grasping both and the relation between them. It is conscious of a totality embracing organism and environment in a single system, in which the conscious subject cannot, therefore, be restricted to the organism alone. It is, in short, the self-consciousness of the entire system, aware of its own self-differentiation, by which the person whose ego is thus aware is able to objectify not only the world and his or her own place in it but also his or her own mental states and the part they play in his or her own character. The person thus becomes aware of his or her own feelings and can influence them by reflecting upon them, of his or her own appetites and the objects that will satisfy them, so converting them into desires. These can be objectified and so either indulged or restrained, modified when they conflict so as to attain a satisfaction more complete than could be gained by allowing them free play. Thus the person is able to formulate principles of conduct conformity to which will ensure the greatest happiness. Similarly, he or she becomes aware of his or her own percepts and judgments and so of the concepts by which they are ordered, and can modify them in the light of their mutual compatibility. The person thus becomes self-critical both of practice and of theory. Accordingly, only at the self-reflective level are morality and science possible, as well as all other truly intellectual pursuits.

A conscious personality aware of self and its own ideas can obviously not be wholly identified with any one of its own states or activities, or with any collection of them simply as a succession or as a coincident group, for to each and any of them the self can stand opposed as subject to object. So far as these states and activities are spatiotemporal events occurring in the stream of consciousness, the self-conscious ego must transcend space and time, for it is aware of space and time as relational wholes that contain the events in question, and that would be impossible if the conscious subject were wholly confined to any one of them as it occurred. This transcendence of consciousness is apparent in memory, which occurs now but the object of which is in the past. The subject must, therefore, be at once both past and present, or else neither; and memory permeates all other mental functions, perception, imagination, and thinking.

The transcendence is due to the operation and immanence, in the finite organism as self-conscious person, of that whole of which it is the focus, through sentience, and which has brought itself to consciousness at the level of the human mind—a self-awareness that comes to fruition, in an appropriate degree, in the higher reflective activities of science, philosophy, art, and religion. Here the mind contemplates objects so much wider in scope than its own physiological basis that to identify this phase of its awareness with its neural activity becomes plainly ludicrous and unmeaning. At this level of awareness, transcending even the finite self, the organism is no more than the channel or instrument through which the all-embracing totality makes itself apparent by means of the self-consciousness of the organic unit.

I said earlier that relations could not be fully actualized until they were grasped as such in consciousness. A whole is a relational complex, so it follows that the whole cannot be fully realized until it is consciously apprehended; and the condition of that is a conscious subject which cannot be confined to any single term within the complex, although it can supervene upon all of them as the form of the whole. Such a subject emerges at the level of self-consciousness. The whole that is the physical universe is not, as we saw, adequately actualized physically. But the physical entity (atom and molecule) becomes self-enfolded in the macromolecules of organic compounds and comes alive. As a living, self-maintaining system, the whole realizes itself more adequately. But metabolism and homeostatic chemical cycles in an organism are still insufficient to fulfill the nisus of the differentiated unity of the organic whole toward total completion. For this, what is alive must become aware of its surround and of itself as related to it—of the whole of which it is a member—and must become a self-conscious subject.

In becoming conscious of itself, the organism ipso facto becomes conscious of the world of which it is a part, and the manifold influences from which, impinging upon it, are registered in its sentience. These are then distinguished and interrelated to constitute the perceived world. To be held together as one complex, however, the terms of relations must be cognized by a single subject, the identity of whom throughout the whole of its experience must be indefeasible. If the subject is not the same throughout, the experience cannot be one experience. Consequently, the unity of the perceived and conceived world is dependent on the unity of the subject of the awareness; in fact, in the experience, they are identical.

This profound insight, of supreme importance for all epistemology and metaphysics, was achieved by Kant and established in his Transcendental Deduction.[8] Fichte went further and identified subject and object in the Ego, which was next taken over by Schelling as "the original act of cognition" and identified by him with the Absolute. It was Hegel who then came to see that the ego was the whole, as Concept and Idea, and that its activity was that of speculative reason, seeing things together, recognizing the interdependence of differences, and identifying opposites in their complementary interrelations.

In Part 5, I shall argue (in agreement with Hegel) that reason operates on two levels: that of ratiocination, or understanding, at which differences and distinctions are emphasized in the pursuit of precision—the level typical of the so-called scientific outlook; and that of speculative reason, in which the nature of wholeness is comprehended, and the oppositions highlighted by the understanding are reconciled. At both levels, however, reason is the active principle of organizing, of differentiating, and of systematically unifying. This is exactly what has been the dynamic character of the universal principle of order pervading the dialectical movement within reality as a whole. That movement proceeds through a scale of forms successively expressing more adequately the true nature of the universal, and now it has transpired as reason, the activity of self-consciousness. Philosophers of the tradition will remember that Aristotle concluded that active reason was the sole occupation of God, *noésis noéseōs*, the knowing that knows itself, an activity that all lower beings imitated in their own way, appropriate to their own level in the hierarchy of being, and which was the supreme aspiration of human desire. The recognition that self-conscious reason is the universal principle of order has profound consequences for both human existence and for the conception of deity.

8. CONCLUSION

We can now see that the activities of mind range themselves in a series of wholes, each composed of lesser configurations, but all exemplifying the same principle of holism that we found operative throughout nature. The activity at every stage is one of self-organization. Sentience is the form of integration of physiological self-organization, which, by turning reflexively in upon itself, through the felt impulse of instinctive urges,[9] directs attention to particular elements and organizes its own content as perception.

Perception is the construction of *Gestalten*, each determined by the total organized sense field to become the apprehension of distinct objects, the nature and meaning of each of which depend on its relations to the experienced context and the funded knowledge acquired in the course of experience—its relation, in fact, to the whole experienced life-world.

The commonsense world is a whole of objects and situations that are perceived as wholes. And in the course of the self-specification of the sense field, having become aware of ourselves as members of this world, when contradictions arise in our experience of it, we reorganize our conceptions of it in scientific theory, which are also systematic wholes and ultimately coalesce into a single conception of nature. Similarly, our practical activity generated by our instinctive urges and appetites is organized at the self-conscious level, by rules of morality aimed at producing a way of life satisfactory as a whole.

Art, religion, and philosophy are all further ways in which, in intellectual activity, we strive to unify and organize our lives in coherent harmony with one another and with the Absolute, expressing the vision of the whole perceptually in *objects d'art*, in reverence and worship of the transcendent divine creative power of the universal principle of order, and in synoptic conception.

So there is a scale of mental and ideal forms, the earlier and more rudimentary being less adequate and the later and more developed more adequate awareness of the totality of the real, the entire cognitive scale originating in, and thence elaborating, the effects upon the organism of the entire environing world. Accordingly, the ultimate whole is immanent in every phase and brings itself to clearer consciousness through the dialectical process, in human self-awareness.

Each stage presents one version or exemplification of the whole that is developing. Each stage is made up of wholes, each of which is a specification of the universal organizing principle. They are thus related to one another as specific differentiations of a universal generic essence.

There is a sense in which the successive phases are mutually opposed to one another. Sentience, as qualitative, is opposed to the abstraction of the schemata or configurations into which it is organized: "Intuition without concepts is blind; concepts without intuition are empty"—but perception is their unification. In the same way, observation, or common sense, opposes itself to theory,

and theory to practice; yet, in fact, the opposites are always mutually complementary, interdependent, and ultimately united in a single whole. They are,
moreover, all continuous and overlap one with another: perception being the
organization and interpretation of sentience, theory being the organization and
interpretation of what is perceived. Similarly, philosophy and science are mutually opposed, yet also mutually continuous and interdependent; and the
same sort of opposition, overlap, and complementarity exists between art, and
religion, religion and science.

The activities of mind thus constitute a scale of forms, graded in their adequacy to the ultimate whole that they specify. They are degrees as well as
species of the ultimate universal, distincts and opposites, yet mutually complementary elements within a unitary whole. Each successive phase sublates, preserves, yet transforms its predecessors in the scale, so that the whole dialectical
process is summed up and consummated in its final fulfillment. The end is at
one and the same time the consummation of the scale and the whole of the
process.

Notes

1. This matter is more fully treated in, *The Foundations of Metaphysics in Science*, chap. 19.
2. See S. Katner, ed., *Vision and Action*, p. 204.
3. R. G. Collingwood, *Principles of Art*, pp. 235–6.
4. Cf. Sigmund Freud, *The Ego and the Id*; K. Koffka, *Principles of Gestalt Psychology*, pp. 319–33; Russell Brain, "The Concept of Schema in Neurology and Psychiatry," in *Perspectives in Neurophysiology*.
5. Cf. P. F. Strawson, *Individuals*.
6. Russell Brain, *Mind, Perception and Science*, p. 14.
7. Benedict de Spinoza *Ethics*, pt. II, prop. XIII, Cf. H. R. Hallett, "On a Reputed Equivoque in Spinoza," *Review of Metaphysics*, vol. 3, no. 10 (1949), and E. E. Harris, *Salvation from Despair: A Reappraisal of Spinoza's Philosophy*, chap. 5, and *The Substance of Spinoza*, chap. 4.
8. Immanuel Kant, *Critique of Pure Reason*, B 132ff.
9. Cf. H. H. Jasper, "Ascending Activities of the Reticular System," in *Reticular Formation of the Brain*, chap. 15, and E. E. Harris, *The Foundations of Metaphysics in Science*, pp. 327, 329ff.

Part 5

Reason

14

Reason as Principle of Order

1. THE TRADITION OF REASON

Throughout the history of philosophy, the province of metaphysics, as well as its primary agency, has been thought of as reason. For Plato, the highest exercise of the mind was the grasp of that which was purely intelligible, "which the reason lays hold of by the power of dialectic";[1] and the philosopher was for him one who could see all things together—"the spectator of all time and all existence." For Aristotle, the culmination of human and cosmic activity was *noésis noéseōs*, the pure activity of God, the unmoved prime mover, the source of all power and all activity.[2]

The Stoics identified the law of reason with the law of nature, which they regarded as the criterion both of truth and of morality; and in this they were followed by the medievals, for whom the Law of Nature was the law of God, a system of universal law, the rational foundation of ethics, the ideal of jurisprudence, and the objective standard of justice.

Descartes held "good sense or reason (*bona mens*)" to be the fountain of all true knowledge, especially metaphysics, or first philosophy.[3] Spinoza taught that the consummation of all philosophy and the only satisfying object of human endeavor, the full realization of human freedom, was achieved through *ratio* and *scientia intuitiva*, leading to *amor intellectualis Dei*:

> The love towards a thing eternal and infinite alone feeds the mind with pure joy and is free from all sorrow, and so it is much to be desired and to be sought after with all our might.[4]

Leibniz continues the same tradition: the appetition of the monad is perpetually toward the resolution of confused perceptions into what is clear and distinct (appperceptions), the transformation of passivity into activity, approximating (as with Aristotle) to the pure activity of God, whose understanding is the region of eternal truths, and who is the sufficient reason of all things.[5]

Even Kant, who denies to pure reason any constitutive function and refuses to allow metaphysics the ability to determine objects (whether phenomenal or real), still reserves for the Ideas of Reason a regulative function governing all natural science, and an imperative determination of moral action, as well as a critical and inspirational validity in art. For Hegel, the real is the rational and the rational is real, and whereas Kant's dialectic of pure reason merely set limits to the understanding, Hegel's is "the principle of all movement, all life, and all activity in the actual world."[6]

Perhaps the most influential conception of reason, right up to the present day, has been Aristotle's, but he did not give the same account of it in all his treatises. For the most part it has been, and still is, equated with logic; and Aristotle's most influential theory of logic is contained in his *Prior Analytics*, which has, ever since, been the basis of formal logic. He gives rather a different presentation (especially of the universal) in the *Posterior Analytics*; and in *De Anima*, in the tenth book of the *Nicomachean Ethics*, and in the *Metaphysics*, we find yet another rather more profound statement of the nature of reason. The *Prior Analytics*, however, taken over by later thinkers and especially by the medieval Schoolmen, seems to have had the most lasting influence; and reason has come almost automatically to be identified with formal logic, ever since. Especially Empiricist philosophers have made this identification, which has had drastic effects upon their attitude toward the status of reason. Hume's assertion that reason is the slave of the passions is typical—but more about that anon.

2. THE ECLIPSE OF REASON

Present-day philosophers have ceased to value reason, and by most people it has been downgraded or even despised. With it has gone the respect for and the practice of metaphysics. It is no longer customary to speak of Reason with a capital *R*, or even respectable to use the word as a noun. One is still permitted, in certain contexts, to reason, and what is done on these occasions is still called reasoning, but for the most part, it is a subsidiary activity with no very substantive capacity, a merely formal procedure of only instrumental value. As Hume averred, reason serves, at best, as a means, with the help of which ends that have been selected by passion and desire (about which argument would be futile) may best be pursued. Reasoning is identified with formal logic and calculation, something that can be carried out by a machine which, properly operated, will unerringly give the right answer to any formal problem fed into it. The prevailing tendency is to reduce all thinking to a computer program and to regard the brain, the organ of thinking, as a computer, if only we knew enough about its workings. Modern symbolic logic is usually described as "a powerful instrument," although it is admitted to be powerless to discover new information, being purely analytic in its procedure, which is that of a formal calculus operated according to conventional rules of transformation, by which formulae are converted by substitution for variables into other formulae. It is thus tautological throughout.

Such a formal calculus is deductive logic. But another sort of reasoning is also countenanced: inductive logic, the only sort reputed to be capable of dealing with matters of fact, which, according to current doctrine, are altogether contingent and logically unconnected, so that none can be deduced from any other. Inductive inference assesses the probability with which factual conjuctions will recur, on the basis of the freqency with which they have occurred in the past. But this too tells us nothing new; it only estimates the chances that what has happened before will happen again. Powerful instruments, though they are held to be, these methods of reasoning are not instruments of discovery, for which, we are told, there is no logic—and so, presumably, no rational procedure. Induction as said to discover laws, but it results only in the enunciation of lawlike statements of frequent concomitances and discloses no necessary connection between facts (for there is supposed to be none), only more or less constant conjunctions. Further, its validity as reasoning was discredited by Hume and has never been satisfactorily established by any subsequent thinker.

Deduction is held to be necessary because it is tautologous, but tautology is empty of content and, to some philosophers (Hegel and F. H. Bradley, for instance) has seemed meaningless or merely silly. Induction generalizes from past occurrences but exerts no compulsion, for there is no necessity that what has happened in the past will happen in the future. Where the power of the allegedly powerful instrument lies, then, remains completely obscure.

Marxists have continued to espouse what they call dialectic, but it is a truncated and distorted sort of dialectic divorced from its true source (the self-specifying whole) and apostate to its ultimate outcome. Their doctrine is dialectical materialism—a dialectic that renounces or degrades consciousness and derogates thinking. Consciousness and all theory are thus reduced to by-products of economic necessity and its consequent social arrangements. The products of reasoning are devalued as ideology, at best a psychological outcome of material conditions, deserving no respect and without claim to truth.

Another detractor of reason is Freudianism, of which a somewhat shallow and popular version enjoys widespread following. This represents reason as a bogus self-justification of desire (or *libido*), the genuine character of which has been repressed. Philosophical doctrines and other professed beliefs are held to be simply rationalizations without authenticity or solid foundation. The springs of all thought and conduct are set in blind, unconscious appetite, and the rest is mere window dressing and deception.

Authenticity, however, is revered and sought after by existentialists, who find it in free choice, for which reason is, at best, only one option. Commitment and acceptance of responsibility are taken to be the hallmarks of the authentic, but what commitments are to be undertaken may not be prescribed. Free choice

remains entirely arbitrary, and the free self is absolved from all principle—
except that the choice be unrestricted by preconceived imperatives.

The lay public retains due deference to science, but this is recognized only
as pursuing a method of observation and experiment in which reasoning, so far
as it plays a legitimate part, is confined to mathematics; and that, like formal
logic, is a calculus which formulates equations between observed quantities and,
by its own operation, discovers no empirical facts. Scientists themselves, meanwhile, are often among the chief antagonists of reason. Along with some contemporary philosophers, many scientists are engaged in an ardent advocacy of
materialism and mechanism, assimilating human thinking to digital computation. Many biologists pursue the goal of explaining all biological phenomena
in terms of physics and chemistry. Reductionism is the order of the day, and
all vestige of teleological explanation is eschewed (such terms as "function,"
"adaptation," "selection," and "survival value" notwithstanding). Similarly, for
the most part, psychologists' consciences are easiest when reference is made to
nothing other than observable behavior, which can be reduced ultimately to
mechanical action. Consciousness, thought, reason—*ils n'ont pas besoin de ces
hypothèses.*

The prevailing opinion, these days, is that feeling and passion dominate behavior
to the exclusion of reason, which neither has nor ought to have any influence.
The claims of reason are considered futile and ineffective, and its recommenda-
tions utopian and impracticable. Established authority appeals only to interest,
and the not uncommon revolt against it has nothing better to offer than the
anarchy of free choice, or is simply an appeal to confused sentiment. Thus is
reason eclipsed, and the dignity and authority with which past philosophers
endued her are treated (if ever noticed) as empty and ridiculous pomposity.

3. THE SELF-DEFEAT OF IRRATIONALISM

It should be immediately apparent that the rejection of reason, on whatever
pretext, is self-defeating. Deductive formalisms have been shown to rest upon
arbitrary conventions: the choice of axiom set, the adoption of transformation
rules, the stipulative definition of key terms, and the like. No solution of any
problem by such means has validity beyond the particular logic game in which
it is formulated. The selective use of any such calculus is equally arbitrary and
has no rational basis; so no solution of a substantive problem by the help of
this kind of logic can be regarded as in any significant sense true. Alternative
theorizations may have similar validity, and one is left to choose whichever
one finds convenient or most appealing. But to construct theories to suit one's
convenience or satisfy one's taste is to be unscientific at best, and dishonest at
worst. If deductive logic has no imperative authority, no purpose is served by
using it, and its instrumental function is otiose. If at this point one were to

find the entire theory of deductive logic unpalatable or inconvenient, one would be justified in substituting for it whatever one wished.

As for inductive logic, not the most assiduous and ingenious proponent of its fundamental principle has yet revealed any flaw in the argument by which Hume, in equating necessary connection with customary association, and belief with forcefulness of impression, showed that it reduces science to the same status as superstition and abandons us either to paralysis of judgment or to "carelessness and inattention."

Materialism, dialectical or any other, in reducing all the products of consciousness and reason to epiphenomenal ideology, must include itself, as a theory of nature and society. It then has as little claim to our respect, or our belief, as any other ideology. Its claim to be scientific, which must rest on the objectivity and superior cogency of scientific method, then goes by the board, for ideology has no cogency apart from emotional appeal. The theory that all theory is but the ideological product of economic arrangements then loses all credibility and is exposed as mere propaganda for a political stance prompted by class interests. This conclusion, of course, would not disconcert the Marxist, who abjures objectivity as surely as rationality. But then every other class ideology has, for its own exponents, similar claim to advocacy, and the final arbiter can only be violent confrontation.

Perhaps science, as one of the foremost deracinators of reason and consciousness, provides the most spectacular evidence against itself. First, it professes to be based on observation, but observation without consciousness is blind. Next, it prides itself on being the most meticulous of systematic thinking, never dreaming that its reduction of the brain to a digital computer calls in question its own capacity to theorize. For digital computers can do no more than operate algorithms, and algorithms not only have to be invented, but also to be interpreted, for which there are and can be no algorithms. For this, as Roger Penrose has demonstrated, insight and inventiveness are required, which no algorithm, and so no computer, can produce.[7] Grant scientists the thesis that the human organism, including its brain, is no more than a machine, and the science that formulates the thesis disappears. Again, scientist frame speculative hypotheses and have to assess the evidence that supports or refutes them. This cannot be done without judgment; but apart from consciousness, self-awareness, and self-criticism, there can be no such judgment. The theorizing that results in mechanistic and materialistic theories, therefore, by its very pronouncements, refutes its own thesis.

If the Freudian reduction of reason to "rationalization" of repressed emotional complexes is strictly adopted, all theory, Freudian or whatever, will have the same subjective and irrational status, including psychology along with the other sciences. The theory then loses all its authority and refutes itself in its own contempt for reason.

If in practice reason and rule are abandoned in the pursuit of complete freedom and so-called authentic choice, no principle is left by which the authenticity of the choice can be determined. If it is held to authenticate itself, simply by being free, then there is nothing to distinguish between any action and any other, for all deliberate choices are free, whether in obedience to or in violation of rules. Good and bad faith in action can be distinguished only with reference to some criterion of goodness, and if reason is ruled out, nothing is left to authenticate the criterion. One may adopt whatever criterion one fancies and is abandoned to sheer caprice. Every choice then becomes as authentic as every other, whether from imputed ulterior motives or not.

The renunciation of reason is a path that, in all its branchings, leads only to dead ends, and the way of life it fosters is liable to destroy itself. In C. S. Lewis's long-forgotten allegory *The Pilgrim's Regress*, the hero, John, is imprisoned by the giant Zeitgeist, from whom he is at last released by Reason in the guise of a Titaness in shining armor on a white horse. Reason sets a riddle to the giant, failure to answer which costs him his head:

> There was a certain man who was going to his own house and his enemy went with him. And his house was beyond a river too swift to swim and too deep to wade. And he could go no faster than his enemy. While he was on his journey his wife sent to him and said, You know there is only one bridge across the river; tell me, shall I destroy it that the enemy may not cross, or shall I leave it standing that you may cross? What should this man do?

Zeitgeist cannot answer and pays the forfeit. Reason explains the riddle to John as follows:

> The bridge signifies Reasoning. The Spirit of the Age wishes to allow argument and not to allow argument. . . . You must ask . . . whether any reasoning is valid or not. If they say no, then their own doctrines, being reached by reasoning fall to the ground. If they say yes, then they will have to examine your arguments and refute them on their merits.[8]

The followers of the giant had maintained that all argument was merely the rationalization of desire. This illuminating allegory predates many of our modern philosophers, but it teachers several lessons they would do well to heed.

4. *CORRUPTIO OPTIMI PESSIMA*

All these forms of rejection of reason are but disguised manifestations of the drive of reason herself. It is by argument that the philosophers and scientists reach and defend their theories, and often the kind of logic they advocate is not used in their own reasoning. No analytic theory is ever demonstrated entirely in symbolic logic—not Russell's *Logical Atomism*, Carnap's *Logische Aufbau der Welt*, Ayer's *Logic, Truth and Language*, nor Wittgenstein's *Tractatus*. This is not surprising, because no significant metaphysical or epistemological theory could be demonstrated by a deductive calculus in which all transformation of sentences was purely tautological. Nevertheless, the theories are demonstrated by argument, the soundness of which is assumed by their authors and must be tested by those to whom they are addressed in accordance with rational standards.

If we accept Hume's account of inductive reasoning, the final appeal is to custom and a feeling of expectation. Accordingly, he tells us: "'Tis not solely in poetry and music we must follow our sentiment, but likewise in philosophy." (Hume, *Treatise of Human Nature*, Book I, Part III, Section viii). He claims that his own method is that of "experimental philosophy," which presumably is inductive. Yet where can one find closer reasoning, more rigorous or more ruthlessly consistent argument?

The Marxist, who sees consciousness as a by-product of material economic arrangements, claims at the same time that those processes are dialectical. But dialectic is the activity par excellence of reason and thought, and the synthesis of opposites can be made intelligible only by the operation and in the light of speculative reason, as will presently become more apparent. Moreover, the Marxist claims superiority for the theory of dialectical materialism on the ground that it is scientific, not merely ideological.

It is, however, science that, in its very denials of spontaneous awareness, draws most copiously from that very spring, and displays most ostentatiously the prowess of original insight. Polanyi has demonstrated very cogently that all scientific skills involve unspecified and unformalized thinking, without which the formal and mechanical cannot be performed;[9] and so likewise has Penrose shown that mathematical proof is undeniably dependent upon unformalizable insight, and that no algorithm can be constructed, understood, or interpreted without conscious thought irreducible to algorithm. Popper has insisted that hypotheses are the fruit of speculative thinking (conjectures, he calls them, but no guesswork is ever devoid of all rational guidance). Hypotheses must be tested, but without judgment, the results of the tests could not be attained; without insight, the devisal of experiments would be futile, nor could their relevance to the problem be recognized.

Psychological arguments, in the same way, although they are sometimes used to depreciate reason, claim to do so on strict scientific grounds. In particular, psychoanalysis gives testimony to the persistent domination of conscious rationality. It assures us that our conscious mind will accept and acknowledge the effects of our subconscious urges only if it can give them rational form and the appearance (at least) of rational justification. It prescribes as the treatment of psychoses a method of making the subject aware of the subconscious motivation of the aberrant behavior; once this motivation is brought to consciousness and acknowledged, the behavior is restored to rational control.[10] Reason cannot be foresworn. She returns upon her own repudiation and proves it false; yet at the same time, she is its source and its sustaining inspiration.

5. WHAT IS REASON?

Up to this point, the meaning of the term reason, has merely been assumed. It has been taken to be that given it by the philosophers quoted at the outset, or by their critics, or in whatever sense is assumed by those who deny its claims or ignore its accomplishments. Now we must try to be more specific and to decide more precisely what reason is and does. Earlier philosophers, Plato and Aristotle, Descartes and Locke, for example, tended to accept a view of the mind as a collection of faculties: the senses, the memory, the imagination, the will, and the intellect; and reason, for them was either synonymous with, or the defining character of, the intellect. Hegel, however, introduced a different conception. For him, reason is no mere faculty or special function; it is the whole activity of the mind at a certain level of development, bringing to fruition the principle operative at all the prior levels—a principle immanent and at work in every phase and aspect of consciousness, as well as throughout life and nature. This principle is dialectic or, alternatively, negativity—that which delimits, defines, distinguishes, and opposes, yet at the same time unites and synthesizes.

We have already discovered that dialectic is the manner of self-differentiation and self-specification of a whole structured by a universal principle of order. Clearly, what distinguishes as well as unites is a principle of organization, which constitutes a unity out of a multiplicity by way of distinction and systematic correlation. It is no mere theoretical method but is a dynamic power of organizing, which by the very nature of wholeness and system tends toward completion and self-maintenance. The whole cannot be at the same time whole and incomplete, nor can it be undifferentiated, for it must have parts; so its essential unity is correlative to an equally essential multiplicity of mutually and internally related differences. The dialectic therefore, runs through a proliferating variety of manifestations of the unitary principle—what, in other contexts, I have called relevant variations—each and all contributing significantly to the overall wholeness (which is never mere abstract unity). Hegel's declaration that dialectic is the principle of all movement, all life, and all activity in the actual world has been confirmed as an unerring insight by contemporary science, as was illustrated above in an earlier chapter; when it reaches the self-conscious level in the human mind, it becomes aware of itself as reason. Reason, above all, is a principle of organization implicit in all natural activity and, at the mental level, is a conscious faculty of relating, coordinating, and systematizing. Here we are concerned only with its operation in this highest phase.

If one accepts this view, it will not be surprising to find reason at work even in those modes of thinking that strive to degrade, belittle, or altogether to repudiate what they (mistakenly) take to be reason. Nor is it surprising that, being themselves a manifestation of the ordering and systematizing activity of thought, their denials and abjurations are self-refuting. What they mistakenly take to be reason is what Hegel called the understanding, a necessary and important stage in the process, but not yet fully developed reason. The difference between understanding and reason and their respective products we may now try to elucidate more fully.

The understanding, Hegel explained, is that mode of thinking that attends to the variety of things and to their differences. It draws sharp distinctions, meticulously sorts out the diverse elements, and separates the distincta. This is an essential phase in the process of explanation, for precision requires that differences should not be blurred or confused together. The understanding, therefore, abhors vagueness, deplores woolly-mindedness, and insists on exactitude. Consequently, it identifies explanation with analysis and seeks to break down all complexes into their most elementary parts. Its ideal of elucidation is reductionism.

This manner of thinking is typical of Newtonian science, and is encouraged by an atomistic metaphysics. It thus infects all empiricism, as we find it especially in Hume, in Russell and in the early Wittgenstein. Its characteristic logic is formal symbolic logic, the latent presupposition of which is that reality consists of separate particulars, externally related to one another and to their inhering properties, which can be subsumed under common properties represented by abstract (or general) terms. It is the logic of the abstract universal. In this logic the primary propositions are held to be atomic, to have no intrinsic or logical connection with one another, and to state facts that are similarly atomic and related to one another entirely contingently.[11] Their truth value is assumed to be derived from observation, with which they must be compared in order to determine whether they are true or false. As statements of fact, however, their purport is to report observation, so how the comparison is to be made can never be consistently explained. One may misreport an observation, but to test the accuracy of reporting, all that can be done is to observe again and report more carefully. One can compare two such reports, but there is no way of comparing any one with the observation it is ostensively reporting. The correspondence test of truth has long since been proved untenable, for to compare a statement of direct experience with the fact it claims to report, one would have to have access to the fact independently of the experience, and there is none. Modern science has, meanwhile, demonstrated the undeniable interdependence of physical facts and the consequent inseparability of the statements that report them. The logic and metaphysics of the understanding, accordingly, collapse irretrievably and must be superseded by a more holistic approach.

It is because digital computation depends on formal logic that those who equate formal logic with reason tend to consider the brain a computer and thinking the operation of a program, forgetting that programs are written by human beings who first have to invent the computer "language" and construct the algorithm.

If, however, too much emphasis is placed on differences, and the distinguished opposites are segregated and held in isolation, they contradict themselves, because what gives them their distinctive character and what defines them is what negates them, what gives them definite outlines and demarcates their limits. Their precise character, accordingly, depends upon what they are not, and it cannot be affirmed without the implication of their relation to what is other. In short, they are inextricably interwoven into a systematic pattern, without which they cannot be what is claimed for them. In presumed isolation, therefore, they at once both deny and affirm this connection, and so contradict themselves. For the contradiction to be resolved they must be seen in interconnection, in the context of the whole to which they belong, and grasping them in this holistic perspective is the work of reason proper, in its speculative phase.

What the understanding overlooks is that differences and distinctions always imply mutual relationships and that they are always made within a context held together as a whole. The contrasting opposites are therefore always mutually complementary. It follows that atomic propositions can have no truth value, because what determines their truth or falsehood is their implication of other statements about interrelated facts. It is the coherence of these intermeshed relationships that establishes their truth, and the clash of incompatible statements that reveals their falsity.

6. REASON AND RATIONALISM

Empiricism is blind to the difference between understanding and reason, and the oversight of the difference has marred even more perspicacious theories. Those that give major respect to reason are usually called rationalist, and what is called rationalism has had a long history in which the term has assumed a variety of different meanings. First, there is the rationalism of the Stoics, for the most part following the view of reason propagated by Plato and Aristotle, which gives precedence to form over matter. Much the same view of reason (we have observed) was taken over by the medieval Schoolmen. But Aristotle's ambivalence with respect to reason and logic infected their conception, confusing the work of the understanding with that of reason proper. Descartes inherited much from these sources, and it is his epistemology that is primarily credited as rationalism. Its weaknesses have been brilliantly exposed by H. H. Joachim, who shows that it depends too strongly on the notion of "simple natures," which are, in fact, neither simple nor mutually independent, and so implicitly confuses the work of the understanding with that of reason proper.[12]

Descartes's followers, Spinoza and Leibniz, are usually classed with him as rationalists, but their conception of reason differs significantly from his and is much more defensible. My present purpose does not require discussion of these philosophers, and I may simply refer the reader to what I have written about them elsewhere.[13]

There is another type of thinker who lays claim to the title rationalist: those who profess to believe only what reason sanctions and to reject what is supported by nothing more than faith (generally disparaged by them as superstition). Many such writers tend to give prominence and preference to science and to scientific theories. Depending upon the scientific theories to which they defer, their approach may be more or less respectable, but in general, they tend toward the more empiricist attitude in science and fail, once again, to notice that the rationalism of the understanding falls short of devotion to reason in its maturest form.

We need not explore the whole extent of this kind of rationalism, but there is one outstanding thinker, Brand Blanshard, whose writing on the nature of thought (in a treatise of that name)[14] is remarkable, seminal, and eminently commendable, expounding a doctrine of truth as coherence to which it would be difficult to take exception—a topic to which a subsequent chapter will be devoted. But in a later work, *Reason and Belief*, Blanshard seems to revert to a conception of reason that is neither viable in itself nor consistent with what he has said elsewhere. Examination of his position will bring out the main point I am concerned to emphasize.

Most of what Blanshard maintains is so sound and well founded that to cavil at his position might seem to be mere carping, and indeed the bulk of his contentions are not to be contested. My sole misgiving is that his account of rationality in this work is at variance with his oft-repeated view about coherence, both as the nature of truth and of the world at large. Here he contends that reason demands that no conclusion should be accepted that is inconsistent with the best available evidence, and that contradiction is not to be tolerated, because two mutually contradictory statements cannot both be true. Being rational is thus being self-consistent. Few would wish to dissent from these assertions.

Blanshard espouses self-consistency not just as a canon of right thinking and belief but as an ontological principle, which is the ground and support of right reasoning. In his words:

> We are committed to a world that is rational to this extent, that nothing in it is either self-contradictory or contradictory of anything else. The real world is a coherent world, in the sense that it is at least self-consistent.[15]

Blanshard concedes that this does not mean that self-contradictions are never asserted or that conflicts never occur. It means only that the world is such that it cannot have incompatible attributes, and, in consequence, no two self-contradictory assertions about it can both be true.

As far as this goes, it is unexceptionable, but much depends on how one understands self-consistency and its relation to coherence, and how one interprets the Laws of Thought, of Identity, and of Contradiction. If one adheres to the interpretation typical of the understanding, the laws themselves become self-contradictory, and the demand for consistency conflicts with the requirements of coherence.

Coherence is the distinguishing (in fact, the defining) characteristic of ordered wholeness, involving structure and organization—a coherent unity of differences. But this concept is by no means simple, for there are different types and degrees of wholeness, exemplifying on different levels the universal concept of order. Consequently, as we have seen, unified wholeness is hierarchical, ranging from more abstract to more concrete and integrated forms. This, in itself, militates against the notion of consistency demanded by the understanding, although it tolerates and requires consistency in another sense, a consistency that varies according to the level of concretion contemplated.

Self-consistency, in the abstract, requires noncontradiction. It does not require, and at least *prima facie* conflicts with, unity in and through difference. For unity and difference are at first sight mutually contradictory. Hence self-consistency is, *prima facie*, incompatible with coherence, which is the unification of differences. For the understanding, identity tolerates no difference whatever, and the Law of Identity prescribes sheer monotonous repetition: A is A. Gertrude Stein's insistence that "a rose is a rose is a rose" reveals no variety and is the acme of consistency, but it is hardly coherent. Featureless uniformity involves no contradiction and is immaculately self-consistent, but it does not consitute a whole and is the opposite of differentiated unity. If rationality requires the latter, it must reject the former. In fact, featureless uniformity cannot maintain itself and collapses into nonentity, for what is real must have some distinguishing character, and what is featureless has none.

Furthermore, when we look more closely, abstract identity, uniform consistency, is seen to contradict itself. "A is A is A is A"—the uniform sameness of distinct entities—is a contradiction in terms, for distinct elements, to be distinguished, must differ, and so cannot be the same. Whatever occurs in such a string of professedly identical terms must be the same as A; but the second and the third As are not the same as the first, and so of them we are compelled to judge that A is not A, violating the law of contradiction. Yet if the successive As are in no way distinct, the proposition cannot be proponed; and if they are, they cannot be strictly and abstractly identical. A must be other than A, it must be not-A, or the law of identity cannot be enunciated.[16]

So likewise the law of contradiction becomes self-contradictory, for if A is not not-A, A and not-A must be different and opposed, but the difference must be significant if they are to be distinguished. We could write not-A is not A, and we would have an identity, not simply because what is not A is identical with not-A (which makes the proposition self-consistent), but because there is no difference between the proposition and its converse, hence no significant difference between the terms. If so, the difference between A and not-A as distincta has been overridden. Either is not the other, so each is other than the other, and they may be transposed. For the purpose of mutual exclusion, they are the same; so the assertion contradicts itself, and the Law of Contradiction is contraverted.

This result, however, is only the consequence of taking identity and difference as abstractly excluding each other. If we recognize that identity always involves difference and vice versa, the Laws of Thought retain their validity. If they did not, all discourse would be at an end, for then we could not even assert that the laws were self-consistent. These laws, however, must be understood and interpreted always in relation to a systematic structure of meaning and fact, without reference to which the terms "identity" and "difference" lose any clear meaning.

An identity cannot be maintained in isolation, because nothing in isolation has identifiable character. What identifies it is what distinguishes it from what it is not, the other that defines it. To be identical, it must be distinguished from everything else. Similarly, difference can be discerned and distinction made only if and because identities have been established, which they can be only within some systematic structure. It is insistence on bare, unqualified identity in total isolation from every determining relation, and on sheer difference divorced from the background structure always tacitly and necessarily presupposed, that subverts the Laws of Thought and leads to self-contradiction (a submission, clearly, that nobody could make if those laws did not hold). The subversion of its own logic is the effect of the abstraction on which the understanding insists, unmindful of the systematic implications of the very terms that it idolizes. This blind separation of identity and difference, and the consequent demand for unrelieved consistency, is what contradicts coherence. The former is never prior to the latter, for coherence alone can give significance to consistency, which is always derivative from it.

Again, for the understanding, coherence must contradict consistency, for coherence is characteristic of order and structure, of unified differences and of unity in difference. An ordered system is a one of many, a unification of diverse elements or parts. But, for the understanding, to unify differences is to contradict oneself. It is to find an identity where only differences exist. What is one, we are told by philosophers who think on this level, cannot be many, nor what is many one. Nor is an organized system simply the juxtaposition of opposites (one and many), for its unity is constituted by the interconnection of its parts, and its integrity consists in their intermesh. Apart from the differences, there is no unity, for they alone are united in it. To the understanding, this makes no sense; it declares that the parts are simply together, and it is just their togetherness that makes the collection a whole. Accordingly, the coherence of a system in which the nature of the elements depends on their interrelations and the relations between them are determined by their several natures is, for the understanding, meaningless, self-contradictory, or circular nonsense. For consistency (the allegation is), each part must be exclusively itself, and its relation to the others purely exteral. Blanshard advocates a coherence theory of truth, but he makes coherence secondary to consistency, falling back inadvertently to the level of the understanding and betraying his own best insight. We shall presently see the devastating effects this defection has upon his metaphysics.

In an organized system, the diverse elements are mutually adapted, and not only is their determination of one another reciprocal, but it is governed by the principle of structure universal to the whole. Only what conflicts with this principle is self-contradictory, and what conforms to it consistent. Order and system require more subtle and complex relationships than blank identity and bare negation, relationships of which these are but inadequate representations and abstract figments.

A whole that is organized and coherent is of necessity internally differentiated, for without diversity there would be nothing to cohere. Diversity implies distinction, and that again negation. But only in a coherent system is negation significant, for significant negation always rests upon a positive base. To negate *A* is to assert *B*, or *C* or *D*, and to these, if we refrain from specifying, we apply the compendious term not-*A*. But because these distincta are the differentiations of an integrated system, they are not separable or altogether exclusive of one another. Their participation in the system is reflected in the special character of each of them, and their mutual relations determine their very particularity and distinctiveness. Hence their mutual distinction is at the same time a mutual intercommunion, and their mutual negation an affirmation of the identity in which they all share. None of this would be so, however, unless identity and difference were themselves distingishable and opposed concepts. But they can be so only on the same condition: that they are interdependent and complementary aspects of one unitary system.

What is self-contradictory is what disrupts the system—what at one and the same time posits the system (implicitly affirming and exemplifying its principle of organization) and conflicts with that principle so that implicitly the structure is wrecked. *A* is what it is in virtue of its relationships to *B*, *C*, and *D*. It is not self-subsistent but depends for its being and character on its place in the prevailing order. Affirm *A* in isolation, as self-maintaining and independent, and, while implicitly invoking the structure that gives it meaning, you explicitly deny or suppress the principle of order giving the system structure. Accordingly, the implicit principle will assert itself in the affirmation of *A* as *A*, and its suppression will produce a contradiction. Alternatively, assert *A* in place of *B* and you at once implicitly affirm the principle of order that makes each of them what they are, and also deny it by relating *A* to its neighbors according to a different principle, placing it where only *B* can be affirmed, where it could not be *A*. It is not that *A* and *B* sheerly exclude each other. They do not, for they are intrinsically related. But that very interconnection between them forbids their transposition.

Not even such self-contradiction would, however, be possible unless the principle of order is at the same time and in all cases instantiated. Otherwise nothing could intelligibly be enunciated at all, not even something intelligibly false. Nothing intelligible is utterly absurd or false. What is so is what has been displaced within the system, or isolated from it. The most blatantly false statement of fact presumes and affirms by implication a whole structure of truth on the basis of which its very falsehood rests, for its falsehood consists in its unwarranted claim to truth, a claim that can be made only in a presupposed context of reality that must be concurrently affirmed. "Washington is to the north of New York" is false only on the basis of a presumed topography of the United States, the main structure of which must be accurate. If that is not concurrently affirmed by implication, the proposition cannot have the purport that is impugned. Falsehood and contradiction, therefore, involve truth and consistency in what seems to the understanding to be an inconsistent manner.

What, to philosophers of the understanding, and even to Blanshard, seems worse, is that truth cannot avoid contradiction. For the whole, the structure of which demands and determines coherence, cannot be explicitly posited as a whole all at once. Its wholeness necessitates its differences, but its differences cannot all be contracted to a point or be asserted in extenso in an instant. For the whole to be adequately cognized, they must be run off or spelled out. Thus each, as it is affirmed, is bound to be only partial and inadequate to the whole that is immanent in it. As such, it necessarily involves contradiction and must, for that very reason, be superseded—must, to form a more adequate whole, be united with what it negates and excludes. The exposition of the whole can only be dialectical, and dialectic both posits and reconciles opposites, in a process that cannot avoid contradiction; but that again stimulates further efforts to remove the discord, to resolve the conflict and advance to a higher degree of unison. Contradiction and coherence are therefore so far from incompatible that they are mutually involved. Without a coherent system contradiction has no force or meaning, and without contradiction the dialectical self-specification of the whole cannot proceed. Blanshard's rigid refusal to tolerate contradiction in any form or sense, his rejection of dialectic, therefore, involves his own theory in the very inconsistency that he strives to avoid. In the metaphysical position he develops, this becomes sorely apparent, as will be demonstrated in the following chapter.

The rationalism that sticks fixedly to abstract consistency has not advanced beyond the initial phase of reason, that of the understanding. In contrast, what gives precedence to genuine coherence is the true rationalism of speculative insight, of reason proper, which is the dialectical process become self-conscious and self-critical, the operation of the universal principle of organization generating and constituting the ultimate whole.

Notes

Some of the material in this chapter was taken from the presidential address to the Metaphysical Society of America in 1968, published in *Review of Metaphysics*, vol. 22, no. 4 (1969), and from "Reason and Rationalism," *Idealistic Studies*, vol. 9, no. 2 (1979).

1. Plato, *Republic*, VI, 511b.
2. Aristotle, *Metaphysics*, 1072b18–30, 1074b35.
3. René Descartes, *Discours de la Méthode*, I.
4. Benedict de Spinoza, *Tractatus de Intellectus Emendatione*, and cf. *Ethics*, Pt V, props. 25–32, 42S.
5. Cf. G. W. Leibniz, *Monadology*, 43, and *Theodicy*, 20.
6. G. W. F. Hegel, *Encyclopaedia of Philosophical Sciences*, I, §81, *Zusatz*.
7. Cf. Roger Penrose, *The Emperor's New Mind*, p. 42.
8. C. S. Lewis, *The Pilgrim's Regress*, pp. 72, 81f.
9. Cf. Michael Polanyi, *Personal Knowledge: Towards a Post-Critical Philosophy*.
10. Cf. Sir Malcolm Knox, *Action*, pp. 155f.
11. Cf. E. E. Harris, *Formal, Transcendental and Dialectical Thinking*, pt. 1, chap. 1.
12. H. H. Joachim, *Descartes's Rules for the Direction of the Mind*.
13. Cf. E. E. Harris, *Nature, Mind and Modern Science*, chap. 9; *Salvation from Despair: A Reappraisal of Spinoza's Philosophy*, chaps. 2 and 8; *The Substance of Spinoza*, chaps. 1 and 10; "Leibniz and Modern Science," in *Metaphysics as Foundation*.
14. Brand Blanshard, *The Nature of Thought*; cf. my essay "Blanshard on Perception and Free Ideas," in *The Philosophy of Brand Blanshard*.
15. Brand Blanshard, *Reason and Belief*, p. 479.
16. Cf. G. Frege, *Foundations of Arithmetic*, pp. 47f: "The symbols i', i'', i''' tell the tale of our embarrassment. We must have identity—hence the i; but we must have difference—hence the strokes; only unfortunately, the latter undo the work of the former." (John Austin's translation). The entire section is apposite.

15

A "Rationalist" Metaphysic

1. CAUSATION AND THE UNIFORMITY OF NATURE

If one ignores or neglects the dialectical character of reason, whether as expressed in thought and discourse or as immanent in all nature and all existence, one tends to restrict oneself to a relatively low level in the scale of forms and to claim as rational what, when pushed to its implied conclusion, becomes absurd. This, unfortunately, seems to be the fate of the ontology offered to us in brief outline by Blanshard in *Reason and Belief*, despite its professed rationalism. The position he advocates is hardly consistent with that so eloquently defended in his earlier work. He still professes a coherence theory of knowledge and reality, and with it the implied doctrines of internal relations and degrees of truth, which should lead to a rather different metaphysic from the one here outlined (and of which he sometimes drops hints, that should lead to serious modifications of its apparent meaning). These reservations notwithstanding, what is presented in the later work is a view of the world that is far from rational and harbors glaring inconsistencies.

The real world is said to be coherent because it involves no inconsistencies of fact. Nothing in it contradicts anything else. This conjunction of coherence with noncontradiction is subject to the strictures voiced in the previous chapter but is so far acceptable, as it makes coherence the hallmark of rationality. The nature and extent of the noncontradiction remain to be investigated. The second characteristic of a rational world, on Blanshard's view, is the uniformity of nature. This means that all things behave lawfully and that the laws are universal and necessary. Prima facie, Blanshard's account of these laws suggests that they are all laws of efficient causation, but he does allow that final causes operate in human purposive behavior, which is nevertheless determined, although, if rationally determined, it is "free." As the rationality of nature consists in its being entirely determined by universal causal laws (presumably efficient), how the exception occurs in the case of human conduct is not made clear, nor is it obvious how the rationality of free action differs from that of natural determinism. Blanshard says that the determination of human action is incom-

220

patible with human dignity only if the determination is purely mechanical, implying that it is not, but he does not carify the difference and tells us only that "the line of causality runs, not around or beneath the human spirit, but through it."[1] To the anticipated objection that this would make human beings only mental or spiritual robots instead of mechanical ones, his reply is that the alternative (indetermination) would be worse. With this last contention we may agree, but it is far from clear what kind of causation is contemplated as mental or spiritual. Meanwhile, the picture we are given is of a completely determined universe, governed, at least on the physical level, by efficient causation.

Unfortunately, this is not a coherent ontology, not for any reason offered us by Hume, but for one that goes much further back in the history of philosophy and was adumbrated by Plato in the *Phaedo*. Every effect has a cause, and every cause an effect, but every cause is also an effect, and every effect is also a cause. The "system" is thus open-ended and open at both ends and is not, therefore, a whole. Nor is it coherent, because if the ground of any existent or event is its cause, and the series of causes regresses infinitely, however universal and necessary causal laws may be, no ultimate ground either of the series as a whole (for it is not a whole) or of any item in it is ever forthcoming. What we have is what Hegel called the bad (or the false) infinite, an endless regress in which the finite is never transcended and the infinite never reached. Kant showed that such a conception of the world leads to insoluble antinomies, so we are left with a thoroughly inconsistent and incoherent conception of the universe.

The medieval theologians sought to resolve the antinomy by postulating the existence of God—a necessary being—as the ground of all finites and the source of all causation. But Kant rejected the Cosmological Argument as invalid, and Blanshard firmly refuses to contemplate the necessary existence of an omnipotent being in a flawed world (as it will shortly appear). He is thus left advocating a conception of the universe that is incoherent, even if typical of science at a certain level and generally espoused by the understanding.

Blanshard might have pleaded in defense that nobody is wholly rational[2] and no metaphysic completely coherent. But if one professes to be a rationalist, one may not tolerate an incoherent account of the world and so ought to reject one that presents it in the way it has been described. On the other hand, if rationality is a matter of degree, and if we conceive the universe as a whole of interdependent parts (accepting the view of the physical world currently advocated by many eminent physicists), we shall adopt a different theory. In a coherent universe, the principle of order may well specify itself in particular events that are, accordingly, subject to univeral and necessary laws, and these may manifest themselves at a certain level as causal laws. But the causality will not be exclusively efficient. It will also be teleological in the sense proposed in Chapter 10 above (which is not incompatible with efficient causation)—that the universal principle of organization determines the connection between things and events. Such a theory, however, would lead to conclusions very different from what Blanshard was prepared to contemplate.

The failure of a system of laws of efficient causation to produce a rational conception of the universe once again is the result of the conflict between coherence and abstract formal consistency. A causal series is apparently self-consistent; it involves no obvious contradictions, but it cannot constitute a self-sustaining coherent whole. Blanshard declares that it is coherent (*op cit.*, Ch. XIII, §§5–6), but does not show how it can be.[3] The notion of efficient causation implies something beyond its conceptual limits that is needed to make it wholly intelligible, and this is the idea of system fully explicated. If so, to be properly rational, a more developed theory is required than Blanshard offers, with implications for the world and for religion that he is unwilling to accept.

2. PERCEPTION

There are, moreover, further inconsistencies in the cosmological schema offered by Blanshard in this book, which militate against its rationality and which become apparent when we examine the account he gives of perception and of values. Blanshard's theory of perception, as set out in *The Nature of Thought*, has much to recommend it. Its one major defect is its failure directly to address the question how we are assured of perceptual veridicality.[4] In *Reason and Belief*, this question is, if anything, further obscured by the suggestion of a correspondence theory of truth quite foreign to and inconsistent with Blanshard's general position.

There is no call to demur at the statement that our perceiving is the judgment that we make on the warrant of what is presented to us sensuously in consciousness. To be consistent, we must affirm only what the evidence justifies, and so (Blanshard holds) we should follow in Berkeley's footsteps, for he is especially careful to appeal only to the evident phenomena and to eschew whatever cannot be asserted on their warrant. Accordingly, Blanshard adopts a Berkeleyan epistemology, although he rejects Berkeley's metaphysical conclusion that *esse* is *percipi*. Our perception of the world is wholly subjective to each one of us, who "cannot share the contents of another's field of consciousness." But, Blanshard goes on to assert, what perception reveals to us, contrary to commonsense belief, is not the world as it is in itself, but simply the phenomena resulting from effects upon our bodies. Even our perception of our bodies, like that of all other material objects, is purely subjective, and our belief in their existence apart from what we perceive of them is entirely inferential. This is as true of the scientist's observations as of common experience. To suppose otherwise, we are told, would throw into hopeless confusion the very theory of perception adopted by surgeons and (presumably) physiologists.[5]

But we can and do infer to one another's experience and to an external world of physical reality. The basis of this inference, he appears to be saying, is empirical science: "Science does attempt this differential explanation of things." And science, though it can give no finally demonstrable proof of its conclusions, can show them to have been "far too massively confirmed for philosophers to ignore."[6] In fact, it seems to be on the strength of the neurosurgeon's conviction that whatever we perceive is due solely to our brain states that Blanshard concludes to the necessity of epistemological idealism.

Yet it seems hardly consistent to accept as massively convincing the evidence offered by the scientist of the existence of an external world independent of human perceiving, if it is also admitted that all scientific observation is subjective to the scientist's mind. We can and do infer to the existence of our own and other people's bodies, to external existences, and to the contents of others' experience, but this cannot make the conclusions we reach any less subjective.

That perception is based on sensation and that sensation in its phenomenal aspect is mental it would be foolish to deny; but that much more is required for perception we have learned not only from Kant and Hegel but also in persuasive detail from Blanshard himself. The "much more" is still the work of the mind as it constructs from the contents of its psychical field a world of objective fact, and this construction is not arbitrary or factitious. It involves principles of organization implicit in the sensory material itself. But all the work of science is included in this constructive ordering and systematizing, and no appeal can consistently be made to anything outside it for a test of its truth. That depends on nothing other than its comprehensive coherence—and it is to Blanshard as much as to any thinker that we owe this insight. Any theory of perception that seeks to validate perceptual judgment by comparison with or inference to an external and independent body of "fact" is at once involved, as was Bertrand Russell's, in insuperable difficulties.[7] But here Blanshard seems to have moved to a position much nearer to, if not the same as, Russell's, one that assumes a knowledge of the physical world and its effects on our bodies, a knowledge independent of our immediate perception, to which we can appeal in order to correlate our perceptual experience with that exterior world.

Moreover, the theory of perception usually adopted by most surgeons and neurophysiologists, to which Blanshard seems to be deferring, is indeed a mass of hopeless confusion, because they begin by assuming the reality of material objects as they are ordinarily perceived, including living bodies on which they experiment; they then observe that their subjects' awareness of things outside these bodies is dependent on the neural discharges in their brains caused by the external things; then, finding that their subjects report similar sensations when the brain is similarly stimulated by different causes, they conclude that the qualities experienced are dependent only on the neural activity, irrespective of the original causes. They then maintain that the external bodies are devoid of the qualities we perceive and that all we can ever know of them is what our senses reveal and what we may infer from that. This should lead to a Berkeleyan metaphysic that would run counter to the original assumptions from which they began.

If our perception is wholly subjective and unlike things as they really are, if this is true equally of our awareness of our own bodies, how can we base the conclusion that it is so subjective on what we observe of "external" bodies? On the other hand, if we can know that external things are other than they appear to us in perception, it can only be because we know those things by some other means. But we have no other means. We must assume that our perception of the world and of our own bodies somehow reveals them to us as they really are (even if they are not as they appear) if we are to demonstrate from our scientific knowledge of the effects of external bodies on our nervous systems and brains that our perception cannot so reveal them to us.

Here then we have both inconsistency and incoherence consequent upon too rigid a separation of mind from the physical world, coupled with an equally firm determination to be consistent about the subjectivity of consciousness, leaving on one's hands two separate spheres that must, yet cannot, be related except by some external correspondence which will not serve to explain the possibility of knowledge. These faults are features of a correspondence theory of perception that, in all his other writings, Blanshard has sedulously avoided, yet here he seems explicitly to embrace:

> The universe is an order in which all events are interconnected by links of causation and necessity. In this universe there have emerged conscious minds, each limited in immediate awareness to the qualities and structures that appear in its own experience. *From these qualities and structures it is possible to infer certain causes and certain abstract corresponding structures in the external world*, though this world is cut off from direct access, and seems bound to remain only dimly and inferentially known. (Ibid, my italics).

How, we may ask, is it possible to infer to causes external to our perceptions, which, as even Locke confessed, "appear not to our senses to operate in their production"? We do infer from our perception of physical things and effects produced upon our sense organs that what we sense is the result of neural processes, but this cannot enable us to infer that these perceptions themselves are caused by corresponding external processes, especially when we conclude from the dependence of the sensations on neural activity that they do not necessarily correspond to any external causes. Our conviction of the existence of an external world corresponding to our perception of it, and of the veridicality of that perception, must be rooted in more consistent reasoning.

What lies suppressed in this theory of perception and of the world is the insuperable mystery of how, from a causally determined physical world, conscious minds could emerge. And that brings with it a further question: How does a chain of physical and physiological causes give rise to appearances in consciousness? How can the perceptual world apparent to me (and none other is) be related to the physical world of mechanical causation in one coherent and rational system? No answer is to be found in Blanshard's professed rationalism. He can see nothing in the nature of the causal system of the world to compel or incline him to believe that it involves mentality—certainly not its being governed by mathematical laws, from which it does not follow that it can exist only in some consciousness (so he maintains in response to Eddington and Jeans). The physical world thus remains apart from and irreconcilable with the existence of human awareness, and the conversion of physical causation into human mentation remains unintelligible. In the words of Joseph Glanvil:

> How the purer spirit is united to this Clod is a knot too hard for fallen Humanity to untie. How should thought be united to a marble statue or a sun-beam to a lump of clay! The freezing of words in the air in the northern climes, is as conceivable, as is this strange union.

Is the final response to be Blanshard's confession that man is but "brokenly and imperfectly rational"? No doubt, but can he afford to be brokenly and imperfectly rationalist? If we are rationalists, on his own plea, we must reject the incoherent and self-contradictory, and if we do, we cannot accept the metaphysical position he offers in this book.

We should reach a more rational theory by advancing from the admirable foundation laid down in *The Nature of Thought* to the recognition that the truth of perceptual experience is to be found in its self-reflective development, which proceeds dialectically, presenting us in science with a theory of the world as an undissectable whole, within which an evolutionary (and similarly dialectical) process produces intelligent life, integrating in sentience its own metabolic and physiological activity in response to the effects upon it of its environment. The dialectical structure of this experience and knowledge is then direct evidence for the dialectical structure of the world, making both our perception of it and of our membership in it together rationally intelligible.[8]

3. MORALITY AND VALUE

Difficulties of a like kind assail us when we turn to Blanshard's account of values and morality. On the side of intellect, the human mind seeks satisfaction in the conception of the world as a coherent system. On the practical side, we are told, it seeks the fulfillment of impulse. But human fulfillment is not limited to the satisfaction of blind appetite or mere instinctive urge. We become conscious of our appetites and their objects, converting them into desires, and we organize our impulses to attain ends consciously pursued. The conscious and deliberate ordering of means to achieve ends is purpose, and the organization of purposive activities subordinate to a supreme objective is morality. Choice between major policies involves the conception of value, which is a function of the fulfillment of human needs. We find experience good because it is fulfilling, not fulfilling because we find it good. Value is thus neither a nonnatural quality nor a mere feeling; although an essential feature of the fulfillment necessary to value, is pleasure, what makes it valuable is not pleasure by itself. Value, then, is the pleasurable fulfillment of human nature.

Blanshard does not insist, like Kant, that the nature to be fulfilled is and must be only the rational nature of humankind. But he does claim that his theory of value is rationalistic because it requires a rational determination of means to ends, rational assessment of the consequences of action, and rational comparison and appraisal of the ends pursued. He also claims that it is objective, for what really does satisfy can be judged objectively, judged though it must be in the light of long experience. Similarly, it can be objectively and rationally determined what will prove most satisfying to the greatest number. Moreover, reason prescribes the rule that we should seek the greatest net good of all affected by our action.

Most of this doctrine is sound and acceptable. That value is inseparable from human desire and purpose is not to be denied. That it is limited to the fulfillment of human impulse may be questioned, but there can be little doubt that human impulse raised to the conscious level and organized to fulfill the aspirations of a self-conscious personality is the basis of morality and the root of value. What, in Blanshard's statement, remains obscure is (1) the ultimate object that would finally satisfy, and (2) the nature whose needs are to be fulfilled. It seems to be, when all is said and done, solely or mainly the affective and impulsive nature of humankind. Blanshard has always been a staunch opponent of emotivism, but here we must ask what criterion of satisfaction is being offered other than feeling. If ultimately none is, we are committed to a noncognitive ethic, the ultimate values of which can be dictated only by sentiment, or some mysterious form of intuition, the rationality of which is restricted to the instrumental function of intelligence estimating consequences and fitting means to ends. The ends themselves seem not to be determined by reason, except so far as reason can decide which of any two is the more fulfilling—and that again depends in the last resort on experience. Why, under these conditions, reason should prescribe the pursuit of the good of others, the greatest net good of all affected by the action, is not immediately apparent, unless it is maintained that human nature is such that it cannot otherwise be fulfilled; and that, if individual nature is meant (to which alone we can attribute impulse), is not immediately obvious from experience. Such an ethic is only secondarily rationalistic, for what satisfies impulse—not reason is the ultimate end.

This point we may pass over to consider a more important issue: the relation of human aspirations and values to the "rational" system of the universe—the "causal whole." In that system, Blanshard finds no evidence of value, apart from what human beings seeking self-fulfillment conceive. He views with sympathy but skepticism the attempts of Royce and Bosanquet to demonstrate goodness of the Absolute and finds neither fact nor theory supporting the view that the universe is in any sense good, even in being logically complete and coherent. How then should one view one's place in this neutral, indifferent world? For us it can have no value. Its laws are indifferent to our aims and aspirations, except fortuitously to thwart or to facilitate their attainment. If the fulfillment of our nature is a rational end, the world is not designed to achieve it and, to that extent, cannot be seen as rational. Yet that same world is what has generated human beings as intelligent persons. Under the conditions it has provided, they have evolved as organisms with appetites and desires craving fulfillment, for which, however, the world does not specifically provide. For the most part, the struggle for that fulfillment is frustrated by natural circumstances. Human desire, therefore, seems to introduce a contradiction into the system of the world, standing in conflict with the cosmos we inhabit. For we are self-conscious, aspiring, craving beings with a rational capacity, who find ourselves in an indifferent, neutral, and even hostile world. If so, neither is the universe rational nor is the human situation.

Further, we must ask if, in this predicament, human desire itself can be considered rational, and what, so circumstanced, human fulfillment could be. Human needs are the necessities for survival, and their supply ministers to our self-preservation, but of what value is survival in an alien world, and why should we endeavor to persist in our own being? On Blanshard's view, the world rationally conceived provides nothing that makes survival in it worthwhile. Are we to say that life is intrinsically good? If so, on what grounds? It cannot be simply because it is pleasant (even if that were true), first, because we have been told that pleasure, although a condition of value, is not its constitutive essence, and second and more important, because pleasure can never be an end in itself, for it supervenes upon success in the achievement of ends desired independently. Unless such ends can be identified and their attainment can be seen as possible, life can scarcely be pleasant. And even if pleasure could be an end in itself, its enjoyment would not be a *rational* fulfillment. What then could constitute a rational fulfillment of human nature? The good of others? But that only raises the same question over again and launches us on an infinite regress.

Fulfillment can only be the filling out of defect and the supply of deficiency. It must supplement the finite and develop it into the self-sufficient and complete. The finiteness of human nature is what generates desires, and their fulfillment must involve the reconciliation of that nature with the infinite of which we find ourselves a part. But if our nature is rational and purposive and the world is mechanical and valueless, no such reconciliation seems conceivable and no fulfillment possible. What then could be a rational aim for human desire? If the world, as rationally conceived, proves indifferent to human values, if it is opposed and foreign to our rational aspirations, it is one in which we can find no rational satisfaction. It is a world into which, as Heidegger would say, we have been thrown and to which we cannot rationally belong. In short, it is an absurd world in which our situation as desiring beings seeking fulfillment, yet at the same time as products of an indifferent nature, is totally absurd.

In relation to our longing for self-realization, the vast irrelevance of interstellar space oppresses the imagination. The laws of nature seem blindly indifferent to the attainment of our goals; the forces they generate are monstrously destructive of the products of our feeble efforts. When we strive to harness them in our service, they turn against us and threaten our survival. Even our own natural desires militate against our endeavor to find peace and contentment, for they conflict and drive us into mutual enmity, prompting us to savagery and vandalism. Nature, as envisaged by Blanshard, whether inanimate or human, seems, in reference to our finer aspirations, to be wholly irrational.

What grounds, then, does Blanshard have for maintaining that to be moral is rational?[9] Morality is rightly said to be the coherent organization of our impulses in subordination to a supreme objective. But that would be rational only if the supreme objective were dictated by reason and only if it were in principle attainable. Blanshard contends that a coherent fulfillment of one's desires in common with those of other people is what would satisfy our purposive and emotional nature. So far, there can be little doubt that he is right. No fulfillment would be complete or coherent, however, either for oneself or for others, unless intellectual satisfaction were attainable in harmony with practical and aesthetic. And if what satisfies the understanding is the conception of a deterministic world indifferent and mainly hostile to our objectives, it is one that could never be reconciled with our moral and aesthetic aspirations. For into such a world rational beings would feel that they had been gratuitously thrown, and in such a world, coherent fulfillment would ipso facto be defeated. Even to desire it would be irrational, because it would be futile and in vain.

The cosmology here being contemplated is one in which the physical universe is irrelevant, or opposed, or both, to human fulfillment, and in such a world, value, as Blanshard has defined it, could not be realized. Moreover, the facts of common experience suggest that, in a determined world governed throughout by causal laws, the natural obstacles to human wishes, to say nothing of our own recalcitrant passions, must constantly frustrate our endeavors, and we should have no clear goal to strive for. Unlike Aristotle, whom in much else he seems to follow, Blanshard postulates no Prime Mover, no God whose activity is active reason, which human beings along with the entire cosmos seek to imitate, and in the contemplation of whom their happiness consists. Consequently, we seem to be abandoned to inevitable frustration. It may be that in this vale of tears our sole consolation is to seek what comfort we can for ourselves and our fellows, but to many, suicide might seem more rational. Yet neither palliatives nor death could persuade us of the rationality of the conception of the world we have been offered.

4. TRUE RATIONALISM

Blanshard might quite justly have replied that however desirable a universe in harmony with our aesthetic and moral needs might be, we have no right to assume that the world is so without, or against, the evidence. Indeed, to do so would be mere wishful thinking. The evidence at our disposal, however, runs counter to mechanical determinism in the physical universe and supports the notion of a coherent and indivisible physical whole. This, as has been argued above, must by its very nature be complete and will develop dialectically, as recent scientific advances give copious evidence that it does. Blanshard himself allows that at least in one point in the value-neutral world an excrescence develops containing life, mind, and purposive action, generating rational values. In that case, it is his general cosmological scheme that is contrary to the evidence, and so rationally inadmissible. It needs correction and modification to accommodate organism, which, even if it can be analyzed into physicochemical processes, is not exhausted by that analysis, because in living things the integration of physicochemical processes is organismic and teleological. The living system maintains itself auturgically through the mutual adjustment and shifting balance of its constituent physical processes, not through the merely random play of chemical reactions. Organisms, moreover, are sentient, and from sentience develops consciousness and intelligence. The self-organization of chemical cycles is metabolism, the complexification of which is physiological activity, and that is the foundation of instinct, which becomes intelligent as purposive behavior.

Reductionists and behaviorists seek to deny that the higher forms are anything but the merely physical; but none more persuasively and eloquently than Blanshard has demonstrated that they ignore the relevant evidence and that their doctrine leads to incoherence.[10] In truth, the dialectical structure of the universe precludes reductionism, for the dialectical relationship ensures the determination of the part by the whole, the more elementary by the more developed, and the rudimentary by the mature. What emerges at the top of the scale is the truth and explanation of what is inchoate at the beginning, so that any reductionism will commit the genetic fallacy.

Because the scale of natural forms is continuous without a break, there can be no unbridgeable gulf between the physical, the organismic, and the mental. When he postulates an irreconcilable opposition between our intellectual conception of the universe and our purposive and moral impulses, Blanshard contradicts his own best insights. Consequently, the sketch of a metaphysic that he offers in *Reason and Belief* is inconsistent with itself and fails to do justice to the evidence at his disposal—evidence from which elsewhere he has drawn conclusions implying a different ontology from the one which, as it stands here, subverts his rationalism.

These shortcomings, however, do not leave reason bankrupt, as some may think and others have independently concluded. Nor does it follow that Blanshard's insights are altogether futile and void. The world, to be intelligibly conceived at all, must be conceived as a coherent whole, and if so conceived, it will be such that, without contradicting its intrinsic nature, physical reality can produce life and mind. The emergence of consciousness must bring with it a perception of the world that is necessarily related to its object, and a nisus to self-fulfillment that will actualize the totality immanent within it. Values will then indeed be the fulfillment of human need, and that must include the need to find intellectual satisfaction in harmony with moral and aesthetic, so as to become a unified and freely self-determining personality. That, again, will prove possible only in social harmony with others, and finally it will point to the development of a common consciousness of belonging to a reality that transcends the merely finite.

With most of this Blanshard would most likely have agreed. But then the coherent world cannot be limited to what he has described in *Reason and Belief.* If conscious minds with immortal longings are to emerge from physical beginnings, inanimate nature cannot be wholly foreign to human aspirations. From the sheerly mechanical and material without a spark of life, no life could evolve. From blind oblivion, no consciousness can arise. The rational conception of the world must therefore be one that finds the potentiality of mind and its fulfillment in the very elements of the physical world and that traces their development through a continuous scale of forms to its ultimate consummation. The whole cannot be dead, unconscious, mindless, and devoid of value; for if it were, none of these characteristics could come into being within it. It must be, as even Kant recognized and as Hegel openly declared, of the nature of mind or spirit. That is the paradigm of the self-differentiating universal which is immanent in all its differentiations. It is, therefore, as has been argued above, actualizable only as and through a hierarchical scale of forms, from the lowest to the highest degree of perfection. And such a scale of forms, while it provides a place for humanity and its self-fulfillment, transcends both, pointing to a divinity that Blanshard fails to recognize and refuses to acknowledge. Yet if we do not conceive the universe in this way, we cannot conceive it coherently; nor unless we do conceive it coherently, can we lay claim to a consistent rationalism.

Genuine rationalism will conceive the world as a dialectical process, for the coherent whole can only specify itself dialectically. Explicated in this way, it can find room for everything that Blanshard sought, as well as much else that he would not admit. Moreover, dialectical interrelation between mind and its object can make sense of an idealistic theory of perception on a realistic foundation, and can marry felicitously correspondence with coherence in epistemology.[11] A dialectical explication of value theory would show that it is indeed the fulfillment of human nature but equally, and as much, the fulfillment of the self-developing world; this fulfillment, however, does not and cannot rest in the finiteness of humanity, and proleptically seeks an ultimate realization of all values in an infinite transcendent reality. The religious dogmata that Blanshard convicts of inconsistency may, therefore, be no worse than efforts to express, in symbolic and metaphorical representation, this transfiguration of the finite, and the theologies that he castigates may be merely one-sided strivings of their devotees to formulate the ultimate truth.

Notes

This chapter is taken from "Reason and Rationalism," *Idealistic Studies*, vol. 9, no. 2 (1979).

1. Brand Blanshard, *Reason and Belief*, p. 489.
2. Ibid., p. 478.
3. Ibid., chap. 13, §§ 5–6.
4. Cf. E. E. Harris, "Blanshard on Perception and Free Ideas," in Schilpp (ed.), *The Philosophy of Brand Blanshard*.
5. Blanshard, *Reason and Belief*, pp. 505ff.
6. Ibid., p. 508.
7. Cf. B. Bosanquet, *Three Chapters on the Nature of Mind*, chap. 3, and E. E. Harris, *Nature, Mind and Modern Science*, chap. 14.
8. Cf. E. E. Harris, *The Foundations of Metaphysics in Science; Hypothesis and Perception*, and *Perceptual Assurance and the Reality of the World*. chap. 12.
9. Blanshard, *Reason and Belief*, p. 543.
10. Cf. also Harris, *Foundations of Metaphysics in Science*, pt. II, and "Mind and Mechanical Models," in Scher (ed.), *Theories of the Mind*
11. Cf. Harris *Hypothesis and Perception*, pp. 384–5.

16

Coherence and Its Critics

1. EPISTEMOLOGY AND METAPHYSICS

The shortcomings of Blanshard's metaphysics are simply the consequence of his failure to free himself completely from the influence of nineteenth-century scientific presuppositions (a failure common to most of his philosophical contemporaries), and his confessed inability to appreciate the implications of twentieth-century physics. He was, nevertheless, acute enough to realize that even Newtonian science involved the universal interconnection of all physical facts (undeniable if only pervasive gravitational attraction is assumed) and the consequent necessary causal connection of all events. This meant that relations between facts must be internal, and the universe must be a single coherently systematic whole. It follows that experience of such a world must also be coherent if it is to be true. But critics have argued that coherence is not enough to ensure truth, for even coherent theories may be false if they do not correspond to the facts. That Blanshard could not concede, because his epistemology, being Berkeleyan, provided no channel other than perception itself by which to discover whether the perceived world corresponded to anything external to the mind, so coherence had to be the final resort. Nor is there any means of discovering what the world is like apart from perception, a fact that in its turn proves a stumbling block to the captious critic of coherence. The strength of Blanshard's position is his insistence on coherence, but his failure to accept the necessary dialectical structure of the universal whole leaves his theory incomplete, actually inconsistent, and incommensurate to his own insight.

The coherence theory of truth does not stand upon its own feet; it is the corollary of a metaphysic, without which it has no cogency. Likewise, no critique of the theory can have weight against it if it merely assumes an incompatible metaphysic, which it does not establish, and unless it can demonstrate the falsity of that on which the coherence theory rests. Were metaphysics simply a matter of taste and temperament (as some have alleged), discussion and criticism would be futile, but that metaphysics is simply a matter of taste and sentiment has shown itself to be a self-refuting and self-contradictory doctrine, itself presupposing a metaphysic. If an epistemological theory like that of coherence is to be examined, therefore, some way must be found to assess the truth of the metaphysic upon which it rests, and this the extant critique of the theory never attempts. It is, on the contrary, founded upon a rival metaphysical assumption that it makes no effort to validate but merely takes for granted. No such critique, however, is legitimate.

Philosophers who assume without critical reflection a particular metaphysical position are apt to use their own "philosophical language" appropriate to the presuppositions they are making, and as R. G. Collingwood perspicaciously maintained in his *Principles of Art,*

> ... the use of a special "philosophical language" commits the user, possibly even against his will, to accepting the philosophical doctrines which it has been designed to express, so that these doctrines are surreptitiously and dogmatically foisted upon every disputant who will consent to use the language . . . (p. 174).

So it is with the critics of the Coherence Theory.

The metaphysic lying behind the coherence theory has already been set out in some detail, but it may here be summarized as the concept of the universe as a single whole of multifarious interdependent parts so related that the nature and occurrence of each are determined by its relations to all the rest, and so by the overall structure of the system. The doctrine of internal relations is integral to the coherence theory, and to reject either is to reject both; but if such rejection is to be made, it should not be merely capricious and must be firmly grounded.

What critics of the coherence theory have almost invariably done, however, is (either tacitly or openly) to reject the doctrine of internal relations on the basis of an alternative metaphysic, which they merely assume without justification or demonstration, and which contradicts the holism presupposed by coherence. The criticism that results is then easy, but is totally invalid. By and large, this rival metaphysic is that most succinctly stated by Wittgenstein in his *Tractatus*: the world is everything that is the case, that is, the totality of facts; and the world divides into facts, of which any one can either be the case or not be the case, and everything else remain the same.[1] This is the doctrine of atomic facts, which is openly espoused by Wittgenstein, Russell, and Ayer, and which many other writers assume without acknowledgment. It is not difficult to show that all the main criticisms of the coherence theory have relied on the assumption of this doctrine. Let us take as an example that of C. I. Lewis, which is one of the most persuasive and includes arguments common to several other writers.[2] Although it does not explicitly confess adherence to the doctrine, that it presupposes the logical independence of facts soon becomes apparent.

2. THE GENERAL CRITIQUE

The first and main contention of this criticism is that the mutual consistency of propositions, even if they are deducible one from another, cannot assure us of the least degree of probability for the whole body of beliefs that they express, unless we have some other reason for believing any one of them.[3] Mutual coherence, or (what is somewhat less) mutual congruence of statements (or beliefs), is inadequate to enhance the probability of any of them unless at least one has some antecendent probability. For it is possible to concoct a group (or even a system) of statements, all mutually consistent, that are all, or many of them, false. This can be done by a sufficiently skillful liar.

Apart from the fact that the exponents of the coherence theory have never maintained that mutual consistency of statements (though necessary) is sufficient by itself and without comprehensiveness to establish truth, the objection raises a serious question of what is meant by, and what is the basis of, antecedent probability. The clue given us by Lewis comes in his statement that "all knowledge has an eventual empirical significance in that all which is knowable, or even significantly thinkable, must have reference to meanings which are sense-presentable" (p. 127). It is not immediately clear how meanings can be sense-presentable, but the suggestion is strong that if and as far as they are, such presentation in itself gives them some probability. As sense-presentations have no obvious or directly presentable connection with one another (a point established by Hume), this initial probability of a "meaning" is logically independent of any other, and the theory of atomic propositions is implied.

Whether or how a sense-presentation can give probability to a meaning is a question to which we shall return. For the moment, let us pursue the last contention further. Lewis asserts that the belief in coherence is based on a paralogism, for all empirical truths are logically contingent, which means that the contradictory of any empirical statement as well as the statement itself is consistent with any other. Thus, if P and Q are mutually consistent empirical statements, any further contingent statement of as yet undetermined truth value is consistent with P and not-Q or with not-P and Q, as long as neither not-P nor not-Q is self-contradictory, which must be the case if P and Q are logically contingent.

To assert that empirical truths are all logically contingent is precisely the same as to say that the fact that any one of them asserts may be the case or not be the case while the rest remain the same. In other words, statements of empirical fact are all logically independent or atomic. The metaphysical presupposition of the coherence theory, however, is the denial of such logical independence. For it, contingency results only from deficiency of our knowledge, because (the theory holds) all facts are mutually determining and are what the universal system of order in the universe requires. The more we find out about facts, the more we see that they necessitate one another, and we discover this by developing the implications of what we already know. To argue on that assumption that mutual compatibility of statements of fact is presumptive evidence of their truth is no paralogism. It is so only on the assumption of atomic facts. What remains to be decided is which of the metaphysical positions is sound.

If facts are atomic, the conception of probability that applies to them will be what is commonly known as the probability of chances, based on the assumption that the events whose probability is under consideration are all equally possible. In that case, of course, all concomitant events must either be irrelevant or (if not) ignored. That this is the concept with which Lewis is working is shown by his illustration of the dealing of cards from a new pack. If a pack has been shuffled, the order in which cards fall when dealt is normally assumed to be haphazard, that is, logically undetermined. If they fall in a set order (known to be that in which new packs are issued from the factory), the appearance of each successive card increases the probability that the pack is new and has not been shuffled. This, however, says Lewis, is not proved by the appearance of any one card nor even by a succession in the right order, until the entire pack has been dealt, because no logical connection is initially presumed between the successive appearances of any of the cards. Only on this assumption does Lewis's argument hold, and the assumption is that of the atomicity of facts.

An adherent of the coherence theory would say that shuffling cards is intended to disrupt any systematic order among them, but the order in which they appear, even so, will be determined by a complex of causes. We regard the succession as haphazard because we cannot know more than an insignificant fraction of the causal determinants; but if we know enough, we can predict the way the cards will appear, as is the case in many card tricks. If we assume that they are arranged in a systematic order, then the appearance in the right order of (say) the first ten will be evidence of the way the rest will occur and, as the sequence increases, the existence of the assumed order becomes more certain. If we have good reason to believe that the pack is new and has not been shuffled, we shall know after the appearance of relatively few cards that the order in which the rest will appear is not only probable but necessary. Whether the reason for our initial assumption is good enough will depend on the extent of our knowledge.

Lewis insists that the probability of evidence is not increased by the corroboration of witnesses' stories, unless, in the first place, the story has some antecedent probability (raising the earlier question of its source), and, in the second place, the witnesses are "independent." Here again the suggestion is strong that observations by the witnesses are atomic facts. He seems to infer from the agreement of testimony only that there has been collusion among those testifying. But surely this is the reverse of the natural order of inference. We normally consider that if witnesses agree, their story is true, and we regard them as unreliable only if we have further evidence of collusion. Lewis objects that if coherence were a reliable test, collusion between liars would turn falsehood into fact.[4] On the contrary, if there were adequate evidence of collusion and of the reputation of the witnesses as liars, their agreement would be presumptive proof of falsehood. The same sort of rebuttal applies to Lewis's assertion that on the coherence theory it would be in the interests of truth for a scientist to cook experimental results. Any evidence of such dishonesty immediately disqualifies the reported results as spurious.

Moreover, by "corroboration" Lewis appears to understand nothing more than repetition of similar reports, whereas the more appropriate meaning of the word is the fitting together, interlocking, and mutual support of *different* stories, as when one witness testifies to seeing the accused near the scene of the crime immediately before it was committed, another testifies to seeing him running away from the area immediately afterward, and a third reports that when sought at his home at that time he could not be found.

Like H. H. Price, Lewis assumes that antecedent probability springs from direct perception, and that without it, corroboration of statements is of no value. Yet oddly enough, both of these writers confess that direct perception gives no assurance of fact without what Lewis calls "congruence" and Price calls "confirmation," so that antecedent probability must in the last resort depend on prior coherence. Before looking into this circumstance more closely, let us notice another argument frequently brought against the coherence theory.[5]

3. ALTERNATIVE GEOMETRIES

However coherent and tightly locked a system of propositions may be, it has been argued, it can at most represent a possible world, not necessarily the actual one. There are numerous alternative geometries, each of them thoroughly coherent yet mutually incompatible. Not all of them, therefore, can represent actual physical space, and it is not their coherence that enables us to decide which one does.

This argument draws its plausibility from two connected sources. One is the doctrine of atomic facts, none of which entails any other; the other is the corollary that, if propositions do entail each other logically, it can only be because they are analytic and tautological. This is supposed to be true of all mathematics and is the reason why geometries are internally coherent deductive systems. Such systems, however, are devoid of empirical content and are developed from arbitrarily stipulated axioms by the application of transformation rules arbitrarily adopted. Accordingly, deductive systems have none but a purely accidental relation (if any) to actual fact. Consequently, pure geometry tells us nothing about the real world, and whether it applies to physical space will depend only on empirical evidence. In that case, it is not surprising that the "coherence" of pure geometry is no evidence of anything but "logical" truth, which, for the type of philosopher who uses this argument, is purely tautological.

The coherence theorist, however, would reject the entire doctrine. Tautology, he or she would declare, is empty and meaningless. If $A = A$ is to have the least significance, there must be some difference between the first A and the second, if only one of position in space or occurrence in time, otherwise the assertion of identity is a meaningless sham. The coherence philosopher would contend that no significant statement is ever purely analytic, not even in mathematics. At least one eminent mathematician has emphatically asserted that the propositions most fundamental to mathematics are synthetic a priori.[6]

Alternative geometries, moreover, are not mutually incompatible throughout, for one may define a limiting case of some principle developed further in another (as Euclidean geometry coincides with Riemannian at very short intervals), or two geometries may diverge along alternative routes of implication (as Euclid and Lobachewski each develop the consequences of a different version of Playfair's axiom). Sir Edmund Whittaker has drawn attention, further, to the fact that Euclidean geometry is not as coherent as is commonly believed, but contains gaps and inconsistencies due to the oversight of topological conditions and of its own tacit assumptions in which incoherencies are implicit. The development of new geometries has taken these defects into account and sought to remedy them, so they are not simply independent systems but rather more coherent corrections of Euclid's.

There is indeed good reason to maintain that all mathematics constitutes a single body of interrelated reasoning founded ultimately on the series of natural numbers, which seem to be something inherent in the real world, and no mere conventional set of postulates.[7] In short, the coherence of mathematics and its consequent cogency are typical of the coherent world in which they hold good, although they are purchased at the cost of extreme abstraction, and, for truth, mere consistency is not enough; concrete comprehensiveness is also required. To decide between alternative mathematical systems, like geometry, therefore, which best represents physical space, it is necessary to discover with which the physical motion of bodies is consistent.

Much the same sort of rejoinder might be made to the argument about possible worlds. If facts are atomic, it is conceivable that they could be grouped in many alternative ways without conflict. In fact, if any one could be the case or not be the case and the rest remain the same, they could be grouped together in any way whatsoever without mutual inconsistency. But this would indicate only different possibilities, and some other criterion would be needed to discover which concatenation was actual. On the other hand, if all facts are interconnected and are determined by their interrelations, possibility becomes what Leibniz called "compossibility" and coalesces with necessity (imposed by interdetermination). Nothing would be possible that was not permitted by existing conditions. "Possible worlds" would then be impossible flights of fancy, harboring some clandestine oversight, or tolerating some unwarranted abstraction, which, when revealed, would disclose an incoherency that forbids realization. For example, a hippogriff, at first blush, might appear to be a possible animal. On consideration of its anatomical arrangements and physiological needs, however, conflicting requirements soon interdict its actualization.

4. WHICH METAPHYSIC?

The more fundamental question must now be faced: how, if at all, can we decide between the metaphysical presupposition of the coherence theory and that of its opponents? By what criterion can we judge whether the world is a system of interlocked and mutually determining facts or a loose collection of atomic *Sachverhalten* of which any may be or may not be the case without alteration of any other? To appeal in the first case to coherence would obviously be question-begging. Would it be equally question-begging for the opponents of coherence to appeal to experience? Can we learn from experience whether, if a presented fact were not the case, other things would remain unchanged? Hardly, because experience can reveal only what is the case, not what would be the case if what is experienced were other than it is. Further, to discover by experience whether a change in events would result in a concomitant change in other events, we should, presumably, have to use inductive reasoning, and Hume has demonstrated incontrovertibly that without petitio principii, inductive reasoning can be validated neither by reason nor by experience.

Are we then in an insoluble dilemma? Fortunately, we are not, because we should not beg the question if we tested the metaphysic of empiricism by its coherence, nor if we appealed to experience for evidence of the truth of dialectical holism.

The empiricist metaphysic, however, fails the test of coherence at almost every turn, as the impasse of inductive reasoning illustrates.[8] Moreover, it asserts that all knowledge derives from sense perception and claims truth for sense perception on the ground of correspondence with fact, a correspondence that, on its own principles, is impossible to ascertain (sense perception being the sole avenue to fact). Or else, sense perception is itself offered as the criterion of truth, while it is admitted sometimes to be deceptive. Locke, seeking the test of real truth, fell into logomachy; Berkeley, to avoid Locke's predicament, had to appeal to coherence ("the settled order of nature"); and Hume, although demonstrating admirably our reliance on coherence for the interpretation of sense perception, dismissed the entire system of belief in an external world as a texture of illusion and subsided into skepticism[9]—a self-refuting and incoherent conclusion. Contemporary empiricists, in attempts to avoid these pitfalls, have embraced (at times unwittingly) doctrines consorting ill with their professed empiricism. Russell declared the principle of induction to be a priori; Price not only followed suit but espoused a quasi-coherence theory of perceptual assurance as well; Wittgenstein (in the *Tractatus*) discovered that his conclusions invalidated the premises from which they were drawn and later (in *On Certainty*) conceded that assurance depended upon systematicity; and Ayer became entangled in phenomenalism and failed to extricate himself from the egocentric predicament.[10] Judged by the criterion of coherence, therefore, the metaphysic of empiricism signally fails and must be pronounced false.

May one appeal to experience to justify the metaphysical backing of the coherence theory or, for that matter, to support any metaphysical theory? Empiricists, of course, vehemently deny any such possibility, but if what has been said above is sound, they have already been heard and found wanting. Proponents of coherence, however, may submit unperturbed to the test of experience, for they contend that experience is of a coherent world and is itself a coherent system. It should then reveal the truth of their theory, and if experience does not bear it out, the theory will be in jeopardy.

There are three ways in which experience should be relevant. First, empirical science should shed light on the question of the interrelatedness of facts and the internality (or otherwise) of relations. Secondly, the history of science should reveal the criteria that scientists themselves adopt for the acceptability of theories. And thirdly, empirical psychology should be able to throw light upon the nature of perception and show whether sense experience serves as an ultimate source of assurance, or if some other criterion is implicit in perceptual acceptance itself.

5. WITNESSES FOR THE DEFENSE

The evidence available from the first witness, empirical science, has already been examined. That physical facts are mutually constitutive has been clearly established by the special and general theories of relativity. The fact that light travels at a finite velocity, which is unaffected either by the motion of the source or by the relative velocity of the observer, makes it impossible to determine simultaneity of events at a distance. Accordingly, lengths in space and lapses in time vary with the velocity of the frames of reference in which they are measured, and this velocity can be determined only relatively to other frames and never absolutely. It follows that the results of measurements of any of these quantities are inseparably dependent on the discoverable values of all the rest. It is therefore patently false that any of them can be other than what it is observed to be by any investigator if other measurements remain the same. They are essentially interrelated: the Lorenz transformations correlate the entire variegated system of systems in such a way that measurements in any one Galilean frame can be converted into corresponding measurements in any other. All physical facts are recorded in such measurements—one may properly say that the measurements are the facts. They are therefore not atomic, and their mutual relations are incurably internal. The universe, in consequence, is seen as a single unbroken four-dimensional continuum of space-time in which reference frames moving at different velocities relative to one another represent different coordinate analyses.

General relativity establishes a more deep-set interdependence between mass and space-time measurements of velocity and acceleration, mass and energy ($e = mc^2$), field and space-time curvature. Every statement of length, time, velocity, mass, energy, or momentum entails some statement about all the others. A. J. Ayer was, therefore, plainly wrong to hold it a "logical truism that if two states of affairs are distinct, a statement which refers to only one of them does not entail anything about the other,"[11] because statements about every distinguishable physical state of affairs entail statements about numerous others.

We need not linger to recall D. W. Sciama's demonstration that centrifugal and Coriolis forces are dependent on the motion of the fixed stars, Eddington's demonstrations of what he said was "the wide interrelatedness of things," or E. A. Milne's proof that "the rest of the universe" was involved in the motion (and its observation) of every particle. We have seen how the quantum theory has shown the inseparability of conjunct quantities and the interdependence of particle and wave motions. We now have the more cogent evidence of the EPR (Einstein, Podolsky, and Rosen) experiment and the consequences of Bell's Theorem that faster-than-light influences, which are not signals, inseparably connect distant quantum events, and the nonlocal effects thought by Roger Penrose to be involved in the formation of certain quasi-crystalline substances.

The biological sciences provide copious evidence augmenting that of the physical. In the light of their findings there can be no question of the inseparability and interdependence of the overlapping metabolic cycles in the living cell, nor of the interdependence and interdetermination of the segmentations and convolutions of cells in orthogenesis, nor of the mutual interplay of physiological processes that maintain the homeostasis of substances and their relative quantities in the living body. Although the organism is markedly self-contained, self-maintaining, and self-reproductive, it is so only by virtue of the fact that it is an open system ceaselessly interchanging energy and matter with its immediate surround. The organic (mutually determining) relations are not limited to the confines of the living creature, but pertain equally between organism and environment, so that no rigid distinction can be drawn between them. If any one state of affairs in the metabolism of the living thing could be different without requiring changes in innumerable others, the entire organic system would be disrupted, resulting in disease or   death.

The science of ecology assures us further that all life is in some degree symbiosis. Every organism depends for its survival on other organisms in every conceivable variety of mutual relation—parasitic, phagocytic, colonial, predatory, protective, imitative, and countless other ways. In consequence, ecosystems are as integral and organic as their constituents, and the living systems within them are equally interdependent. Change any one, and the complete complex has to change in response. If one predatory species is annihilated, others multiply and consume the sustenance of those with which they compete, altering the conditions for survival of virtually every species of flora and fauna in the region. Hence we find inexhaustible evidence that biological facts are far from atomic and that the coherence of the biosphere is pervasive and all-embracing.

The second witness for the defense is the historian of science, who discloses instances belying the persistent declaration of empiricists that facts, being contingent, cannot be deduced one from another. C. I. Lewis, as we have observed, contends that even if it be conceded that "the whole of truth" is a tight-locked system in which all facts are mutually fixed, yet the mutual consistency of all true statements (which must obviously be presumed) and their systematic interconnection do not help us to determine the truth of empirical statements concerning facts yet perceptually undiscovered. Why Lewis should persist in this belief in the face of numerous instances to the contrary in the history of science is difficult to understand. Adams and Leverrier's deduction of the existence of Neptune before it was observed is only one of the better known instances. Nevertheless, and despite such contrary cases, the accepted view of scientific method has long been that hitherto unknown facts can be inferred from those already observed only by inductive reasoning. But inductive argument has never been successfully validated, and contemporary philosophers of science, Karl Popper, N. R. Hanson, J. O. Wisdom, Thomas Kuhn, and Imré Lakatos have all abandoned the doctrine and sought alternatives that have brought them to the brink of adopting the coherence theory.[12]

Further, the historian of science discovers that scientists themselves use the criterion of coherence to recommend their theories, and that from Kepler and Galileo to the present day, they have sought in their research to marshal diverse but convergent evidence-forming systems, such that no factor can be denied without invalidating all the rest, so that their conclusions are seen, in the light of the evidence, to be not just probable but necessary.

This description fits the researches and reports of such innovators as Kepler, Harvey, Newton, Lavoisier, and Darwin, as I have shown at some length in *Hypothesis and Perception* (chapter 6). What is written there need not be repeated here, for even more convincing evidence comes from the profession of the scientists themselves of their persuasion that the world is a coherent system and that coherence is the mark of the best theories about it. Copernicus, writing to Pope Paul III concerning his own heliocentric hypothesis, complains that the Ptolemaic astronomers use different principles of explanation for the motion of different heavenly bodies, and even so are unable to explain or observe the constant length of the seasonal year; whereas, on the contrary, he can claim for his own theory that

> I have at last discovered that, if the motions of the planets be brought into relation with the circulation of the Earth and be reckoned in proportion to the circles of each planet, not only do their phenomena presently ensue, but the orders and magnitudes of all stars and spheres, nay the heavens themselves, become so bound together that nothing in any part thereof could be moved from its place without producing confusion of all the other parts of the Universe as a whole.

Kepler was a notorious believer in *harmonia mundi* and judged all scientific theories according to their mathematical unity and elegance. His aim, he said, was to show why the facts "are as they are and not otherwise," clearly revealing his belief in a systematically determined world. But more general and more confident support for the conception of the world as a coherent system and of coherence as the proper test for the acceptability of theory comes from scientists of our own day. Einstein writes:

> All these endeavours are based on the conviction that existence should have a completely harmonious structure. Today we have less ground than ever before for allowing ourselves to be forced away from this wonderful belief.[13]

Niels Bohr testifies in support that Einstein's reinterpretation of classical concepts effected a higher degree of unity in the description of nature. He adds that the quantum theory had a similar consequence:

> Perhaps the most distinguishing characteristic of the present position of physics is that almost all the ideas which have ever proved to be fruitful in the investigation of nature have found their right place in a common harmony without thereby having diminished their fruitfulness.[14]

Einstein and Infeld, writing in conjunction, express the same opinion. Modern physics, they say, is simpler than classical—a surprising remark on the face of it, but not when we realize that simplicity (always considered a *disderatum* of sound scientific theory) is nothing other than freedom from conflict in application to a wide area of fact and is really the same as coherence.[15] The simpler our picture of the world, Einstein and Infeld maintain, the more facts it embraces and the more strongly it reflects the harmony of the universe.[16] The criteria they recognize and seek are those of comprehensiveness and coherent unity.

Louis de Broglie professes the same adherence to the coherence ideal: "The fundamental postulates [of quantum theory] are justified by the possibility of founding on them a coherent theory, compatible with all the experimental facts."[17]

There is another aspect of the coherence theory that modern scientists endorse with singular unanimity. The theory requires that the advance of knowledge should proceed by progressive correction of earlier theories, removing inconsistencies, and in every case, coherence is the criterion for preference of the newer theories over those superseded. The critics object that theories of outstanding completeness and coherence are often abandoned and replaced by others no more complete or coherent, for the sole reason that the new theories can explain freshly observed facts that the former theories could not. The favorite example is classical Newtonian mechanics, an exemplary case of coherent elegance now superseded by relativity and quantum theory. The adherent of coherence would have to retort by showing that Newtonian mechanics was not completely coherent and that relativity and quantum theory supplement its deficiencies and fill out its inadequacies.

That classical physics harbored inconsistencies galore is by now well known. The theory of the ether and the attempts to explain electrodynamic phenomena by mechanical models led to notorious incoherencies, but even prior to that, the theory of gravitation with its implication of action at a distance troubled Newton himself, and the apparently more tenable idea of transmission of motion by impact was no less bewildering.[18]

There is an extraordinarily wide consensus among modern physicists that succeeding theories have not simply superseded their predecessors but have developed and completed earlier concepts. Let us again hear Einstein and Infeld:

> ... it would be unjust to consider that the new field view freed science from the errors of the old theory of elastic fluids, or that the new theory destroys the achievements of the old. The new theory shows the merits as well as the limitations of the old theory and allows us to regain our old concepts from a higher level. This is true, not only for the theories of electric fluids and field, but for all changes in physical theories however revolutionary they may seem. . . . To use a comparison, we could say that creating a new theory is not like destroying an old barn and erecting a sky-scraper in its place. It is rather like climbing a mountain, gaining new and wider views, discovering unexpected connexions between our starting point and its rich environment.[19]

Next, Louis de Broglie:

> It is just by this process of successive approximations that science is capable of progressing without contradicting itself. The structures that it has solidly built are not overthrown by subsequent progress, but rather incorporated into a broader structure.

In the same work, he says:

> ... the theory of relativity, while pushing them to their extreme consequences, retains the guiding ideas of the old physics. Thus it can be said that, despite

the so-new and almost revolutionary character of the Einsteinian conceptions, the theory of relativity is in some ways the culmination of classical
physics.

The same applies to quantum physics:

> The structure of quantum physics would seem to be built round classical
> physics and to have enveloped it within a wider framework. So, in all the
> long history of science, progress is made by successive approximations.[20]

Max Planck is in full agreement: "The Theory of Relativity . . . has proved to
be the completion and culmination of the structure of classical physics."[21]

If this testimony is accepted for the way in which scientific knowledge is
progressively developed and supplemented, it carries with it significant implications for the much criticized doctrine of degrees of truth, another corollary
of the coherence theory, following naturally from the account of the scale of
forms given in an earlier chapter, which is also a scale of degrees.

The third witness for the defense is empirical psychology and its discoveries
about the nature of sense perception. Its special relevance lies in its bearing on
the contention of critics such as C. I. Lewis that the final appeal in deciding
the truth of statements must be to what is sense-presentable. The criticism
simply plays into the hands of those criticized if it transpires that what is
immediately presented in sense does not and cannot serve as a criterion of
veridicality or rank at all as knowledge, unless it involves in itself an implicit
inference from cohering evidence (either concurrent or successive)—if, that is,
perception proves to be implicit judgment, as alleged by the proponents of the
coherence theory. Here the philosophical case will not be argued (whatever its
merits); the empirical evidence will be left to speak for itself.

Much of this evidence I have marshaled in chapter 20 of *The Foundations of
Metaphysics in Science*, reporting, among many others, the contribution of the
Gestalt psychologists, in particular, K. Koffka. The views of Egon Brunswik,
Adelbert Ames, H. Cantril, J. S. Bruner, and L. Postman are especially illuminating, and the work of Sir Frederick Bartlett is revealingly supportive. But the
experimental evidence extends considerably further than what has been con-
tributed by these investigators. The results of numerous investigations by all
these and several other experimentalists may be summarized briefly as follows.
Perception is never instantaneous, and in the short interval between the presentation of an object and the apprehension (or recognition) of it by the subject, the mind goes through an activity of structuring the contents of the perceptual
field according to schemata, some of which are (or may be) innate and others
acquired in the course of experience, but all subject to modification through
learning. The processes of structuring involve selection and correlation of elements, and although much of it goes on subconsciously, it is akin to, and
continuous with, what, when raised to the level of explicit consciousness, is

judgment and inference. To this structured background, the presented datum is referred in an effort to identify and characterize it. Several psychologists refer to the activity as the entertainment of hypotheses for the identification of sensory cues and the revision of the hypotheses in accordance with success or failure in the recognition of objects, or with other appropriate reactions to them. Success is found to depend on the coherence of cues, and failure results from conflict among them: the final result of the perceptual process is the achievement of recognition, which is, in effect, the conclusion of an inference and is a judgment based on the structure, both spatial and temporal, of the sensory material in the light of past experience.

In general, the experimental results point to the conclusions that immediate presentation to the senses does not produce any intelligible object that could serve as an indication of an actual state of affairs or the truth of a judgment of fact; and what does result is largely the product of a mental activity, akin to judgment, which is for the most part founded upon inherited and acquired schemata. But even this in the first instance is nothing that can serve as a criterion of truth, for although it is an inchoate judgment, it is frequently liable to error. The correction of the error when it occurs is shown to be effected by the correlation of cues until they prove to be mutually harmonious.

It is not possible in a short space to review the mass of experimental work issuing in these results, but a few of the more telling examples may be cited. Experiments by W. H. Ittelson on the visual perception of distance provide convincing evidence of the liability to error of primary perceptual judgment.[22] Ittelson presented subjects with isolated test objects illuminated in a dark surrounding and required them to estimate the distance of the presented objects. They indicated their assessment by placing a comparison object on a scale at the estimated distance. The test object was viewed monocularly and the comparison object and the scale binocularly. The experiment produced two visual fields, one of which was divided into two parts: one containing the test object (the experimental field), and the other containing the comparison object (the companion field). By means of an arrangement of half-silvered mirrors, the two fields could be viewed together so that correlation could be more accurate.

The test objects presented in one experiment were (1) playing cards, one three-quarters the normal size and one one-and-a-half times the normal size; (2) two indefinitely shaped cards referred to as "inkblots," both alike except that one was half the size of the other; and (3) one small and one large diamond-shaped card. In a second experiment, a normal-sized playing card, a double-sized one, and a half-sized one were used, as well as a typed business letter and a matchbox. In each experiment, the test objects were all presented to the subject at the same actual distance, nine feet in the first, and seven-and-a-half feet in the second. None of the subjects reported any awareness of the differences in size of the test objects, and all placed the smaller objects at proportionately greater distances than the larger. The distances of the smaller test objects were consistently overestimated and those of the larger ones consistently underestimated. Ittelson found that the assessment of distance was significantly influenced by the assumed objective size of the presented object, that is, the size the observer assumed it to be from familiarity with things of the same kind (e.g., playing cards). The cards, he points out, were placed at the distance at which a normal-sized card would have to be placed in order to produce a retinal image of the given size. The apparent distances of the normal playing card, the letter, and the matchbox, though of very different sizes and producing differently sized retinal images, were not significantly different. In summing up his results, Ittelson writes:

> Size operates as a cue to distance in the following manner. A perceptual integration is reached between the physiological stimulus-size and the assumed-size related to that particularly characterized stimulus-pattern. The object is localized by O at a point at which an object of physical size equal to the assumed-size would have to be placed in order to produce the given retinal-size.... Discrete changes in the size of the physiological stimulus related to a physical object will be perceived as discrete changes in the apparent-distance of that object, provided the assumed-size remains constant.... Discrete changes in the characteristics of the physiological stimulus-pattern resulting in changes in assumed-size will be perceived as discrete changes in apparent distance even though size remains constant.

What the experiments show is that a sense-presentable object in isolation provides no reliable criterion for judgment either of size or of distance. The apparent distance of objects depends not simply on their immediate sensible appearance but upon other factors, such as prior knowledge of the kind of object and its normal size. In the absence of other cues, distance is liable to be grossly misjudged. The experiment does not show how a correct judgment would be reached, but it gives reason to suppose that it would require a correlation of numerous cues in a coherent system. Nor does it throw light on how prior knowledge of the type and normal size of the test object is acquired, but the assumption is well justified that it would require the correlation and comparison of innumerable sensuous occurrences.

Another very revealing experiment was performed by Bruner and Postman on the perception of incongruity.[23] These investigators presented subjects with playing cards, some of which were normal and some with the usual colors reversed: spades red and hearts black. The cards were presented tachistoscopically, in mixed groups of five cards each, some consisting of four normal cards and one trick card, some consisting of four trick cards and one normal card.

The significant findings, for our purpose, were that thresholds for recognition of normal cards were four times lower (28 milliseconds) than for that of incongruous cards (114 milliseconds), and incongruous cards were seen as modified in the direction of normality according to whether the subject's reaction was dominated by form or by color. A red six of spades would be identified with assurance as the six of hearts by some observers and as the six of spades by others. In one case, form dominates and color is suppressed; in the other, form is suppressed in favor of color. In another type of reaction, subjects saw the incongruous cards as intermediate between what they normally expected and the actually presented object, for example, purple hearts or spades or gray hearts. Yet a third kind of reaction was called by the experimenters "disruption"—the complete breakdown of perceptual organization "at the level of coherence normally attained . . . at a given exposure level." The subject, having failed to resolve the stimulus in terms of his available perceptual expectation, exclaimed: "I don't know what the hell it is now, not even for sure whether it is a playing card." Actual correct recognition of the incongruous object required by far the longest exposure.

From this we learn, as the authors point out, "that perceptual organization is powerfully determined by expectations built upon past commerce with the environment." (Note that perception is described as "organization" and that expectations are generated by "commerce," that is, correlations and comparisons of environmental influences.) Moreover, these expectations may, in certain circumstances, falsify perception in various ways. If the presented clues clash with them too severely, the perceptual organization on which veridicality depends breaks down. The psychologists use the word "coherence" in this connection without hesitation, the attainment of which is assumed to be a condition of successful perception. The experimental results leave little doubt that perception involves interpretation of cues and judgment in accordance with acquired knowledge and is no mere passively accepted datum. It is itself dependent on other criteria for the attainment of truth and is not, in any purified form, the sole touchstone of veridicality.

That correct perception depends on the correlation of many different cues and not on the mere sensuousness of presentation is well illustrated by M. D. Vernon's summary of a great mass of experimental work on shape and size constancy. This author is fully aware that all perception is judgment and makes no scruple to use the word. She writes:

> The adult will actually see in one case a tilted square, in the other a distant object of constant size. If he is asked to make a judgement of the shape of an object seen sideways, his judgement will not correspond to the shape projected on the retina, but will to a greater or less extent resemble the shape of the object if viewed from directly in front of it.

Notice that the visual appearance of the object as actually perceived is described indifferently as "his judgement" or what he "will actually see." Vernon proceeds:

Thus it seems that normally we relate the size of any object to the size of all other objects in the total surroundings at that distance; and the size is perceived in relation to the size scale of objects at that distance. We perceive these surroundings as extended all round us in space, and fit each object into this total pattern, at its appropriate position.

One can hardly require clearer evidence that perceptual judgment depends on coherent coordination of sensuously apprehended cues.

It is not only size and comparison that are involved in distance perception but also texture and clarity of outline. Only with the correlation of all these varied clues comes veridical perception, and without them, as Vernon remarks,

> if the surroundings of an object are concealed from the observer, so that he cannot see whether it is tilted in space, nor what its distance is, then he is forced to rely on the projected image, and his judgement will be made in accordance with that alone.[24]

And then, as Ittelson's experiments demonstrate, that judgment is likely to be false.

So our third witness testifies amply to the facts that sensuous presentation alone does not and cannot serve as a test of truth or probability and that sense perception itself involves judgment relying on the congruence of clues for veridicality. Experience itself, therefore, in all the ways in which we have appealed to it, upholds the coherence theory of knowledge and reveals a world of interrelated and mutually constituting facts such as the coherence theory presupposes, and at the same time, that same experience confounds the critics.

6. THE DYNAMIC PRINCIPLE OF ORGANIZATION

Coherence is order and organization. We perceive and come to know the surrounding world by organizing the contents of the sensuous field into an orderly and coherent system. The activity that does this is judgment, and the faculty is reason. It is the same dynamic principle of wholeness that is active at lower levels in the gamut of natural forms, which, in the course of self-specification, has brought itself to consciousness in the percipient animal. When it becomes self-conscious in the human mind, it reveals itself as reason and as dialectically continuous with the organizing principle operative in the physical and the biological phases of reality.

From the subjectivity of consciousness there is no escape, but the wholeness of the sensuous field and the dialectical structure of the noosphere that develops out of it, as well as that of the conceived world that it reveals, together vouch for the reality of the physical and the biological phases as dialectically continuous with the psychological. We are assured of all this by the consistency and coherence of the dialectical interpretation of our experience, as we could be in no other way.

Notes

This chapter is revised and largely rewritten version of what was published in *Idealistic Studies*, vol. 5, no. 3 (1975).

1. Ludwig Wittgenstein, Cf. *Tractatus Logico-Philosophicus*, 1.2, 1.21.
2. C. I. Lewis, *An Analysis of Knowledge and Valuation*, chap. 11.
3. The same criticism can be found in H. H. Price's *Perception*.
4. Lewis, *Analysis of Knowledge and Valuation*, pp. 352–3.
5. Cf. C. R. Morris, *Idealistic Logic*, and Lewis, *Analysis of Knowledge and Valuation*.
6. See H. Poincaré, *Science and Hypothesis*, chap. 1.
7. Cf. H. van Os, *Tijd, Maat en Getal*, pp. 14–6.
8. Cf. E. E. Harris, *Hypothesis and Perception*, pt. I.
9. Cf. D. Hume, *Treatise of Human Nature*, bk. I, pt. IV, sec. 2, "Scepticism with Regard to the Senses."
10. Cf. E. E. Harris, *Nature, Mind and Modern Science*, pt. IVC; J. O. Urmson, *Philosophical Analysis*; G. J. Warnock, *English Philosophy Since 1900*; A. J. Ayer, *Foundations of Empirical Knowledge*.
11. A. J. Ayer, *The Problem of Knowledge*, p. 29.
12. Cf. E. E. Harris, "Epicyclic Popperism," *British Journal for the Philosophy of Science*, vol. 23 (1972).
13. Albert Einstein, *The World as I See It*, p. 141.
14. Niels Bohr, *Atomic Theory and the Description of Nature*, pp. 4–5, 9, 101.
15. Harris, *Hypothesis and Perception*, pp. 354–7.
16. A. Einstein and I. Infeld, *The Evolution of Physics*, p. 226.
17. L. de Broglie, *The Revolution in Physics*, p. 205; cf. Sir Arthur Eddington, *The Nature of the Physical World*, pp. 254–5; W. Heisenberg, *Physics and Philosophy*, p. 60; cf. also W. Heisenberg, *Philosophical Problems of Nuclear Science*.
18. Cf. *The Correspondence of Sir Isaac Newton*, vol. 3, p. 254; Harris, *Hypothesis and Perception*, pp. 214f., and Émile Myerson, *Identity and Reality*, chap. 2.
19. Einstein and Infeld, *The Evolution of Physics*, pp. 158f.
20. De Broglie, *The Revolution in Physics*, pp. 20–1, chap. 5, p. 211.
21. Max Planck, *The Universe in the Light of Modern Physics*, pp. 17f.
22. H. W. Ittelson, "Size as a Cue to Distance: Static Localization," *American Journal of Psychology*, vol. 64 (1951), pp. 54–67.
23. J. S. Bruner and L. Postman, "On the Perception of Incongruity," *Journal of Personality*, vol. 18 (1949), pp. 206–23.
24. M. D. Vernon, *The Psychology of Perception*, pp. 66, 69, 68.

17

Practical Reason

1. SUBJECTIVE AND OBJECTIVE ACTIVITY

The activity of reason is far from being purely theoretical. If, as has been claimed, it is the universal dynamic raised to the level of self-consciousness, then not only physical activity but all biological process is implicitly (Hegel would have said *an sich*) reason. Reason is, in fact, the subjective aspect of human conduct, and all living activity (possibly all activity whatsoever) has a subjective side—from the evident sensitivity of the protozoan *Volvox*, the sentience that may confidently be presumed in arthropoda and cephalopods, to the percipience of instinctive behavior in vertebrates and the patent intelligence of birds and mammals. It is natural for the animal psychologist and the animal trainer to find the marks of intelligence in animals' behavior and their capacity to modify it by learning. Thus, while intelligence is commonly thought of as a subjective activity of thinking, it is clearly just as much practical. Humans, having become self-conscious, can objectify their own impulses and appetites and deliberately indulge or restrain them, so that instinctive behavior is converted into rational conduct. The exercise of reason is, accordingly, both intellectual and practical at once.

The activity of organizing, which is the function of reason, is the setting of distinct objects and events in orderly relation. I maintained earlier that relations could not be explicitly realized, but remained merely implicit until they were cognized. For a relation to be explicitly actual, it must be (once again to use Hegelian language) not simply *an sich* but *an und für sich*. This means that the terms in relation are distinguished and held together as a single complex as the object of awareness of a conscious subject. The subject cannot be exclusively identified with any one of the terms, for if it were, the relation could not be cognized. It must therefore distinguish itself from both (or all) the related terms in order to apprehend the relation between them. It is, accordingly, only at the level of self-consciousness that the activity of organizing can become overt and deliberate. It is then practical reason.

2. HUMAN CONDUCT

The springs of living behavior, as far down as we need to penetrate in this discussion, are the appetites and instinctive urges of the natural animal: hunger and thirst, sex, combativeness, fear, submissiveness, curiosity, and the like—all of them closely associated with pleasure and pain, vigor and fatigue. They are always both conative and affective, two aspects that can never be wholly separated. Thus they all have both active and passive characters. At the human level, the passions and their corresponding impulses combine to form various sentiments, such as love and hate, gratitude and resentment, modesty and pride. As they may be variously combined, so appetites and passions occasionally conflict. When they do so, on the level of instinct, the stronger overcomes the weaker, or, if they are of more or less equal force, the resulting behavior is ambivalent and vacillating.

Self-consciousness transforms all this from simple behavior into rational conduct, converting feeling and impulse into passion and desire. The human subject can objectify its appetites and become aware of their goals. Being itself *ego*, both subject and object in one, it distinguishes itself from its own feelings and sets them in relation. Hence, when they conflict, as they frequently do, the self is able to compare them and their objectives and to give precedence to one over another, preferring the first to the second in accordance with a chosen standard of value. This is the operation of practical reason, involving value judgment and deliberate choice.

Natural appetites have natural goals, which satisfy them when attained. But the goal of the self-conscious ego is to satisfy not just its desires but itself as a whole. It seeks to realize *itself*, and as it is necessarily one, its constant and typical spontaneous drive is to coordinate the content of its entire experience into a single system. In human self-awareness, the nisus to the whole has become conscious of itself, so the self, being apprised of its own desires and their aims, strives to organize them, in order to attain coherent wholeness, in which it can find complete self-satisfaction; that is, to make them mutually compatible, so as to remove the frustration inherent in internal conflict. It is this self-realization that determines the ultimate standard of value.

3. INDIVIDUAL AND SOCIETY

The term "self-realization," however, may be somewhat misleading, for its initial suggestion is of exclusiveness, smacking of egoism and even of selfishness. But this is a misapprehension, for the self cannot be exclusive. Consciousness of self is correlative to consciousness of other; and, in the first instance, the other is always animate—an other self. Not only is the infant's earliest awareness that of contact with and ministrations from its mother, but in early childhood all objects are at first regarded as animate. It is in relation and opposition to such animate, or quasi-animate, others that one becomes aware of oneself.

The human self, therefore, is always a social self, and the satisfaction of desires is rarely if ever possible without the cooperation of others, even when it is not in competition with and opposition to theirs. Human beings are from the first dependent for their survival on the ministrations of other human beings, so that no personal satisfaction is ever possible in total isolation. Desires, when they conflict, are not only those of a single agent, but commonly, if not invariably, the conflict is between the desires of different agents, which, if any is to be satisfied, must somehow be reconciled. In fact, conflict between the desires of a single person usually originate in conflict with the interests of others to which they must be adjusted if mutual harmony is to be achieved. Consequently, the organization of conduct is always social organization, and rational action is always social action. Practical reason is thus as much social and political as personal, nor can the individual and the societal aspects ever be separated. The attempt to make such separation in political theory always leads to disastrous abstraction and the distortion of the legitimate claims either of the citizen or of the state.

4. VALUATION AND OBLIGATION

Setting objectives in an order of priority in the interest of achieving harmony and wholeness necessarily results in the imposition upon conduct of rules, permissions and prohibitions formulated as "do's" and "don'ts," "thou shalts" and "thou shalt nots," the observance of which is obligatory. And for obedience or disobedience to the rules we are held morally responsible. The source of the obligation is the requirement of coherence or, as it has been called, consistency of the will. What we will to do is what we deliberately choose to do. If we act impulsively, without deliberate intention, we are not strictly responsible for the deed, although we may be responsible as rational persons, for failing to control the impulse. A reflex nervous reaction is not an act for which one can be held responsible, and the control we can exert over our action is (up to a point) a matter of degree. When we are in control of ourselves and act with deliberation and from choice, we are morally responsible.

The attainment of wholeness and harmony in life, in which the self can find ultimate satisfaction, is (we have said) what sets the standard of value. It is to this end that we order our desires and regulate our conduct. We do so because we are rational beings, and our rational nature imposes the objective upon us as a necessity—a categorical imperative. This is the source of the obligation to observe the rules and is what we acknowledge as moral obligation, and it springs directly from the evaluation of the desired end. I am morally obliged to do what is best, and if the action, for whatever reason, can have no value, there can be no obligation to perform it. Of course, actions may have value for any number of different reasons, and some actions may be obligatory even though their immediate consequences may not seem to be in any way beneficial, as, for instance, when one feels obliged to fulfill a promise detrimental to oneself although the person to whom it was made will gain little or nothing in consequence. The obligation, in such a case, derives from the general insecurity that would prevail if people could not be trusted to fulfill promises. Here, as ever, the imperative is imposed by the need for coherence of the will. A promise is an undertaking to do what one has been trusted to carry out. To break it would convert the undertaking into a lie, and that would, in principle, undermine trust in all communication between persons dependent on one another for the success of every enterprise. Consequently, not only social harmony but one's necessary reliance upon others for one's own satisfactions would suffer if, in general, promises were not kept.

5. "The Goal of Our Great Endeavor"

Because rational conduct is always social conduct, the ultimate aim of rational (or moral) action is always at once social and individual self-realization. The good of the community is nothing other than the good of each and all of its members, but the good of none of its members can be assured in separation from the others, because the satisfaction of any depends on the cooperation and solidarity of purpose of the whole community. The good life, for each person, is thus the sort of social intercourse and social order that has been found, in the course of time and within the limits of current knowledge and belief, to be the most satisfactory on the whole. This is what is called the culture of the community concerned. But we cannot stop here, especially today, for cultures are not self-sufficient, nor can the organized life of any one community be made wholly satisfactory within its own boundaries. Every community and every culture is in commerce with, and is dependent for its welfare upon, other communities. The whole, the realization of which is to be sought by any, must embrace them all and cannot be restricted to the confines of any one or of any limited group.

6. Understanding and Reason in Practice

Even on the plane of self-consciousness, reason operates on different levels—that of understanding and that of speculation—and these are displayed in both practical morality and in the ethical theories that philosophers propound. The characteristic of the understanding is its insistence on sharp and rigid distinctions, its tendency to oppose one to another and to emphasize one at the expense of its opposite, although in truth they are complementaries, each demanding the other in reconciliation within a single whole. In morality and ethics the understanding is wont to distinguish sharply and then to separate obligation from goodness, subordinating one to the other, or concentrating attention upon one to the neglect of the other. In practice this leads to the pursuit of advantage with scant consideration of the demands of duty; or, alternatively, the insistence on duty without regard to advantage. In ethical theory, hedonistic and utilitarian theories correspond to the first, and deontic to the second. Again, morality has two aspects: subjective, focusing on the importance of conscience, and objective, stressing the universality and strict invariability of the moral law. Different and opposing theories represent each of these aspects to the neglect, or suppression, of the other; and in practice, there are those who follow conscience in disregard of convention or statute, while others unbendingly require conformity to an accepted code.

In politics, similar dichotomies tend to be made by the understanding. The rights and interests of the individual are divorced from the demands and the legitimacy of law and government, resulting, both in theory and in practice, in doctrines of limited as opposed to those of absolute, sovereignty, in libertarianism as opposed to authoritarianism.

As always, the rigid separations of the understanding lead to a dialectic: each of the separated moments, when driven to extreme, turns into its opposite and contradicts itself. So, on the one hand, untrammeled respect for conscience leads to social dissent and disorder, prompting the forcible imposition of moral and political authority; while, on the other hand, with unquestioning submission to authority and to a rigid moral code, conscience atrophies, casuistry and corruption tend to flourish, and hypocrisy to become rife.

The escape from the resulting impasse is the recognition of the mutual supplementation of the opposites in harmonious complementarity. In practice, this is the realization that what duty requires is what ultimately satisfies (the service of God is perfect freedom), that universal respect for persons, love, and devotion, in which law and conscience are reconciled, are what secure the good of all. The corresponding theory is that of "my station and its duties," in which conscience is reconciled with what society expects and requires (including criticism and, when necessary, reform). The theory goes on to show that this leads necessarily to universal trust and genuine devotion to the welfare of others, the features of an ideal morality of devoted self-giving in which benevolence, duty, and self-realization merge.

On the side of politics, demands for complete liberty tend to anarchy and inequality, which defeat the aims of the libertarian. Anarchy generates conflict in which the use of force tends to triumph and, in the end, the strongest prevails and tyranny is reinstated. Or, alternatively, to counteract unrest, demand increases for stronger exertion of the law's authority, and totalitarianism results. Arbitrary rule, again, breeds discontent and resistance, fomenting revolution. The resolution of this self-frustration is the recognition that rights and duties are correlative and exist in practice only when recognized; that individual rights are the incidents of social function and can be preserved only if protected by the law, which can best be guaranteed in a constituted democracy governing by popular consent.

It is hardly possible here to discuss in detail all these facets and phases of practical reason, but some indication may be given of how the dialectic unfolds and is exemplified in different theories that have been espoused in the past, as well as in those advocated in recent times, and how they relate to the contemporary metaphysics.

7. UTILITARIANISM

Hume's declaration that reason is the slave of the passions makes reason purely instrumental, confusing it with understanding. His consequent argument that morality is a matter of sentiment and his postulation (following earlier moralists) of a moral sense emphasize the subjective aspect of morality at the expense of the objective. The same is true of the utilitarian doctrine of Bentham and the Mills which highlights happiness and the feeling of pleasure, to which duty is made ancillary. These thinkers assert that the pursuit of pleasure is the spring of all action, and that pleasure is the end at which all action should aim. Inclination and obligation thus become one and the same, and prudence takes the place of conscience. But this immediately undermines the whole concept of morality, which stems from the distinction between one's inclination and the duty one is obliged to fulfill whether or not one is inclined to do so.

Moreover, the supposed end is held to be the greatest sum of pleasures; but pleasures cannot be summed, for as each is past and gone, it cannot be revived to combine with the next. Further, as the unreserved pursuit of personal pleasure would result in conflict between different individual enterprises, defeating the universal aim, utilitarians prescribed, as the good to be sought, the greatest pleasure of the greatest number. This, however, is a sum that cannot be computed or assessed, and so cannot serve as a standard of moral worth. Further, in the attempt to achieve it, utilitarians tend to recommend a legalism involving the regulation of individual choice, which runs counter to their professed liberalism.

Finally, the whole doctrine of hedonism is undermined by the fact that pleasure is experienced only on success in achieving some other end desired independently. If sought for its own sake, pleasure eludes the pursuit. It is enjoyed only when it is not the aim of the successful venture. Accordingly, if pleasure is the moral end, it is one that ought not to be pursued—a self-contradictory and paradoxical conclusion.

8. THE MORAL LAW

The opposing theory declares, with Kant, that nothing is good, without qualification, except the good will—the will that obeys the categorical imperative of morality. The imperative is that one should act for no other reason than that the act is morally right, but what makes it right is that the motive is morally pure; so we have moved in a circle. This precept, therefore, is apt to abandon the moral agent to arbitrary choice.

Kant's ethics is far from being exhausted by this assertion, and may not summarily be swept aside in virtue of this denouement, for it contains much more of weight and substance. It is not, however, our immediate purpose to examine it for its own sake. His requirement that the maxims of action must be universalizable without self-contradiction has some merit, but it fails in the end, because any maxim that contains sufficient qualification can be so universalized. Moreover, as Plato showed in the opening of the *Republic*, universalizability cannot guarantee moral rectitude, for circumstances alter cases and may at times render obedience to a rule that is generally salutary morally inadmissible.

Kant's argument is based on the spontaeous activity of the transcendental *ego*, who acts freely and whose will is autonomous. An autonomous will necessarily wills its own freedom. Only such autonomous action is rational, and only rational action is moral; hence nothing is morally good, without qualification, except the freely autonomous will. It obeys a categorical imperative, because to be free it may not be influenced by any natural sensuous inclination, which would make it heteronomous. Thus its action is self-determining and unconditioned. It follows that every rational being is an end in itself and may not be treated merely as a means. So to treat all humanity, however, gives us little guidance, unless we know what the practical end of any rational being ought to be. Kant maintains that the necessary object of a will determined only by the moral law is the highest good, which, he asserts, is human happiness proportionate to desert. Morally right conduct deserves happiness, but that assumes that happiness is desirable. As all human experience, according to Kant, is sensuous and only of phenomena, all human desire is naturally conditioned and involves the heteronomy of the will. To will the highest good, therefore, if that is the deserved happiness of all rational beings, implies the heteronomy not only of the will of the agent acting to produce it, but of all human willing. The categorical imperative has now become its opposite—a hypothetical imperative—and the doctrine contradicts itself.

The solution to these paradoxes is the recognition that happiness and moral rectitude are one and the same; that true advantage is mutual service and beneficence, harmonious (that is, rational) living: as Plato maintained, a harmony in the soul conditional on a harmony in the social order. The ethics that provides this insight is of the kind offered by Hegel, T. H. Green, and Bernard Bosanquet, which reconciles conscience with law and self-realization with self-giving. The one-sided theories are those of the understanding, and their reconciliation is effected by speculative reason.

9. THE BACKGROUND METAPHYSIC

Thinkers of the the the seventeenth to the nineteenth centuries all wrote under the influence of the metaphysical presuppositions of Newtonian science, either in accordance with them or in reaction against them. Their direct product was empiricism, of which Hume and the utilitarians offer examples. Those who found their implications troublesome and sought an alternative were Spinoza, Leibniz, and Kant,[1] but Kant never freed himself from them entirely. He realized, after Hume had awakened him from his dogmatic slumber, that the objective claim of Newtonian science could not survive on the foundation of unqualified empiricism, and that it presupposed a transcendental unity of apperception to introduce into the manifold of sense the organizing principles of the categories of understanding. But he refused to relinquish the limitation set to human knowledge by its dependence on sense perception. While the ethics of utilitarianism is the direct consequence of empiricist premises, Kantian ethics follows from his dichotomy between conception and perception, between reason and sense, prompted by the Cartesian dualism of thought and extension, which in turn was the result of the Newtonian exclusion of mind from the celestial mechanism.

Kant, however, provided Hegel with the clue to progress in the dialectic. The synthetic unity of apperception ensured that experience was, in Kant's own words, a whole of related and connected representations. Hegel, therefore (following Fichte and Schelling) developed the implications of this holism, to which twentieth-century science, replacing the classical physics of Newtonianism, impels us to return at the present time.

10. NONCOGNITIVISM

For Newtonian science, the world is a material mechanism observed from without. To use A. N. Whitehead's phrase, it is closed to mind. All objective fact is therefore devoid of everything mind-dependent; it is the record of what is "given," free from any subjective coloring or wish. It is, and must be, value-free. Valuation derives only from human desire and willing, which depend solely on the mind, and goodness is what appeals to our tastes, not what derives from natural properties. Hume, the empiricist, acknowledges as matter-of-fact only what is given in sense impressions, and these have value only as colored by emotion and sentiment. What we seek, and what we feel ought to be, is that to which we are subjectively inclined, to which actually existing circumstances are indifferent. Hence, what we think ought to be cannot be derived from what is. There are no oughts in nature. Kant followed Hume in declaring that the *ought* cannot be derived from the *is*, because he too believed that all objective fact was phenomenal, though formed by the categories of the understanding. Human inclination was a natural phenomenon and was causally determined, whereas the categorical imperative derived solely from the autonomy of the will and the spontaneous activity of the ego, which is the source of the categories and cannot be brought under them. Accordingly, an unbridgeable cleft was cut between fact and value that has confronted moralists ever since.

11. THE NATURALISTIC FALLACY

Contemporary ethicists, inclined toward empiricism, follow this lead and inveigh against the naturalistic fallacy that seeks to deduce the good from the natural properties of the objects valued. The question why these properties themselves are good can never be answered objectively. So G. E. Moore maintained that goodness was a "non-natural" property independent of the natural (or objective) character of the object valued. The medieval doctrine of Natural Law, prescribing an objective moral order continuous with and integral to nature as such, has, accordingly, been castigated as fallacious. This doctrine was derived from the ontological presumption of the Ancients that Nature was a living creature with a soul of its own, and that the souls of animals and humans were individual centers of the world-soul. The medievals modified this worldview in the light of the Judeo-Christian belief that God had created the world as a rational and moral order, in which the divine law was one and the same throughout. Natural Law was thus held to be at once the law of God, of reason, and of moral requirement. But as soon as the physical world was seen (though still the creation of God) as a machine, the laws of whose working were automatic and inviolable, natural law became purely descriptive of the regularities occurring among natural events, whereas the moral law was prescriptive by moral and social authority. In contrast to the laws of nature, as they were now conceived, the moral law could be and frequently is violated and had to be otherwise explained. Hence the persistent question in ethics of the source of moral obligation. The explanation offered was, in the main, that human beings in the pursuit of happiness devised rules of conduct to ensure advantage and satisfaction. Thus the moral law became subjectivized, as dependent upon human desire and sentiment, and social laws were relative to the community on whom they were imposed.

The tradition of Natural Law persisted, however, among Roman Catholic writers who followed Thomas Aquinas and among jurists and political theorists seeking a standard by which to criticize existing codes. But it has been widely subjected to attack, whether as the basis for ethics or as a doctrine in jurisprudence. Fact and value are firmly held apart by contemporary thinkers. According to Bertrand Russell:

> A judgement of fact is capable of a property called "truth," which it has or does not have quite independently of what anyone may think about.... But ... I see no property, analogous to "truth," that belongs or does not

belong to an ethical judgement. This, it must be admitted, puts ethics in a different category from science.[2]

Karl Popper asserts:

Perhaps the simplest and most important point about ethics is purely logical. I mean the impossibility to derive non-tautological ethical rules—imperatives—. . . from statements of fact.[3]

So, likewise, Margaret Macdonald, discussing natural rights, says:

The statements of the law of Nature are not statements of the laws of nature, not even the laws of an "ideal" nature. For nature provides no standards or ideals. . . . Natural events cannot tell us what we ought to do until we have made certain decisions when knowledge of natural fact will enable the most efficient means to be chosen to carry out those decisions. Natural events themselves have no value, and human beings as natural existents have no value either, whether on account of possessing intelligence or having two feet.[4]

(Note that knowledge of natural fact is said to enable us to choose the most efficient means only after we have made certain decisions that we wish to carry out, so that value depends on our wishes and decisions, and is to that extent subjectivized.)

The jurist Julius Stone adopts the same attitude. In his book *Human Law and Human Justice*, he asks the rhetorical question: "Have the natural lawyers shown that they can derive ethical norms from facts?"

John Finnis, defending the Natural Law doctrine, concedes that *ought* cannot be derived from *is* but alleges that the accusation is unfounded that Aquinas committed the fallacy, although he convicts some of his followers (such as Suarez) of misinterpreting Aquinas and of making the error.[5] As will presently appear, neither side of the argument is justified in maintaining the rigid division between fact and value. Aquinas certainly did not commit that error, nor did Suarez diverge from his master's doctrine.

That *ought* cannot be derived from *is* follows from the view that statements of fact are either true or false, whereas statements of value are neither. The latter, it is alleged, are not descriptive; they express only preference, approval, or imperative. In short, statements of value are expressions, in one form or another, of feeling, which is subjective to the person speaking. Consequently, the prevalent ethical theory has been emphatically noncognitive and has ranged from the emotivism of C. L. Stevenson and A. J. Ayer to varieties of utilitarianism, some of them more latent than open, as may be discerned in the case of Kurt Baier's book *The Moral Point of View*, where "enjoyment" is given as the primary "reason" for action, and the explanation of obligation and the superiority of "moral reasons" is the desire to avoid the anarchy and terror of

Hobbes' state of nature. The appeal is to pleasure and the avoidance of pain—once more, a purely subjective basis for moral evaluation.

Deontic theories (like those of W. D. Ross and H. A. Prichard), which oppose utilitarianism, still resort to some kind of moral intuition that recognizes "prima facie duties" as imperative. They assert that the content of moral requirements is self-evident. Yet they confess, in the end, that intuitions differ from one person to another and that what is held to be obligatory in one society is not the same as, and may conflict with, what is required in another. Morality remains subjective.

12. RELATIVISM AND ITS CONSEQUENCES

In all these theories the criterion of value and the moral standpoint is subjective, with the inevitable result that morality becomes radically relativized, not just to the society and the period, but also to the individual. This relativism, moreover, is reinforced by another effect of the Newtonian paradigm, which, in the physical sciences, had so great and such rapid success that it proceeded to embrace every sphere of investigation and to reduce the subject matter of all other sciences to the objective status assumed in physics: that is, externality to mind. Every science became value-free. Even psychology externalized its subject and became behavioristic, and it was to psychology that thinkers turned for the explanation of moral convictions. The explanation that science offered was that moral attitudes were the results of social conditioning. At the same time, sociologists discovered that in different cultures different and incompatible moral codes were observed, between which there was and could be no standard by which to judge one superior to any other; and historians found the same to be true of different historical periods. Moral judgments, in consequence, were pronounced relative to the time, to the society, and finally to the person.

Relativism degenerates into skepticism. If moral obligation is relative in this way, it is open to every person to adopt whatever course of action he or she prefers—in short, there is no real obligation upon anybody to observe any one code rather than any other, or any at all, and morality proper goes by the board. This is what has, by and large, happened at the present time. Few writers have revealed this more convincingly than Alasdair MacIntyre in his book *After Virtue*, where he describes the modern ethos and its relation to current ethical theories; although he attributes the prevailing situation rather to the influence of the Enlightenment than to Newtonian science. However, as the Enlightenment was itself the consequence of the metaphysical presuppositions implicit in Newtonianism, MacIntyre's position does not really contradict what is being argued here. Rather, he confirms the contention I am making when he asserts that the separation of fact from value (on which, he says, modern ethics is wrecked) is far from being a logical truth, that it follows simply from a change in the use of evaluative expressions which occurred in the seventeenth (or early eighteenth) century, such that what ranked as factual could no longer entail what now pass for value judgments.

MacIntyre agrees that contemporary ethics is emotivist, even in the hands of the existentialists, and he avers that Kant and the deontologists have consistently failed to vindicate conventional morality. At least since Nietzsche, the traditional morality inherited from the Greeks and Christianity is seen to have broken down, and the current worldview provides no rational basis for respecting it. MacIntyre illustrates vividly how the common moral outlook of today presupposes the absence of all objective standards. Commitments are partisan and incommensurable, and the only ultimate end envisaged for human endeavor is "success." Manipulation of persons takes the place of respect for persons; and, in consequence, the current use of moral terms and the professed deference to rational precepts have become largely a front for propaganda (as the theorists themselves admit) serving personal preferences and partisan social aims. In general, the present age is abandoned, whether in theory or in practice, to prejudice, relativism, and ethical skepticism.

To all this we may add that the Copernican-Newtonian view of the universe as a machine generates the attitude that physical and nonhuman nature is and may legitimately be exploited for human purposes, while the success of Newtonian science in the eighteenth and nineteenth centuries has given rise to an ever-advancing technology that is now destroying the life-supporting environment of the planet. Today we are faced with global problems that demand decisions based on universal criteria of value (for deference to partisan or parochial beliefs is quite inadequate), and we need objective standards most when they have lost all credence.

13. RESOLUTION OF THE IMPASSE

MacIntyre's remedy for the parlous situation in which we now stand is a return to the Aristotelian tradition of virtue founded in community, the modern critique of which he holds to be self-defeating. Commendable as this would be, it is unlikely to occur if the influence of Newtonian presuppositions continues to prevail. It is, moreover, high time that that influence began to wane, for the science that generated the metaphysical background has been superseded by a new physics and a new biology requiring a very different metaphysic. Once the unity of the universe and of the biosphere has been fully grasped, and the consequent dialectical structure of the universal system appreciated, morality will be seen as the practical exercise of reason, which is itself the conscious operation of the organizing principle active throughout nature. The new metaphysic abolishes the opposition of fact to value, for the criterion of truth and of value is the same: coherent order and unity. No fallacy is involved in deducing what ought to be, and to be done, from the general nature of the world and of its organizing principle, which, when it becomes self-conscious, characterizes and defines human nature. For what ought to be done is what promotes health, unity, and harmony, as well in the biosphere, as in human society. This is the dictate of practical reason, no less than of theoretical; and the notion of Natural Law can now be resuscitated on a new and more solid foundation.

Practical reason is indeed essentially social in character, but it is now evident that it cannot be restricted to single communities, but must embrace all. For today, all communities and nationalities are interdependent, and all have a common interest in the conservation of the planetary ecosystem vital to human survival. This cannot be ensured by the uncoordinated action of separate national communities. Organization of human purposes and activities, therefore, cannot be confined to the limits of any one society, nor within the frontiers of any one nation, but must extend to the entire world and encompass all humankind.

The demands of practical reason at the present time go far beyond the questions that formerly prompted ethical speculation. In the past, philosophers asked what was the best way for the individual to live. Ethical inquiry centered on the person and the immediate community. Never until now has it extended beyond the limits of the national state. Today, however, while all the old questions remain pertinent, new ones have arisen concerning the rights of future generations as well as of species lower than the human, concerning duties not merely to one another and to the state but to the global environment. Political theory is faced with questions concerning world order and the maintenance of peace, which is perpetually menaced by a power struggle between sovereign nations armed with weapons of mass destruction. The purview of moral philosophy today extends far beyond the concerns of former ages, requiring a holistic outlook exceeding the horizons even of Hegel and his immediate followers.

14. The Limits of Morality

The universal principle that organizes the physical world as a unified whole and generates life within it on planets where the physicochemical conditions are appropriate, evolving creatures capable of intelligent behavior and bringing itself to consciousness as reason, expresses and strives to realize itself in the social and moral conduct of human beings. But morality is not enough. The finite nature of the animal organism, which is the vehicle of intelligent, self-conscious reason, opposes and restricts the efforts of the moral agent. This is why moral effort is always very demanding and commonly falls short of what is required. "The spirit is willing but the flesh is weak." Spinoza justly observed that human power is extremely limited and is far surpassed by the power of external causes. As finite modes, human beings are never free from external pressures, hence they are always subject to passion, which their reason, although it can do much, can never wholly overcome. To that extent, Kant's insight was right that human desire, being merely natural, is a constant obstacle to practical reason.

Nor can the enshrinement of moral rules in social institutions and legal enactments suffice to remedy this defect. The state can appeal only to the wrong motives for obedience. The moral law requires willing compliance, but the law of the state can be enforced only by fear of punishment or, more rarely, hope of material reward, neither of which is a pure moral motive. Citizens cannot be made moral by act of parliament. The ultimate aim of practical reason is thus unattainable solely by the effort of the natural human animal, even with the help of secular institutions.

What is ultimately desired is union with the absolute whole, which transcends the human intellect and the finite human will; although both of these can be cognizant of it, because its principle of unity and order is immanent in them both. Accordingly, humankind seeks, in religion that reveals a perfection transcending the merely human, the "at-one-ment" with the whole that cannot be achieved by unaided moral effort.

Notes

1. Cf. E. E. Harris, *Nature, Mind and Modern Science*, chaps. 10, 11.
2. Bertrand Russell, "Reply to Criticisms," in Schilpp (ed.), *The Philosophy of Bertrand Russell*, p. 723.
3. Karl Popper, "What Can Logic Do for Philosophy" in *Proceedings of the Aristotelian Society*, sup. vol. 22 (1948), p. 154.
4. Margaret Macdonald, "Natural Rights," *Proceedings of the Aristotelian Society*, 1947–48, reprinted in *Philosophy, Politics and Society*, ed. Peter Laslette, p. 44.
5. Cf. John Finnis, *Natural Law and Natural Right*, pp. 17, 33.

18

Religion

1. REASON AND RELIGION

Commonly, reason and religion are supposed to be in mutual opposition, or at least are contrasted as different sources of enlightenment, the one by means of argument and inference, and the other by direct revelation. Devotees of the first are often disposed to belittle the second as self-deception and superstition. These are the "rationalists" of whom I spoke in Chapter 14, who take the understanding to exhaust the range of reason and fail to comprehend speculative synopticism, which they reject as mysticism. But although much superstition, self-deception, and wishful thinking frequently pass for religion, there is a genuine religious phase of self-consciousness that is not opposed to, but is in fact identical with, speculative reason.

The assumed conflict between reason and religion is often identified as that between science and religion. Here again, reason is confused with understanding; it is the reason of the Enlightenment, identified with Newtonian science, that has been superseded and is now outdated. In fact, not even Newtonianism, in its earlier pronouncements, was opposed to religion: Newton declared space to be the sensorium of God, and other seventeenth-century scientists declared that what their science revealed was the glory of God's creation. He was conceived as the divine architect who had created the celestial machine and set it in motion. Not even the dispute between Galileo and the papacy was really a conflict between science and religion, although the church was involved. It was a dispute between Aristotelian science, which the church had espoused, and Copernican science, which had just emerged—the sort of debate that is typical of every scientific innovation, whenever it occurs, although it is not always accompanied by the ecclesiastical censure that descended upon Galileo. The real opposition to religion was posed by the Darwinian theory in the mid-nineteenth century, because it undermined the teleological proof of God's existence in the form it had taken in William Paley's *Natural Theology*, which had then seemed to prevail over even Hume's skepticism. Paley's argument, supported by telling examples from natural history and anatomical structure,

264

had proved cogent until Darwin's theory showed that everything Paley had attributed to divine providence might be accounted for by chance variation and natural selection.

Today, all this has changed. Contemporary biology has revealed cases of living process and behavior the evolution of which cannot credibly be accounted for by the accumulation of chance variations (which according to Darwinism, is all that is responsible for innovation), and biologists have calculated that the probability of such nicely adjusted complications arising solely by that means is less than minuscule, so that some additional factor of self-organization has to be presumed. The science of the twentieth century has opened up a new vision of the universe, a holistic conception in both physics and biology, the philosophical implications of which render complete reconciliation between religion and science possible, as long as superstition and the various degenerate forms of pseudo-religion are eschewed.

2. THE CONCRETE UNIVERSAL

Reason is the self-conscious, self-critical activity of self-reflective mind, which is the precondition of all intellectual pursuits—science and morality no less than art, religion, and philosophy—all of which are no more nor less than dialectical moments in the self-specification of the concrete universal, in its later phases. The concrete universal is the principle of organization governing the structure of the entire universe. It specifies itself first in and as the physical world, then in the biosphere, and finally comes to consciousness of itself in the noosphere. This, as I explained in Chapter 8, is the necessary deployment of the whole, which contemporary science has discovered the physical universe to be, a whole that does not realize itself explicitly as a relational complex until it is cognized, as it comes to be at the level of reason in science and philosophy (to which social order and morality are prerequisite).

The dialectic of the noosphere begins with sentience, in which the physical whole, sublated in the biosphere, is internalized by the living organism. First, sentience becomes object to perception, affording the content of consciousness. Next, consciousness, enfolding itself yet again, reflects upon the content of perception in understanding. Each phase is a whole in itself: the felt whole of indiscriminate sentience, the life-world of percipient common sense, and the scientific worldview. In each case it is the same whole raised successively to a higher degree of adequacy to the integral, diversified unity of the concrete universal.

The necessary social character of reflective self-consciousness asserts itself at the level of conscious reason as it organizes conduct, along with knowledge, in morality and social order. Morality is the quest for wholeness in human life, bringing harmony within both the person and the community, but it falls short of its ultimate purpose, owing to the finiteness of the individual and the conflict that the finite self can never wholly overcome between natural passion and rational aspiration—an aspiration for complete unity and conciliation of moral, intellectual, and aesthetic satisfactions, which cannot be achieved unless the self-conscious person can grasp and experience its own identity with the absolute (infinite) totality, within which it is comprehended (in which it lives and moves and has its being). What is ultimately sought is a unity and reconciliation between the finite and the infinite. It is this relationship of atonement that constitutes the goal and specific character of religion.

3. FINITE AND INFINITE

Religion originates in the recognition by human beings of their finitude. The early tribal hunter, pastoralist, and agriculturalist were all made painfully aware, on the one hand, of their abject dependence upon natural processes for their survival and, on the other, of the inimical forces of nature. As the ego automatically projects its own self-reflective capacity upon its other, these forces were personified, and the attempt was made to placate and to identify with the powers controlling them. Thus *Homo sapiens*, from the moment that epithet becomes appropriate, is aware of his own finitude, by virtue of a concomitant awareness of what limits and opposes him, defining and supplementing his own deficiency. To be conscious of deficiency is ipso facto to be conscious, however vaguely, of a standard of adequacy and completeness. So the sense of finitude is wedded to a premonition of the infinite and evokes a feeling of deference and subjection to it. Further, as the transcendental ego is the immanence of the whole within the part, the *conatus* to self-maintenance in the animate self is a nisus to wholeness and unification, which generates, in the premonition of the infinite, a presentiment of its absolute governance.

Inchoate rationality, therefore, from its earliest emergence, is religious, first identifying the individual with the tribe (the proximate whole) and then, through the totem, the tribe with nature (dimly conceived as all-encompassing). Religion is ubiquitous in human civilization and has characterized its entire history. The consciousness of finitude and deficiency, with its concomitant sense of the numinous in the universal totality, is detectable in all the major world religions: in the conception of *Brahma* in Hinduism, in contrast to the illusory *Maya*; of *Dharmakaya* in Buddhism, with the inadequacy of the finite mind and the prescription of the eightfold way to the attainment of *Nirvana*; and of the *Tao*, uniting the finite opposites of *yin* and *yang*, in Taoism. In the West, Judaism envisages one all-powerful, all-creative, and all-righteous God in contrast to whom the princes and judges of the earth are as vanity (Isaiah 40:23); and Paul, proselytizing Christianity, is acutely aware of his own finitude and bewails the law in his members, which he finds warring against the law of his mind (Romans 7:23), for which the remedy is to walk after the Spirit of God and Christ. Correlatively, the philosophizing Descartes finds the idea of a perfect being in his mind implicit in his awareness of his own deficiency and finitude (*Meditations*, III).

The immanence of the whole in the self-conscious subject is the source of the inherent awareness of a transcendent reality that surpasses the limits of the finite self and toward which the drive of the finite to fulfill itself is directed. Religion, therefore, is the natural and logical outcome of the necessary self-specification of the universal organizing principle, as it proceeds through the experience of rational beings. This self-specification is dialectically continuous from the physical to the biotic and thence to the noetic; and the dialectical structure follows directly from the conception of the unity of the universe disclosed by the new physics. Religious consciousness, accordingly, is a dialectical consequence of contemporary physical theory.

4. RELIGION AND ART

In their beginnings, art and religion are one and the same. The cave paintings of the Dordogne and Altamira were the religious practice of Stone Age hunters. The sculpture of totem poles and the modeling of ritual masks were the expression and representation of religious beliefs. The graven image and the sculptured idol became objects of worship. When Moses had extirpated the worshippers of the golden calf before Mount Sinai, he gave elaborate instructions for the design and adornment of the tabernacle and ark of the Lord, which must have been consummate works of art, as were the vestments, breastplates, and headdresses of the priests. We read in the second book of Chronicles (29: 27–8) how Hezekiah commanded a burnt offering to be made:

> And when the burnt offering began, the song of the Lord began also with the trumpets, and with the instruments ordained by David king of Israel. And all the congregation worshipped, and the singers sang, and the trumpeters sounded.

Art, in its origins, is the outward sensible expression of religious worship and fervor, from which the beautification of everyday utensils and instruments for its own sake, and the representation of the artist's own vision of the inner significance of the objects made and the events represented are derivative.

The subject matter of art was almost exclusively religious, right up to the Renaissance. The epics of ancient Greece were their scriptures; Hesiod and Homer were revered as sages, and their writings recorded the actions of the gods and demigods. Greek architecture was of temples, and their statues were of divine persons, their painted ceramics showed the activities of nymphs and maenads in religious or quasi-religious practices. Greek tragedy presented the conflict between religion and the secular law, and drama was performed as part of a religious ceremony. The art of the Middle Ages depicted sacred and demonic figures, medieval architecture was of churches and cathedrals, the sculpture was of saints and devils (gargoyles); modern drama originated in the passion play, in morality-plays and in miracle-plays. Almost universally, secular art is derived from religious art.

From the other side, art is the medium of presentation of religious teaching and beliefs. In ancient Greek religion, the gods and goddesses were imaginative symbolic personifications both of untamed natural processes (cosmic and human) and of moral qualities, as well as of the conflict between them. They and their transactions with human beings and among themselves were proclaimed in myth and allegory by poets and dramatists. The Hebrew Scriptures are epic and dramatic narrative, they rejoice and celebrate with hymns and psalms, they teach in parables, and most of their declamation is metaphor. Much of what the prophets write is poetry, for prophecy, as Spinoza saw, is the intellectual gift presenting the truth in the medium of the imagination; and religious leaders "speak in tongues."

The opening verses of Genesis are pure poetry:

> In the beginning God created heaven and earth.
> And the earth was without form, and void;
> And darkness was upon the face of the deep.
> And the Spirit of God moved upon the face of the waters.

The book of Job is a dramatic dialogue written in a poetic vein that is the virtual equivalent of blank verse. The visions of Ezekiel and Zechariah are artistic imagery, as is the eleventh chapter of Isaiah. A great deal else is expressed metaphorically, which is the genre of religious language in general. The common "rationalist" criticism of religion, therefore, which discredits religious doctrine as literally meant, is generally as misguided as is the ranting of the fundamentalists who accept the Scriptures without criticism or elucidation.

Of the descriptions of the miraculous, more needs to be said. Miracles are presented as historical events, but there is little, if any, historical evidence to support them; many of them can be plausibly explained as natural phenomena, and many more, if we could know more detail of the occurrences, might be so explicable. Others may well be exaggerated accounts of unusual happenings given by overexcited witnesses. One must constantly remember the period in which the accounts were written, and that they were written by persons without scientific knowledge for the edification of people who were uninstructed and credulous. They are all subject to historical criticism, and even those that are not metaphorical declarations of the power of God need careful interpretation.

5. Consequences of Literalism

Literal acceptance of religious pronouncements results in two opposed and baneful errors. The first is superstition, the belief in and action upon falsehoods, and credence given to reports of thaumaturgy based on insecure and insufficient factual evidence. The falsehoods arise out of taking literally what are metaphorical statements, and the consequent practices are often barbarous and immoral, including vicious persecution of alleged unbelievers and the committal of violent crimes claimed to have been commanded by God. Such practices have occurred throughout history, from the time of Moses to the present, in the name of Judaism. Because of the belief that the Lord had commanded Samuel to instruct Saul to smite Amalek and "slay both man and woman, infant and suckling, ox and sheep, camel and ass" (I Samuel 15:3), the Amalekites were slaughtered; based on that same belief, that God had commanded it, Yigal Amir murdered Prime Minister Yitzhak Rabin. In the past, the followers of Mohammed have perpetrated similar massacres, and to this day, from Algeria to Pakistan, they continue to commit terrorist atrocities in the name of Allah. The Christian church butchered the Albigensians and burnt reputed heretics at the stake in order to save their souls, and nowadays, religious fundamentalists plant bombs in public places that kill hundreds of innocent people. Such blinkered malevolence and violence toward putative opponents have given religion a bad reputation that, in its true form, it does not deserve, for the actual culprits are bigotry, fanaticism, and superstition. Nor is the conduct of religious institutions necessarily the same as the genuine practice of religion. At times, not infrequently, the first runs counter to the precepts of the second and to the professed commitments of the devotees: Christians, for instance, enjoined to love their enemies, have instigated crusades and waged religious wars. Similar examples from other institutionalized religions are not hard to find.

So religion has been brought into disrepute, and the inconsistencies in and with its precepts have induced many freethinking people to reject it and call its dogmas into question. Especially under the influence of the Enlightenment, the "rationalism" of the eighteenth and nineteenth centuries prompted agnosticism and atheism. So Nietzsche, on the strength of scientific enlightenment (although, with characteristic inconsistency, he also disparaged reason), declared that God is dead. Freud attempted to explain away religious belief as an infantile psychosis, and Marx to discredit it as "the opium of the people" used by established capitalism to placate the workers. Others, like Darwin and Samuel Butler, rejected religious dogma as incredible and self-contradictory. Contemporary thinkers (e.g., Bertrand Russell) have drawn attention to and condemned the misconduct of the Churches in the past, the social chaos and human suffering caused by religious wars, and the massacres committed in religious persecutions. The philosophical inconsistencies and shortcomings of such atheistic attacks need not detain us here. In *Atheism and Theism* I have discussed them at some length, as well as their salutary effects in counteracting superstition. The point presently being underlined is their common failure to interpret what is metaphor and allegory. Such criticism and rejection, when they are not induced by failure to distinguish between the conduct of religious dignitaries and what genuine religion requires, result, in large measure, from understanding literally what is actually figurative representation.

6. RELIGION AND THE NEW SCIENCE

The tension between science and religion was occasioned, for the most part, by the intellectual attitude engendered by Newtonian science. Laplace rightly responded to Napoleon's question that his science had no need of the hypothesis that there was a God. Scientists, if they raise the question at all (which, as scientists, it is not their business to do), tend to treat the existence of God as a hypothesis, whereas, in truth, it is a metaphysical necessity. All science, Collingwood argued, in its implicit and indispensable faith in the rational order of the universe, absolutely presupposes the monotheistic conception of an all-wise creator.[1] Contemporary physicists, moreover, have recently become more sensible of the religious implications of their science. Einstein, in particular, was insistent that modern physics led him to the conviction that God existed, and Jeans speculated that in the light of contemporary physical discovery, God must be a supreme mathematician. Paul Davies has explicitly raised and considered the question whether today's science gives grounds for the belief in a divine creator.[2] These, however, are only peripheral indications of the actual implications of recent developments.

Contemporary physics, we have observed, has abolished the classical materialism and has made it impossible any longer to maintain the sharp separation between the physical object and the observer. It has established the internal character of physical relations and the unity of the physical universe. Philosophically considered, the essential nature of the whole so revealed requires a dialectical structure that leads inevitably to religious conclusions.

A whole, I have argued, must be differentiated; and the parts must be systematically interrelated, the disposition and intrinsic nature of each being dependent on its relations to all the rest, as the parts and events of the physical universe have been discovered by contemporary physicists to be. This systematic structure is, accordingly, governed by a universal ordering principle that is dynamic in nature, because it cannot be fully actualized in any one point or moment or in any limited manifestation. As every such limited phase is defined by its relations to what lies beyond its limits, in accordance with the principle of organization, it is driven to unite with its opposite to constitute a more adequate expression of that principle and a less incomplete phase of its self-specification. The consequent process is dialectical, generating a scale of forms, each relating to the next as opposite, as complement, as a distinct specification of the universal, and as a gradation in the more or less adequate expression of the pervasive wholeness. Each form sublates the predecessors that it supersedes, at once canceling their previous pretensions and incorporating them within itself, modified by the new and more coherent context.

Such a scale is teleological, because the full character of each phase is revealed in its successors, in which its potentialities are realized more fully. The process is teleological because of this continuous fulfillment, and each phase is a stage in the generation of a whole, the nature of which governs both the immature form and the course of its development. Hence explanation is teleological, for the truth of each phase is revealed in what it becomes.

Being a scale of progressive realization of wholeness, it cannot continue endlessly, for at each stage the completion of the whole is more adequately actualized. The scale could not proceed, and its dynamic would evaporate, if all forms were destined to remain open-ended. For it is powered by the organizing principle governing the complete (perfected) structure. It must, therefore, eventually culminate in closure in an all-embracing, fully developed totality, which, moreover, is "eventual" only with reference to its undeveloped parts, but is equally necessarily real and complete throughout the process; for unless this were so, none of the immature phases could be what it is. In fact, because each successive phase sublates its predecessors in the scale, the final consummation is both end and process in one, comprehending as well as fulfilling all the specific forms in which it has differentiated its unity. To this overlap of process and end human experience at each moment is analogous, as it sublates all its previous knowledge and practice in present cognition and action.

The reality of the absolute whole, along with its perpetual activity of self-specification, engendered and directed by the organizing principle universal to the entire gamut of phases, is indispensable to the existence of any and every form in the scale—is indefeasible and undeniable. The absolute whole, however, is precisely what conforms to Anselm's definition of God: "that than which a greater cannot be conceived." No greater can be conceived, because only through it can anything lesser (or anything at all) be conceived. The universal principle of organization (the concrete universal) is the explanatory principle of everything, hence nothing more universal is conceivable. It is the ultimate teleological explanation, "the truth of" everything, the Truth with a capital T (what Augustine identified with God).

Because this whole and its principle of organization are what come to consciousness as reason, reason cannot deny them without denying itself. And as reason is the self-conscious unity of apperception that grasps all experience as a whole of interrelated representations, bringing the universe to consciousness as a whole, the existence of that whole cannot be rationally denied without sacrificing rationality itself. The denial, to be rationally justified, would require the affirmation of what is denied. The very nature of the consummated whole, its essence, involves its existence, which is presupposed in all existence and by any conceivable proof of existence. Thus the Ontological Proof of the existence of God, so often affirmed in the past and as often contested, is revalidated by the implications of contemporary science.

In the same way, because every causal process is powered and regulated by the universal principle of order, the Cosmological Proof can be reestablished in a new form; and because every evidence of order and purpose is evidence of the whole of which it is a dialectical phase, the Teleological Proof is also restored to respectability. The nerve of the reasoning in all three proofs is the same—the indispensability of the absolute whole to the reality and nature of every finite entity, to every process of generation and development, to all order, to all reasoning, and to all understanding.

If contemporary physics has thus revitalized a metaphysic that can validate afresh the proofs of God's existence, is the resulting conception of God, even if it be that of the philosophers, the God of religion? Is it the God of Abraham, Isaac, and Jacob, the Christian Trinity, the Allah of Islam, not to mention the gods of Hinduism and the objects of worship of Buddhism and Shintoism? Of course, not every conception of God is an adequate and worthy object of worship, but the question remains whether the sort of absolute whole postulated in the above argument is an appropriate object of worship at all.

Clearly, the consummation of the cosmic scale of forms cannot be reduced to a mere formula or abstract principle. It must be the most comprehensive and concrete being conceivable. Further, we have insisted repeatedly that, as a relational complex, it cannot be fully actualized until brought to consciousness, and consciousness involves life. The realization of the integral wholeness of things impels the merely physical to the biotic. The whole cannot be less than alive, and it must be alive to become conscious. It does so in the human mind, and of this more will be said below. But the human mind is finite and is far from attaining the completeness and perfection toward which the dialectical process moves. Nevertheless, the self-conscious reflective capacity of human personality is an indication and a warrant that the absolute whole cannot be less than a mind, cannot be less than a person. It must be alive, conscious, and self-aware in an experience comprehending all reality. We may conclude, therefore, that not only does the absolute whole conform to Anselm's definition but it must also be of such a nature that it is at least prefigured in the God of religion. The various religious representations of deity are, for the most part, artistic and imaginative representations, sometimes in finite and anthropomorphic pictures of the ultimate infinite and absolute being.

That the concept of the Absolute is prefigured in the major world religions has already been indicated. Fritjoff Capra has argued persuasively that the Eastern mystical religions propagate a concept of reality analogous to the view of the cosmos entertained by contemporary physics.[3] Jehovah of Judaism and Allah of Islam is an omnipotent creator of the world, as is the universal principle of organization generating the scale of forms postulated in the metaphysical system outlined in this book and demanded by current scientific ideas. That principle has transpired as the concrete universal, a rational, self-conscious and personal activity, immanent in all reality and knowledge, corresponding to the omniscient deity of traditional religion. Its immanence in human reason, which is nurtured only in organized society, makes it the inspiring mainspring of morality and righteousness, as the traditional God is held to be, and provides a sober interpretation of the belief that God created humankind in his own image. This too offers some justification for the persistent tendency in many religions to imagine an anthropomorphic God. The finitude of human nature and the failure of the natural human animal to live up to its own aspirations are allegorically represented in Judeo-Christian teaching as the fall of Adam and Eve, redemption from which is sought in repentance and atonement.

That human self-consciousness is the immanence in the human mind of the absolute whole makes intelligible the possibility that these traditional beliefs should foreshadow the scientific discovery of the unity of the universe in the present century, and that earlier philosophical systems, such as those of Plato and Aristotle, Spinoza and Hegel, should, in various ways and degrees have anticipated the metaphysic warranted by that discovery.

In the course of the dialectical process, at an appropriate stage in the scale of forms, the self-specification of the principle of wholeness (the concrete universal) becomes conscious and self-reflective. The internalization of the physical and biological world in the sentience of the living organism, by self-enfoldment, becomes aware of itself as "I", both subject and object on one. Henceforth, the *ego* constitutes, through its spontaneous activity of organizing, every intentional object and all the relational structures involved. Accordingly, it is necessarily transcendent beyond all intentional objects and the terms of every relation. The transcendental subject is the principle of order itself; it is immanent in human personality, and although the individual is finite, being subject to the limitations set by the biological conditions of organic life, the transcendental subject is in principle infinite as the conscious subject of a potentially all-inclusive whole of experience. It is only in and through this transcendental Ego that the absolute whole becomes explicit; hence, the culmination of the scale of forms, which transcends all finite (including human) beings, must be a (or rather *the*) self-conscious Ego—the epitome of all personality. This consummation of the scale is that than which no greater can be conceived—what we mean by God, who must, therefore, be a self-conscious personality.

It follows that the God of the metaphysician is indeed the same as the God of Abraham, Isaac and Jacob, as He was revealed to Moses in the burning bush:

And Moses said unto God, Behold, when I come unto the children of Israel, and shall say unto them, The God of your fathers has sent me unto you; and they shall say to me, What is his name? what shall I say unto them? And God said unto Moses, I AM THAT I AM; and he said, Thus shalt thou say unto the children of Israel, I AM hath sent me unto you. (Exod. 3; 13,14)

The same concept seems to have been present in the mind of Christ when he declared: "I am the way." "I am the resurrection and the life."

In the later philosophy of Fichte, the absolute Ego is explicitly identified with God; and Constantin Brunner maintained that the divinity of Christ consists in his realization of the identity in God and man of the transcendental Ego (the Cogitant).[4]

Nobody should be misled by this submission into concluding that God is the supreme egotist. The transcendental Ego is the epitome of the self, but there can be no self which is indistinguishable from a not-self. The divine I-am-I is constituted by its activity of creation (as, in the case of the finite human self, the transcendental subject is itself constituted by its own spontaneous activity of constituting its objects). God creates His own Other in the existent universe which culminates in intelligent life and in the person of Christ, and then each identifies with its other in perfect love. If God is the absolute "I am," He is by the same token identical with that dialectical process from the physical to the personal through which God, as concrete universal and creative principle, is brought to consciousness. This identity of Self and Other is absolute love. The infinite, God, is identical with the finite in Christ, who identifies himself with the Father ("I am in the Father, and the Father is in me . . ." John, 14; 11.) and with all other persons: "Verily, I say unto you, Inasmuch as ye have done it unto one of the least of these my brethren, ye have done it unto me." (Matt. 25; 40). The supreme commandments are to love God with heart, soul, and might, and to love one another as God loves you; the self, whether finite or infinite, finds its fulfilment in identification with its other, in which it finds itself at home.

The difference between God and humankind is that between the infinite and the finite, and their mutual complementarity through the order of Nature (the creation) is the basis of their identity. Here we come upon another feature of contemporary physical cosmology indicating the convergence of science and religion at the present time.

7. THE ANTHROPIC COSMOLOGICAL PRINCIPLE

The covergence of science with religion is even further facilitated by another recent development in physical cosmology: the pronouncement by physicists of what they call the Anthropic Cosmological Principle. The forms in which they have stated it and the interpretation given to it are in the first instance, unsatisfactory, but taken in conjunction with the view of the universe as a single, indivisible whole, and the consequences following from that, the principle states an important and fruitful insight.

There are four ways in which the principle has been formulated: weak, strong, participatory, and final. The weak anthropic principle, as first stated by Brandon Carter, is that "what we can expect to observe must be restricted by the conditions necessary for our presence as observers." The strong anthropic principle declares "that the Universe (and hence the fundamental parameters on which it depends) must be such as to admit the creation of observers within it at some stage." The participatory anthropic principle arises from the Copenhagen interpretation of the quantum theory, according to which a constitutive parameter of the quantum system comes into being only when actually measured by an experimenter, that is, when the psi-function (expressing the probability amplitude within which the parameter may be found) collapses. This form of the principle states, accordingly, "that observers are necessary to bring the Universe into being." The final anthropic principle goes even further, contending that "intelligent information-processing must come into existence in the Universe, and, once it comes into existence, it will never die out."[5]

The shortcomings of these statements are fairly obvious. If there are to be observers at all, the conditions necessary for their existence will, of course, pertain, so what they will observe cannot but be restricted by those conditions. What we observe, in short, is necessarily a universe such as permits our own existence. But this is a truism. The strong version is not a truism as Carter states it, for it is not obvious, at first sight, that the universe should be such as to admit the creation of observers—except, of course, that we must exist in order to make the statement, and as we do, there can be no question but that the universe must be such as to admit our existence. The participatory version seems to state a paradox. If the constituent parameters of the quantum system on the micro level of elementary particles do not come into existence until observed, how can the observers, on the macro level, who are made up of elementary particles, ever come into existence? The final anthropic principle is predicated on the claim that computer science and information theory have already established the possibility of constructing machines capable of doing whatever can be done by an intelligent human, including self-reproduction. These so-called von Neumann probes, once constructed, will be able to launch themselves into space and colonize the entire universe, making themselves impervious to adverse conditions. They will therefore keep intelligence of some kind active and in being perpetually. This claim seems extravagant and has been castigated by some scientists as completely ridiculous. But even if it were justified, what it tells us about the universe is no more than what we already know, namely, that it contains intelligent beings (ourselves), and if we can construct and launch von Neumann probes, it will continue to do so.

On the other hand, if one considers the philosophical consequences (developed in Part 2 of this book) of the contemporary discovery of the undissectable unity of the physical universe, the Anthropic Cosmological Principle takes on an impressive and illuminating significance. The systematic relational complexity of the totality, we have said, remains merely implicit and potential (like Aristotle's prime matter) until it is made explicit in the consciousness of an intelligent mind. Prior to the evolution of human self-reflection this does not occur; yet it is necessary to the dialectical self-specification of the concrete universal—the principle of systematic structure of the whole. It follows that the universe is such that intelligent life and critical scientific observers must emerge at some stage in its self-unfolding. And what will be observed will inevitably be an integrated, undisseverable universe, in which the conditions of their own evolution and existence obtain. Accordingly, both the weak and the strong forms of the anthropic principle hold. Further, because the unity of the merely physical is only implicit before it is cognized, as indeed is the human body itself, the physical whole is not explicitly actualized until it is observed, measured, and consciously ordered in a scientific theory (the truth of all the prior phases in the cosmic scale), so the participatory form of the principle is also justified. Finally, because the evolution of self-conscious rational beings is dialectically necessary in the course of self-specification of the universal principle of wholeness, whatever we on this planet may do—even if, in our folly, we destroy our own life-supporting environment or annihilate ourselves in a nuclear holocaust—intelligent life will emerge elsewhere in the universe (as well it may already have done) wherever the physicochemical conditions are favorable. So we may also accede to the final anthropic principle.

Intelligent scientific observers, however, do not simply spring up like mushrooms wherever physicochemical conditions permit. They have to be nurtured in a rationally ordered society. Social and political organization, an advanced civilization, is prerequisite to scientific research, and scientists must be educated in a highly developed intellectual milieu. This further involves moral probity, intellectual integrity, and all the other intellectual and practical virtues that contribute to and make possible a scientific community. The implications of the anthropic principle, therefore, are not only that the universe is a physical and organic system but also that the pervasive organizing principle requires and prescribes a moral order, as well as religious consciousness (as we found above). It is in this religious consciousness that humanity seeks its ultimate self-realization, which morality alone cannot achieve—"that peace that the world cannot give." This aspiration can be realized only in the reconciliation and unification of the finite with the infinite: humankind's "at-one-ment" with God.

The full entailment of the Anthropic Cosmological Principle, then, is that life, intelligence, rational self-awareness, critical scientific expertise, social and moral order, and religious consciousness, which finds ultimate self-realization in the unity of the human with the divine—all these—are intrinsic to the very nature and substance of the physical universe. The dynamic principle of organization constituting the whole and, in its self-specification, creative of all the constituent parts is active and brings itself to fruition in human reason, which, in its transcendental synthesis of sensuous and perceptive content, is in principle all-embracing and portends the infinity of the absolute totality. The transcendental ego is the immanent concrete universal, the final consummation of whose self-specification is the absolute whole itself. That again, being whole and absolutely concrete is no abstract, pure "perfection," but by its own nature it must differentiate itself and manifest itself in and as the scale of natural (physical, chemical, biotic, and noetic) forms, from elemental physical energy to rational, self-cognizant knowledge, artistic vision, and religious conviction.

The absolute consummation of the scale of forms is God, who by His very nature specifies its universal principle as a physical, a biotic, and a noetic world—creates all things "visible and invisible." It is immanent in the human mind and inspires all its intellectual prowess, its morality, its artistic imagination, and its religious fervor. In the last of these, finite and infinite unite through human penitence and worship in the person of Jesus Christ, and divine grace, descending on the human religious community, imbues it with that solidarity of love which the Bible calls the Holy Spirit. In this manner, the Christian doctrine of the Holy Trinity can be given philosophical interpretation and rational justification.

The implicit identity of finite and infinite is manifested in Christ, who is at once human and divine. This is the religious version of the anthropic principle, declaring that the nature of the universe implies the presence in it of human self-consciousness, which is the coming of the whole to self-awareness. The self-reflective experience thus intrinsic to the physical world is in principle identical with the world that is its object (for that is what has come to consciousness in it), and in this union the human spirit finds its ultimate rest and destiny.

This scientific-philosophical statement is paralleled in the poetic religious pronouncement of the opening chapter of St. John's Gospel. The Greek word *logos* is translated "word," but its philosophical meaning (especially for Aristotle) is "ration" or relational principle. "In the beginning," writes St. John,

> was the *Logos* and the *Logos* was with God, and the *Logos* was God. . . . All things were made by him and without him was not anything made that was made. In him was life; and the life was the light of men. . . . That was the true Light that lightest every man that cometh into the world. . . . And the *Logos* was made flesh, and dwelt among us (and we beheld his glory the glory as of the only begotten of the Father) full of grace and truth.

The *Logos*, or relational principle, is the concrete universal, which is the principle of organization of the whole and its creative power (from the beginning it "was with God") and is identical with the whole ("and was God"). It is the creative principle of all things ("All things were made by him and without him was not anything made that was made"). Its self-specification in the physical world burgeons out into the biotic ("In him was life"), and that becomes sentient and intelligent ("and the life was the light of men"). So the universal ordering principle is immanent in rational humanity ("the *Logos* was made flesh"), and that involves sociality ("and dwelt among us"), morality, and religion ("and we beheld his glory, the glory as of the only begotten of the Father . . . full of grace and truth"). The Father is, of course, God, the absolute truth of everything and of the whole, and His grace is bestowed upon and is manifest in rational, moral, and religious human nature in its perfection and self-realization—which is Christ.

The universal dynamic principle of organization, which specifies itself progressively and is constructive of every successive whole, comes to consciousness in human self-awareness and seeks the comprehension of the whole in which finite and infinite are reconciled and united. As the principle is one and the same throughout the dialectical scale of forms, the identity is already presaged, as the immanence of the whole in every part. And, at the self-conscious level, this union is variously expressed as the divine spark in human artistic genius; as the gift of prophesy in religion; as the love of God, of one's fellow humans, and of all God's creatures. The identification of the finite with the infinite makes itself felt as the yearning of the religious worshipper for at-one-ment with God; but above all, it is figured forth in the identity of human and divine nature in Christ, which is the supreme object of religion.

Historically this is recorded as having occurred in the life and ministry of Jesus, and the belief that he was the Christ, the Messiah expected by the Jews, rests upon the impression made upon his disciples, who narrated the events of his personality, his teaching, and his reappearance after the Crucifixion. Accordingly, the vindication of that claim calls for critical historical assessment of the surviving evidence, limited almost entirely to the Gospel stories. Such historical criticism is not the purpose of the present discussion.[6] The term of its reference is to demonstrate the contemporary accord between science and religion.

The implications of the Anthropic Cosmological Principle are thus convergent with the religious teaching of Christianity, and there is no irreconcilable conflict between science and religion, once the metaphysical significance of the contemporary scientific worldview is recognized and properly developed. Sincere scientists and devout religious believers are no longer, as they were in the nineteenth century, at odds, and they are not called upon to try to adjust to a divided intellectual milieu in which the scientist could not accept religious dogma without hypocrisy and the believer in God and His revelation in Christ were subject to the accusation of obscurantism, if not of superstition.

APPENDIX

Something needs to be said in response to the various arguments that have been advanced against the Anthropic Cosmological Principle, on the grounds that circumstances are conceivable that would render the existence of intelligent life in the universe merely contingent. For our main purpose, this is a somewhat peripheral discussion, for the theories concerned are not scientifically established and, at least, up to the present, remain purely speculative.

Although it is obvious that intelligent observers will discover that they inhabit a universe in which the conditions essential to their existence obtain, it does not follow with equal necessity that their encompassing universe is special or unique. Other universes, it has been maintained, may be possible in which those conditions are absent, and, of course, they will not be observed at all. Some cosmologists have surmised that this is in fact the case. If the expansion of the universe is at some period reversed (which will happen under certain conditions that are, in principle, discoverable), the universe will proceed to contract and will eventually collapse in a "Big Crunch." A subsequent expansion may produce a new universe with different initial conditions or different fundamental physical constants (or both) in which no observers can be accommodated. If, however, such alternating expansion and contraction occur through infinite time, universes in which intelligent observers can exist may arise by pure chance, separated, no doubt, by enormous intervals. Our own universe might be one of these, and our existence in consequence could be entirely fortuitous.

One interpretation of quantum mechanics leads some physicists to contend that all the possibilities, over which the psi-function of any quantum prediction ranges, are in fact actual, and that each exists in a separate universe. We experience only one of these, because it is we who make the measurements in which the probability amplitude collapses. Whether conditions favorable to life obtain in the other universes is a contingent matter, and that they do in ours is obvious, but may be pure luck.

Such speculations, however, give rise to serious difficulties that ought to be faced, the least of which is, perhaps, terminological. The universe, strictly speaking, is all there is and ever has been or will be; there cannot be more than one. Even if there were many distinguishable worlds, they would all belong to the one universe. We could adjust our language to accommodate this restriction, but the caveat is not simply linguistic, for if the distinct worlds were totally separate, without any relation to one another, we could not even conceive their multiplicity. Nor are they so separate and unconnected in the theories proposed. The possible alternation of expansion and contraction is postulated on the strength of pervasive quantitative properties of this universe that could be ascertained. The parallel universes envisaged by some quantum theorists are related in the psi-function calculated from observations made by homegrown scientists. Even so, as they are, in principle, unobservable, their scientific reputation is questionable, and their postulation violates Occam's rule of parsimony.

Further, if one takes seriously the current conviction that the universe is a single unified whole in which distinct and distant events are integrally interconnected, relations must be regarded as universally internal; and if many worlds are presumed, they should be as necessarily interrelated as everything that we observe in this world. In that case, it would hardly be appropriate to regard a world in which the conditions were congenial to intelligent life as occurring (in whatever fashion) by pure chance. That it should occur at all immediately establishes the anthropic principle not just for one particular world but for the universe as such, whether or not it is diversified into different worlds, because it is *we* who observe our own universe and speculate about others.

The most recent physical theories, moreover, have brought physicists to the conclusion that nature not only tolerates but demands a fundamental symmetry, and that if all divergences and anomalies are to be removed, only one coherent theory is possible.[7] If so, it would seem somewhat rash to contemplate many different and incompatible "universes"—at least, we could hardly regard the occurrence and interrelation of such worlds as random or, in consequence, the emergence of intelligent life as fortuitous. Certainly, it is possible that the human form taken on Earth by intelligent life is conditional upon special and accidental circumstances. It could conceivably take other forms in different environments elsewhere in the universe. But that would make no difference in principle. The important point is that reflective intelligence and reason are seen as intrinsic and essential to the universe as a whole, in the way we have argued that it must be.

Notes

1. Cf. R. G. Collingwood, *An Essay on Metaphysics*.
2. Cf. Paul Davies, *God and the New Physics*. On the flyleaf, Einstein is quoted: "Religion without science is blind. Science without religion is lame." Cf. by the same author, *The Mind of God: The Scientific Basis for a Rational World*.
3. Cf. Fritjoff Capra, *The Tao of Physics*.
4. Cf. J. G. Fichte, *Die Wissenschaftslehre im allgemeinen Umriss* (1810); and Constantin Brunner, *Our Christ: The Revolt of the Mystical Genius*, Trans. G. Harrison and M. Wex (Van Gorcum, Assen/Maastricht, the Netherlands, 1990), pp. 19, 39 and 128f.
5. The last two formulations are due to J. D. Barrow and F. J. Tipler, *The Anthropic Cosmological Principle*, pp. 22–3.
6. I have paid some attention to this matter in *Revelation Through Reason*, chap. 5; *Atheism and Theism*, chap. 7; *Cosmos and Theos*, chap. 13.
7. Cf. Michio Kaku and Jennifer Trainer, *Beyond Einstein: The Cosmic Quest for the*

Theory of the Universe, pp. 108f.; Barrow and Tipler, *The Anthropic Cosmological Principle*, pp. 257–8, citing S. Weinberg, *The 1979 Nobel Prize Lecture*; J. A. Wheeler, "The Universe in the Light of General Relativity," in *The Monist*, vol. 47, (1962), p. 40; B. S. de Witt, "Quantum Theory of Gravity I, The Canonical Theory," in *Physical Review*, vol. 160 (1967), p. 1113.

19

Conclusion

1. RÉSUMÉ

Philosophy in the twentieth century has been characterized predominantly by attacks on, and renunciations of, metaphysics, all of which, however, have themselves depended upon a latent and unacknowledged metaphysic. The positions adopted, moreover, have entailed, and have led to, an assortment of skeptical conclusions that are self-refuting. Virtually all the antimetaphysical schools have continued to assume, if only surreptitiously, the worldview introduced at the Renaissance by the Copernican revolution in science, which segregated the physical world, as mechanically conceived, from the mind of the observer, so as to establish a matter-mind dualism. As any such dualism leads to insuperable problems, philosophers have tended to deny, or explain away, one side of the dichotomy and to espouse (not always overtly) a form either of materialism or of idealism. The results invariably prove ultimately fatal, as each of the contrary doctrines tends to revert to its opposite before complete dissolution in relativism and skepticism. We have seen this happen in the case of positivism and analysis, first becoming ensnared in the egocentric predicament, with a reluctant but unavoidable committal to solipsism, and then declining into relativism and nihilistic skepticism. We have seen it happen with phenomenology and existentialism, the initial idealism of which reverted, in hermeneutics, to relativism and, in structuralism and poststructuralism, to materialistic positivism, ending in the skeptical attitudes of postmodernism,

2. METAPHYSICS REHABILITATED

What has gone unnoticed is that the twentieth-century revolution in physics has abrogated the Newtonian paradigm, introducing a holistic worldview that requires a new metaphysical endeavor. The discovery of the integral wholeness of the physical world demands of philosophers the task of analyzing and laying open the logical implications of holism, which reveal the dialectical structure intrinsic to every whole—a structure that the sciences have themselves disclosed, each in its own field and together in the universe as a whole. The resulting metaphysic is holistic, dialectical, and, in consequence, teleological, reconciling the opposition of materialism to idealism, of matter to mind, and of body to soul.

The metaphysic is holistic because the universe has been shown to be woven of seamless cloth (to use a somewhat inadequate metaphor, as all metaphors are inadequate). It is dialectical because every element and part contradicts itself, being at once dependent for its intrinsic nature on its relations to other parts and, in the final issue, on the whole and yet also in itself only partial. The contradiction invokes and forces it into its other, with which it unites to form a larger whole, less inadequate to the universal holistic principle of organization, but still incomplete. The process repeats itself to generate a scale of provisional wholes ascending in degrees of adequacy to the universal essence that each of them exemplifies in some measure. The metaphysic is teleological because the truth of each phase is what succeeds it in the scale, and each phase as well as the whole series is directed and governed by the whole that embraces them all. The reconciliation of materialism and idealism is achieved because the lower stages are physical and biological (constituting "the external world"— external in that it is extended in space and time), but as relational complexes they can become properly explicit only as cognized. Hence they must, to fulfill their potentiality and the holistic nisus of the dialectic, become self-conscious, which they do in our minds, so that the truth about them is realized in idea— for it could otherwise not be realized at all. Truth, to be truth, must be known (when we say that we don't know the truth, we mean that we don't know the whole—if we knew nothing, we could not make that confession). It follows that the final consummation of the scale of forms is a self-conscious experience of the whole, encompassing the entire scale. Reality is thus both material and ideal, the corresponding phases being related to each other dialectically as degrees of exemplification of the concrete universal. The ultimate universal self-conscious experience is that beyond which nothing is conceivable—it is the infinite whole to which everything that can be attributed to finite minds in some degree can be ascribed absolutely. It is, therefore, God, and the metaphysic cannot but be theistic. Moreover, as it is rooted in scientific theory, science and religion are not in mutual conflict.

3. EVIL AND ERROR

Some qualification is needed to what has just been said: that whatever can be attributed in some degree to finite minds is attributable absolutely to God. This does not mean that human errors and misdoings are to be ascribed absolutely to the Deity. It refers only to positive epithets, whereas errors and evils are no more than the truncation of positive propensities and the misplacements and distortions that result. Accordingly, it will not come amiss to add a word here as it were, in parenthesis, about error and evil (for these are attributable to finite minds but not to the divine).

Evil and error are incident and consequent upon finitude; they are due solely to privation. However unfortunate an event or depraved a person's conduct and character, the resulting constraint on progress toward perfection (which constitutes evil) is due to limitation, whether of self-control or of insight and knowledge or of both. Suffering in general is the consequence of finitude—although not all suffering is evil—for what is not finite is impassible, and so cannot suffer. Whatever in the unfortunate event or in the delinquent person is positive is not evil. The energy, emotion, or judgment involved is wrong and bad only so far as it is misplaced, distorted, or exaggerated due to lack of knowledge or self-control (i.e., to defect and deprivation). On the other hand, strength in distress and courage in the face of danger and disaster are virtues. Error, likewise, is lack of knowledge or abridged content; the garbled or curtailed information constituting error is, in its proper context and full exposition, correct.

Error and evil, then, may be equated with finitude, which, as the scale of forms unfolds, is progressively overcome. But finitude is inevitable wherever differentiation occurs, and differentiation is indispensable to wholeness. Hence the presence of evil and error in the world is unavoidable. Only in this regard are they attributable to God, who could not create a world at all, the necessary differentiation of the concrete totality, without the mutual limitation of the parts and phases. Nevertheless, although evil and error are necessary in a finite world, as Spinoza asserts: "God did not lack means for the creation of every degree of perfection from the highest to the lowest" (*Ethics*, I Appendix). And the exercise of God's power is the perpetual overcoming of evil, for evil and error are continuously sublated, remedied, and corrected as the dialectic proceeds, and in the Absolute, they are transcended altogether and finally canceled out. As St. Paul tells us: "When that which is perfect is come, then that which is in part will be done away" (I Corinthians 13:10). And Habakkuk says of God: "Thou art of purer eyes than to behold evil" (Habakkuk 1:13).

4. THE TRUTH IS THE WHOLE

The whole, to be whole (no mere blank uniformity nor undimensional point), must be systematically differentiated, structured by an ordering principle that specifies itself progressively in a scale of forms dialectically related—God, by the necessity of His nature, creates a universe. The ordering principle, fully manifested only in the whole, is the concrete universal, the truth and the source of explanation of all that is. Hence the teleological character of all process and all explanation. Consequently, Heisenberg tells us that the physicist seeks

a fundamental law of motion for matter from which all elementary particles and their properties can be derived mathematically.

The final equation of motion for matter will probably be some quantized non-linear wave equation for a wave field of operators that simply represents matter, not any specific kind of waves or particles. This wave equation will probably be equivalent to rather complicated sets of integral equations, which have "Eigenvalues" and "Eigensolutions," as the physicists call it. These Eigensolutions will finally represent the elementary particles.[1]

Today, S-Matrix theory, Grand and Unified Theories, and Superstring theory have brought scientists nearer to this goal, to a universal formula representing a unified field covering the whole physical universe from which all types of matter and energy can be derived. Thus the whole explains the part and the processes within it at the physical level. At the biological level, it is the biosphere as a whole in which the explanation of the parts and processes is to be sought, even though, as yet, no mathematical formula is available from which to derive the details. In the noosphere, the situation is more complex; but without reason, there can be no noosphere, and without reason there can be no explanation; in the final issue, reason and the concrete universal are one and the same.

5. CONTINUITY OF THE SCALE OF FORMS

The physical world is a single unity, diversified into distinct forces and entities, ranging continuously from energy to elementary particles, which graduate from gluons to protons and neutrons, from electrons to hadrons. These combine to form atoms, which again are ranged in the periodic table of elements. Atoms combine into molecules, and molecules into crystals; elements combine into compounds, and compounds into polymers, forming the basic substances of living cells—amino acids to form proteins, nucleic acids to form chromosomes.

The biosphere is a whole on a new level, differentiated into a similar scale of living forms—from viruses to bacteria, and from protozoa to metazoa; from colonial combinations of cells to creatures with specialized organs; from asexual to sexual; from invertebrate to vertebrate. Species have evolved continuously, becoming progressively more versatile and relevantly responsive to environmental influences, until animals with the intelligence of apes and hominids have developed into *Homo sapiens*.

Sentience, common to animals and humans, is objectified in perception, and perception is further organized by intelligence. Human self-reflection has burgeoned out into the noosphere, in which the experience, knowledge, and skills of each individual are engendered through social intercourse and, by communication, are shared to constitute a single common body of experience available to all (though not immediately enjoyed by each in its entirety). Practical reason manifests itself in morality and social order, theoretical reason in science and philosophy, and both practical and theoretical combine in art and religion.

Each of these moments of the noosphere is at once the whole and one branch or phase. Each is distinct from all the others, yet the objects of each include all of experience, and each depends upon and is interwoven with all the rest. The dialectic at every successive level becomes more complex, and at the noetic stage it becomes especially intervolved because of the self-referential and reflective character of human reason. In every department of its operation, it is aware of every other and subordinates all the rest to its appropriate method and genre.

At every stage the dialectic is continuous within each major phase and between successive phases—despite mutual distinction and opposition, between inorganic and organic, between body and mind. The entire gamut of forms is one whole, constituted of a series of wholes—physical, biotic, and noetic— each similarly differentiated internally. The structure of the whole is analogous to that of a fractal set, displaying the same contour on every scale and on each level.

6. THREE IN ONE

Each of the three major phases of the scale is a whole on its own level. They are not three wholes, but one: first, they are mutually continuous; secondly, through the physicochemical conditions prevailing on the earth, the whole physical universe is registered in the biosphere and in each and every organism within it. Further, the multifarious influences impinging upon the organism are interiorized in sentience, which, as the felt body, sublates in the whole of feeling the effects of the universal environment. So the whole is the same throughout the scale of its self-specifications, each of which is a distinct manifestation of its immanent totality.

Immanent though it is, and come to consciousness in the human mind, the whole is not fully realized in the noosphere constituted by finite subjects. It transcends the merely natural and human and must exist complete and perfect as the source of all being, all self-awareness, and all knowledge. As thus both immanent and transcendent, it is God, toward whom all things strive, each in its own way and according to its own level in the scale of being. The physical universe, in its vastness and in its detail, manifests the universal order at the primary level and proliferates a series of forms tending toward life and mind: "The heavens declare the glory of God; and the firmament sheweth his handiwork: (Psalms 19:1).

Human endeavor aspires to perfection. In art, it strives to portray the beauty in all things, which is nothing less than the immanence in them of the whole:

> Flower in the crannied wall,
> I pluck you out of the crannies,
> I hold you here, root and all, in my hand,

Little flower—but *if* I could understand
What you are, root and all, and all in all,
I should know what God and man is.
                    Alfred Lord Tennyson:

In morality, struggling to overcome the conflict within human nature between body and soul, passion and reason, humankind cannot succeed without religion, through which the soul seeks that peace which the world cannot give, in atonement with God, attained in the person of Christ, in whom the immanence of the divine as well as the grace of its transcendence is revealed.

So the universe, in all the stages of its evolution, through the scale of forms that is generated at every level, tends toward God, who creates and sustains all things and in whom all things find their unification and fulfillment.

7. THE IDENTITY OF SUBJECT AND OBJECT

That unification and fulfillment involves the identification of subject and object, for each of these finds its ultimate realization in its other. In the first place, the dialectical process, through which physical and biotic actuality are brought to self-consciousness in human self-reflective mentality, objectifies in human experience that same process: the evolution of the human mind. The content of human knowledge is the physical world and the biosphere, which together are the process of its own generation. Thus human knowledge, which is at the same time the awareness by the subject of itself as a member of the world that it perceives and conceives, is the effective union and identity of both. The subject and its experience are one, and its experience is of an external world that is actually that same subject in becoming. The object is only fully explicated in being cognized by the subject: and the subject only attains truth in the recognition of the object as its own self-generation. The full philosophical realization of this dialectical relation is thus the identity of subject and object.

In the second place, in practical life, the ultimate objective of the moral agent is self-realization, which it can approach only by imposing its own rational nature on its own conduct and the social context that molds its personality. This is already an identification of subject and object. Furthermore, personal and social harmony and order require the recognition of the other as of equal status and value as oneself, the identification of oneself and one's interest with that of others in the community by which one is sustained. So far as that can be achieved, it is the identification of subject and object. But so far as it cannot be achieved, due to the finite status and natural limitation of human nature, it is to be sought in atonement with God—the unity of finite and infinite, of the religious subject with the religious object.

In the third place, God is the ultimate union of subject and object, in which each finds its satisfaction in identification with its other. God is that union, because God is the absolute self-conscious subject who specifies Himself, as concrete universal, in the external world and brings it back to Himself, via biological evolution and noetic self-awareness. As immanent in the world, He is object; as transcendent, He is subject; and thus, as absolute, He is the identity of subject and object. As the organizing principle, He finds fulfillment in self-specification as the objective world, which, through its dialectical development, finds fulfillment in His transcendent glory, each in its identification with the other. Thus identity of subject and object is the goal of the *conatus* to self-specification and self-maintenance and the nisus to the whole, in which the entire scale of forms attains its completion and culmination.

8. THE RESTITUTION OF METAPHYSICS

The twentieth-century revolution in science requires that restitution be made to metaphysics for its vilification (as nonsense) and for its abrogation in contemporary philosophy. Its function as revealing, criticizing, and tracing the development of the absolute presuppositions of science, to which Collingwood drew attention, must be recognized afresh. Its reinstatement as the queen of the sciences is to be celebrated anew. It can now be restored as the warranty of objectivity in knowledge, as the buttress of objective morality, and as the vindication of genuine religion.

Note

1. Cf. W. Heisenberg, *Physics and Philosophy*, p. 60, and *Philosophical Problems of Nuclear Science*, p. 103.

Bibliography

Adrian, Lord E. D. *The Physical Background of Perception*. Oxford: Clarendon Press, 1947.

Alexander, S. *Space, Time and Deity*. London: Macmillan, 1920, 1929.

Allport, Floyd H. *Theories of Perception, and the Concept of Structure*. New York: Wiley, 1955.

Alston, W. P. *Religious Belief and Philosophical Thought*. New York: Harcourt Brace, 1963.

Ames, Adelbert. "Reconsidertion of the Origin and Nature of Perception." In *Vision and Action*, ed. S. Katner. New Brunswick, NJ: Rutgers University Press, 1953.

———. "Visual Perception and the Rotating Trapezoid Window." *Psychological Monographs*, vol. 63, no. 7 (1961).

Anselm, St. *Cur Deus Homo*. In *Basic Writings*, trans. S. W. Deane. La Salle, IL: Open Court, 1962.

———. *Monologion*. In *Basic Writings*, trans. S. W. Deane. La Salle, IL: Open Court, 1962.

———. *Proslogion*. In *Basic Writings*, trans. S. W. Deane. La Salle, IL: Open Court, 1962.

Aquinas, St. Thomas. *Basic Writings*, ed. A. C. Pegis. New York: Random House, 1945.

———. *Philosophical Texts*, selected and trans. T. Gilby. London and New York: Oxford University Press, 1951, 1952.

Aristotle. *De Anima*. In *Basic Writings*, ed. Richard McKeon. New York: Random House, 1941.

———. *Ethica Nicomachea*. In *Basic Writings*, ed. Richard McKeon. New York: Random House, 1941.

———. *Metaphysica*. In *Basic Writings*, ed. Richard McKeon. New York: Random House, 1941.

Armstrong, D. M. *Perception and the Physical World*. London: Routledge and Kegan Paul; Atlantic Highlands, NJ: Humanities Press, 1961.

Augustine, St. *Basic Writings*, ed. W. J. Oakes. New York: Random House, 1948.

Austin, J. *Sense and Sensibilia*. Oxford: Clarendon Press, 1964.

Ayers, A. J. *Foundations of Empirical Knowledge*. London: Macmillan, 1940.

———. *Language, Truth and Logic*. London: Macmillan, 1946.

———. *The Problem of Knowledge*. Harmondsworth: Penguin Books, 1956.

———. *Thinking and Meaning*. London: Macmillan, 1947.

Baier, K. *The Moral Point of View*. Ithaca, NY: Cornell University Press, 1955.

Barnes, Winston H. *The Philosophical Predicament*. London: A & C Black, 1950.

Barrow, J. D. *Theories of Everything*. Oxford: Clarendon Press, 1991.

Barrow, J. D., and Tipler, F. J. *The Anthropic Cosmological Principle*. Oxford and New York: Oxford University Press, 1986, 1988.

Bartlett, Sir Frederick. *Remembering*. Cambridge: Cambridge University Press, 1961.

Bates, M. *The Forest and the Sea*. New York: Random House, 1960; Vintage Press, 1965.

Bergman, Gustav. "The Revolt Against Logical Atomism." *Philosophical Quarterly*, vols. 7, 8 (1957–58).

Berkeley, George. *Works*, ed. T. E. Jessop and A. A. Luce. London: Nelson, 1948.

Blake, R. R., and Ramsey, G. V., eds. *Perception: An Approach to Personality*. New York: Ronald Press, 1951.

Blanshard, Brand. *The Nature of Thought*. London, Allen and Unwin, 1939.

———. "The Philosophy of Analysis." *Proceedings of the British Academy*, vol. 38.

———. *Reason and Analysis*. La Salle, IL: Open Court, 1962.

———. *Reason and Belief*. New Haven, CT: Yale University Press, 1974.

Bogard, P. A., and Treasch, G., eds. *Metaphysics as Foundation*. Albany, NY: State University of New York Press, 1993.

Bohm, D. *Fragmentation and Wholeness*. Jerusalem: Van Leer Foundation Series, 1976.

———. *Wholeness and the Implicate Order*. London and Boston: Routledge and Kegan Paul, 1980, 1983.

Bohm, D., and Aharonoff, Y. "Discussion of Experimental Proof for the Paradox of Einstein Podolsky and Rosen." *Physical Review*, vol. 103 (1957).

Bohm, D., and Hiley, B. J. "Non-relativistic Particle Systems." *Physics Reports*, vol. 144, no. 6, (1987).

———. "On the Intuitive Understanding of Non-Locality as Implied by Quantum Theory." *Foundations of Physics*, vol. 5. (1975).

Bohr, N. *Atomic Theory and the Description of Nature*. Cambridge: Cambridge University Press, 1934.

Bolzmann, I. *Vorlesungen über die Principien der Mechanik*. Leipzig, 1897.

Bonner, J. T. *Evolution of Development*. Cambridge; Cambridge University Press, 1958.

———. *Morphogenesis*. Princeton, NJ: Princeton University Press, 1952.

Borel, E. *Space and Time*. London: Constable, 1931; New York: Dover, 1960.

Borger, R., and Seaborne, A. E. M. *The Psychology of Learning*. Harmondsworth: Penguin Books, 1966.

Borresen, C. R., and Lichte, W. H. "Shape-Constancy: Dependence upon Stimulus Familiarity." *Journal of Experimental Psychology*, vol. 63 (1962).

Bosanquet, B. *Three Chapters on the Nature of Mind*. London: Macmillan, 1923.

Bradley, F. H. *Appearance and Reality*. Oxford: Clarendon Press, 1897, 1930.

———. *Essays on Truth and Reality*. Oxford: Clarendon Press, 1914.

———. *Ethical Studies*. Oxford: Clarendon Press, 1927.

Brain, Sir W. Russel. "The Concept of the Schema in Neurology and Psychiatry." In *Perspectives in Neuropsychiatry*, ed. D. Richter. London: H. K. Lewis, 1950.

———. *Mind, Perception and Science*. Oxford: Blackwell, 1951.

Braithwaite, R. B. *Scientific Explanation*. Cambridge: Cambridge University Press; New York: Harper and Row, 1953.

———. "Teleological Explanation." *Proceedings of the Aristotelian Society*, vol. 47 (1946–47).

Bridgeman, P. W. *The Logic of Modern Physics*. New York: Macmillan, 1951.

Bruner, J. S., and Krech, D. *Perception and Personality*. Durham, NC: Duke University Press, 1949.

Bruner, J. S., and Postman, L. "On the Perception of Incongruity." *Journal of Personality*, 18 (1949).

Brunner, Constantin, *Our Christ. The Revolt of the Mystical Genius*, Trans. G. Harrison and M. Wex, Assen/Maastricht, Van Gorcum, 1990.

Caird, E. *The Evolution of Religion*. Glasgow: James Maclehose, 1894.

Campbell, C. A. "The Mind's Involvement with 'Objects,' an Essay in Idealist Epistemology." In *Theories of the Mind*, ed. J. Scher. London: Macmillan, 1962.

Capra, Fritjoff. "The Role of Physics in the Current Change of Paradigm." In *The World View of Contemporary Physics, Does It Need a New Metaphysics?* ed. R. Kitchener. Albany, NY: State University of New York Press, 1988.

———. *The Tao of Physics*. London: Wildwood House; New York: Random House, 1975, 1983.

Collingwood, R. G. *An Autobiography*. Oxford: Clarendon Press, 1939.

———. *An Essay on Metaphysics*. Oxford: Clarendon Press, 1940.

———. *An Essay on Philosophical Method*. Oxford: Clarendon Press, 1934, 1965.

———. *The Idea of Nature*. Oxford: Clarendon Press, 1945.

———. *The New Leviathan*. Oxford: Clarendon Press, 1942.

———. *Principles of Art*. Oxford: Clarendon Press, 1938, 1947.

———. *Speculum Mentis, or the Map of Knowledge*. Oxford: Clarendon Press, 1924.

Copernicus. *De Revolutionibus Orbium Coelestium*. Brussels: Culture et Civilization, 1966.

d'Abro, A. *The Evolution of Scientific Thought from Newton to Einstein*. New York: Dover, 1950.

———. *The Rise of the New Physics*. 2 vols. New York: Dover, 1951.

Darwin, Charles. *The Origin of Species*. London: John Murray, 1859, 1888; Watts and Co., 1929; New York: Modern Library, 1936.

Davies, Paul. *God and the New Physics*. London: Dent, 1983; Harmondsworth: Penguin Books, 1984, 1986.

———. *The Mind of God: The Scientific Basis for a Rational World*. New York and London: Simon and Schuster, 1992.

de Broglie, Louis. *The Revolution in Physics*, trans. R. W. Niemeyer. New York: Noonday Press; London: Routledge and Kegan Paul, 1953, 1954.

Descartes, R. *Philosophical Works*, trans. E. S. Haldane and G. R. T. Ross. Cambridge: Cambridge University Press, 1931.

DeWitt, B. S., and Graham, N. *The Many-Worlds Interpretation of Quantum Mechanics*. Princeton, NJ: Princeton University Press, 1973.

Donagan, A. *The Later Philosophy of R. G. Collingwood*. Oxford: Clarendon Press, 1962.

Dreyfus, H. L. *What Computers Can't Do*. New York and London: Harper and Row, 1967.

———. "Why Computers Must Have Bodies in Order to Be Intelligent." *Review of Metaphysics*, vol. 21 (1967).

Duprés, L. *Passage to Modernity*. New Haven, CT: Yale University Press, 1993.

Eddington, Sir Arthur. *The Expanding Universe*. Cambridge: Cambridge University Press, 1952.

———. *The Nature of the Physical World*. Cambridge: Cambridge University Press, 1928.

———. *New Pathways in Science*. Cambridge: Cambridge University Press, 1935.

———. *The Philosophy of Physical Science*. Cambridge: Cambridge University Press, 1939.

———. *Space, Time and Gravitation*. Cambridge: Cambridge University Press, 1953.

Einstein, A. *The Meaning of Relativity*. London: Methuen, 1956.

———. *Relativity, the Special and General Theories*, trans. R. W. Lawson. London: Methuen, 1954.

———. *The World as I See It*. London: Watts, 1935.

Einstein, A., and Infeld, I. *The Evolution of Physics*. Cambridge: Cambridge University Press, 1938; New York: Simon and Schuster, 1954.

Einstein, A., Podolsky, B., and Rosen, N. "Can Quantum Theory Description of Physical Reality be Considered Complete?" *Physical Review*, vol. 47 (1935).

Feigl, H. "Logical Empiricism." In *Twentieth Century Philosophy*, ed. D. D. Runes. New York: Philosophical Library, 1943.

Feigl and Brodbeck *Readings in the Philosophy of Science*. New York Appleton, Century, Crofts, Inc.

Fichte, J. G., *Die Wissenschaftslehre in allgemeinen Umriss* (1810).

———. "The 'Mental' and the 'Physical.'" *Minnesota Studies in the Philosophy of Science*, vol. 2 (1958).

———. "Mind-Body, Not a Pseudo-Problem." In *Dimensions of the Mind*, ed. Sidney Hook. New York: New York University Press, 1960.

Finnis, J. *Natural Law and Natural Right*. Oxford: Clarendon Press, 1979.

Flew, A. *Logic and Language*. Oxford: Blackwell, 1952.

Frank, P. *Between Physics and Philosophy*. Cambridge, MA: Harvard University Press, 1931.

Frege, G. *Grundlage der Arithmetik* trans. John Austin as *Foundations of Arithmetic*, Oxford: Blackwell, 1950.

Freud, Sigmund. *The Ego and the Id*. London, 1927.

Gale, G. "The Anthropic Principle." *Scientific American*, vol. 154 (1981).

Galilei, Galileo. *Dialogue Concerning the Two Chief World Systems*, trans. Stillman Drake. Berkeley: University of California Press, 1962.

———. *Dialogues Concerning Two New Sciences*, trans. Henry Crew and Alfonso de Salvio. Evanston, IL: Northwestern University Press, 1968.

Gibson, J. J. *Perception and the Visual World*. Boston: Houghton Mifflin, 1950.

Gleick, J. *Chaos: Making a New Science*. New York: Viking Press; Harmondsworth: Penguin Books, 1987.

Grier, P., ed. *Dialectic and Contemporary Science*. Lanham, MD: University Press of America, 1989.

Guthrie, E. R. "Purpose and Mechanism in Psychology." *Journal of Psychology*, vol. 21, no. 25, (1924).

Haldane, J. S. *Organism and Environment*. New Haven, CT: Yale University Press, 1917.

Hallett, H. R. "On a Reputed Equivoque in Spinoza." *Review of Metaphysics*, vol. 2, no. 2 (1949).

Hampshire, Stuart. *Thought and Action*, London, Chatto and Windus, 1959.

Hanson, N. R. *Patterns of Discovery*. Cambridge: Cambridge University Press, 1958.

Harris, E. E. *Atheism and Theism*. New Orleans, LA: Tulane University Press, 1977; Atlantic Highlands, NJ: Humanities Press, 1993.

———. "Blanshard on Perception and Free Ideas." In *The Philosophy of Brand Blanshard*, ed. Paul Schilpp. La Salle, IL: Open Court, 1980.

———. *Cosmos and Anthropos*. Atlantic Highlands, NJ: Humanities Press, 1991.

———. *Cosmos and Theos*. Atlantic Highlands, NJ: Humanities Press, 1992.

———. "Epicyclic Popperism." *British Journal for the Philosophy of Science*, vol. 23 (1972).

———. *Formal, Transcendental and Dialectical Thinking*. Albany, NY: State University of New York Press, 1987.

———. *The Foundations of Metaphysics in Science*. London: Allen and Unwin, 1965; Lanham, MD: University Press of America, 1983; Atlantic Highlands, NJ: Humanities Press, 1993.

————. *Hypothesis and Perception: The Roots of Scientific Method.* G. Allen and Unwin, 1970. Atlantic Highlands, NJ: Humanities Press, 1996.

————. *An Interpretation of the Logic of Hegel.* Lanham, MD: University Press of America, 1982.

————. "Leibniz and Modern Science." In *Metaphysics as Foundation*, ed. P. A. Bogard and G. Treasch. Albany, NY: State University of New York Press, 1993.

————. *Nature, Mind and Modern Science.* London: Allen and Unwin, 1954.

————. "Objective Knowledge and Objective Value." *International Philosophical Quarterly*, vol. 15 (1975).

————. "Objectivity and Reason." *Philosophy*, vol. 21, no. 116 (1956).

————. *Perceptual Assurance and the Reality of the World.* Worcester, MA: Clark University Press, 1974.

————. "Political Power." *Ethics*, vol. 68, no. 1 (1957).

————. *The Problem of Evil.* Milwaukee, WI: Marquette University Press, 1977.

————. "The Problem of Self-Constitution in Idealism and Phenomenology." *Idealistic Studies*, vol. 7, no. 1 (1977).

————. *The Reality of Time.* Albany, NY: State University of New York Press, 1988.

————. *Revelation Through Reason.* New Haven, CT: Yale University Press; London: Allen and Unwin, 1958.

————. *Salvation from Despair: A Reappraisal of Spinoza's Philosophy.* The Hague: Martinus Nijhoff, 1973.

————. *The Spirit of Hegel.* Atlantic Highlands, NJ: Humanities Press, 1993.

————. *The Substance of Spinoza.* Atlantic Highlands, NJ: Humanities Press, 1995.

————. *The Survival of Political Man.* Johannesburg: Witwatersrand University Press, 1950.

Harrison, E. *Masks of the Universe.* London and New York: Macmillan, 1985.

Hegel, G. W. F. *Encyclopaedia of Philosophical Sciences: Logic*, trans, W. Wallace. Oxford: Clarendon Press, 1892; revised by A. V. Miller, with a foreword by J. N. Findlay, 1975.

————. *Encyclopaedia of Philosophical Sciences: Philosophy of Mind*, trans. W. Wallace; *Zusatze* trans. A. V. Miller. Oxford: Clarendon Press, 1975.

————. *Encyclopaedia of Philosophical Sciences: Philosophy of Nature*, trans. A. V. Miller. Oxford: Clarendon Press, 1975.

————. *Enzyklopädie der Philosophischen Wissenschaften, Werke*, vols. 6–8. Frankfurt-am-Main: Suhrkamp Verlag, 1971–78.

————. *Gesammelte Werke*, ed. F. Hogemann and W. Jeaschke. Hamburg: Felix Meiner Verlag, 1981–.

————. *Lectures on the Philosophy of World History, Introduction: Reason in History*, trans. H. B. Nisbet, with an introduction by Duncan Forbes. Cambridge: Cambridge University Press, 1975.

————. *Phänomenologie des Geistes, Werke*, vol. 3. Frankfurt-am-Main: Suhrkamp Verlag, 1971–78.

————. *Phenomology of Mind*, trans. J. Baillie. London: Allen and Unwin, 1910, 1931, 1955–56.

————. *Phenomenology of Spirit*, trans. A. V. Miller. Oxford: Oxford University Press, 1977.

————. *The Science of Logic*, trans. A. V. Miller. London: Allen and Unwin, 1969; Atlantic Highlands, NJ: Humanities Press, 1991.

Heidegger, M. *Being and Time*, trans. J. Macquarrie and E. Robinson. London: S. C. M. Press, 1962.

————. *Einfuhrung in der Metaphysik*, trans. Ralph Manheim as *Introduction to Metaphysics*. New Haven, CT: Yale University Press, 1959.

————. *Holzwege*, Frankfurt-am-Main, 1952.

Heisenberg, W. *Philosophical Problems of Nuclear Science*. London: Faber and Faber, 1952.

————. *The Physicist's Conception of Nature*. New York: Harcourt Brace, 1958; Westport, CT: Greenwood Press, 1970.

————. *Physics and Philosophy: The Revolution in Modern Science*. London: Faber and Faber, 1952; New York, Harper and Row, 1959, 1962.

Hirst, R. J. *The Problems of Perception*. London: Allen and Unwin, 1959.

Hobbes, T. *Leviathan*, ed. M. Oakshott. Oxford: Clarendon Press, 1946.

Hook, S., ed. *Dimensions of the Mind*, New York, New York University Press, 1960.

Holt, E.B., *The Concept of Consciousness*, London, G. Allen and Unwin, 1914.

Hume, D. *Dialogues Concerning Natural Religion*, London, Nelson and Sons, 1947, Indianapolis, IN., Bobbs-Merrill Co., 1981.

————. *Enquiries Concerning Human Understanding and Concerning the Principles of Morals*, Oxford, Clarendon Press, 1902, 1955.

————. *Treatise of Human Nature*, ed. L.A. Selby-Bigge, Oxford, Clarendon Press, New York, Oxford University Press, 1978.

Husserl, E. *Cartesian Meditations*. The Hague: Martinus Nijhoff, 1960.

————. *The Crisis in the European Sciences*, trans. D. Carr. Evanston, IL: Northwestern University Press, 1970.

————. *Formal and Transcendental Logic*, trans. D. Cairns. The Hague, Martinus Nijhoff, 1969.

————. *Ideas*, trans. W. Boyce Gibson. London: Allen and Unwin, 1931, 1956.

————. *Logical Investigations*, trans. J. N. Findlay. Atlantic Highlands, NJ: Humanities Press, 1982.

————. *Phenomenology of Internal Time Consciousness*, trans. S. Churchill. Bloomington: Indiana University Press.

Ittelson, H. W. "Size as a Cue to Distance: Static Localization." *American Journal of Psychology*, vol. 64 (1951).

Ittelson, H. W., and Cantril, H. *Perception, a Transactional Approach*. Garden City, NY: Doubleday, 1954.

Ittelson, H. W., and Kilpatrick, F. P. "Experiments in Perception." *Scientific American*, vol. 185, no. 2 (1951).

Jasper, H. H., Proctor, L. D., et al. *Reticular Formation of the Brain*. Henry Ford Hospital International Symposium. Boston and Toronto: Little, Brown, 1958.

Joachim, H. H. *Descartes's Rules for the Direction of the Mind*, ed. E. E. Harris. London: Allen and Unwin, 1957; reprint, Westport, CT: Greenwood Press, 1979.

————. *The Nature of Truth*. Oxford: Clarendon Press, 1924.

————. *Logical Studies*. Oxford: Clarendon Press, 1942.

Jonas, H. *The Phenomenon of Life*, New York, Harper and Row, 1966.

————. *Philosophical Essays*, Englewood Cliffs, NJ., Prentice Hall, 1974, Chicago: Chicago University Press, 1980.

Joseph, H. W. B. "A Plea for Free-thinking in Logistic." *Mind*, vols. 41, 42, 43 (1931–1933).

Kafatos, M., ed. *Bell's Theorem and Conceptions of the Universe*. Dordrecht, Boston, and London: Kluwer Academic, 1989.

Kafatos, M., and Nadeau, R. *The Conscious Universe: Whole and Part in Modern Physical Theory*. New York: Springer Verlag, 1990.

Kaku, M., and Trainer, J. *Beyond Einstein: The Cosmic Quest for the Theory of the*

Universe. London, New York, and Toronto: Bantam Books, 1987.

Kant, I. *Critique of Judgement*, trans. J. H. Bernard. London: Macmillan, 1914.

———. *Critique of Practical Reason*, trans. L. W. Beck. New York: Liberal Arts Press, 1956.

———. *Critique of Pure Reason*, trans. N. Kemp Smith. Atlantic Highlands, NJ: Humanities Press, 1992.

———. *Religion Within the Limits of Reason Alone*, trans. T. M. Greene and H. H. Hudson. New York: Harper, 1960.

Katner, S., ed. *Vision and Action*. New Brunswick, NJ: Rutgers University Press, 1953.

Kaufman, S. *The Origins of Order: Self-Organization and Selection in Evolution*. Oxford: Oxford University Press, 1993.

Kitchener, R., ed. *The World View of Contemporary Physics: Does It Need a New Metaphysics?* Albany, NY: State University of New York Press, 1988.

Knox, Sir Malcolm. *Action*. London: Allen and Unwin, 1968.

Koffka, K. *Principles of Gestalt Psychology*. London: Routledge and Kegan Paul; New York, Harcourt Brace, 1935.

Kuhn, T. *The Structure of Scientific Revolutions*, Chicago: University of Chicago Press, 1962, 1970.

Langer, S. *Mind: An Essay on Human Feeling*. 3 vols. Baltimore, MD: Johns Hopkins University Press, 1967–83.

———. *Philosophical Sketches*. Baltimore, MD: Johns Hopkins University Press, 1962.

Le Gros Clark, W. E. "Anatomical Perspectives in Neuropsychiatry." In *Perspectives in Neuropsychiatry*, ed. D. Richter. London: H. K. Lewis, 1950.

Leibniz G. W. *Discourse on Metaphysics*. Manchester: Manchester University Press, 1953.

———. *The Monadology and Other Philosophical Writings*, trans. R. Latta. Oxford: Clarendon Press, 1898.

Lévi-Strauss, C. *The Savage Mind*. London: George Weidenfield and Nicholson; Chicago: University of Chicago Press, 1966, 1968.

Lewis, C. I. *An Analysis of Knowledge and Valuation*. La Salle, IL: Open Court, 1946.

Lewis, C. S. *The Pilgrim's Regress*. London: Dent, 1933.

———. *The Problem of Pain*. London: Centenary Press, 1942; New York: Macmillan, 1962.

Locke, J. *An Essay Concerning Human Understanding*, ed. A. Campbell Fraser. Oxford: Clarendon Press, 1894; New York: Dover, 1959.

Macdonald, Margaret. "Natural Rights." In *Philosophy, Politics and Society*, ed. Peter Laslett. Oxford: Blackwell, 1956–70.

MacIntyre, A. *After Virtue*, Notre Dame: University of Notre Dame Press, 1981.

Margenau, H. "The Exclusion Principle and Its Philosophical Importance." *Philosophy of Science*, vol. 11 (1944).

———. *The Nature of Physical Reality*. New York: McGraw-Hill, 1950.

Mascall, E. M. *Christian Theology and Natural Science*. London: Longmans, Green and Co., 1956.

McTaggart, J. E. *The Nature of Existence*. Cambridge: Cambridge University Press, 1927.

Merleau-Ponty, M. *Phenomenology of Perception*, trans. C. Smith. London: Routledge and Kegan Paul, 1962.

Monod, J. *Chance and Necessity*, trans. A. Wainhouse. London: Collins, 1972.

Moore, G. E. *Philosophical Studies*. London: Kegan Paul, Trench and Trubner, 1922.

Morris, C. R. *Idealistic Logic*. London: Macmillan, 1933.

Mure, G. R. *Idealistic Epilogue*. Oxford: Clarendon Press, 1978.

Myerson, É. *Identity and Reality.* London: Allen and Unwin, 1930.

Needham, J. *Order and Life.* New Haven, CT: Yale University Press, 1936.

Paley, W. *Natural Theology.* New York: S. King, 1824; London: R. Faulder, 1802; Chilworth, 1879; Boston: Gould and Lincoln, 1869; selections reprinted by Bobbs-Merrill, 1963.

Penrose, R. *The Emperor's New Mind: Concerning Computers, Minds, and the Laws of Physics.* New York and Oxford: Oxford University Press, 1989.

Pepper, Stephen. "A Neural-Identity Theory of Mind." In *Dimensions of the Mind,* ed. Sidney Hook. New York: New York University Press, 1960.

Place, U. T. "Is Consciousness a Brain Process." *British Journal of Psychology,* vol. 47 (1956).

Planck, M. *The Philosophy of Physics.* London: Allen and Unwin, 1936; New York: Norton and Co., 1936.

———. *The Universe in the Light of Modern Physics.* London: Allen and Unwin, 1937; New York: Norton and Co., 1951.

———. *Where Is Science Going.* London: Allen and Unwin, 1933.

Plato. *The Works of Plato,* ed. E. Hamilton and H. Cairns. Princeton, NJ: Princeton University Press, 1963.

Poincaré, H. *Science and Hypothesis.* New York: Dover, 1952.

Polanyi, M. *Personal Knowledge: Towards a Post-Critical Philosophy.* London: Routledge and Kegan Paul, 1958.

Popper, Sir Karl. *The Logic of Scientific Discovery.* New York: Harper, 1959.

Popper, Sir Karl. "What Can Logic Do for Philosophy." *Proceeding of the Aristotelian Society,* Supplementary vol. 22, 1948.

Price, H. H. *Perception.* London: Methuen, 1950.

Pringle-Pattison, A. S. *Studies in the Philosophy of Religion.* Oxford: Clarendon Press, 1930.

Quinton, A. M. "The Problems of Perception." *Mind,* vol. 64 (1955).

Raven, C. E. *The Gospel and the Church.* New York: Scribner's, 1940.

———. *Experience and Interpretation, Natural Religion and Christian Theology.* vol. 1. *Science and Religion*; vol. 2. Cambridge: Cambridge University Press, 1953.

———. *Science, Religion and the Future.* Cambridge: Cambridge University Press; New York: Macmillan, 1944.

Reichenbach, H. *The Rise of Scientific Philosophy.* Berkeley and Los Angeles: University of California Press; London and Cambridge: Cambridge University Press, 1951.

Richter, D., ed., *Perspectives in Neuropsychiatry.* London: H. K. Lewis, 1950.

Rorty, R. *Philosophy and the Mirror of Nature.* Princeton, NJ: Princeton University Press, 1979.

Runes, D. D. *Twentieth Century Philosophy.* New York: Philosophical Library, 1943.

Russell, Bertrand. *Human Knowledge: Its Scope and Limits.* London: Allen and Unwin, 1948.

———. "Logical Atomism." In *Contemporary British Philosophy.* Series I. London: Allen and Unwin, 1924.

———. *My Philosophical Development.* London: Allen and Unwin; New York: Simon and Schuster, 1959.

———. *Mysticism and Logic.* London: Allen and Unwin, 1919.

———. *Our Knowledge of the External World.* New York: Norton, 1929.

———. *The Philosophy of Logical Atomism.* Minneapolis: University of Minnesota Press, 1959.

———. "Reply to Criticism." In *The Philosophy of Bertrand Russell,* ed. Paul Schilpp. Evanston, IL: Open Court, 1946.

Russell, B., and Whitehead, A. N. *Principia Mathematica*. Cambridge: Cambridge University Press, 1925, 1927.

Ryle, G. *The Concept of Mind*. London: Hutchinson, 1949.

Scher, J., ed. *Theories of the Mind*. New York: Free Press of Glencoe, 1962.

Schilpp, P., ed. *Albert Einstein, Philosopher Scientist*. La Salle, IL: Open Court, 1949; New York: Harper, 1951.

——. *The Philosophy of Bertrand Russell*. Evanston, IL: Open Court, 1946.

——. *The Philosophy of Brand Blanshard*. La Salle, IL: Open Court, 1980.

——. *The Philosophy of G. E. Moore*. New York: Tudor Publishing Co., 1952.

Schroedinger, E. *Science and Humanism*. Cambridge: Cambridge University Press, 1952.

——. *What Is Life? and Other Scientific Essays*. New York: Doubleday, 1956.

Schwartz, J. *Superstrings*. Singapore: World Scientific, 1985.

Sciama, D. W. *The Unity of the Universe*. Garden City, NY: Doubleday, 1959, 1961; London: Faber and Faber, 1959.

Sinnott, E. W. *Cell and Psyche*. New York: Viking Press, 1950.

Smart, J. J. C. *Philosophy and Scientific Realism*. London: Routledge and Kegan Paul; Atlantic Highlands, NJ: Humanities Press, 1963.

——. "Sensations and Brain Processes." *Philosophical Review*, vol. 68 (1959).

Sorley, W. R. *Moral Values and the Idea of God*. Cambridge: Cambridge University Press, 1918, 1935.

Spinoza, B. de. *Chief Works*, trans. R. H. W. Elwes. 2 vols. London: George Bell and Sons, 1889; New York: Dover, 1955.

——. *Collected Works*, trans. and ed. E. Curley. Princeton, NJ: Princeton University Press, 1985.

——. *Ethic of Benedict de Spinoza*, trans. W. Hale White and A. H. Stirling. London: T. Fisher Unwin, 1894.

——. *Ethics and de Intellectus Emendatione*, trans. E. Boyle. London: Dent, 1910.

——. *Ethics and Selected Letters*, trans. S. Shirley. Indianapolis, IN: Hackett, 1982.

Stapp, H. P. "Are Faster-than-Light Influences Necessary." In *Quantum Mechanics Versus Local Realism: The Einstein, Podolsky and Rosen Paradox*, ed. F. Salleri. New York: Plenum Press, 1987.

——. "Quantum Mechanics and the Physicist's Conception of Nature: Philosophical Implications of Bell's Theorem." In *The World View of Contemporary Physics: Does It Need a New Metaphysics?* ed. R. Kitchener. Albany, NY: State University of New York Press, 1988.

Stone, J. *Human Law and Human Justice*. London: Steven and Sons; Stanford, CA: Stanford University Press, 1965.

Strawson, P. F. *Individuals*. London: Methuen, 1959.

——. *Introduction to Logical Theory*. London: Methuen, 1952.

Taylor, A. E. *Does God Exist?* London: Macmillan, 1948.

——. *Elements of Metaphysics*. London: Methuen, 1903, 1916.

Taylor, R. *Metaphysics*. Englewood Cliffs, NJ: Prentice-Hall, 1963.

Teilhard de Chardin, P. *The Phenomenon of Man*, trans. B. Wall. London: Collins; New York: Harper and Row, 1959.

Thomas, Lewis, *The Lives of a Cell*. New York: Viking Press, 1974.

Urmson, J. O. *Philosophical Analysis*. Oxford: Clarendon Press, 1958.

van Os, H. *Tijd, Maat en Getal*. Leiden: Mededelingen vanwege het Spinozahuis, 1946.

Vernon, M. D. *The Psychology of Perception*. Harmondsworth: Penguin Books, 1962, 1968.

Vernon, M. D., ed. *Experiments in Visual Perception*. Harmondsworth: Penguin Books, 1970.

von Bertalanffy, L. *Modern Theories of Development*. Oxford: Oxford University Press, 1933; New York: Harper, 1962.

Warnock G. J. *English Philosophy Since 1900*. Oxford: Clarendon Press, 1958.

Weinberg, J. H. *An Examination of Logical Positivism*. London: Kegan Paul, Trench, 1936.

Wells, G. P., and Huxley, J. *The Science of Life*. London: Cassell, 1938.

Whitehead, A. N. *Adventures of Ideas*. Cambridge: Cambridge University Press: New York: Macmillan, 1933.

————. *Process and Reality*. Cambridge: Cambridge University Press, 1929; New York: Free Press, 1978.

————. *Science and the Modern World*. Cambridge: Cambridge University Press, 1926; New York: Macmillan, 1925, 1948; New American Library, 1953.

Whiteley, C. H. *An Introduction to Metaphysics*. London: Methuen, 1950.

Whittaker, R. H. *Communities and Eco-Systems*. New York: Collier-Macmillan, 1975.

Whittaker, Sir Edmund. *From Euclid to Eddington*. Cambridge: Cambridge University Press, 1949.

Widom, J. "Metaphysics and Verification." *Mind*, vol. 47, (1938).

Wittgenstein, L. *On Certainty*. Oxford: Blackwells, 1969.

————. *Philosophical Investigations*. London: Routledge and Kegan Paul, 1967.

————. *Tractatus Logico-Philosophicus*. London: Routledge and Kegan Paul, 1960.

Index

Boldface numbers indicate pages where a topic is treated more fully.